Timeless Service

IN

GAMMA SIGMA OMEGA CHAPTER

Alpha Kappa Alpha Sorority

EMMA JEAN HAWKINS CONYERS

iUniverse LLC
Bloomington

TIMELESS SERVICE IN GAMMA SIGMA OMEGA CHAPTER ALPHA KAPPA ALPHA SORORITY

iUniverse books may be ordered through booksellers or by contacting:

iUniverse
1663 Liberty Drive
Bloomington, IN 47403
www.iuniverse.com
1-800-Authors (1-800-288-4677)

Because of the dynamic nature of the Internet, any web addresses or links contained in this book may have changed since publication and may no longer be valid. The views expressed in this work are solely those of the author and do not necessarily reflect the views of the publisher, and the publisher hereby disclaims any responsibility for them.

Any people depicted in stock imagery provided by Thinkstock are models, and such images are being used for illustrative purposes only.
Certain stock imagery © Thinkstock.

ISBN: 978-1-4917-1429-4 (sc)
ISBN: 978-1-4917-1431-7 (hc)
ISBN: 978-1-4917-1430-0 (e)

Library of Congress Control Number: 2013920810

Printed in the United States of America.

iUniverse rev. date: 12/06/2013

Timeless Service in Gamma Sigma Omega Chapter
Alpha Kappa Alpha Sorority

Author
Emma Jean Hawkins Conyers

Editors
Sheila Burton Hutcherson
Virginia Annette Mercer Parham

Assistant Editors
Charlene E. Jones
LaShawna K. Alderman-Mullgrav
Taqwaa F. Saleem

Contributors
Patricia J. Clark
Dr. Clemontine Freeman Washington
Audrey Barnes Singleton

Support
Queen E. Barnes
Tara Scott-Brown
Zena E. McClain, Esq., President
Marsha Lewis Brown, South Atlantic Regional Director
Carolyn House Stewart, Esq., International President

December 31, 2012

Dedication

Dr. Albertha E. Boston and Frances Clarke Dye

Dr. Albertha E. Boston

TIMELESS SERVICE IN *Gamma Sigma Omega Chapter* is dedicated to two Alpha Kappa Alpha Sorority members. They are Albertha E. Boston and Frances Clarke Dye. These two sisters represent unsung heroes in Gamma Sigma Omega Chapter of Alpha Kappa Alpha Sorority. They were quiet, steadfast, workers, behind the scene, who ensured that service projects and programs were successfully done not only for chapter recognition but for the good of the community.

Dr. Boston was the driving force behind the chapter's first publication, *Gamma Sigma Omega Chapter of Alpha Kappa Alpha Sorority, Inc., 1943-2002.* Having served as President and Historian, she knew the value of preservation. At her 90th birthday, her nieces and nephrews honored her: Nathaniel, Melvin, Cheryl, Kelvin, Zandra, Waymonn, Lenora, Charletta, Robert, Charles, and Karen. Sometime after this celebration, her vision began to fail. In spite of the odds, with the help of chapter members, she attended sorority meetings. Her handicap did not diminish her great heart, astute intellect, and love for Alpha Kappa Alpha. Participating with silent support, humbly and attentively, she sat in chapter meetings. Affectionately called, "Bert," she became an Ivy Beyond the Wall on October 1, 2012.

Frances Clarke Dye's persona depicts one of intelligence and alertness, an ardent reader, motivator, organizer, and beauty. Having never seen her nor known of any AKA living today who has, for me and other Gamma Sigma Omega members, these attributes have been perceived by readers of GSO's history. We know that it was she who informed the chapter about Adeline Graham's Will. Martha Wilson's obituary informs us that Frances C. Dye served as the first President of Greenbriar Children Center's Board and that Mrs. Wilson succeeded her when Ms. Dye moved to New York in 1944.[1] The chapter's history does not indicate anything of her family nor marital status, but the chapter knows that she had to be a servant of Jesus Christ, used by Him for that present age. Whatever her mortal or immortal status, Gamma Sigma Omega Chapter thanks God for the life that she shared with the members and the Savannah community.

Emma Jean Conyers
Sheila Hutcherson
Virginia M. Parham

Contents

Foreword

G AMMA SIGMA OMEGA is one of many chapters of the first Black
female Greek-letter organization, Alpha Kappa Alpha Sorority.
The preservation of Gamma Sigma Omega's history is not only a mission
of our national office but of the chapter's as well. It is our prayer that all
who choose to read and partake in such an accomplishment will do so
with a heart of love and understanding that a project of this magnitude
was completed with the best interest of the chapter and the sorority as
a whole in mind. We hope that you find the reading enlightening. We
are extremely proud of the history that we have embarked upon and
even more proud of the sisterly efforts that intertwined to ensure its
documentation was a success.

As one can imagine, it takes a team of dedicated individuals
to complete a task of this magnitude. There are several members
of the chapter who have willingly supported this project and have
unselfishly devoted their free time to its success: Emma Jean Conyers,
Virginia M. Parham, Queen Barnes, Patricia Clark, Clemontine F.
Washington, Charlene Jones, LaShawna K. Alderman Mullgrav,
Taqwaa F. Saleem, Audrey B. Singleton, Tara Scott-Brown, and yours
truly. This team researched the history of past presidents, the history
of our undergraduate chapters, collected and compiled surveys for
informational purposes as well as serving as editors. Although the
responsibilities sometimes became time consuming and may have been
overwhelming, the responsibilities of this team were met with great
enthusiasm and diligence in order to complete the one common goal,
retaining Gamma Sigma Omega's history.

The desire to publish our history did not just begin with this team of
individuals. A passion to organize the history of Gamma Sigma Omega

began with our very own Virginia M. Parham, Albertha E. Boston, and Emma J. Conyers who saw the need and met the challenge with a publication entitled *Gamma Sigma Omega Chapter of Alpha Kappa Alpha Sorority, Inc. 1943-2002*, a history book that was used as the main source of information for this great project you now have before you.

Our founders have given us a legacy of which to be proud, one we will continue to preserve through our devotion to the sorority and with the integrity required to maintain its accuracy and retention. It is the responsibility of Gamma Sigma Omega Chapter of Alpha Kappa Alpha Sorority, Inc. to ensure that future sorority members and the community are made aware of this legacy through our chapter's service, achievements, and the documentation there of. This is only the beginning of several history books to come from a chapter that has been and will continue to be of "service to all mankind."

Sheila Burton Hutcherson, Historian (2012), Editor

Acknowledgements

THE MEMBERSHIP OF Gamma Sigma Omega Chapter of Alpha Kappa Alpha Sorority, past and present, is deeply indebted and very grateful to all the sorors who have helped to foster "Service to all Mankind" throughout the chapter's history and especially the initial and abiding interest in Greenbriar Children's Center, Inc.

Special thanks and appreciation to the author, Emma Jean Hawkins Conyers, for her untiring research and retrieving efforts of chapter documents (newsletters, minutes, the previous history book, archives of local news paper articles, etc.) and of Corporate Office documents (Boule minutes, Ivy Leaf editions, and other archived corporate materials) that served as the foundation of this publication.

Gamma Sigma Omega Chapter of Alpha Kappa Alpha Sorority, Inc., 1943-2002 served as the springboard for this second edition. The early history (1943-1965) was compiled mostly from individual members' personal knowledge and memories presented orally to the authors. Much of the information for the second phase of the history (1966-1982) was gleaned from chapter minutes, local news paper articles and active participation of the authors. From 1978 thru 2012, each chapter Basileus provided information highlighting her respective term in office. These efforts were augmented by the author's research of archived records. Thank you to everyone who helped to make this project a success.

The author and the editors sincerely thank the chapter and the current leadership for entrusting the publication of the Second Edition of Gamma Sigma Omega Chapter's history to us. We hope and trust it will meet your expectations. It has been our privilege TO SERVE OUR CHAPTER in this effort.

Virginia M. Parham, Editor

Governance and Operation

G AMMA SIGMA OMEGA Chapter (GSO) is governed by *Alpha Kappa Alpha Sorority, Inc. Constitution and Bylaws, Alpha Kappa Alpha Sorority, Inc. Manual of Standard Procedures*, and any other approved documents recommended by Alpha Kappa Alpha Sorority, Inc.; Gamma Sigma Omega's *Chapter By-Laws, Policies and Procedures Manual, Campaign Guidelines;* and *Robert's Rules of Order.*

The purpose of Gamma Sigma Omega Chapter of Alpha Kappa Alpha Sorority is to cultivate and encourage high scholastic and ethical standards, to promote unity and friendship among college women, to study and help alleviate problems concerning girls and women in order to improve their social stature, to maintain a progressive interest in college life, and to be of service to all mankind as stated in the *Constitution and Bylaws of Alpha Kappa Alpha Sorority, Inc.*[2]

The chapter is structured where the membership sets the rules and regulations that do not conflict with Alpha Kappa Alpha Sorority. Presently, membership is composed of graduate members graduating and transferring from an undergraduate chapter into the chapter, Membership Intake Process (MIP) for graduate initiates, and transferring AKAs from General Membership of Alpha Kappa Alpha Sorority and other chapters of Alpha Kappa Alpha Sorority. The leaders of the chapter are officers and committee chairmen, comprising the Executive Committee that meets prior to chapter meeting, normally the Thursday before the 1st Saturday at 6:00 p.m. Chapter meeting is held the 2nd Saturday of the month at 10:00 a.m. Committees may meet at anytime chairmen designate or upon recommendation of the Basileus. An emergency meeting may be called by the Basileus with members given a twenty-four hour prior to meeting notice.

The officers serve for two years with the following officers as officers-elect: Anti- Basileus, Anti-Grammateus, and Anti-Tamiouchos. The Basileus determines the direction for the Standing Committees and/or Ad Hoc Committees with the exception of Program and Nomination. The Anti-Basileus determines the direction for the International Program of Alpha Kappa Alpha Sorority, the chapter local programs, and formulates committees accordingly.

Members seeking to run for an office in the chapter must adhere to the rules in the *Campaign Guidelines* for a fair and equitable election process.

The chapter has a Program Account and an Operation Account. The International Program service programs and the local community service programs are budgeted under the Program Account. The other Standing and Ad Hoc Committee events and activities are budgeted under the Operation Account. In order to be an active member of the chapter, a member must pay all chapter assessments and dues before her per capita tax is submitted to the International office.

At Founders' Day, the chapter honors members in three standing categories: (1) Soror of the Year Award (2) Countess Y. Cox Sisterhood Award (3) Evanel Renfroe Terrell Scholarship Award. Also, the Mozella Gaither Collier Community Volunteer Service Award is given to the most worthy community applicant.

M.A.R.T.H.A., Inc. is a 501 (c) (3) organization established as a Corporation to support the charitable, educational and community programs andinitiatives of Gamma Sigma Omega Chapter of Alpha Kappa Alpha Sorority, Chatham County, Georgia, including: the organization's educational initiatives for at-risk children and their parents in the organization's mentoring of Middle School Girls, the organization's health, economics, and arts initiatives, and the organization's procurement of property for literacy and educational programs.[3] This organization is structured, with the exception of financial officers, where the officers of Gamma Sigma Omega Chapter are the same officers of M.A.R.T.H.A., Inc.

There is an annual assessment that each member must pay to M.A.R.T.H.A., Inc.

The heartbeat of Gamma Sigma Omega Chapter (GSO) in the Savannah community is Greenbriar Children's Center, Inc.; therefore, GSO is governed (the planning and strategizing of projects) by the needs of the Center. GSO Chapter is dedicated to the successful operation of the Greenbriar Children's Center. This Center was the initial service project (home for Negro Orphans) for the chapter. The chapter's budget includes Greenbriar Children's Center first on the list of financial recipients. Upon Greenbriar's request or other known needs, the chapter, within its budget, meets the need. Since the existence of Greenbriar Children's Center, an Alpha Kappa Alpha woman has served on its Board of Directors. They are Frances Dye, Martha Wilson, Leila Braithwaite, Louise Owens, Mattie B. Payne, Mary McDew, Countess Cox, Ouida Frazier Thompson, Luetta Milledge, Virginia Parham, Johnye Gillans, Shirley McGee Brown, Clemontine F. Washington, Dorothy B. Wilson, and Deborah Ellington Wilson (not GSO member). Some of these GSO members have served for many consecutive terms and some have repeated more than one term of service. Today serving on the Board of Directors is Clemontine F. Washington. It is Gamma Sigma Omega Chapter's belief that a member of GSO should always be on the Board of Directors to perpetuate the legacy of the chapter's initial service project.

AKA International Historical Perspective for Timeless Histories

ALPHA KAPPA ALPHA SORORITY, INCORPORATED

A Legacy of Sisterhood and Timeless Service

CONFINED TO WHAT she called "a small circumscribed life" in the segregated and male-dominated milieu that characterized the early 1900s, Howard University co-ed Ethel Hedgeman dreamed of creating a support network for women with like minds coming together for mutual uplift, and coalescing their talents and strengths for the benefit of others. In 1908, her vision crystallized as Alpha Kappa Alpha, the first Negro Greek-letter sorority. Five years later (1913), lead incorporator Nellie Quander ensured Alpha Kappa Alpha's perpetuity through incorporation in the District of Columbia.

Together with eight other coeds at the mecca for Negro education, Hedgeman crafted a design that not only fostered interaction, stimulation, and ethical growth among members; but also provided hope for the masses. From the core group of nine at Howard, AKA has grown into a force of more than 265,000 collegiate members and alumnae, constituting 972 chapters in 42 states, the District of Columbia, the US Virgin Islands, the Bahamas, Germany, South Korea, Japan, Liberia, and Canada.

Because they believed that Negro college women represented "the highest—more education, more enlightenment, and more of almost everything that the great mass of Negroes never had— Hedgeman and her cohorts worked to honor what she called "an everlasting debt to raise them (Negroes) up and to make them better." For more than a century, the Alpha Kappa Alpha Sisterhood has fulfilled that obligation by becoming an indomitable force for good in their communities, state, nation, and the world.

The Alpha Kappa Alpha program today still reflects the communal consciousness steeped in the AKA tradition and embodied in AKA's credo, "To be supreme in service to all mankind." Cultural awareness and social advocacy marked Alpha Kappa Alpha's infancy, but within one year (1914) of acquiring corporate status, AKA had also made its mark on education, establishing a scholarship award. The programming was a prelude to the thousands of pioneering and enduring initiatives that eventually defined the Alpha Kappa Alpha brand.

Through the years, Alpha Kappa Alpha has used the Sisterhood as a grand lever to raise the status of African-Americans, particularly girls and women. AKA has enriched minds and encouraged life-long learning; provided aid for the poor, the sick, and underserved; initiated social action to advance human and civil rights; worked collaboratively with other groups to maximize outreach on progressive endeavors; and continually produced leaders to continue its credo of service.

Guided by twenty-eight international presidents from Nellie M. Quander (1913-1919) to Carolyn House Stewart (2010-2014), with reinforcement from a professional headquarters staff since 1949; AKA's corps of volunteers has instituted groundbreaking social action initiatives and social service programs that have timelessly transformed communities for the better— continually emitting progress in cities, states, the nation, and the world.

Signal Program Initiatives

2000s—Launched Emerging Young Leaders, a bold move to prepare 10,000 girls in grades 6-8 to excel as young leaders equipped to respond to the challenges of the 21st century; initiated homage for civil rights milestones by honoring the Little Rock Nine's 1957 desegregation of Central High (Little Rock, Ar.) following the Supreme Court's 1954 decision declaring segregated schools unconstitutional; donated $1 million to Howard University to fund scholarships and preserve Black culture (2008); strengthened the reading skills of 16,000 children through a $1.5 million after school demonstration project in low-performing, economically deprived, inner city schools (2002); and improved the quality of life for people of African descent through continuation of aid to African countries.

1990s—Built 10 schools in South Africa (1998); added the largest number of minorities to the National Bone Marrow Registry (1996); Became first civilian organization to create memorial to World War II unsung hero Dorie Miller (1991).

1980s—Adopted more than 27 African villages, earning Africare's 1986 Distinguished Service Award; encouraged awareness of and participation in the nation's affairs, registering more than 350, 000 new voters; and established the Alpha Kappa Alpha Educational Advancement Foundation (1981), a multi-million dollar entity that annually awards more than $100,000 in scholarships, grants, and fellowships.

1970s—Was only sorority to be named an inaugural member of Operation Big Vote (1979); completed pledge of one-half million to the United Negro College Fund (1976); and purchased Dr. Martin Luther King's boyhood home for the MLK Center for Social Change (1972).

1960s—Sponsored inaugural Domestic Travel Tour, a one-week cultural excursion for 30 high school students (1969); launched a "Heritage Series" on African-American achievers (1965); and emerged as the first women's group to win a grant to operate a federal job corps center (1965), preparing youth 16-21 to function in a highly competitive economy.

1950s—Promoted investing in Black businesses by depositing initial $38,000 for AKA Investment Fund with the first and only Negro firm on Wall Street (1958). Spurred Sickle Cell Disease research and education with grants to Howard Hospital and publication of *The Sickle Cell Story* (1958).

1940s—Invited other Greek-letter organizations to come together to establish the American Council on Human Rights to empower racial uplift and economic development (1948); Acquired observer status from the United Nations (1946); and challenged the absence of people of color from pictorial images used by the government to portray Americans (1944).

1930s—Became first organization to take out NAACP life membership (1939); Created nation's first Congressional lobby that impacted legislation on issues ranging from decent living conditions and jobs to lynching (1938); and established the nation's first mobile health clinic, providing relief to 15,000 Negroes plagued by famine and disease in the Mississippi Delta (1935)

1920s—Worked to dispel notions that Negroes were unfit for certain professions, and guided Negroes in avoiding career mistakes (1923); pushed anti-lynching legislation (1921).

1900s—Promoted Negro culture and encouraged social action through presentation of Negro artists and social justice advocates, including elocutionist Nathaniel Guy, Hull House founder Jane Addams, and U. S. Congressman Martin Madden (1908-1915). Established the first organizational scholarship at Howard University (1914).

—Earnestine Green McNealey, Ph.D., AKA Historian August 2013

The South Atlantic Perspective

The South Atlantic Region is the largest region of all ten regions in Alpha Kappa Alpha Sorority, Incorporated. Initially, the original South Atlantic Region was composed of three states—Virginia, North Carolina, and South Carolina. Six graduate chapters and four undergraduate chapters in South Carolina were in the original South Atlantic Region.

South Carolina Chapters in Original South Atlantic Region

Graduate

Chartering Year	Chapter	Location
1934	Beta Zeta Omega	Orangeburg, South Carolina
1942	Gamma Nu Omega	Columbia, South Carolina
1942	Gamma Xi Omega	Charleston, South Carolina
1949	Epsilon Beta Omega	Spartanburg, South Carolina
1952	Epsilon Chi Omega	Florence, South Carolina
1952	Epsilon Tau Omega	Greenville, South Carolina

Undergraduate

Chartering Year	Chapter	School and Location
1938	Beta Sigma	South Carolina State College (University) Orangeburg, South Carolina
1947	Psi	Benedict College (University) Columbia, South Carolina
1947	Mu	Allen University Columbia, South Carolina
1949	Gamma Nu	Claflin College (University) Orangeburg, South Carolina

Chapters in Georgia and Florida were a part of the South Eastern Region, which was comprised of five states—Tennessee, Mississippi, Alabama, Georgia, and Florida. Those chapters in Georgia and Florida were as follows:

Graduate

Chartering Year	Chapter	Location
1923	Kappa Omega	Atlanta, Georgia
1940	Gamma Zeta Omega	Miami, Florida
1940	Gamma Theta Omega	Tampa, Florida
1941	Gamma Mu Omega	Daytona Beach, Florida
1943	Gamma Rho Omega	Jacksonville, Florida
1943	Gamma Pi Omega	Fort Valley, Georgia
1943	Gamma Sigma Omega	Savannah, Georgia
1943	Gamma Tau Omega	Columbus, Georgia
1947	Delta Iota Omega	Pensacola, Florida
1947	Delta Kappa Omega	Tallahassee, Florida
1947	Delta Eta Omega	Albany, Georgia
1947	Delta Omicron Omega	Orlando, Florida
1952	Epsilon Omega Omega	Macon, Georgia

Undergraduate

1930	Alpha Pi	Clark College (Clark/ Atlanta University) Atlanta, Georgia
1932	Beta Alpha	Florida A & M University Tallahassee, Florida
1942	Gamma Gama	Morris Brown College Atlanta, Georgia
1943	Alpha Beta	Fort Valley State College (University) Fort Valley, Georgia

1949	Gamma Sigma	Albany State College (University) Albany, Georgia
1949	Gamma Upsilon	Savannah State College (University) Savannah, Georgia
1949	Gamma Tau	Bethune-Cookman College (University) Daytona Beach, Florida

The South Eastern Region, which was composed of Tennessee, Mississippi, Alabama, Georgia, and Florida, was considered too large. Therefore, a Constitutional Amendment for realignment of the two Regions of South Atlantic and South Eastern was voted upon at the 1953 Boule in St. Louis, Missouri. The "New" South Atlantic Region removed North Carolina and Virginia from the South Atlantic Region and added Georgia and Florida to the region. The new South Atlantic Region would consist of three state—Florida, Georgia, and South Carolina. Zatella R. Turner was the Regional Director before the realignment, and A. Kathryn Johnson from Atlanta, Georgia, had been elected South Eastern Regional Director; however, she was appointed the new South Atlantic Regional Director (1953-1958). Lois Daniels of Nashville, Tennessee, was appointed to Regional Director of the South Eastern Region.

The First Regional Conference

A. Cathryn Johnson requested permission to plan and have the first South Atlantic Regional Conference as a joint Regional Conference with South Eastern. The request was granted, and the conference was held at Alabama A and M College (University) April 15-18, 1954. The joint regional conference was presided over by both A. Cathryn Johnson and Lois Daniels; there were approximately 200 in attendance. Gamma Mu and Epsilon Gamma Omega chapter were hostesses. (*Ivy Leaf,* June 1954).

The First Regional Report to Boule

The first South Atlantic Regional Report to the Boule was made at the 1954 Boule in Nashville, Tennessee, by A. Cathryn Johnson. She reported the following: "The new Undergraduate Cup was named 'The Mayme E. Williams Cup' for former South Eastern Regional Director. The Cup was awarded to Gamma Tau, Bethune-Cookman College, Daytona Beach, Florida. The Graduate Cup was named 'The Marie Woolfolk Taylor Cup' for the Founder. The Cup was awarded to Delta Omicron Omega, Orlando, Florida." (Minutes 1954 Boule).

The Regional Directors

Georgia Schank (1958-1959) succeeded A. Cathryn Johnson as South Atlantic Regional. She became an Ivy Beyond the Wall on April 29, 1959, while serving her first term. The Supreme Basileus, Marjorie H. Parker, appointed Mayme E. Williams (1959) to serve in an interim position until the appointment of Suzette F. Crank (1959-1964) who served in the remaining one and half years for Georgia Schank and was later elected as the South Atlantic Regional Director. Exhaustive research did not reveal or produce a photograph or any information about Georgia Schank other than her death date.

Since 1953, seventeen courageous, outstanding, and dedicated women have served as South Atlantic Regional Directors. Presently, Marsha Lewis Brown from Florida leads this region as Regional Director. Since 1953, the South Atlantic Region has increased in membership making it the largest region. As of June 28, 2013, the region had 107 graduate chapters, 58 undergraduate chapters, which totals 165 chapter with a membership of 1,113 undergraduates and 8,658 graduate members totaling 9,771. (Patricia A. Watkins, Director of Membership)

Honor is given to those who have served with distinction as South Atlantic Regional Directors.

Names	Years of Service
A. Cathryn Johnson	1953-1958
Georgia Schank	1958-1959
Mayme E. Williams	1959 (Interim)
Sujette Crank	1959-1964
Odessa Nelson	1964-1968
Margaret Roach	1968-1970
Homie Regulus	1970-1974
Norma Solomon White	1974-1978
DeLoris Ham Oliver	1978-1982
Mary Shy Scott	1982-1986
Frederica S. Wilson	1986-1990
Vertelle M. Middleton	1990-1994
Lucretia Payton-Stewart	1994-1998
Sonja W. Garcia	1998-2002
Irene W. McCollom	2002-2006
Ella Springs Jones	2006-2010
Marsha Lewis Brown	2010-Present

Two Regional Directors have gone on to become International Presidents of Alpha Kappa Alpha Sorority, Incorporated.

The 23rd International President (1990-1994) was Mary Shy Scott of Atlanta, Georgia. She completed the addition of the third floor to our Corporate Office (debt free) by instituting an assessment as part of the members' annual dues. She remains a popular International President.

The 25th International President (1998-2002), was Norma Solomon White from Jacksonville, Florida. She was Program Chairman during Mary Shy Scott's administration. One of White's programs, "On Track," focused on keeping our youth "on track" in reading, math, and other studies. She also coined "AKA Coat Day." Over 75,000 coats were donated to those in need.

Other former Regional Directors have served with distinction as international committee and special chairmen, on special committees, and in other leadership roles.

The Region is proud that the 28th International President, Carolyn House Stewart (2010-Present), is from the South Atlantic Region. Her program theme, "Global Leadership Through Timeless Service," has engaged chapters and members with programs and activities for youth leadership development, health, global poverty and economic security, human rights, and environmental sustainability.

Cluster Concept Creation

The creation of the cluster concept originated in the South Atlantic Region during the administration of Suzette Crank. The Neighborhood Concept was created to allow members who could not attend Regional Conferences or Boules an opportunity to attend a one-day, drive-in meeting. As the region continued to grow, the Neighborhood Concept expanded and included additional guidelines.

- The Neighborhood groups were realigned and renamed "Clusters." Chapters were assigned to eight clusters with eight appointed Cluster Coordinators during Norma Solomon White's administration.
- Guidelines for the election of Cluster Coordinators were adopted during the administrations of DeLoris Ham Oliver and Mary Shy Scott.
- The election of Cluster Coordinators was terminated and replaced with appointments by the Regional Director during the administration of Frederica S. Wilson.
- During Vertelle M. Middleton administration, Cluster Coordinators duties expanded and the Cluster Coordinators Council, chaired by Ella Springs Jones, assisted with the supervision and monitoring of chapters and hosting of Regional Conferences. Cluster Coordinators In-Training was created to prepare the appointees for the role of Cluster Coordinator.

- The role of Cluster Coordinator was expanded even more to assist with concerns of the undergraduate chapters during the administrations of Lucretia Payton-Stewart and Sonja W. Garcia.
- As the region continued to grow, Irene W. McCollom utilized the Cluster Coordinators in maintaining open communication, assisting with the interpretation of policies and program, and hosting of Regional Conferences.
- The advent of electronic communication meant instant information to chapters during Ella Springs Jones' administration through the Cluster Coordinators. Cluster conference calls were initiated and utilized extensively. Cluster Coordinators planned the Regional Director's VIP Dinner, hosted the Regional Suite during Regional Conferences and Boules, and planned the Boule South Atlantic Luncheon.

To date, Cluster Coordinators are appointed by the Regional Director; a nomination letter from the chapter, an application, and documentation are required for the process.

Significant Highlights of the South Atlantic Region

- ➤ Woolfolk Taylor, founding member, was a charter member of Kappa Omega, the oldest chapter in the South Atlantic Region
- ➤ Broke through segregation during the 1960s and integrated downtown hotels in the Region
- ➤ Cluster Concept established and introduced in other regions
- ➤ AKA at the State Capitol was designed by Marjorie H. Young and implemented throughout the Sorority
- ➤ "100 Years of Service: The Alpha Kappa Alpha Story" Centennial Traveling Exhibit was hosted in Atlanta, Georgia, and Tampa, Florida
- ➤ First Place winners in PIMS competition at the 57th Boule (1996), Baltimore, Maryland from Zeta Xi Omega Chapter, Augusta, Georgia, and 58th Boule (1998), Chicago, Illinois, Beta Zeta Omega Chapter, Orangeburg, South Carolina

- First Place Entrepreneurship Youth Business Plan Award, 64th Boule (2010), St. Louis, Missouri, from Upsilon Sigma Omega Chapter
- Regional EAF winner for largest contributions at Boules
- Four Boules hosted in the Region
    - 36th Boule (1956, Clark University, Atlanta, Georgia)
    - 46th Boule (1974, Fountainbleu, Miami Beach, Florida)
    - 49th Boule (1980, World Congress Center, Atlanta, Georgia)
    - 60th Boule (2002), Orange County Convention Center, Orlando, Florida)
    - scheduled for the 2016 Boule in Atlanta, Georgia
- Other Directorate Members
    - First Supreme Anti-Basileus: Mayme E. Williams (1954-1958), Mary Shy Scott (1986-1990), Norma Solomon White (1994-1998), and Carolyn House Stewart (2006-2010)
    - Second Supreme Anti-Basileus: Rosalind Fripp (1994-1998), Angela Okunsanya (1998-2002), and Jatisha Marsh (2002-2006)
    - Supreme Grammateus: Freddie L. Groomes (1986-1990) and Carolyn House Stewart (2002-2006)
    - Supreme Anti-Grammateus: Earnestine Green (1970-1974)
    - Supreme Tamiouchos: Delores Y. McKinley (2010-Present)
    - Supreme Parliamentarian: Patricia Russell (1978-1982), Lucretia Payton (1982-1986), Freddie L. Groomes-McLendon (2006-2010)
    - Undergraduate Member-at-Large: Dawn Adams (1974-1978), Delta Springer (1978-1982), Diedre Barrett (1982-1986), Chandra Dillard and Traci Williams (1986-1990)

- Editors-in-Chief, *Ivy Leaf*
    - Lucille McAllister Scott (1949-1953) and Earnestine Green (1974-1978)

- ➤ Executive Directors
  - ○ Alison Harris Alexander (1989-1996)
  - ○ Earnestine Green McNealey (1980-1985)

- ➤ Largest Region in Alpha Kappa Alpha Sorority, Incorporated

- ➤ Home of three the International Presidents
  - ○ Mary Shy Scott, 23rd
  - ○ Norma Solomon White, 25th
  - ○ Carolyn House Stewart, 28th

Honorary Members

- ❖ Coretta Scott King, Civil Rights Actives, Atlanta, Georgia, 1967
- ❖ M. Athalia Range, Secretary of Human Affairs for Florida, Miami, Florida, 1975
- ❖ Gladys Knight, Music Legend, 1984, Atlanta, Georgia
- ❖ Elena Diza-Verson Amos, Humanitarian and Volunteer, 1986, Columbus, Georgia
- ❖ Alice Coachman Davis, Olympia Gold Medalist, 1998, Albany, Georgia
- ❖ Valda S. Flewellyn, Poet, Author, and Storyteller, 2002, Sanford, Florida

Ella Springs Jones
August 2013

Introduction

The Climate of the Period/The Worth of a Child

ALPHA KAPPA ALPHA Sorority has 900 plus chapters of rich and illustrious histories, and Gamma Sigma Omega Chapter is one of those chapters. Gamma Sigma Omega Chapter proudly presents the chapter's history, encouraged by Supreme Basileus, Carolyn House Stewart, Esq. and Regional Director, Marsha Lewis Brown, to do a printed edition. This foresight perpetuates a revolving cycle for information to be beacons of light for legacies.

The chartering year, 1943, for Gamma Sigma Omega Chapter, in Savannah, GA, was inclusive of World War II, economics, and the concern for children. Franklin Delano Roosevelt, Democrat, was President of the United States. In November of 1943, Churchill and Roosevelt traveled to Tehran to meet with Stalin, and President Roosevelt realized that the peace of the world after the war depended upon the cooperation of the great world powers and that his attempts to build a friendship with Stalin were characterized not by naiveté but by a clash of goals.[4] Roosevelt's farsightedness in foreign policy was demonstrated in his conviction at the International Monetary Conference at Bretton Woods, New Hampshire, in July of 1944, a meeting that created the International Monetary Fund to stabilize world currencies and aid in reconstruction and development of nations.[5] Ellis Gibbs Arnall, Democrat, was Governor of Georgia, and Thomas Gamble, Jr., Democrat, was Mayor of Savannah.

Volunteerism and service to the community were welcoming venues for anyone. The *Savannah Morning News* columnist, Angelo Patri, wrote "Our Children" where the worth of a child was celebrated. This column must have touched the hearts of Gamma Sigma Omega's chartering members. January 1, 1943, a quote from the article says, "Children cannot go on working without attention from some respected older person. 'Come and see what I have done,' is a plea of recognition which must never be denied."[6] May 29, 1943, the article extols parents. However, Negro orphans don't have parents. This insight for service was the stepping stone for Gamma Sigma Omega Chapter to be the answer for a greater cause in the Savannah community, a home for neglected Negro children.

Marjorie Parker on Greenbriar and its Incorporation

The words of Marjorie Parker, author of *Alpha Kappa Alpha, 1908-1958*, express the major significance of Gamma Sigma Omega Chapter. She writes that in 1943, a report in a Savannah newspaper of a small bequest to "whoever" might start a movement to establish an orphanage for Negro children came to the attention of members of this chapter. For a long time, these women had been aware of the urgent need for a local institution designed for the care of orphans and other destitute children, for at that time these children were either neglected or housed with delinquents. To meet the stipulations of the bequest, it was necessary for Gamma Sigma Omega to make the initial move toward establishing the institution and to secure the support and cooperation of other community groups, especially the pastors of Protestant churches.[7] Ms. Parker continues that the chapter raised funds to purchase a half-block of land as the first step. Then in June, 1944, eight members of Gamma Sigma Omega incorporated as Greenbriar Children's Center, Inc, so that community members might be included. She said that between 1945 and 1948, the group raised more than $50,000, and was able to establish the Home at Hunter Field. When expansion of Hunter Field made it necessary for them to give up that property, Gamma Sigma Omega members led the campaign for funds for a new location. In October, 1955, a new Greenbriar, completed at a cost exceeding $250,000 was opened.[8] The new Greenbriar is the only institution in Chatham County, Georgia, which serves dependent and neglected

Negro children. Continuing to write, she says the new institution has always had an interracial Board of Directors, and the President has always been a member of Gamma Sigma Omega Chapter. One of the cottages of the Center is named for Alpha Kappa Alpha member, Martha W. Wilson. Mrs. Wilson served as President of the Board of Directors during the formative years.[9]

Timeless Service in Gamma Sigma Omega Chapter will present the National program foci that solidified Gamma Sigma Omega Chapter's challenge to be that voice for homeless Negro children in Savannah. Gamma Sigma Omega Chapter has not only served Greenbriar Children's Center but has mentored middle school girls, provided reading and math tutorials, reading initiatives, voter registration drives, health initiatives, economic initiatives; showcased oratorical talent and cultural awareness; and has given financial donations to institutions, organizations, and individuals. The profiles of different administrations and the membership will give a capsule of our service and our talents.

Emma Jean Conyers, Author

Chapter I

THE CREATORS

Martha W. Wilson

Chartering

> To the Basileus, [Beulah Tyrell Whitby], Directorate,
> Delegates, and visitors of the Twenty-fifth Annual Boule
> Session of Alpha Kappa Alpha Sorority now in session in
> Chicago, Ill, I bring you greetings from the Southeastern
> Region...May 29, 1943: a trip was made to Savannah, Ga.,
> where plans had been completed at the Directorate Meeting
> to establish a graduate chapter. That night, six sorors took
> the vows and one Ivy was initiated, Gamma Sigma Omega.[10]

THE REPORT OF Irma F. Clark, Supreme Grammateus, highlighted
Gamma Sigma Omega (GSO) by saying that at the Twenty-Fifth
Annual Boule the new chapters chartered in 1943: Alpha Beta, Fort

1

Valley College, Fort Valley, GA, April 23, 1943; Beta Theta Omega, Wheeling, West Virginia, March 27, 1943; Gamma Sigma Omega, Savannah, GA, May 29, 1943; Gamma Tau Omega, Columbus, GA, July 16, 1943. She writes that the charter for the chapter at Savannah, GA had been granted at the Twenty-Fourth Boule, but due to difficulties in securing transfers, the chapter was not established until 1943 and that the last chapter to be established in 1943 was Gamma Tau Omega.[11]

In September 1943, the *Ivy Leaf* reported that Gamma Sigma Omega Chapter was being enthusiastically received and the year's program of activities was already beginning. The chartered members were sorors Irene Alexander, Frances Dye, Juanita Jennings, Mattie Paine [Payne], Mamie Russell, and Martha Wilson. Associated with the chapter were Lenore Blackshear, Angeline Brown, and Dorothy Jamerson.[12] *Gamma Sigma Omega Chapter of Alpha Kappa Alpha Sorority, Inc.* reports there were seven charter members. Six were listed on the charter.[13] The obituary of Martha Wilson reports that the chartering was done in her living room. Wilson was the first President.[14]

Initial Service

At the September 1943 meeting of the chapter, Frances Dye told the other members that she had learned from a newspaper notice that the deceased woman, Adeline Graham, had left property and funds "to whoever might start a movement to establish an Orphanage for Negro Children." A committee composed of Dye, Martha Wilson, and Dorothy Jamerson investigated the bequest, reported to the chapter their findings, and thus the chapter's first project was undertaken.[15]

The National focus of Alpha Kappa Alpha Sorority gave an impetus to Gamma Sigma Omega to answer the challenge of Adeline Graham. The Regional Director, Collye Lee Riley, reported topics discussed at the Southeastern Region to the Twenty-Fifth Annual Boule: "Effects of War and Defense Program Upon Economic Conditions," and "Nutrition and Post War Planning." Such topics gave impetus to Gamma Sigma Omega's decision to answer the call of Adeline Graham's.[16]

Also, the following statement, "Report of National Non-Partisan Council on Public Affairs," by Norman E. Boyd, 1944, suggested an awareness to Gamma Sigma Omega's members of children and health needs: "We have co-operated with our Health project in trying always to get any health legislation passed, as well as co-operating in trying to devise ways and means of supplementing the National treasury and in the execution of these plans through voluntary activity of the chapter."[17]

In addition to Boyd's article, the comment, in 1944, "There has never been a time in the history of the world when the need of our drastic action where the health of the nation, and particularly the health of the Negro, is more apparent than now."[18]

These positions by Alpha Kappa Alpha Sorority were the foundation that gave the women of Gamma Sigma Omega the inspiration to promote the need for an orphanage for Negro children.

With the National Office emphasizing the health of the Negro, the ladies of Gamma Sigma Omega Chapter were compelled to offer service to the Negro orphans in Savannah, GA. The National Health Committee set as its objectives at the Twenty-Fifth Annual Boule, 1944 the following:

1. To improve health standards among Negroes throughout America.
2. To train in methods of disease prevention.
3. To introduce new techniques for solving food and household problems.
4. To teach Health and Hygiene habits.
5. To stress the importance of eating the right kinds of foods.
6. To bring needed relief from physical suffering to people of low income groups in remote rural areas.
7. To aid making available to Negroes such resources for health that are provided through Federal, State, and other agencies.[19]

The ladies set out to work, and according to article, "Gamma Sigma Omega Chapter," March 1944:

> Each member is enthusiastic because of the great need for
> such an institution in the city of Savannah. With the aid
> of the colored Protestant churches much progress has been
> made and Gamma Sigma Omega is looking forward to the
> establishment of a modern institution to meet the needs of
> homeless colored children. On Friday, February 11, 1944, a
> mass meeting was held for the purpose of acquainting every
> citizen with the progress made and steps taken by the chapter
> as sponsor of this project.[20]

Greenbriar: The Name and Incorporation

With Gamma Sigma Omega's members at the helm, community support was sought and received, the provisions of the deceased woman's Will carried out, and an institution for orphaned and destitute Negro children began to take organizational shape. "The group called its project the Greenbriar Children's Center."[21] Frank Rossiter writes in article, "Neglected Negro Children May Get Overdue 'Break,' " that the name "Greenbriar was selected to get away from the need of referring to it as a home or orphanage.[22] On June 8, 1944, Greenbriar Children's Center, Incorporated came into being, just one year after Gamma Sigma Omega Chapter was chartered. On July 15, 1949, the Center's first building opened for occupancy.[23] There were twenty children and accommodation for a housemother, all through the efforts and leadership of Gamma Sigma Omega's members.[24] Thus for many years, Gamma Sigma Omega Chapter of Alpha Kappa Alpha Sorority and Greenbriar Children's Center, Inc. were almost synonymous. Greenbriar was the Chapter's primary project, which included fundraising, leadership, personal involvement, and service from the beginning until approximately 1966 when Federal, State, and City funding became more readily available to the Center.[25]

Wilson's obituary reports that Frances Clarke Dye served as the first Board President of Greenbriar. When Dye moved to New York in the fall of 1944, Martha Wilson was elected Greenbriar Board President in 1946 and served as President until 1956. She was succeeded by Countess Y. Cox in 1956.[26]

Minutes of the Twenty-Seventh Annual Boule in 1947 explained that Gamma Sigma Omega, Savannah, Georgia had done an outstanding civic service to the community by answering the call of a wealthy white citizen who had left in her Will funds for a Negro Orphanage. The article said when several months had elapsed and no group had accepted the responsibility, Gamma Sigma Omega carried through the provision of the Will.[27]

"Greenbriar Children's Center Orphanage Built by Sorority Dedicated," 1949, reports that formal dedication exercises were held recently to launch the official operation of Greenbriar Children's Center, a home for orphans. The article says the home represents a seven year project completed by eight members of Gamma Sigma Omega of Alpha Kappa Alpha Sorority who saw its need in Chatham County. Under the leadership of Mrs. Martha Wilson, faculty member of Georgia State College and chairman of the Center's Board of Directors, the chapter raised $5,000.00. The article continues that the building is located on a ten acre lot at Hunter Field, formerly the WAC (Women Army Corp) Headquarters. It was completely renovated at the cost of $35,000 and can accommodate eleven girls and nine boys. It is attractively decorated in green and ivory [ivy] and was furnished largely with equipment donated by the public-spirited citizens. Adjacent to the Center is the former WAC recreation building which is to be converted into a recreation center for the occupants of the home. The article reported that the present staff consists of Miss Frances Nichols, house maker; Miss Dorothy M. Littles [Little], housemother; Nathaniel Little, maintenance man and Miss Minnie Smith, dietician.[28]

From the Minutes of the Twenty-Ninth Annual Boule, December 27-30, 1949, in Houston, Texas the Southeastern Region gave as its highlight of Community and Inter-racial interest, the opening of the Greenbriar Orphanage. It was reported that eight "sorors" of Savannah, Georgia started the movement which became a Community-wide project and in a two-week drive, fifty thousand ($50,000) dollars were raised. The opening was July, 1949.[29]

The September – December 1950, *Ivy Leaf's*, article "Gamma Sigma Omega Notes" indicated several activities of the chapter, including a campaign for Greenbriar Children's Center. The article said that on Saturday, June 10, 1950, the chapter met at the home of Ernestine Bertrand for their last meeting of the official term. The members congratulated Mary McDew, who served as acting Basileus the past year. Wilson, Pike, and King were presented gifts of appreciation for their loyalty and courage. The sorority also paid high tribute to Martha Wilson for her outstanding contribution to the Savannah community, especially to Greenbriar Children's Center. The article said that during the war, the Chapter raised $5,000. After the close of the war, a campaign was started to raise $50,000 for Greenbriar to be built. In the spring of 1950, the article continues that $1500 was raised for the American Cancer Society. The newly elected officers were listed as follows: Basileus, Kathryn Bogan; Anti-Basileus, Muriel King; Grammateus, Helen Walker; Tamiouchos, Violet Singleton, Epistoleus, Ouida Thompson; Parliamentarian, Martha Wilson; and Ivy Leaf Reporter, Mary E. Williams.[30]

Public Awareness

Many in the Savannah community took note of the ladies in Gamma Sigma Omega Chapter because of their service. One avenue for public awareness is an annual Founders' Day Observance.

"Founders' Day was observed February 6, 1944, when the chapter worshipped at First Congregational Church. The main address was delivered by Soror Mattie Payne who has had many years of experience and association in Alpha Kappa Alpha." [31]

Founders' Day celebration was reported in the *Ivy Leaf,* June 1946. The article, "Gamma Sigma Omega Chapter, Savannah, Georgia" reads that the thirty-eighth anniversary of the founding of the Alpha Kappa Alpha Sorority was celebrated with a musical at St. John's Baptist Church on Sunday, February 21 at 5 o'clock. Members of the Chapter offered numerous musical selections. Those appearing on the program were Lula Lafayette, Jane Parker, Amy Bailey, Elizabeth Kendrick, and Mary McDew.[32]

Also the article reported that on March 1, three hundred persons were reported as guests at the first formal dance which was given at the Cocoanut Grove. The flowers used for decorations were later donated to the charity ward of a local hospital.[33]

In addition in 1946, the article describes the play, "His Women Folks," presented by the members during the third week in May at Georgia State College [Savannah State University].[34]

New Members

Johnnie Lockett Fluker and Jamie Reddick Graham were listed in the March 1946 Ivy Leaf as Neophytes.[35]

In 1948, Gamma Sigma Omega Chapter initiated two new sorors, Louise Lautier and Florence Fonielle [Fonvielle] according to article "Gamma Sigma Omega Chapter Initiates Two." It says that Lautier received her Master's Degree from the University of Michigan and served as critic teacher in Powell Laboratory School at Georgia State College and that she did her undergraduate work at Georgia State College. At the time she was employed as an instructor of English at Georgia State College. It was also reported that Fonvielle received the bachelor of arts degree with a major in biology at Livingstone College, Salisbury, N. C. and that prior to coming to Savannah, Fonvielle was a teacher in the elementary schools in Gastonia, North Carolina.[36]

The Pan-Hellenic Council

The Pan-Hellenic Council was created on the campus of Howard University, May 10, 1930, in Washington, DC as reported in the Mission of the Pan-Hellenic. The charter members were Omega Psi Phi and Kappa Alpha Psi Fraternities, and Alpha Kappa Alpha, Delta Sigma Theta and Zeta Phi Beta Sororities. In 1931, Alpha Phi Alpha and Phi Beta Sigma Fraternities joined the Council. Sigma Gamma Rho Sorority joined in 1937, and Iota Phi Theta Fraternity completed the list of member organizations in 1997. The National Pan-Hellenic Council (NPHC) promotes interaction through forums, meetings and other mediums for the exchange of information and engages in cooperative programming and initiatives through various activities and functions.[37]

Supreme Basileus, Maudelle Bousfield records in the Minutes of the Thirteenth Annual Boule, December 28-31, 1930, that Bobbie Scott was appointed to represent Alpha Kappa Alpha at the Pan-Hellenic Council held in Washington, May 10, 1930. A constitution was adopted and that AKA paid $25 dues, to be a yearly amount. She indicated that the following organizations were represented: Kappa Alpha Psi, Omega Psi Phi, Alpha Kappa Alpha, Delta Sigma Theta, and Zeta Phi Beta.[38]

Recognizing the importance of such an organization, the members of Gamma Sigma Omega Chapter took the lead to establish a local chapter of the National Pan-Hellenic Council in Savannah. "Gamma Sigma Omega in Pan-Hellenic Organization" states that the members of Gamma Sigma Omega are proud of the fact that they were instrumental in organizing a chapter of the Pan-Hellenic Council in Savannah.[39] According to "Gamma Sigma Omega Notes," Dorothy Jamerson conceived the idea for a Pan-Hellenic Council in Savannah.[40] The local chapter consists of representatives from seven Greek letter organizations and that Martha Wright Wilson, Mary Williams, and Mattie B. Payne were the AKA representatives. Payne was Chairman of the Pan-Hellenic group.[41]

"Greenbriar Children's Center Orphanage Built by Sorority Dedicated" reported that the members of Gamma Sigma Omega are working untiringly with the Pan-Hellenic Council with Sorors Martha Wilson, Quiddo [Ouida] Thompson and Mary E. Williams as members of the Council. The Council presented an Art exhibit at the West Broad Street Y.M.C.A. featuring AKA, Erline Simms, who headed the Art Department that year [1949] at Georgia State College.[42]

On May 28, 1950, "Gamma Sigma Omega Notes," Gamma Sigma Omega presented a radio program at the Pan-Hellenic Council Art and Hobby Show. Dorothy Jamerson who conceived the idea of a Pan-Hellenic Council was the reader for this radio program with songs by Mary McDew, Agatha Curley, Johnnie Fluker, Marian Roberts and Violet Singleton, and Jane P. Starr at the piano.[43]

Chapter II

THE BUILDERS

Gamma Upsilon

> "to cultivate and encourage high scholastic and ethical standards, improve the social stature of the race, promote unity and friendship among college women…" (Alpha Kappa Alpha Sorority, Inc.). An Alpha Kappa Alpha Sorority interest group was organized in 1948, and Grace Hunt, a faculty member of Georgia State College, was appointed as sponsor. For administrative reasons, Dr. Colston inactivated Miss Hunt, which automatically stopped the formation of the organization until another sponsor could be chosen. The interest group stayed intact under the guidance of Mattie B. Payne, Basileus, Gamma Sigma Omega Chapter.[44]

IN 1948, DR. James A. Colston, President, Georgia State College (now Savannah State College*) [Savannah State University] undertook the establishment of the Pan-Hellenic Council for the purpose of spearheading the formation of chapters for all academic Greek letter organizations on the campus. The organization would also be known as the Greek Letter Governing Board.[45]

Dean William Kenneth Payne, the successor to Dr. Colston in 1949, requested that steps be taken to establish the undergraduate chapter during the Fall Quarter 1949. Evanel Renfrow, transferred from Gamma Epsilon Omega Chapter, was appointed sponsor.[46]

Although ten candidates were required by the Boule for initiation, Mayme E. Williams, South Eastern Regional Director, gave permission for seven young women with appropriate academic averages of no less than a B- be formed into an Ivy Leaf Club. On a 3-point scale, one candidate had a cumulative grade point average of 2.9; two candidates had an average of 2.7.[47]

Charter fees, per capital tax, and pin costs were duly sent to Carey Maddox, Administrative Secretary, National Office, and with the discriminating and knowledgeable assistance of Mattie B. Payne and Mayme Williams, the pledging ceremony, probation period activities, and responsibilities were completed.[48]

The candidates for membership into Gamma Upsilon Chapter of Alpha Kappa Alpha Sorority were initiated November 26, 1949. Following the initiation, a very lovely candlelight dinner with ivy and pink carnation decorations was held in Hodge Hall. Mayme Williams was the Banquet speaker. Sunomia Lewis was elected as first Basileus.[49]

"Gamma Upsilon Set up at Savannah State College," describes the sponsorship of this Chapter by Gamma Sigma Omega Chapter. The March 1950 *Ivy Leaf* says that seven co-eds were initiated in Alpha Kappa Alpha Sorority November 26. The seven were the Charter members of Gamma Upsilon: Jessie R. Collier, Savannah; Helen S. Dilworth, Savannah; Marie Farley; Jewel Gamble, Vidalia; Sunomia Lewis, Savannah; Dorothy Y. Singleton, Augusta; Dorothy D. McIver, Savannah. They were introduced and initiated by Mamye E. Williams, Southeastern Regional Director from Miami, Florida. Mattie B. Payne was Basileus of GSO, and Evanel Renfrow was sponsor of Gamma Upsilon Chapter.[50]

Fashionetta

Fundraising for Greenbriar Children's Center was paramount for the chapter. In December 1951, the *Ivy Leaf* reports that Gamma Sigma Omega met in September at the home of Eleanor Bryant Williams and that Teddy Martin was a graduate of Talladega College with plans to transfer to Gamma Sigma Omega and also Vandelle planned to transfer to the chapter. The chapter planned to introduce to Savannah for the first time, Fashionetta, a social and fundraising event. Officers elected to fill out the terms left vacant were Grammateus, Edwina Ford and Epistoleus, Eleanor Bryant Williams.[51]

GSO's first Fashionetta was held November 30, reported "Fashionetta Held at Savannah, GA," March 1952 *Ivy leaf.* It was held in the auditorium of Beach High School. "All who attended came away saying Savannah had never witnessed such a beautiful affair before and that no one should miss it this coming year."[52] The winners were Dorothy Davis, Senior Fashionetta, sponsored by Stella Reeves; and Edwina Simmons, Junior Fashionetta, sponsored by Violet Singleton and Jane Parker, raising the largest cash amount.[53]

"Gamma Sigma Omega Gives $500 to Charity," 1953, explains that a goal of $500 for others was reached here at the end of the year by Gamma Sigma Omega. Over $150 went into the preparation of Christmas baskets by GSO members to the needy through the public welfare agencies and Family Service December 23. Earlier, December 21, a community carol sing was held at the Greenbriar Children's Home. Members also decorated a beautiful tree for the appreciative youngsters. Basileus, Jane Parker, told the local press of the chapter's fundraising success and pledged that Alpha Kappa Alpha would take increase responsibility in service in 1953. The remainder of the chapter's $500 was ear marked for Girl Scoutcamperships, student scholarships, funds for NAACP, the Boys Industrial Farm and United Community Services. The article explained that Gamma Sigma Omega's fundraising goal was attained by its successful second annual Fashionetta which featured the glamorous Miss Dororthy McDavid of New York City. The Charleston, SC chapter very kindly permitted Gamma Sigma Omega to follow their previously successful Fashionetta theme of "A Symphony in Color." Miss Bernice Washington was presented as "Miss Fashionetta." Little Miss Emily Stevens was presented as "Junior Miss Fashionetta." Gamma Upsilon Chapter of Savannah State College cooperated with the graduates. Gamma Upsilon served as ushers and provided the affair's narrator, Miss Phoebe Robinson.[54]

Gamma Sigma Omega and Gamma Upsilon Resume [Resume'] of Activities

The year 1957 was another eventful one for the chapter. "Gamma Sigma Omega and Gamma Upsilon Give Resume [Resume'] of Activites," was presented in *Ivy Leaf,* June 1957. The article states that the graduate chapter, Gamma Sigma Omega and the undergrads, Gamma Upsilon, gathered together to observe Founders' Day. It was distinctively an impressive affair at which A. Catherine Johnson was featured speaker. One other highlight of the occasion was selections by the "Alphaettes" which was composed of members of Gamma Upsilon and Gamma Sigma Omega, article says. It continued to describe the entertainment with Gamma Sigma Omega's sparkling version of "Fashionable." "Easter Parade" was the theme, and the program was divided into 4 (four parts): (1) Easter morning (2) Cocktails (3) Easter Monday (sportswear) and (4) Let's Dance. The fourth part consisted of dancing.[55]

A New Region for Gamma Sigma Omega

The year 1953 became a transitional period for Gamma Sigma Omega Chapter. Boston, Conyers, and Parham write that in December 1953, the 33rd Boule held in St. Louis, Missouri, voted to establish the new South Atlantic Region, comprising the states of Florida, Georgia, and South Carolina. The original South Atlantic Region was comprised of the states of Virginia, North Carolina, and South Carolina. This realignment was the result of growth in the number of chapters. In 1954, the South Eastern and the new South Atlantic regions held a Joint Regional, the only joint Regional in the history of the Sorority.[56]

A. Cathryn Johnson, Regional Director, at the Thirty-third Boule reported twenty-five graduate chapters in the South Eastern Region, in 1953 that included Alabama, Florida, Georgia, Mississippi, and Tennessee.[57] At the Thirty-fourth Boule, 1954, Johnson gave greetings from the new South Atlantic Region to Florida, Georgia, and South Carolina, twenty graduate chapters. She said the Region through

12

planning was smaller, more friendly, potentially closer-knit, and perhaps more easily organized. She said the Region had enjoyed and benefitted by two Regional Conferences this year: Easter week-end at Normal, Alabama. On this occasion, the New South Atlantic and the New South Eastern groups held joint conferences.[58]

Members and Events

The Minutes of the Thirty-six Boule reported that Gamma Sigma Omega, Savannah, GA, Dr. Mary Williams, P.H, Chairman, conducted physical therapy program to help individuals suffering with such diseases as arthritis, neuritis, rheumatism, nervous and accident cases.[59] In March, 1956, the *Ivy Leaf,* "Health News," acknowledged Gamma Sigma Omega as one of the contributing chapters to donate gifts to Veterans Administration Hospital. The gifts from chapters included wrappings, money, time and energy that brought Christmas cheer to some six hundred patients of the Veterans Administration Hospital, Tuskegee, Alabama and to their relatives and friends in twenty-eight states.[60]

In 1959, Jimmie C. Tiggett reports in article, "Gamma Sigma Omega," that Ouida Thompson served as Basileus and that a joint meeting was held with Gamma Upsilon, the undergraduate chapter. It said that as part of the health project, Christmas gifts were collected from members and sent to patients at Milledgeville State Hospital. The article continues by reporting that members were still working at Greenbriar Children's Center. The chapter held their annual Christmas party for members and guests, December 22. The article reported that Louise Lautier Owens was delegate at the Cincinnati Boule and that the fundraising project for 1959-1960 for scholarships was Fashionetta, Ernestine Betrand, Chairman.[61]

1959 South Atlantic Regional Conference in Savannah

The Minutes of the Thirty-eight Boule of Alpha Kappa Alpha Sorority, Inc., Cincinnati, Ohio, December 26-30, 1959 reports that the South Atlantic Regional Conference, March 27-28, 1959 was held in Savannah, GA with Gamma Sigma Omega and Gamma Upsilon Chapters as Hostesses. The minutes read that no effort was spared in making the visiting AKAs feel welcome and comfortable at Savannah State College. The minutes stated that the Alpha Phi Alpha Regional was held at the same time, so a joint Public Meeting took place. Supreme Anti-Basileus Mayme Williams was banquet speaker. There were 144 registered delegates in attendance. At the time, Georgia Schanck was Regional Director, her last Regional Conference. Because of Schanck's death, Sujette Fountain Crank was appointed Regional Director in July, 1959.[62]

Chapter III

THE VISIONARIES

Greenbriar for All Children and the Formulation of the Foundation

I N 1960, THE Greenbriar Children's Center was opened to all children.[63] According to "Greenbriar Foundation Is Organized" April 1961, A Pratt Adams, a Savannah Attorney, announced the organization of the Greenbriar Foundation, Inc., a corporation established to receive bequests or gifts of money to be used for the benefit of Greenbriar Children's Cnter. Adam emphasized that the funds of the Foundation would not be used for operating expenses, since Greenbriar is supported by Chatham County and the United Community Services. The first gift of $500 to the foundation was given by Gamma Sigma Omega Chapter, Leila Braithwaite, Basileus, Ms. J. W. Wilson (Martha Wilson), Vice President of Foundation and Ms. S. M. McDew Jr. (Mary McDew) Secretary.[64] Because Greenbriar was now supported by Chatham County and the United Community Services, the chapter was able to make more substantial donations to other charities. However, GSO Chapter continued to make annual financial donations to Greenbriar, and Alpha Kappa Alpha women (AKAs) continued to serve as members of the Board of Directors.

Gamma Sigma Omega bemoans the appearance of Greenbriar Children's Center and is moved to make a difference. The article, "Gamma Sigma Omega," listed the new officers of the chapter: Lelia Braithwaite, Basileus; Louise Owens, Anti-Basileus; Kay Francis Stripling, Grammateus; Laura Martin, Epistoleus; Lillie A. Powell,

Tamiouchos; Martha Wilson, Graduate Dean/Undergraduate Advisor, Carolyn Stafford, Ivy Leaf Reporter; and Violet Singleton, Parliamentarian. Also, the article explains the condition of Greenbriar. It said though Greenbriar may seem finished to on lookers, chapter members were not completely satisfied. Greenbriar Children's Center had five cottages and housed sixty children. One of the cottages was named for Martha Wilson. At that time, members serving on the Greenbriar Board were Mary McDew, Martha Wilson, Ouida Thompson, Countess Cox, Louise Owens, Mattie Payne, and Leila Braithwaite. Wilson and Cox were former Board Presidents. The chapter started work on a new building for Greenbriar, one that would accommodate ten emotionally disturbed children. It would cost approximately $35,000. The article continued to inform readers that GSO not only gave service to Greenbriar but to other charitable causes, scholarships to graduating students from high schools, contributions to the NAACP, support in the student "sit-In" movement, assistance to the TB campaign, Christmas gifts to hospitals, curtains for Mills Memorial Hospital.[65]

The Central Administration building at Greenbriar Children's Center was named Ivy Hall in 1966 in honor of "the initial and abiding interest" of Gamma Sigma Omega Chapter of Alpha Kappa Alpha Sorority, Inc. The ivy leaf is the symbol of Alpha Kappa Alpha Sorority.

Virginia M. Parham and the Completion of Hettie Copeland's Term

In 1963, Virginia Mercer writes in the *Ivy Leaf* that the chapter was having a busy year. A Scholarship Dance was given in October. Members worshipped together the third Sunday in November and for Thanksgiving bought tickets for twenty children from the Greenbriar Children's Center, Inc. for the Thanksgiving Azalea Classic football game. Other children from the Center were Thanksgiving Dinner guests of various members. She reported that the chapter was hostess to Gamma Upsilon for the first joint meeting of the year in December. The meeting was business and social where parts of "To Capture A Vision Fair" were discussed and Christmas gifts were exchanged. She included that the chapter's main project, Fashionetta 1963, was held March 1, 1963. The proceeds went to Greenbriar Children's Center, Inc. The Basileus was Hettie F. Copeland who represented the chapter at the 1962 Boule.[66]

Virginia Mercer Parham, as Anti-Basileus, completed Hettie Copeland's term when Copeland relocated from Savannah to Augusta, Georgia, in 1963. Also, effective January 1, 1964, Alpha Kappa Alpha Sorority, Inc. changed its term of office for chapter officers from a fiscal year, July-June, to a calendar year, January-December.[67]

1964 Membership Intake

On January 5, 1964, the chapter initiated Sylvia Bowen, Mozella Collier, Mattie Leftwich, and Willie Mae Patterson. Parham had just begun her first full calendar year as Basileus.[68]

Following Parham's term of office as Basileus, she embarked upon the task of writing the chapter's first set of By-Laws. Violet Singleton and Mary McDew provided guidance and secured copies of by-laws from other chapters and the National documents as guides.[69]

During the tenure of Mozella G. Collier, the chapter supported the national projects: the Cleveland Job Corps, the United Negro College Fund Drive, and the National Council of Negro Women.[70]

1970 Membership Intake

The chapter increased its membership from 16 to 26 by initiating 10 ladies on June 2, 1970. They were Albertha E. Boston, Albertha W. Collier, Agatha Cooper, Ethel Gibbs, Leona B. Henley, Merdis Lyons, Freddie Pippen, Onnye Jean Sears, Annette Taylor, and Margaret Washington.[71]

Project SEARCH

With emphasis from the Alpha Kappa Alpha Sorority National Office being placed on Personal Involvement Now (P.I.N), on January

7, 1973, Gamma Sigma Omega's members launched project SEARCH (Service through Emulation, Action, Resources, Counseling, and Humanity). The target area for this project was a neglected black community known as Ogeecheeton.[72]

The Spring 1974 *Ivy Leaf* reports that P.I.N. program was known locally in Savannah, GA as Project SEARCH (Service through Emulation, Action, Resources, Counseling and Humanity). There were four general objectives and four specific objectives that were concentrated in one deprived community known as Ogeecheeton. The objectives were (1) to provide opportunity for the residents to life, liberty and the pursuit of happiness (2) to provide opportunity for the reduction of frustration which exists among residents of this neglected community, and (3) to show humanitarian concern for the welfare of the residents through personal involvement and community action by all sororos of the chapter. Activities implemented: (1) The chapter worshipped with the residents at each of the community churches during January as introductory steps. (2) A Get-Acquainted fish fry was given for the residents in March so they and the sorors could meet. (3) A house to house survey of the community was taken and data from the survey was made to determine the needs and desires of the residents and as guidelines for the chapter in developing the project activities. (4) A play-in and wiener roast for the children of the community were given in May on a nearby vacant lot. (5) During the summer months, five recreational activities were provided for the community's youth: a tour of an industry and museum, two skating outings, a movie party and a picnic. Sewing classes were started for interested pre-teens and teenagers. Bookmobile services for the community were secured, and the members conducted a story hour twice a month for the children. Community workshops began in December. In these workshops, family related topics were discussed, such as preparation of nutritious meals, purchasing items on credit, shopping for insurance and advising of services available from local and educational agencies. Also, an Arts and Crafts Workshop for interested residents was started. These activities, programs, and workshops were the outgrowth of the survey which indicated the interests, needs and desires of the residents of the

Ogeecheeton community to be continued throughout 1974 or as long as there was an apparent need for or interest in all or any aspects of Project SEARCH. The project was chaired by Janie B. Bruen with Johnye P. Gillans as co-chairperson.[73]

In addition to these activities, there were health care services, community beautification, voter registration and education, recreational and cultural activities. Also, workshops informed youth of educational opportunities. Both youth and adults learned to sew and enjoyed arts and crafts as they made ceramic and leather articles as well as things from household throw-a-ways. Residents' children received dental, visual, auditory, and lead poisoning screening. They were checked for proper immunizations, and they were aided in securing their birth certificates needed to enter school. The adults were screened for high blood pressure, diabetes, and cardiovascular disorders. Members participated in Ogeecheeton Community Clean-up Day where they helped to clean the neighborhood and to provide transportation for removal of old appliances, trash, and other debris. The chapter provided funds for complete water hook-ups, including meters and plumbing, for the four homes in the community that did not have any type of running water.[74]

In the four years that project SEARCH in Ogeecheeton was the chapter's major project, much was accomplished in that community, and the members were truly personally involved, rendering time, service, and money. The project was implemented under Basileus, Margaret Chisholm Robinson, and continued under Basileus, Clemontine Freeman Washington.[75]

1975 Membership Intake

In the summer of 1974, under the reign of Basileus Robinson, action was started to initiate new members. On May 9, 1975, with Clemontine F. Washington as Basileus, four ladies were initiated into the chapter. They were Jacquelyn Handy, Mildred Mobley, Serdalia Singleton, and Dorothy Wilson. Virginia Parham, former Basileus, was Dean of Graduate Candidates. Emma Jean Conyers served as Assistant.[76]

1976 Regional Conference in Savannah.

The fall *Ivy Leaf* 1976 reports that the Twenty-Third Regional Conference was held in Savannah, Georgia, April 15-17, 1976, with the members of Gamma Sigma Omega, Zeta Iota Omega, and Gamma Upsilon Chapters serving as hostesses. More than 650 Alpha Kappa Alpha members were in attendance. Gamma Sigma Omega's Mozella G. Collier and Clemontine Washington, Basileus, served as co-chairmen of the conference. Paula R. McNeely was Basileus of Zeta Iota Omega Chapter, and Bronwyn McCall was Basileus of Gamma Upsilon Chapter. Norma S. White was the Regional Director of the South Atlantic Region. The article reports that the national theme was "Greater Involvement: Alpha Kappa Alpha's Responsibility." On Thursday, April 15, 1976, the Supreme Basileus, Bernice Sumlin, was honored at a reception which was held in the Hilton's Harborview Room. More than 350 guests attended the reception.

The article notes that the Savannah Alumni Chapter of Kappa Alpha Psi Fraternity, Inc. provided coffee. Alderman Roy Jackson of the City of Savannah presented the Regional Director the Key to the City.[77]

Tutorial Reading Program

With many of the objectives of project SEARCH having been accomplished and with National's emphasis on the Reading Experience, Gamma Sigma Omega's members sought to combine related parts of project SEARCH with the Reading Experience. The outcome of this merger resulted in a tutorial reading program, opened to any interested child. The Tutorial Reading Program met twice a week, with an arts and crafts program integrated to stimulate and maintain interest. By popular demand, the sewing program for children was continued, with both programs being held in the Social Hall of Butler Presbyterian Church. The chapter's members transported interested children from the Ogeecheeton area to the programs at the Church.[78]

In reference to the Tutorial Reading Program, the article, "Gamma Sigma Omega Sisterhood at Work," explained the Tutorial Reading

Program was now opened to any child in the Savannah Community. It said while working on an approach to cause changes in living conditions, health and safety habits, and nutritional standards, the chapter felt it important to begin by providing recreational, cultural, and reading experiences for youth of the community. A reading program was established and the objectives established were (1) to improve youth and overall community literacy (2) to improve attitudes of the community's youth toward learning by improving basic reading skills and up grading their academic performance (3) to create an early desire to read among young children by showing them that reading is fun. The article continues to say that the community's response to the reading program was good, and the appreciation of the parents was great, and that in conjunction with the reading program, sewing classes and classes in arts and crafts were added. Periodic fashion shows were attended by very proud relatives. The arts and crafts classes were also popular. Ceramic sculpture, macramé, wall hangings, tie-dyeing and silk screen printing were some of the created arts and crafts presented in an exhibition at Carver State Bank. Since the Ogeecheeton project's initiation in January 1973, the chapter expanded its chapter's reading, recreational, sewing, and arts and crafts programs [1977], to forty-five students, attending three times a week in two-hour blocks each. Lydia Young was Basileus, and Jessie C. DeLoach was Anti-Basileus.[79] These activities were funded through the efforts of the chapter's 1977 Calendar Girl Contest.

As a result of project SEARCH and the Tutorial Program, Gamma Sigma Omega Chapter won the 1977 top Chatham Savannah Volunteer Award sponsored by the Voluntary Action Center for the best project and was later honored by Georgia's Governor George Busbee for working with people in the Ogeecheeton and surrounding areas. At the 1974 South Atlantic Regional Conference, the chapter received a third place trophy for the best Program Exhibit, which featured project SEARCH in pictures. At the 1977 South Atlantic Regional Conference, the chapter received recognition for its Tutorial Reading Program exhibit.[80]

The Fall 1977 *Ivy Leaf* reported that the members of Gamma Sigma Omega Chapter had been busy making their influence felt in the community offering their expertise and time by serving youth through the Tutorial Reading Program. The article continued to say that recently Albertha Collier and Willie Mae Patterson had accepted honors at the state capitol building in Atlanta from Governor George Busbee for taking top honors on the local level. The chapter had been chosen by the Savannah Volunteer Action Center, an organization which annually honors outstanding individuals and groups in the community who contribute expertise, time, and effort to helping others. Collier was also present at the luncheon to accept the award for the chapter's project which was judged the community's most outstanding group effort. She explained to the local news media that the winning project helped children and young adults with their reading skills, and in conjunction with the reading program, sewing and arts and crafts classes were conducted. She said that members had logged more than 500 hours tutoring those classes.[81]

1977 Cluster VI in Savannah

Clusters grew out of neighborhood meetings where a group of chapters in immediate vicinity were designated by the Regional Director.

The chapter was hostess for the 1977 Cluster VI Workshop under Basileus, Lydia Young. At the 1977 Cluster VI Meeting, Clemontine F. Washington was elected Cluster VI Coordinator. "Gamma Sigma Omega and Gamma Upsilon Host Neighborhood Meeting," describes Cluster VI in Savannah, GA. Neighborhood Meeting was Saturday, November 5, 1977. Eulalia T. Powell, Cluster Coordinator, presided. The article further described the four workshops around the Cluster theme, "Leadership is the Key to Century III." Workshop I, Strengthening the Leadership Ability of Chapter Officers, led by Johnalee Nelson; Workshop II, Motivating Fellowship of Chapter Members, led by Hettie Copeland; Workshop III, Roles and Responsibilities of Leaders and Followers, led by Melanie Williams; and Workshop IV, Identifying and Developing Potential Leaders, led by Gamma Sigma Omega members, Gwendolyn Harris and Sandra Riley.[82]

Martha Wilson Presents Charter on 70th Founders' Day

The 70th Founders' Day was observed. Marjory Varnedoe served as Chairman of the Founders' Day Observance (February 12, 1978). Under her leadership, a Founders' Day scrapbook was started, beginning in 1973. Rebecca Cooper presided. Johnye Gillans was the eloquent speaker. Virginia Parham was presented a plaque, "Special Award," for outstanding service to the chapter through the years. The Founders' Day Committee designated Albertha E. Boston to conduct the Rededication Ceremony. Boston asked the current Basileus and all past Basilei of Gamma Sigma Omega Chapter to share the experience with her. The response from the Basilei was overwhelming. In addition to Boston, the following Basilei participated in the Rededication Ceremony: Lydia Young, Basileus, and former Basilei Clemontine Washington, Margaret Robinson, Carolyn Gantt (Morris), Mozella Collier, Eudora Allen, Emma L. Preer, Virginia Parham, Inez Williams, Violet Singleton, Jane Parker, Mary McDew, and Martha Wilson, charter Basileus. Wilson presented the Charter to the chapter at the Observance.[83]

Targeting Areas for Service in 1979 and 1980

Jessie C. DeLoach, a charter member of Gamma Upsilon, began her first year as Basileus in January 1979. There were 39 active members. Johnye Gillans, the newly elected Anti-Basileus and Chairperson of Program led her team with much ease and success. In April, 1979, the chapter entered Yamacraw Village to plot, scout, and map out strategic target areas in order to render "service to mankind."[84]

The graduate and undergraduate chapters observed the 71st Founders' Day jointly on February 18, 1979 at the Downtowner Motor Inn, they report. Many active and inactive members paused to celebrate and to pay honor to the courageous Founders of this great sisterhood. Jessie C. DeLoach presided. Michelle Williams introduced the undergraduate speaker, Shirlee Wright, Basileus of Gamma Upsilon, Savannah State College. She gave an inspiring speech on sisterly relations. Virginia Parham introduced the graduate speaker, Clemontine F. Washington who gave a timely speech entitled "Membership: The Highway and the Low." The following members were honored for their achievements: Lydia Young, Outstanding Soror of the Year; Carolyn Bell and Albertha E. Boston, Scholarship; Marjory Varnedoe, Sisterhood; Mozella Collier, Outstanding Service; Jacquelyn Handy and Dorothy Wilson, the Basileus Award.[85] The summer *Ivy Leaf,* 1979, "Gamma Sigma Omega," reports that approximately sixty-five sorors participated in the impressive celebration. Music for the occasion was presented by AKAs Linda Corry and Sandra Riley. Selection by a choral ensemble from both the graduate and undergraduate chapters added to the memorable occasion. The Founders' Day celebration was chaired by Marjory Varnedoe.[86]

Gamma Sigma Omega Chapter of Alpha Kappa Alpha Sorority, Inc. reports subsequent to Founders' Day, several members were certified in Cardiopulmonary Resuscitation (CPR). They were Johnye Gillans, Albertha Collier, Jessie DeLoach, Virginia Parham, Onnye Jean Sears, Marilyn Taylor, and Clemontine Washington. Collier was in charge of arranging the CPR course.[87]

Under the leadership of Emma Preer, Parliamentarian, the chapter's By-Laws were revised. Members on the By-Laws Committee were Mozella Collier, Jeraldine Coleman, Connie Cooper, Jackie Handy, Virginia Parham, Janet Spry, and Jessie DeLoach, Basileus.[88]

Several members attended the 1979 Regional Conference in Hollywood, Florida. With the election of Clemontine Washington as Cluster VI Coordinator, more members started attending the yearly Cluster meetings. Consequently, Gamma Sigma Omega and "first place for attendance" were synonymous.

In 1980, DeLoach began her second year as Basileus. There were 43 active members. The 1980 Reading Program emphasized, "Reading for Pleasure." Each student was given a placement test and an interest inventory test. The results of the tests determined the activities and experiences to which the students were exposed. One segment of the program included a story hour, which provided opportunities for role-playing, communicating verbally and graphically. Members stated that the students, generally, demonstrated improved reading skills and showed overwhelming enthusiasm for the Program. The members of the Tutorial Reading Committee were Charlene Jones, Freddie Pippen, Albertha Collier, Emma L. Preer, Margaret Ann Pearson, Sandra Riley, Johnye P. Gillans, Clemontine F. Washington, and Rebecca Cooper, Chairman.[89]

In February, the Annual Heart Fund Drive found several members actively participating in door-to-door campaigning as well as participation in the jog-a-thon.[90]

Open and Closed Founders' Day/The Mozella Gaither Collier CommunityVolunteer Service Award

Mozella Gaither Collier

Beginning in 1980, the chapter started observing open and close Founders' Day in alternate years; in even years, Founders' Day would be opened; in odd years, Founders' Day would be closed. The citizenship award, namely, "The Mozella Gaither Collier Community Volunteer Service Award," was initially awarded in 1980, and the chapter voted to present this Award every two years at the open Founders' Day observance. Gamma Sigma Omega Chapter initiated this Award to honor Collier for her many years of volunteer service in Savannah and Chatham County and throughout the state of Georgia. The Award recognizes citizens in the community who have given their time and talents to be of service to others. The Awards Committee at that time included Albertha E. Boston, Mozella G. Collier, Albertha Collier, Jessie C. DeLoach, Marjory Varnedoe, Lydia Young, and Onnye Jean

Sears, Chairperson. The 72nd Founders' Day (held at St. Matthew's Episcopal Church on February 17, 1980) was extra special in many ways. The first Mozella Gaither Collier Community Volunteer Service Award was given; the Mayor of Savannah proclaimed Sunday, February 17, 1980 Mozella Gaither Collier Day. The first recipient of this Award was Mrs. Priscilla D. Thomas, Principal of a local elementary school; runners-up were Dr. Clifford Hardwick, III; Mrs. Sadie Stelle, and Mrs. Gertrude Green. A former member of Gamma Sigma Omega, Lillie Gillard, was the 72nd Founders' Day speaker. Mozella Collier was voted Outstanding Soror of the Year. This Founders' Day program was very well attended. It is believed to have been the largest attendance for a Founders' Day celebration in the history of Gamma Sigma Omega Chapter. More than 200 people were present.[91]

At the 1980 Regional Conference in Columbia, SC, the chapter received numerous awards. Mozella Collier was the first-place recipient of the Ruby J. Gainer Human Relations Award. Onnye Jean Sears won second place for the Emory O. Jackson Journalism Award. Basileus DeLoach was a winner of the Homie Regulus Basileus Award. The chapter won The Georgia Schank Innovation Award. Again, the chapter won first place for attendance at the Regional Conference. Albertha E. Boston conducted the "Ives Beyond the Wall" ceremony.[92].

Gamma Sigma Omega's members in attendance were Albertha Collier, Mozella Collier, Jessie DeLoach, Connie Cooper, Agatha Cooper, Leona Henley, Merdis Lyons, Charlene Jones, Onnye Jean Sears, Clemontine F. Washington, Lydia Young, and Albertha E. Boston.[93]

1980 Membership Intake

On June 10, 1980, sixteen ladies were initiated into the chapter. They were Shirley Brown, Alma Chisholm, Audrey Cooper, Lynda DeLoach, Linda Green, Nadine Lewis, Geraldine Mack, Annette Mitchell, Olga Musgrow, Dora Myles, Evadne Roberts, Gwendolyn Smith, Brenda Stevens, Rena Varnedoe, Alice Walton, and Marian Wiles. Connie Cooper served as Dean of Graduate Candidates. For the first time, the active membership of Gamma Sigma Omega exceeded 50 members.[94]

The 49th Boule was held in Atlanta, Georgia, July 19-25, 1980. Twenty-six members attended the Conference. They were Eudora Allen, Albertha Collier, Mozella Collier, Connie Cooper, Rebecca Cooper, Countess Cox, Jessie DeLoach, Johnye Gillans, Jacquelyn Handy, Leona Henley, Annie Jackson, Charlene Jones, Bette Milledge, Dora Myles, Virginia Parham, Henrietta Perry, Sandra Riley, Violet Singleton, Marjory Varnedoe, Rena Varnedoe, Clemontine Washington, Eunice Washington, Marian Wiles, Dorothy Wilson, and Lydia Young.[95]

According to "Workshops Featured at Cluster VI Meeting," on November 15, 1980, Clemontine Washington, Cluster VI Coordinator, presided at the meeting, and that her final act was conducting the Rededication Ceremony. Hettie Copeland, now residing in Augusta, was elected the new Cluster VI Coordinator, approximately 150 attended with 17 chapters.[96]

In January 1981 with Johnye Gillans as Basileus, Gamma Upsilon was invited to attend chapter meeting. At that time, fifty-eight graduate members were active.[97]

The Yamacraw Village Project

On February 19, 1981, the chapter conducted a planning and a "beautify our worksite" meeting at the Yamacraw Village Community Room. Posters and pictures were used as a means of communication. Teaching materials were donated and purchased. Use of these materials depended upon the participant's skill level. Each child received an educational comic book, which Radio Shack ordered free of charge.[98]

As the weeks passed, enrollment at the reading sessions increased tremendously. Nadine Lewis, Marian Wiles, Jessie C. DeLoach, Rebecca Cooper, Marilyn Taylor, Sandra Riley, and Charlene Jones participated in planning and/or implementation of the program.[99]

From June 8-19, 1981, the Summer Reading classes were held daily, Monday through Friday, from 9:00 a.m. until 11:00 a.m. at the Yamacraw Village Center. Forty-five students, ages 7 to 17 participated in the Program. The theme for the summer was "Reading Is Fun, Always Keep Ahead." Students were involved in activities which were designed to emphasize "the reading can be fun" concept. The story hour was broadened to include films, filmstrips, role playing, listening stations, dramatization, community talents, and field trips. Refreshments were served after each session. An outdoor party and picnic, as well as an educational tour of Fort Pulaski, were given as a culminating activity.[100]

Members and Events

At the 73rd Founders' Day Observance, Countess Y. Cox presided. Jeraldine Coleman introduced the speaker, Rebecca Cooper, Anti-Basileus.[101]

In April 1981 (for the first time since April 1971), the chapter chartered a bus to attend the Regional Conference, departing from the same location, Butler Presbyterian Church. Dorothy Wilson was in charge of transportation. The 39-seat vehicle was almost full to capacity with Gamma Upsilon, Gamma Sigma Omega, and visiting AKAs bound for Hollywood, Florida. The chapter won first place for attendance.[102]

"Moving On Up" was a three-act play by Afri Productions of New York. Carolyn Bell served as Chairperson of the Fundraising Committee. This event was a means to receive funds for the chapter to make annual financial donations. Dorothy Wilson was in charge of the souvenir booklet. Three members received plaques for outstanding service, selling the largest number of tickets. The winners were Albertha E. Boston, Carolyn Gantt, and Mozella Collier.[103]

In 1981, emphasis was placed on reclaim and retain. In an effort to reclaim members, the active membership divided into groups: alpha, beta, gamma, epsilon, through nu. Five to six active members were placed into each group. Each group's task was to contact the designated seven to eight inactive AKAs, with the ultimate aim of reactivating the AKAs. At one sorority meeting, inactive AKAs were invited and given special recognition.[104]

In an effort to retain members, games were conducted, and winners were given prizes. Wallet-size calendars and other personal items were given to first arrivals at the meetings. Connie Cooper was Membership Chairperson, and Willie Mae Patterson was Co-Chairperson. Other committee members were Nadine Lewis, Geraldine Mack, Marilyn Taylor, Freddie Pippen, Violet Singleton, Shirley Brown, Olga Musgrow, and Albertha E. Boston.[105] Prior to the official opening of the King-Tisdell House, a Black Heritage edifice on Huntingdon Street, members spent one Saturday in the block cleaning the areas between Price and East Broad streets. Agatha Cooper headed the activities for the King-Tisdell House.[106]

In 1982, there were 56 active members. Johnye Gillans served her second year as Basileus; Rebecca Cooper served as Anti-Basileus and Chairperson of Program. The chapter sponsored the following programs during 1982: a leadership workshop at Tremont Temple Baptist Church, a teen workshop for 65 teens at the DeSoto Hilton Harbor View Room, voter registration, a health fair, and nutrition workshop. Members who assisted with the 1982 Program were Charlene Jones, Rebecca Cooper, Nadine Lewis, Marian Wiles, Margaret Pearson, Emma Williams, Jeraldine Coleman, Emma Preer, and Johnye Gillans, Basileus. Other members served in different aspects of the chapter's activities.[107]

Open Founders' Day was observed at Thankful Baptist Church on February 21, 1982. Carolyn Gantt, delivered a powerful message. Inez Williams presided.[108] Dr. Otis S. Johnson, Professor at Savannah State College, became the second recipient of the Mozella Gaither Collier Community Volunteer Service Award. Members were honored for their chapter achievements. They were Charlene Jones, Outstanding Soror of the Year; Nadine Lewis, Outstanding Service Award; and Albertha E. Boston, Sisterhood Award. Evanel Terrell was presented a special award for her long and continuous service to both the graduate and undergraduate chapters.[109]

Contributions to charitable organizations were made to NAACP, Savannah State College, Greenbriar Children's Center, the Frank Callen Boy's Club, Afro-American Heritage, American Red Cross, Cancer Fund, Carver State Bank's Thanksgiving Drive, Cleveland Job Corps, Coalition of Black Women, Collection of Life and Heritage (Black History Museum), Empty Stocking Fund, Heart Fund, King

Tisdell House, ASALH, Leukemia, Maggie Bozeman Fund, Manual for Chatham County Jurors, March of Dimes, Sickle Cell, United Community Appeal, United Negro College Fund, YMCA, and YWCA.[110]

Twenty-three members attended the 19th South Atlantic Regional Conference in Albany, Georgia. The chapter competed for four awards and placed in all; five members competed in individual awards; four of them placed. Onnye Jean Sears was the recipient of the first-place Emory O. Jackson Journalism Award. The plaque was striking in appearance with a large feather denoting "scribe." The four delegates were Johnye Gillans, Clemontine Washington, Nadine Lewis, and Marilyn Taylor. The alternates were Charlene Jones and Carolyn Gantt.[111]

In July 1982, thirteen members attended the 50th or Golden Boule in Boston, Massachusetts. The delegates were Johnye Gillans, Rebecca Cooper, Charlene Jones, Dorothy Wilson, and Rena Varnedoe. Other members in attendance included Albertha E. Boston, Jessie DeLoach, Leona Henley, Bette Milledge, Henrietta Perry, Violet Singleton, Clemontine F. Washington, and Marian Wiles. Marjory Varnedoe attended as a delegate from Zeta Rho Omega Chapter.[112]

"Radio Man," another three-act play by Afri Productions of New York, was presented as a fundraising project at the Savannah Civic Center on December 6, 1982 under Chairman Carolyn Bell. Vera Young, daughter of Mr. & Mrs. Joseph L. Young (GSO member, Lydia's daughter), was crowned "Miss Pink and Green." Runners up were Crystal Gaulden, 1st place; Patricia Ann Swint, 2nd place; Felecia Walls, 3rd place; and Melanie Hendricks, 4th place. Gillans, the outgoing Basileus, received a plaque for outstanding services as Basileus.[113]

At the conclusion of the December 1982 meeting, Agatha Cooper installed the newly elected officers. Rebecca Cooper began her tenure as Basileus January 1983.[114]

Lambda Kappa

Regional Director, Norma S. White, assigned Clemontine Washington and Dorothy Wilson of Gamma Sigma Omega to advise an interest group at Georgia Southern University in Statesboro, GA. "Report of the South Atlantic Regional Director" in the Minutes of the Forty-Eight Boule of Alpha Kappa Alpha Sorority, Inc. indicates that Lambda Kappa was chartered May 7, 1977.[115]

"Lambda Kappa Chartered" in the Fall *Ivy Leaf*, 1977 describes the chartering of the chapter. It indicated that the chartering marked the establishment of not only the first predominantly Black sorority but the first Black Greek organization at Georgia Southern.[116]

The ceremony was conducted in Statesboro, GA by Norma S. White with the assistance of Gamma Upsilon and Gamma Sigma Omega chapters. The newly installed officers were Basileus, Zelda Vanessa Burke; Anti-Basileus, Andrea Vernita Gardner; Grammateus, Deborah Lynn Tremble; Anti-Grammateus, Elizabeth Hill; Epistoleus, Judith Allyson Clarke; Tamiouchos, Patricia Ann Jones; Parliamentarian, Valerie Dean Minor; Ivy Leaf Reporter, Debra Marie Ellington; Dean of Pledges, Meshelle Marlyn Hudson; Assistant Dean of Pledges, Elease Turner; and Hodegos, Pamela Elaine Williams. Other new sorors were Cheryl Yvette Blank [Bland], Clara Elaine Johnson, Brenda Lee Jordan, Karen Marchelle Lovett, and Jarvis W. Ogletree. The charter was presented to Dr. Nicholas Quick, Vice President of the college by Soror White in the Gold Room of the Rosenwald Building on the campus. Following the event the neophytes celebrated with a banquet luncheon at "Mrs. Bryant's Kitchen," a local restaurant.[117]

New National Headquarters

Responding to National's appeal to build a new headquarters, the chapter made a $2,000 contribution. Each member was asked to contribute $25 and in return would receive a button labeled "I am Making It Happen." The members whose contributions were remitted in December 1981 along with the chapter's were Johnye Gillans, Virginia Parham, Jessie DeLoach, Gwendolyn Smith, Carolyn Gantt, Emma Preer, Albertha Collier, Evadne Roberts, Countess Y. Cox, Leona Henley, Rebecca Cooper, Clemontine F. Washington, and Mozella Collier.[118]

Members contributing in the second mailing included Onnye Jean Sears, Carolyn Bell, Albertha E. Boston, Connie Cooper, Jacquelyn Handy, Charlene Jones, Nadine C. Lewis, Bette C. Milledge, Evanel Terrell, Rena Varnedoe, Alice Walton, Eunice Washington, Inez B. Williams, Dorothy B. Wilson, and Lydia Young. Subsequent to the second mailing, additional members responded to the Capital Improvement Project (CIP).[119]

Chapter IV

MENTORS, 1983-2002

Rebecca R. Cooper, 1983-1984

Chapter Events and Activities

HAVING BEEN INSTALLED by Agatha Cooper, December 1982, Rebecca Cooper took the helm of the sorority by implementing the plans for the 75th Founders' Day to be observed February 20, 1983, at the Downtowner Motor Inn, Regency Room, 4:00 p.m., with Jeraldine Coleman as Chairman.

The 30th Regional Conference of Alpha Kappa Alpha Sorority was held March 10-13, 1983 at Myrtle Beach, South Carolina. The general theme was "Our Diamond Jubilee Promise, Facets of Dynamic Power." AKAs from Georgia, Florida, and South Carolina were honored for outstanding service and achievements. The following awards were presented to Gamma Sigma Omega Chapter: Third Place, Chapter Achievement Award and Second Place, Margaret B. Roach Health Award. Members received the following awards: Dorothy B. Wilson, First Place, Odessa S. Nelson Graduate Advisor Award; Clemontine F. Washington, Third Place, Margaret Davis Bowen Outstanding Alumna Award; Agatha Cooper, runner-up, Ruby J. Gainer Human Relations Award, and Johnye W. Gillans, Third Place, Homie Regulus Alumna Basileus Award. Members attending the Conference were Mozella Collier, Connie Cooper, Jessie DeLoach, Johnye Gillans, Quay Hurt, Charlene Jones, Henrietta Perry, Audrey Singleton, Violet Singleton, Gwendolyn Smith, Eunice Washington, Inez Williams, Dorothy

Wilson, Clemontine Washington, Awards Chairman, and Rebecca Cooper, Basileus. The undergraduate chapter, Gamma Upsilon of Savannah State College, also received several awards: First Place, Georgia Schank Innovative Award; Third Place, Chapter Achievement Award; and First Place, Chapters Under Twenty-Five Attendance Award. Cynthia E. Ellis of Gamma Upsilon won the Mamie E. Williams Outstanding Undergraduate Award and the Homie Regulus Undergraduate Basileus Award.[120]

In the pursuit of service, the chapter with Dorothy B. Wilson, Program Chairman, coordinated a Leadership Seminar on October 22, 1983 at Shuman Middle School from 9:00 a.m.-1:00 p.m. The workshop focused on "teens," tomorrow's future leaders. The theme was "Where Do We Go From Here?" There were two workshops and a panel discussion. A fashion show was the highlight during the luncheon. Dr. Otis S. Johnson, Associate Professor of Social Work/Sociology and Head of the Department of Social and Behavioral Science at Savannah State College, gave the challenge to students to be remembered by making accomplishments and being somebody. His topic was "Who Will Remember?" Joyce McLemore, an AKA, Associate Professor of Reading and Reading Coordinator of Developmental Studies, at Savannah State College, and Connie Cooper, GSO member, School Social Worker with the Chatham County Board of Public Education, conducted the workshops. Emma J. Preer and Clemontine F. Washington were Co-Chairmen of this activity. There were 75 student participants from Chatham County Middle and High Schools, Bradwell Institute of Hinesville, Georgia, and Ridgeland High School of Ridgeland, South Carolina.[121]

The 76th Founders' Day was observed January 22, 1984 at St. Matthew's Episcopal Church. The speaker was Inez B. Williams. Agatha Cooper received the Mozella Gaither Collier Community Volunteer Service Award; Second Place, Mrs. Jewel McDew; and Third Place, Dr. Frankie Ellis. Several members were also honored in various categories. The awards were Soror of the Year, Jessie Collier DeLoach; Outstanding Service Award, Johnye W. Gillans; Sisterhood, Connie Cooper; Excellence in Professionalism, Rena W. Varnedoe; and Scholarship, Charlene Jones. Basileus Rebecca Cooper presented the Basileus Award to Marilyn Taylor. Basileus Cooper presented tokens of appreciation to Linda Alston, Nadine

C. Lewis, Henrietta C. Perry, and Clemontine F. Washington. Emma J. Preer received a certificate for 25 years of service in the Sorority, receiving Silver Star status.[122] She became a Silver Star in 1983; her certificate was given in 1984. Virginia M. Parham received Silver Star status in 1984.

On March 25, 1984, "Facing the Rising Sun," a cultural arts program, featuring youth reciting dramatic monologues and performing vocal and instrumental solos, was showcased in the Savannah community. This dramatic performance was the brainchild of Marjory Varnedoe.[123]

Cooper's second Regional Conference, the 31st Regional Conference, was held in Miami, Florida. Mary Shy Scott was Regional Director. Several of Gamma Sigma Omega Chapter members participated on various committees and programs. Several members were Regional Award recipients: Basileus Rebecca Cooper presented special guests in attendance at the open banquet; Countess Y. Cox served as Chairman of the Resolutions Committee, and Jessie C. DeLoach sang with the Regional Chorus. Members serving on committees were Marian Wiles, Charlene Jones, and Albertha E. Boston. Gamma Sigma Omega received the following Chapter awards: Second Place, Georgia Schank Innovative Award; Second place, Chapter Achievement, Over Forty; and Third Place, Margaret B. Roach Health Award. Individual award recipients were Carolyn Bell, Deloris H. Oliver Service to Mankind Award; Evanel Terrell, Second Place, Ruby J. Gainer Human Relations Award, and Clemontine F. Washington, First Place, Odessa S. Nelson Graduate Advisor Award. Members in attendance at the Conference were Linda Alston, Albertha E. Boston, Rebecca Cooper, Countess Y. Cox, Jessie C. DeLoach, Johnye Gillans, Leona Henley, Charlene Jones, Carolyn Russell, Evanel Terrell, Clemontine Washington, Marian Wiles, Dorothy Wilson, and Lydia Young. Gamma Upsilon Chapter of Savannah State College received the following awards: Second Place, Georgia Schank Innovative Award; Second Place, Margaret B. Roach Health Award; and First Place, Chapter Achievement Award Under Twenty-Five. Only two undergraduates attended: Sybil Bettis who won First Place for the Mamye E. Williams Outstanding Undergraduate Soror and the Basileus, Rosanna Ellis. Charlene Jones was the Graduate Advisor and Clemontine Washington the Assistant Graduate Advisor.[124]

Cooper's quiet but inspiring disposition motivated members to serve. Gamma Sigma Omega Chapter sponsored one of the computer workshops during the summer of 1984 at Savannah State College. Thirty participants in grades 6-12 from public and private schools in Chatham County attended the four-day seminar on word processing/basic programming. Dorothy Wilson, Program Chairman, worked with Dr. Leo Parrish, Dean of the School of Business in setting up the computer workshop. Emma L. Preer and Clemontine F. Washington served as Chairman for the seminar. Johnye W. Gillans, Albertha E. Boston, and Jessie DeLoach were assistants. Culminating activities included a tour of the Computer Center at Citizen & Southern Bank and an afternoon treat at Burger King.[125]

The 51st Boule was held at the Convention Center in Washington, D.C., July 21-27, 1984. Faye B. Bryant, the 21st Supreme Basileus, presided over the meeting. She was the Associate Superintendent for the Houston Magnet School System in Houston. The theme was "Alpha Kappa Alpha Power: Energizing for the Twenty-First Century." Mayor Marion Barry declared July 22-27 as Alpha Kappa Alpha Week in Washington, D.C. in recognition of 76 years of "service to mankind." Members attending were Albertha E. Boston, Mozella Collier, Rebecca R. Cooper, Countess Y. Cox, Jessie DeLoach, Johnye Gillans, Leona Henley, Charlene Jones, Virginia Parham, Henrietta Perry, Carolyn Russell, Marjory Varnedoe, Rena Varnedoe, Clemontine Washingon, Marian Wiles, Dorothy Wilson, and Lydia Young.[126]

1984 Cluster VI in Savannah

More than 200 Alpha Kappa Alpha women attended Cluster VI of the South Atlantic Region at Shuman Junior High School, Savannah, GA, October 20, 1984. Gamma Sigma Omega Chapter, Rebecca Cooper, Basileus, and Gamma Upsilon Chapter, Sharon Lawson, Basileus, hosted the Cluster VI meeting. Irene McCollom was Cluster VI Coordinator. South Atlantic Regional Director, Mary Shy Scott, conducted the business session. Connie Cooper was Chairman, and Marjory Varnedoe was Co-Chairman for the meeting.[127]

Dorothy Boston Wilson, 1985-1986

Soror of Action

Dorothy Boston Wilson, "the soror of action," was installed as Basileus at the December 8, 1984 chapter meeting. She served during the administration of Supreme Basileus Faye B. Bryant and Regional Director Mary Shy Scott. The national programmatic thrust was "Energizing for the 21st Century on POWER."[128]

Wilson in 1985 established a standard meeting schedule for the Executive Board, developed a monthly newsletter, *ECHOES*, as the official communication vehicle for members, implemented a Chapter Retreat with Carolyn Bell serving as Chairman, and strengthened Alpha Kappa Alpha's presence in the Pan-Hellenic Council with the election of Johnye W. Gillians as President. She presided over a closed Founders' Day Observance at the Hyatt Regency Hotel with a record breaking attendance, Freddie Pippen, Chairman and Connie Cooper, Co-Chairman. The members of the chapter contributed $2000 to the Gamma Sigma Omega Foundation and celebrated the Golden Soror status of Evanel Terrell.[129]

Wilson's "soror of action" was evident. With Marjory Varnedoe serving as Program Chairman, the Cuyler Community Project was implemented. It was an outreach project at St. Mary's School: tutorial programs, teen club workshops, field trips for teens, Teenage Pregnancy Counseling, and Senior Citizens Adopt A Grandparent.[130]

South Atlantic Regional Honors and Awards: The Mozella Gaither Collier Community Volunteer Service Award

The Mozella Gaither Collier Community Volunteer Service Award, as a part of the South Atlantic Regional Honors and Awards Program, was established at the 1985 South Atlantic Regional Conference. The Award was to honor Soror Collier for her many years of volunteer service in Savannah Chatham County and throughout the State of Georgia. It was given to recognize citizens in the community who had given of their time and talents in the service of others.[131]

Chapter Events and Activities

Gamma Sigma Omega won the Gold, Silver, and the Bronze in Regional honors and awards competition: 1st place, Odessa Nelson Graduate Advisor Award, Charlene Jones; 1st place, Emory O. Jackson Journalism Award, Theresa White; 2nd place, Ruby Gainer Human Relations Award, Evanel Terrell; 2nd place, Deloris Ham Oliver Service to Mankind Award, Carolyn Bell; 3rd place, Margaret Roach Innovative Award, Clemontine Washington; 3rd place, Margaret Roach Innovative Award, Dorothy B. Wilson.[132]

Desiring to improve leadership of members, Basileus Wilson supported Gamma Sigma Omega Chapter's vision to send delegates to the Leadership Seminar in Chicago, Illinois. Members attending were Dorothy B. Wilson, Clemontine Washington, Charlene Jones, and Johnye Gillans. They participated in the dedication of the mortgage-free, Ivy Center, Alpha Kappa Alpha Corporate Headquarters. Gamma Sigma Omega's members attended the 1985 Cluster VI Conference, hosted by Nu Delta Omega Chapter in Hilton Head, South Carolina to learn more about the Sorority and to promote sisterhood.[133]

In 1986, Basileus Wilson and thirty-seven other committed and financially active members set out for a new year. Gamma Sigma Omega took the word "retreat" to a higher level. The Standards Retreat was held on Cap'n Sam's River Boat with a Dinner Buffet and thirty-one members in attendance. Carolyn Bell served as Chairman. Clemontine Washington initiated the fundraising campaign for support of community service programs. Albertha W. Collier, Albertha E. Boston, Annie C. Jackson, Bette C. Milledge, and Emma J. Preer led the effort to make major revisions to the chapter's By-Laws and to distribute them to all members. Carolyn Bell, Johnye Gillans, Clemontine Washington, Dorothy B. Wilson, and Lydia Young represented the chapter's participation in the United Negro College Fund campaign event at H & H Eagles Nest.[134.]

Founders' Day Observance was held at the St. Philip A.M.E. Church, Freddie Pippen, Chairman and Connie Cooper, Co-Chairman.[135]

Many Gamma Sigma Omega members attended the 1986 South Atlantic Regional Conference in Atlanta, Georgia. Frederica S. Wilson became the South Atlantic Regional Director. In 1986, the chapter won the Gold, the Silver and the Bronze in honors and awards in the Regional competition: 1st place, Connection Award, Jessie C. Deloach; 1st place Homie Regulus Basileus Award, Dorothy B. Wilson; 2nd place Deloris Ham Oliver Service to Mankind Award, Carolyn Bell; 3rd place, Chapter Achievement Award; 3rd place, Mozella Gaither Collier Community Volunteer Service Award, Jessie C. DeLoach. Annie Jackson received Silver Star Soror status.[136]

Gamma Sigma Omega's members attended the 52nd Boule at Cobo Hall, in Detroit, Michigan, July 1986. The delegates were Dorothy B. Wilson, Charlene Jones, Johnye Gillans and Marjory Varnedoe. Others in attendance were Albertha E. Boston, Rebecca R. Cooper, Countess Y. Cox, Carolyn Russell, Evanel Terrell, and Clemontine Washington. At the 1986 Boule, Mary Shy Scott became the 23rd Supreme Basileus. Nu Rho Omega Chapter in Hinesville, Georgia hosted the 1986 Cluster VI Conference.[137]

Marjory Varnedoe, 1987-1988

Marjory Varnedoe held several leadership positions in Gamma Sigma Omega before moving to the helm, including Epistoleus, Ivy Leaf Reporter, Graduate Advisor, Membership Chairperson, Founders' Day Chairperson, and Anti-Basileus for 1985-1986. Varnedoe also received the chapter's Sisterhood Award in both 1979 and 1980.

When Varnedoe took office in January 1987, she sent a letter to the members encouraging them to continue the work already begun: "Our newly elected officers are on task insuring the smooth functioning of our organization. And the retired officers are still 'on the job' lending assistance whenever needed. This executive body is working hard to keep you involved or get you involved."[138]

Shirley Brown was hostess to the chapter's Retreat. Varnedoe described her home as lovely. The Retreat was held September 12, 1987.[139]

St. Mary's School Project

Gamma Sigma Omega Chapter continued its program initiative, a tutorial program at St. Mary's School. The chapter had chosen St. Mary's as a target area, and Varnedoe as Anti-Basileus in 1985-86 was the Program Chairman. A tutorial program in Reading and Math was the prime focus. The students met twice a week from 4-6 p.m. The chapter had an Open House for the AKA Youth Center at St. Mary's School, June 6, 1987. The summer enrichment program began that summer. The members of Gamma Sigma Omega put in many hours at the AKA Youth Center. There was a clean-up day in which members donned the appropriate attire and scrubbed the walls and floors of St. Mary's School. There was also a Black History Celebration at the Center, February 26, 1988. The students in the program did Black History scrapbooks that were judged by leaders in the community.[140]

Bell Resigns as Anti-Basileus/WesleyCommunity Center Project

Carolyn Bell tendered her resignation as Anti-Basileus due to a demanding job. The chapter elected Albertha E. Boston to complete Bell's term. Lydia Young was elected the Tamiouchos.[141]

Local Program Change

In 1988 the program target area changed. Under the leadership of the new Anti-Basileus, Albertha E. Boston, an after school tutorial program was begun at the Wesley Community Center on 32nd and Drayton Streets. The students served were mainly in grades 4-8. Enrichment activities were also a part of the program because the Director of the Center was musically inclined.[142]

Chapter Events and Activities

During Varnedoe's term in office, the following events occurred. The South-Atlantic Regional Conference was held in Greenville, South Carolina, March 18-22, 1987. The 3rd Annual Pan-Hellenic Ball was held at the Savannah Civic Center, Saturday, September 25, 1987. The 1988 South Atlantic Regional Conference was held in Tallahassee, Florida, March 16-20. There was a Regional Conference planning committee meeting in Savannah at the DeSoto Hilton Hotel, September 10, 1988. The 1989 South Atlantic Regional Convention's site was planned for Savannah. The Cluster VI Workshop was held in Savannah, December 3 at the DeSoto Hilton. This Workshop was basically a planning meeting for the South Atlantic Regional Conference. Los Angeles, California was the site of the 53rd Boule, July 9-17, 1988.[143]

"Facing the Rising Sun," 1987, had a dual purpose: to spotlight local talented youth and to honor outstanding students in chorus and band from the local high schools.[144]

At the February 1988 Founders' Day, the following members were honored for their service to the Basileus. Virginia Parham readily agreed to chair a pet project of Basileus Varnedoe's, an AKA Savings Club.

Johnye Gillans, affectionately known as Basileus Varnedoe's "AKA Inspiration" was always a guiding light and a bridge over troubled waters for Varnedoe. Rena Wynn Varnedoe, the mother of Basileus Varnedoe, received the coveted Basileus Award.[145]

At the 1989 Founders' Day Celebration, Lydia Young received the Basileus Award for meritorious service to the Basileus. Young's honor was given for her selfless attitude of picking up the chapter's mail weekly and mailing it to Basileus Varnedoe who lived in Hinesville.[146]

Albertha E. Boston, 1989-1990

Touch Somebody with Your Goodness

After the call to order on January 14, 1989, the first meeting of the new administration opened with the monthly theme: "Touch Somebody with Your Goodness." Eighteen red, long-stem roses were provided for the first eighteen members to arrive. However, the recipient was required to give the rose away and embrace the new recipient. After a few minutes, the emotional inspirational period ended with all members singing "Touch Somebody's Life with your Goodness."[147]

Through the contact of John A. Finney, Director of the Savannah EOA, twenty-two members of Gamma Sigma Omega enjoyed a singular experience when they hosted Dr. Mae Jemison, an AKA, as well as an astronaut, at the DeSoto Hilton Hotel. Jemison was in Savannah to participate in the January, 1989 Martin Luther King, Jr. Birthday Celebration.[148]

In an effort to promote sisterhood among inactive AKAs, the Membership Committee and the Basileus extended invitations to many non-financial members to attend the 81st Founders' Day Program, February 5, 1989 at Butler Presbyterian Church. Martha W. Wilson and seven other inactive AKAs joined thirty-six members of GSO to celebrate the closed activity. Jessie C. DeLoach was the speaker.[149]

On June 6, 1989, a 17-year-old teen, a member of the Philpot Family, of West Savannah perished in a house fire. The chapter voted to assist this family. At the designated date and time, five members: Leona H. Williams, Gwendolyn Cummings, Johnye W. Gillans, Renee' Williams, and Albertha E. Boston met at Marilyn S. Taylor's residence to load furniture, clothing, cooking utensils, etc. to give to Mrs. Philpot, mother of the deceased. The Basileus presented a check to Mrs. Philpot.[150]

Hurricane Hugo, September 23, 1989, caused devastating destruction, especially to the residents of Charleston, South Carolina. Janet Jones Ballard, Supreme Basileus, sent a "SOS" call to all chapters and requested assistance for the Charleston Hugo victims. GSO graciously answered the call by donating major appliances, clothing, bedding, etc. for the designated members. In a sisterly act, the majority of the GSO members agreed to donate their 1989 South Atlantic Regional Rebate to the Hugo Hurricane victims.[151]

1989 South Atlantic Regional Conference in Savannah

On March 23-26, 1989 GSO hosted the 36th South Atlantic Regional Conference at the Savannah Civic Center. Clemontine F. Washington served as Conference Chairman.[152]

Chapter Events and Activities

Women's Walk '89, labeled "Just for the Health of It," was hosted at Savannah State College (now Savannah State University) on Saturday, May 20. Approximately fifteen members participated.[153]

The determining of award recipients and the voting for "Soror of the Year" were to be announced at the 82nd Founders' Day. In 1990, the celebration was opened to the public, and it was observed at Holy Spirit Lutheran Church, East 37th Street. Dorothy J. Gardner, wife of President William I. Gardner of Savannah State College (now Savannah State University) was the speaker. Seven representatives from charitable organizations were present to receive their financial gifts, including Greenbriar Children's Center.[154]

Members participated in the MLK Parade, the Heart Drive and Census. Rev. Thurmond N. Tillman conducted an orientation to the 1990 Census Reporting Session. Seven members of GSO became trained Voter Registrars: Rosa Pringle, Coordinator; Emma Conyers, Connection Chairman; Johnye W. Gillans, Patricia Mincey, Lillian Taylor, Marilyn Taylor, and Albertha E. Boston. In March, members participated in the annual Mother's March for the March of Dimes.

The 37th South Atlantic Regional Conference was held in Orlando, Florida, April 11-15, 1990. The majority of the members rode the chartered bus. Albertha E. Boston, Gwendolyn Cummings, Renee′ Williams, Emily Williams, and Rebecca Cooper were the delegates. Seventeen other members were in attendance.[155]

The 54th Boule, National Conference, was held in Richmond, Virginia, Richmond Coliseum, July 14-22, 1990. Several members of Gamma Sigma Omega journeyed to Richmond to participate in some history making events. Five members served as delegates. They were Albertha E. Boston, Basileus; Renee' Williams, Graduate Advisor for Gamma Upsilon at Savannah State College; Gwendolyn Cummings, Assistant Graduate Advisor; Jeraldine C. Patterson, and Kervia Lemon. Others members attending were Johnye Gillans, Charlene Jones, Nadine Lewis, Merdis Lyons, Linda Owens, Virginia Parham, Marjory Varnedoe, Bonnie Washington, Clemontine Washington, and Dorothy Wilson. Albertha Boston's modeling, at the South Atlantic Regional Luncheon, portrayed Sarah Meriwether Nutter, one of the sixteen Founders of Alpha Kappa Alpha Sorority, Incorporated.[156]

The Connection Committee planned and executed one aspect of its new four-year National Program: World Community Support. The Committee made more than two dozen yellow and blue ribbons that were placed on church doors. The display of ribbons symbolized not only the chapter's concern for the hostages and military servicemen/women involved in the Gulf Crisis but also emphasized the profound care, concern and love for the men and women who had been deployed or who were on alert for the Gulf Crisis. Linda Owens headed this activity, Emma Conyers, Connection Chairman. Members who delivered ribbons were Shirley Brown, Karen Clark, Gwendolyn Cummings, Johnye W. Gillans, Annie Jackson, Charlene Jones, Nadine Lewis, Virginia Parham, Carolyn Russell, Emma J. Preer, Ivy Richardson, Audrey Singleton, Marilyn Taylor, Clemontine Washington, Emily Williams, Renee' Williams, Dorothy Wilson, Lydia Young, and Marjory Varnedoe.[157]

Ella S. Jones, Cluster VI Coordinator, requested all chapters to swap news about outstanding programs, events, members' achievements, etc. via a Chapter SWAP SHEET. Albertha E. Boston, assisted by having some GSO members, compile and present the SWAP SHEET at the Cluster VI Conference, November 18-19, 1990.[158]

GSO continues to work for Greenbriar Children's Center. Four AKAs were Board Members of Greenbriar Children's Center: Shirley

M. Brown, Johnye W. Gillans, Virginia Parham, and Dorothy Wilson. They solicited more than $1000 in new memberships. Residents of Greenbriar Children's Center donned their Halloween Costumes and enjoyed the party and festivities the chapter provided for them. For Thanksgiving, Greenbriar requested the chapter to adopt two families. Anti-Basileus Taylor and her committee responded to this request as well as other requests in the community.[159]

The following agencies or institutions were the recipients of the chapter's financial contributions: Scholarship Fund for SSC, Gamma Upsilon Chapter, Cleveland Job Corps, NAACP, YMCA, Greenbriar Children's Center, Educational Advancement Foundation (EAF), Rape Crisis Center, Safe Shelter, Teen-Age Pregnancy, Frank Callen Boys & Girls Club, Empty Stocking Fund, American Cancer Society, Savannah Chapter of Sickle Cell, Arthritis Foundation, The American Heart Association, and March of Dimes.[160]

Marilyn Taylor, 1991-1992

Chapter Events and Activities

Taylor's tenure as Basileus was a fruitful one in membership. Her theme was "Sorors Working Together To Make Things Happen; Sorors Working Together To Make A Difference." Gamma Sigma Omega Chapter increased by 60% in membership. Members were encouraged to take an active role in leadership positions. The "Willingness to Serve" forms were initiated. The international theme: "Addressing The Crisis of the 1990s" was implemented. Members continued programs at Greenbriar Children's Center and initiated programs at Grace House. Contributions continued to Savannah State College, the American Cancer Society, Boys and Girls Club, May Street YMCA, Sickle Cell Anemia Foundations, and UNCF. The chapter collaborated with the following organizations: Junior League, Pan-Hellenic Council, and the Women's Luncheon of the Martin Luther King, Jr. Observance Day Association.[161]

The Connection Committee, Emma Jean Conyers, Chairman, Annette Mitchell, Time and Place Coordinator, sponsored the First Political Forum, June 13, 1991, including Republican and Democratic candidates for the Mayoral election. Also, the Connection Committee was active in the City's plans for the Area C Neighborhood and the City and State's plans for the 1996 Olympics.[162]

"Immediate Needs": blankets, linens, towels, batteries, paper towels, toilet tissue, etc. were collected and sent to AKAs who were victims of Hurricane Andrew. These items were collected at the 1992 November meeting.[163]

A Ribbon Cutting Ceremony was held at Greenbriar. The chapter presented books and magazines for a section of the library, launching the year of the Lifetime Reader.[164]

Over $200 was contributed to the Grace House Union Mission as a part of AKA Water Day, "Have A Heart." This activity was to support the homeless population.The chapter supported World Food Day with Renee' Williams coordinating the event. The chapter chose to donate can goods to Grace House. Each member brought at least two can goods to the October meeting. The can goods were presented to Jay Davis at Grace House.[165]

In support of Job Corps, Karen Clark, Coordinator, requested all members to contribute a unisex gift to be sent to the Cleveland Job Corps. The chapter also agreed to provide a subscription of *Upscale Magazine* for the Job Corps Center and sent bedspreads to the Center. Charlene Jones, Program Chairman, outlined activities for the chapter to participate in the Sickle Cell Anemia Awareness Program at Butler Presbyterian Church, September 26, 1999.[166]

In an effort to show support for Black businesses, the members spent their dollars at Williams' Accessories.[167]

Taylor and Audrey Singleton attended the 1991 Leadership Conference in Chicago, Illinois, July 20-21. The theme of the Conference was "Leadership Strategies for A Changing Society." The Supreme Basileus was Mary Shy Scott.[168]

The Standards Committee recommended in October 1991 to rent a small self-storage unit and to purchase file cabinets for housing chapter's records and property. It was also recommended that an amount for such storage be included in the 1992 budget and that a committee be appointed to assemble, categorize, and store chapter property. Virginia Parham was Chairman of the Standards Committee.[169]

The fundraising activity for the chapter was Fashionetta. Members were taxed to fund programs that would meet the needs of the community. From Fashionetta's proceeds, money was donated to the local agencies, including Greenbriar Children's Center and allocated for Program activities and contributions in the community.[170]

The 84th Founders' Day speaker was Deloris Ham Oliver. The Program was observed February 2, 1992 at St. James A.M.E. Church. Johnye Gillans was Chairman.[171]

The 1991 Cluster VI was held in N. Charleston, SC, October 4-5. The 1992 Cluster VI was held in Walterboro, SC, October 16-17.[172]

At the 55th Boule held in New Orleans in 1992, all members of Alpha Kappa Alpha Sorority, Inc. were assessed $200 for Corporate Office Improvement Project (COIP).[173]

The 39th South Atlantic Regional Conference, April 2-5, 1992, was held in Macon, Georgia. Gwendolyn Cummings, Vernice Whitfield, Emily Williams, and Ellen Wilson were delegates. Virginia Parham and Jeannette Lincoln were alternates. Marilyn Taylor and Audrey Singleton, Basileus and Graduate Advisor respectively, were also delegates. Thirty-three members attended. Patricia Mincey, Carolyn Russell, Vernice Whitfield, and Ellen Wilson were recognized as Silver Stars.[174]

Patricia Mincey, Constitution/By-laws Chairman, directed the revision of the chapter's By-laws to bring into compliance with the National Constitution. Questions of concern consisted of those pertaining to attendance requirements and specific qualifications necessary for holding an office.[175]

A joint meeting of Gamma Upsilon and Gamma Sigma Omega Chapters was held April 12, 1992 at SSC Student Union Building.[176]

Several other events of Taylor's administration were the chapter's adoption of a Bus Stop at 52nd and Hopkins Streets, Senior Citizens Day, a family picnic, and the publishing of handbook. The chapter was committed to keeping the Bus Stop, identified with chapter's name, cleaned and beautified. Also, the chapter participated in a Senior Citizens Day activity at Chatham Nursing Home. Sixty pairs of white socks were donated to the Nursing Home. The Membership Committee, Clemontine Washington, Chairman, sponsored a family picnic at Skidaway Island State Park on September 27, 1992. A Handbook/Directory was published in 1992, with the purpose of disseminating information to the membership. Dorothy B. Wilson was Chairman.[177]

The *Ivy Leaf* reports in the article, "Gamma Sigma Omega Retreat a Success," that the chapter had a successful retreat that was sponsored by the Standards Committee. The theme was "Creative Strategies Through Sisterhood." The retreat was held on a weekend at the Quality Inn Motel Airport. Planning activities, including plans for the Greenbriar Children's Center and the bonding of members were the emphasis for the retreat. The retreat ended with an inspirational service on Sunday morning. The speaker was Carolyn Bell. Her message was entitled "What does love have to do with it?" All members left the weekend with renewed spirit.[178]

1992 Membership Intake

Clemontine Washington, Membership Chairman, led the induction of thirteen women into the Sorority, January 11, 1992. They were Bernadette Ball-Oliver, Birdie Lee Moore Beard, Jeanette Blount-Lincoln, Martha Dixon Hicks, Bernadine L. Lewis, Yolanda Renee Powell, Isabell Denyce Sanders, Mary Pierce Thomas, Andrea Bowers Williams, Dorothy J. Davis Williams, Sadie B. Bryant Williams, Alvernia Smith Wilson, and Doris Hampton Wood.[179]

GSO Housing Foundation

At the 1992 September meeting, a request was made to chapter members to join Gamma Sigma Omega's Housing Foundation. The requested amount was $100 for membership, but other donations would be accepted. The primary purpose was to obtain land and housing for Gamma Sigma Omega Chapter and its Program of service. The Foundation was established by a resolution February 9, 1985. This Foundation was to be a separate entity from Alpha Kappa Alpha Sorority and Gamma Sigma Omega Chapter. GSO members were not required to be a member of the Foundation. The Foundation needed at least 40 members at $100/year for 5 years to obtain suitable land and housing. The Foundation's assets as of May 29, 1992 were $7,898.15. Officers: President, Lydia Young; Vice-President, Clemontine Washington; Secretary, Onnye Jean Sears; Assistant Secretary, Virginia Parham; Treasurer, Johnye Gillans. Board Members: Rebecca Cooper, Merdis Lyons, Shirley Brown, and Dorothy Wilson, in addition to the above officers.[180]

Charlene E. Jones, 1993-1994

Service Projects

The Executive Meeting was held at home of the new Basileus, Charlene Jones, January 7, 1993, 7:00 p.m. The chapter meeting was held January 9, 1993 at SSC-School of Business. All Standing Committees submitted their goals and objectives to Virginia Parham. Basileus Jones gave a prayer of inspiration. Her theme was "Together By Choice, United We Stand; Divided We Fall." At this meeting there were thirty members present and one visiting AKA, Charlene Townsend.[181]

Ellen Wilson initiated an activity called *Sis*. Each member pulled a numbered brown paper bag from a larger bag. Those members who pulled the same numbered bags became *Sis* to the other. The concept was to keep up with one's *Sis* and to provide needed information about that *Sis*.[182]

Marjory Varnedoe, Fundraising Chairman, invited all members' children to participate in social functions and dutch treats provided for the Fashionetta contestants. The six contestants were Willa Brooks Roberson, Reina Chanel Varnedoe, Serena Sherise Yarbor, Arlethia Brown, Yashica Chevette Davis, and Zakiyya Williams. The culminating activity was the fashion show held at the Alee Temple on Friday night, April 30, 1993. Tickets were $5.00 each. As a result of the financial rewards from the program, the chapter made donations to Greenbriar Children's Center, the American Cancer Society, YMCA, Sickle Cell Anemia Foundation, NAACP, UNCF, Savannah State College Scholarship Fund, and the Frank Callen Boys and Girls Club.[183]

Emily Williams, Anti-Basileus, thanked members for their future participation and cooperation in the activities scheduled for 1993. Williams' goal was to make Gamma Sigma Omega the most outstanding chapter to render service in the South Atlantic Region. Program Chairmen: Education, Freddie Pippen; Health, Alvernia Wilson; Economics, Albertha E. Boston; The Black Family, Dorothy Williams; The Arts, Carolyn Bell; World Community, Marilyn Taylor.[184]

February 14 was AKA Water Day, "Have a Heart." The goal was to support the homeless through an international demonstration of self-denial. The objective was to promote "Have a Heart" by giving generously to the needy. Each member donated the cost of a meal to the Union Mission. The chapter donated turkeys to Grace House of Union Mission, November 23, 1993.[185]

As a part of the IVYAKADEMY participation, members contributed old magazines to the Blackshear Housing Unit. Over 500 magazines were distributed to the residents of Hitch Village for their reading enjoyment.[186]

The Black Family Committee initiated the participation in the 5th Annual Women's Walk for Athletics at the T. A. Wright Stadium and the worship service at Saint Matthew's Episcopal Church. Twenty members and their families worshipped together. The chapter spotlighted Black families. Mr. and Mrs. Frederick Marshall were honored as an "Outstanding Black Family in the Coastal Area."[187]

On June 22, graduate and undergraduate AKAs with members of their families, participated in an AIDS Awareness Workshop held in Hitch Village, one of Savannah's inner city's housing projects. Renee Hunt, a certified AIDS presenter, was the facilitator for this activity. "Gamma Sigma Omega Serves the Community," says that Soror Renee Hunt, a certified AIDS presenter and employee of the housing authority presented information on the AIDS virus and helped to explain and clear up some of the wrong information about the virus. Two videos were shown that were eye-catching for the young people in attendance. Educational materials were also distributed. Undergraduate sorors of Savannah State College and graduate sorors with members of their families, participated in an AIDS awareness workshop held in Hitch Village, one of 10 public housing projects in the area.[188]

On July 17, the chapter participated in Super Saturday II, All Kids Count with the Chatham County Health Department and several other agencies. The chapter hosted an Immunization Health Fair and Fun Day for the Community. GSO sponsored a Balloon-popping booth, and approximately 100 children participated. Also, the chapter collected books on behalf of the statewide ITZAREADER effort to collect books for local libraries. The effort was part of Georgia's planning for the 1996 Olympic games.[189] Approximately 70 books were delivered on August 7, 1993 to the Public Library.[190] "Gamma Sigma Omega Serves the Community," says that the Olympic Force, the volunteer arm of the Atlanta Committee for the Olympic Games, is working with its members, including Gamma Sigma Omega, on this year long campaign to promote reading and literacy.[191]

Senior Citizens Day was observed at Chatham Nursing Home on September 18, 1993. The members of Gamma Sigma Omega and Gamma Upsilon Chapters entertained the residents with music and songs. The residents were presented with flowerpots, plant cuttings, potting soil and three large plants. On December 5, 1993, Gamma Sigma Omega and Gamma Upsilon presented a festival of hymns and hymn stories at the Rose of Sharon Apartments.[192]

GSO participated in the membership Phon-A-Thon for Greenbriar Children's Center: Johnye Gillans, Charlene Jones, Virginia Parham, Ivy Richardson, Carolyn Russell, Mary Thomas, Audrey Singleton, Vernice Whitfield, Emily Williams, Leona Williams, and Renee´ Williams during the week of December 6-10. Also, the members solicited funds in a Phon-A-Thon for the King-Tisdell Cottage Foundation.[193]

Founders' Day and the Golden Chartering Anniversary

Gamma Sigma Omega Chapter celebrated Founders' Day and its Golden chartering anniversary with an open public program. Ellen Wilson served as Chairman. The celebration began with a fellowship at the Holiday Inn-Midtown, February 5, 1993, 5:30 to 7:30 p.m. On February 6, a Fashion Show/Luncheon was held at Alfred E. Beach High School, 12:00 noon to 2:30 p.m. The cost was $6.00. Sunday, February 7, 1993, the celebration continued at First African Baptist Church, 4:00 p.m. The speaker was Lucille Whipper of Charleston, SC. Virginia James was Chairman of Music. Albertha E. Boston provided the organ prelude. Boston and Alvernia Wilson served as pianists for the choral selections. Jane J. Parker played the Greek medley.[194]

Other Events

The 40th Regional Conference was held in Ft. Lauderdale, Florida, April 15-18, 1993, the theme: "Launching: Meeting the Challenges of

Today, Developing Strategies for the year 2000." A chartered bus was secured for transportation to the Regional Conference. "Honey Dos" were invited to ride. Basileus Jones served as the Educational Forum Facilitator. Clemontine Washington conducted the workshop on Grantsmanship. Johnye Gillans served as Special Assistant to the Regional Director. Albertha E. Boston served on the Blue Ribbon Awards Committee. Dorothy Wilson was a panelist for the Economic Development Workshop in addition to being the Regional Financial Director and working with the On-site Registration Committee. Wilson also won the Mozella Gaither Collier Community Volunteer Service Award. Washington won second place, the Frederica S. Wilson Sisterly Relations Award.[195]

Media Appreciation day was held at Alfred E. Beach High School, April 3, 1993. Several members of the media were honored with lunch and a certificate of appreciation. Public Relations Chairman, Vernice Whitfield, presented a copy of *Crusade for Justice: The Autobiography of Ida B. Wells* to the library of the Greenbriar Children's Center in honor of a Media personality.[196]

The Standards and Retreat Workshop, Virginia Parham, Chairman, was held September 11, 1993. Charletta Wilson Jacks, daughter of Dorothy Wilson and a member of Lambda Epsilon Omega Chapter of Atlanta, GA, presented a workshop on mentoring. The theme of the workshop was Creative Strategies for Sisterhood.[197]

Cluster VI was held in North Charleston, SC, October 8-9, 1993. An article in the fall *Ivy Leaf* 1994, titled "Cluster VI Founders' Day Luncheon Held," says the sorors of Cluster VI of the South Atlantic Region celebrated Founders' Day with the first Cluster VI Founders' Day Luncheon at the Omni Hotel at Charleston. Participating graduate chapters were Beta Zeta Omega, Gamma Sigma Omega, Gamma Xi Omega, Kappa Upsilon Omega, Mu Phi Omega, Nu Alpha Omega, Nu Delta Omega, Nu Tau Omega, Nu Upsilon Omega, Omicron Rho Omega, Sigma Upsilon Omega, Zeta Xi Omega and Xi Omega Omega. The article continued by saying that the Regional Director, Vertelle M. Middleton, brought greetings and spoke on the occasion and that Norma S. White, Chairman International Program Committee, delivered the message.[198]

A joint workshop for members of Gamma Upsilon Chapter and Gamma Sigma Omega Chapter was held October 24, 1994, 6:30-7:30 p.m. at the School of Business Auditorium, Savannah State College. Virginia Parham was Standards Chairman, and Dorothy B. Wilson was Workshop Coordinator.During Senior Citizen Month, September, the members brought clothes for recycling to Senior Citizens. In December, the chapter's chorale sang for the residents at Rose of Sharon, a citizen seniors' housing complex, at the invitation of Mrs. Lottie Blake. Also, the members continued to contribute canned food to the 2nd Harvest Food Bank.[199]

The 86th Founders' Day was observed Sunday, February 20, 1994 at 4:00 p.m. in the Mary Clay Torian Auditorium of Savannah State College (SSC), New School of Business Building. Marjory Varnedoe was speaker. The 41st Regional Conference was held in Charleston, South Carolina, March 31- April 3, 1994.[200]

Media Appreciation/Program Declaration Day was held Saturday, April 16, 1994, 12:00 Noon, Weston Savannah Hotel and Convention Center East Boundary Street. Media honored were Kenneth Adams and Jettie Adams, *The Herald*; Theron "Ike" Carter, WHCJ (SSC); Lottie Blake, *The Tribune*; John Jackson, WEAS; Wayne Nix, Cablevision of Savannah; Don Adderton, *News Press*. Vernice Whitfield was Chairman.[201]

The 56th Boule was held in Indianapolis, in, July 9-15, 1994. The theme was "Building the Future: The Alpha Kappa Alpha Strategy, Making the Net Work." The delegates were Virginia James, Charlene Jones, Audrey Singleton, Clemontine Washington, and Vernice Whitfield. Whitfield received the Ida B. Wells Excellence in Media Award at the Boule. At Cluster VI, December 3, 1994, Dorothy B. Wilson won the first Ella S. Jones Outstanding Service Award.[202]

Gamma Sigma Omega Chapter made contributions to the United Negro College Fund (UNCF), Greenbriar Children's Center, participated on Black History radio spots, donated books, gave subscriptions of magazines, gave care packages, and gave comic books to the Cleveland Job Corps, participated in Relay for Life sponsored by the American Cancer Society, sponsored "Facing the Rising Sun," implemented the AKA Communication Fan-Out, and made provisions for a complete Thanksgiving meal for 30 homeless Inner City Night Shelter residents.[203] The article, "Gamma Sigma Omega Walks in Relay for Life" says the chapter participated in the Relay for Life walk-a-thon fundraiser sponsored by the American Cancer Society. The chapter met the goal of $1000 a team. The first lap of the event was set aside to honor those who were battling cancer. There was a candle lighting ceremony to honor those who had lost their battle with cancer and to those who were survivors. The Chapter lit two candles in memory of chapter members Mozella Collier and Ellen Wilson.[204]

Emma C. Williams (Emily), 1995-1996

Chapter Activities and Events

The regular meeting of the chapter was held on January 14, 1995 in the Savannah State College Howard Jordan School of Business, Room 147. The Basileus, Emma C. Williams, called the meeting to order. The National Program's theme was "Building the Future: The Alpha Kappa Alpha Strategy: Making the Net Work." The National Program's emphasis was Mathematics and Science Literacy, co-chaired by Pendar Franklin and Davida Wood; American Red Cross/Health, chaired by Sylvia Perry and Alvernia Wilson; Business Round Table, chaired by Dorothy Wilson; Senior Citizens, chaired by Patricia Clark; the Black Family, chaired by Dorothy Williams; Cleveland Job Corps, chaired by Emily Sanders.[205]

Founders' Day, co-chaired by Sonia Renee Williams Grant and Ivy Richardson, was an exciting time because the Regional Director, Dr. Lucretia Payton-Stewart, was the speaker. The Founders' Day committee felt that the chapter should support Dorothy Wilson's campaign for Cluster Coordinator by having her introduce the speaker. The 87th Founders' Day was held February 5, 1995, 4:00 p.m. in the Savannah State College Jordan School of Business building, the Mary Clay Torian (an AKA) Auditorium.[206]

The 87th Founders' Day committee charged Audrey Singleton, Graduate Advisor, and Emma Conyers to formulate plans to include Gamma Upsilon, the undergraduates on Savannah State College as hostesses. In addition, the undergraduates were assigned to other committees. It was the feeling of the committee that Gamma Sigma Omega should prepare the undergraduates for a smooth transition into Gamma Sigma Omega Chapter. Therefore, mentoring of the undergraduates was highly encouraged. Denise Williams, daughter of Emma Williams, Gamma Sigma Omega's Basilieus, served as Basileus of Gamma Upsilon Chapter, concurrently. Closed Founders' Day, the 88th, was held at St. Matthew's Episcopal Church.[207]

The South Eastern Regional Director of the National Pan-Hellenic Council, Horace Magwood, brought greetings as did Lois

Tate, president of the Savannah Chapter of the Council. The chapter's annual contributions were presented by Emma Williams to Greenbriar Children's Center, the NAACP, the Frank Callen Boys and Girls Club, the YMCA, and the Sickle Cell Anemia Foundation. The Outgoing Basileus Award was presented to Charlene Jones who then presented the Basileus Award to the two members who had assisted her the most during her terms of office, Vernice Pinkston-Whitfield and Dororthy B. Wilson. The Mozella Gaither Collier Community Volunteer Service Award was presented to Debra Simmons of Sigma Gamma Rho Sorority. The Soror of the Year award was presented to Dorothy B. Wilson. During the Greek Medley, the AKA candle was lit by the chapter's charter Basileus, Golden Soror and Life Member, Martha Wright Wilson.[208]

The Founding of the Jr. Debutantes/Precious Gems Mentoring Program

The mentoring of middle school girls, founded by Johnye W. Gillans and Dorothy B. Wilson, was implemented March 1995. This mentoring was called the Precious Gems Mentoring Program. Gamma Sigma Omega initiated the Precious Gems Mentoring Program and invited young ladies in grades 6 and 7 to participate in exposure to social, cultural, educational, and spiritual activities. Letters were sent to churches, and public announcements were made inviting young ladies to participate. The program was designed to aid middle school young ladies in broadening their cultural development, reinforcing self-esteem, enhancing intellectual, spiritual and personal development, and preparing for other life avenues. Mentoring activities included but was not limited to get acquainted, social graces, personal appearance, creative writing, public speaking, and career interests. This committee consisted of the following members: Charlene Jones, Pendar Franklin, Audrey Singleton, Clemontine Washington, Rena Varnedoe, Marjory Varnedoe, Vernice Whitfield, Ivy Richardson, Martha Hicks, Dorothy Williams, Virginia Parham, Alvernia Wilson, and Sylvia Perry.[209]

In addition to mentoring these Precious Gems, Gamma Sigma Omega sponsors a fundraising event where parents, other family members, friends and GSO members make donations to a Precious Gem. The Gem who reports the most funds is crowned Miss Precious Gem at the end of the mentoring year in a formal cotillion. Thus, the Jr. Debutantes/Precious Gems Mentoring Program became the local signature program and fundraising arm of Gamma Sigma Omega Chapter. The chapter returns this public money to the community by donating to charitable organizations: Greenbriar Children's Center, Sickle Cell Association, Scholarships, NAACP, United Negro College Fund, West Broad Street YMCA, EOA, and others.

The Precious Gems/Junior Debs for 1995-1996 included: Charlotte R. Blue, Ashley D. Chisholm, Ariatianca M. Coleman, Giselle P. Davis, Jacqueline Y. Dorsey, Kristin A. Fields, Fallon D. Glover, Lynn A. Harris, Melissa I. Ilugbo, Janell D. Meadows, Khadijah J. Murray, Ebony N. Pough, Adonia L. Roberts, Patricia A. Scott, Candis L. Sears, Joi A. Stevens, Kandyce M. Washington, Caretha S. Williams, Juelea E. Williams, Janine B. Williams, and Serena S. Yarbor. Precious Gem Melissa Ilugbo was crowned Miss Precious Gem at the Junior Debutante Cotillion. This activity was co-chaired by Johnye W. Gillans and Dorothy B. Wilson.[210]

Whitfield Resigns as Anti-Basileus

GSO survives because of great learning from conferences and administrations that navigate successful service projects. Cluster VI Conference was held in Georgetown, South Carolina, September 23, 1995. Dorothy Wilson presided as Cluster VI Coordinator. Nineteen members attended. November 2, 1995, a letter of resignation by Whitfield as Anti-Basileus was read. She resigned to accept a position with Ebon Academy in Forsyth, Georgia. Johnye Gillans was nominated to serve the unfinished term of the Anti-Basileus.

PIMS (Partnership in Mathmatics and Science)

During the administration of Supreme Basileus Eva Lois Evans and National Program Chairman, Gloria Stevens Smith, a national thrust was the emphasis on mathematics and science. Pendar Franklin took up the challenge to lead the program PIMS (Partnership in Mathematics and Science) for Gamma Sigma Omega. Closely working with her were Tracy Anderson, Ivy Richardson, Carolyn Russell, Sonia Renee W. Grant, Lydia Young and Chandra Haines. The PIMS after school program was set up at the St. Pius Community Center; students in grades 4-8 were participants. This enrichment program included, in addition to tutorial, field trips to industries and workshops presented by engineers. Bernie Polite, an employee at Union Camp, secured for PIMS engineers to share their experiences with the students. Tracy Anderson, who worked for Superior Landfill and Recycling Center, invited the students on a field trip to her employment. Other industries visited were Kemira, Gulfstream, Carson Products, and Skidaway National Park. The students spent five days at the Oceanography and Aquarium at Skidaway, studying the life of animals. Each student had to maintain a diary. These students were invited to participate in the Explorer Club at Union Camp.[211]

Other Events

In addition to mentoring, service at Greenbriar, PIMS, and other programs continued to be served. Vernice Whitfield encouraged members to participate in "All Kids Count," an outreach activity of the Chatham County Health Department. The Relay for Life, sponsored by the American Cancer Society, was also a focal activity of Program. Members were again encouraged to volunteer time and finances. In 1995, approximately $1500 was raised on behalf of the Relay for Life. Stephanie Grantham, an AKA, with the Department of Family and Children's Services presented a very informative workshop on Foster Parenting, during Black Family Month, May 14-June 18, 1995. Members participated in the 2nd "Happy Birthday Party for Immunized Two Year Olds." Basileus Williams continued to make the network by inviting Gail Segal of Memorial Hospital to present an overview of the First Steps Program that was designed to provide support, parent education, community resource information, and referral assistance to first time at-risk mothers and their families. Members were encouraged to become First Step volunteers.[212]

Emma C. Williams, Johnye Gillans, and Charlene Jones completed the First Step Volunteer Program of Memorial Hospital. Dorothy Williams encouraged members to volunteer at the Inner City Night Shelter. Ms. Pollet Robinson, R.N. was invited to the chapter meeting by the Health Committee April 20, 1996 to discuss the Bone Marrow Program. The chapter collected $1,483 in pledges for The Relay for Life of the American Cancer Society, and Emma Jean Conyers sang the National Anthem at the opening ceremony. At the All Kids Count, an immunization program for children was held October 26, 1996 at the National Guard Armory, the chapter hosted a finger painting booth for the children.[213]

The Regional Conference was held in Atlanta, GA, April 6-9, 1995. Gamma Sigma Omega won in three categories: First Place in Chapter Program for chapters under 50; Second Place, Attendance Award (twenty-six members in attendance), and Carolyn Bell won First Place, the Ruby J. Gainer Human Relations Award. The Regional Conference was held in Jacksonville, Florida, April 10-14, 1996. Dorothy Wilson, Cluster VI Coordinator, announced that Gamma Sigma Omega Chapter would host the Regional Conference in 1998. The Desoto Hilton was chosen as the Regional Conference Headquarters hotel. The 57th Boule was held in Baltimore, Maryland, July 12-19, 1996. The theme was "Building the Future: The Alpha Kappa Alpha Strategy— Making the Net Work." Delegates were Albertha E. Boston and Patricia J. Clark. Boston was honored at this Boule as a Silver Star for 25 years of dedicated service. Cluster VI was held October 12, 1996, in Goose Creek, South Carolina. Seventeen members attended.[214]

In nurturing undergraduates, on June 1, 1996, the Mentor and Mentorees of Gamma Sigma Omega Chapter and Gamma Upsilon Chapter had dinner at the downtown Morrison Cafeteria.[215]

Andrea Williams, Hodegos Chairman, implemented the Leaders of the Month to assist the chapter in a better recognition of members' illnesses, bereavements, or honors. Members were to contact the Month's leader so that cards, flowers, etc. could be sent in a timely manner.[216]

Johnye W. Gillans, 1997-1998

Chapter Events and Activities

Excitement, involvement, and membership growth certainly are appropriate descriptors of the 1997-98 term in Gamma Sigma Omega Chapter. This term offered a challenging and enjoyable experience for the Executive Board and Johnye Gillans, Basileus.[217] The Executive Board began the term with the officers and committee chairmen's retreat. At this retreat, the officers received their "Accepting The Challenge" team manuals. The Board's theme for the term was "Strengthen The Gamma Sigma Omega Team: Together Everyone Achieves More." The goals were as follows: to promote soror involvement, to improve attendance and punctuality, to expand the Junior Debutante Program, to secure and store chapter materials, and to provide written committee reports for regular chapter meetings.[218]

There were several chapter accomplishments: a successful Retreat Workshop, the securing of storage space for Archives, the implementation of the EOA Homeless Shelter Mentoring Program, the revision of Chapter By-Laws, the presentation of monthly hospitality themes with unique gifts and delicious monthly repasts, the recruitment and reclaiming of members, the Pan-Hellenic Babes and Tots winner, the adoption of a Black Family, contributors to dictionary project, participants in Greenbriar Children's Center and SSU Mentoring Program, the production of "The Green Page," a directory of local African American Businesses, participants in American Relay For Life and All Kids Count, PIMS, the summer project, which won several awards at Cluster VI and the Regional Conference, quarterly visits to Chatham Nursing Home, participants in a Sing-Along at Rose of Sharon Apartments, and in 1997-1998, top contributor to the UNCF among the Pan-Hellenic Council members.[219]

The 89th Founders' Day was observed February 16, 1997, 4:00 p.m., First Bryant Baptist Church, Yamacraw Village. The speaker was Norma S. White, the First Supreme Anti-Basileus of Alpha Kappa Alpha Sorority. The musical ensemble, BRAVO (Black Youth Reaching to Achieve in Vocal and Orchestral Music), performed.[220]

The Executive Board provided leadership in observing and recommending policies for a smooth flow of chapter operations. Recommendations adopted were as follows: the addition of the position of Chaplain as an appointed office, the establishment of separate accounts for Chapter Operations and Program, the development of plans for joint Founders' Day with Nu Rho Omega and Nu Delta Omega Chapters, and the revival of the Sorority Housing Committee.[221]

The Initial Tri-Chapter Founders' Day

The Tri-Chapter celebration of Founders' Day, started with the vision of Basilelus Gillans. The first Joint Founders' Day Program was celebrated among three graduate chapters: Gamma Sigma Omega Chapter of Savannah, Nu Delta Omega Chapter of Beaufort, South Carolina, and Nu Rho Omega Chapter of Hinesville, Georgia. Gamma Sigma Omega Chapter hosted the First Joint Tri Chapter celebration on January 31, 1998 at the Savannah Marriot Riverfront Hotel, Savannah.[222]

1997 Membership Intake

The Membership Intake Process (MIP) was held April 18-20, 1997, at the Quality Inn & Suites. Patricia Clark was Chairman, and Albertha E. Boston was Co-Chairman. Gamma Sigma Omega Chapter initiated twenty-eight candidates into the Sorority: one general member and twenty-seven graduate members. The candidates were the following: Tracy Ann Anderson, Antoinette Yvette Barnes, Anika L. Blackwell, Danette Harden Boston, Felicia Carr, Laquetta P. Daughtry, Virginia Edwards, Victoria Hall-Stewart, Johnnie S. Holmes, Scherherazade Lockhart Hurst, Maxine Jackson, Brenda M. Jenkins, Gail Hall Jones, Vikke Kearse, Lavinea G. Kennedy, Maureen Maxwell, Lois Milton, Emily Maureen Preer, Kimsherion Reid-Mills, Paprice Gresham Roberson, Sharon Savage, Lawanda Tillman, Leslie Denise Vaughns, Delorise Simpson Wilhite, Bernita G. Williams, Dianne F. Williams, Lois Vedelle Williams and a General Member, LaSonda A. Hill. Lorna

Chatman Jackson was unable to participate in the MIP due to illness. Her MIP process was rescheduled.[223]

Conferences

The 44th Regional Conference was held in Greenville, South Carolina, April 24-27, 1997. Nineteen members attended: Albertha E. Boston, Patricia Clark, Connie Cooper, Pendar Franklin, Johnye Gillans, Jacqueline Handy, Johnnie Holmes, Brenda Jenkins, Virginia Parham, Carolyn Russell, Denyce Sanders, Emily Sanders, Audrey Singleton, Gwendolyn Smith, Marjory Varnedoe, Andrea Williams, Leona Henley Williams, Dorothy Wilson, and Charlene Jones. [224]

The Cluster VI meeting was held in Hilton Head, SC, November 21-22, 1997. The 58th Boule was held at the McCormick Convention Center, Chicago, Illinois, July 5-10, 1998. Several members attended.[225]

1998 South Atlantic Regional Conference in Savannah

The 45th Regional Conference was held at the Savannah Civic Center, Savannah, Georgia, April 9-12, 1998. Lucretia Payton-Stewart was Regional Director. At this Conference, Sonja Garcia was elected to succeed Payton-Stewart as Regional Director. Cluster VI Chapters hosted this Conference. Dorothy Wilson was Coordinator of Cluster VI and was the Conference Chairman. At the 1998 Regional Conference, Gamma Sigma Omega sponsored two Quiz Bowl Teams, and the high school team placed 2nd in the tournament. PIMS' first year included only girls, but because of the success of the Program, boys were invited to be participants the second year. For the 1998 Regional Conference, the PIMS students assisted in the publicity of the Conference by creatively decorating a window in a corridor of Oglethorpe Mall.[226]

Jr. Debutantes/Precious Gems Mentoring Program

The Jr. Debutantes/Precious Gems Mentoring Program was the local signature program and fundraising arm of Gamma Sigma Omega

Chapter. The 1996-1997 Precious Gems/Junior Debs included: Renitra L. Baker, Alysha Chapman, Crystal Chisholm, Dia Kiett, Christina Lamar, Marrika Olds, Charmaine Simmons, Reina C. Varnedoe, Christina Watts, Tiffany White, and Tahirah Wilson. Precious Gem Reina Varnedoe, daughter of Soror Marjory Varnedoe, was crowned Miss Precious Gem at the Junior Debutante Cotillion, held at the Howard Jordan School of Business, Savannah State University (SSU), May 30, 1997, 7:30 p.m.[227]

The 1997-1998 Precious Gems/Junior Debs included: Amber Brown, Malary David, Atecia Driessen, Jaleesa Fann, Christy Hardy, Iesha Hills, Kenisha Mobley, Brittany Sawyers, Lori Singleton, and Crystal Tyson. Precious Gem Jaleesa Fann was crowned Miss Precious Gem at the Junior Debutante Cotillion, held at the Howard Jordan School of Business, Savannah State University.[228]

Virginia Mercer Parham, 1999-2000

Chapter Events and Activities

The Officers were elected in December 1998 for two-year tenure. The theme for the chapter was "IT'S A K A TIME – Total Involvement Means Everyone."

The Supreme Basileus was Norma Solomon White of Jacksonville, Florida, and the Regional Director was Sonja W. Garcia of Tampa, Florida. The National Program theme for 1998-2002 was "Blazing New Trails," and the five targets were Education, Health, the Black Family, Economics, and the Arts with Leadership Development as the foundation. Under Education, ON TRACK was the signature program aimed for at-risk children in grades 3 through 6.[229]

The National Program's theme and the chapter's theme for the next two years were introduced to the membership in January 1999. During 1999 and 2000, the following Program activities and events were successfully achieved. In the area of Education, the SCANA/AKA "Homework Center" partnership with Gadsden Elementary School was begun. In the area of the Arts, "Facing the Rising Sun," the annual dramatic monologue cultural program, was presented, and monthly book discussions were held. In the area of Health, the chapter participated in Relay for Life Cancer Walk, All Kids Count immunization party, and Health Awareness--AKA Healthy Notes. Coats were distributed to several agencies each year; projects were done with the families at Austin House and the children at May Street YMCA. Quarterly visits were made to Chatham Nursing Home for members to interact with patients, and expenditures made with Black businesses were recorded during Black Dollar months, all as part of the Black Family Program target. Leadership Development was implemented through several Chapter Leadership Training Sessions, and four members attended the National Leadership Conference. Mini-Workshops were conducted for the members on economic issues. Other chapter successes during these two years included top contributor, each year, to the United Negro College Fund of the local Pan-Hellenic members.[230]

Jr. Debutantes/Precious Gems Mentoring Program

The Jr. Debutantes/Precious Gems Mentoring Program continued to be the local signature program and fundraising arm of Gamma Sigma Omega Chapter. The event culminated with "A Pink and Green Affair," the elegant Junior Debutante Cotillion. Seventeen young ladies made their debut in 1999, and Precious Gem Chelsea L. Williams, daughter of chapter member, Wanda Williams, was crowned 1999 "Miss Precious Gem" at the Junior Debutante Cotillion. Precious Gems/Junior Debs 1998-1999 included Erica D. Benjamin, Hanniyah D. Brown, Ashley N. Bryant, Dominique A. Dixon, Crystal Eady, Christy N. Holmes, J'Aime C. Jennings, Tenah D. McAlmont, Kelli D. Phelps, Sherri N. Pierce, Melanie L. Robinson, Alexis B. Savage, Leslie S. Walker, Keli D. Washington, Chelsea L. Williams, Alicia L. Woods, and Alexis D. Jones. In 1999-2000 twelve young ladies made their debut, and for the first time a junior and a senior were crowned. Precious Gem Valencia Smith was crowned Senior "Miss Precious Gem" 2000, and Precious Gem Brandis V. Smith was crowned Junior "Miss Precious Gem" 2000 at the Junior Debutante Cotillion. The Precious Gems/Junior Debs included SandQuinnetta J. Bryant, Brittany Doctor, Curtisha Dugger, Tiyanna Hurst, Jemella Ingram, Ernestine McCullough, Alexis Proctor, Ashanti Reeves, Arequila Robinson, Brandis Smith, Valencia Smith, and Whitney Ware.[231]

Founders' Day

The chapter observed an outstanding open 91st Founders' Day celebration, February 14, 1999 at St. Philip A.M.E. Church. The speaker was Alpha Kappa Alpha member, Denise Rockwell, member of the National Educational Association Executive Committee, Los Angeles, California. A Tri-Chapter celebration was observed for the 92nd Founders' Day. Chapters, Nu Delta Omega, Nu Rho Omega, and Gamma Sigma Omega met on St. Helena Island, South Carolina at the Brick Baptist Church, Fellowship Hall, Penn Center, January 22, 2000. The host Chapter was Nu Delta Omega.[232]

50th Greenbriar Children's Center Anniversary

Gamma Sigma Omega Chapter sponsored the 50th Greenbriar Children's Center Anniversary Reception, and supported the 50th Greenbriar Children's Center Anniversary Gala in 1999.[233]

Conferences

Members attending the 1999 Regional Conference held in Orlando, Florida, March 31 thru April 4, 1999 were delegates: Basileus Virginia M. Parham, Clemontine F. Washington, I. Denyce Sanders, Maureen Maxwell, Anika Blackwell, Marjory Varnedoe, and Emma J. Preer. Others attending were Antoinette Barnes, Carolyn Bell, Albertha E. Boston, Patricia Clark, Connie Cooper, Rebecca Cooper, Kimberly David, Nicole Fields, Pendar Franklin, Johnye W. Gillans, Chandra Haines, Jacqueline Handy, Leona Henley-Williams, Johnnie Holmes, Annie Jackson, Diane Jackson, Lorna Jackson, Maxine Jackson, Brenda Jenkins, Linda Johnson, Charlene Jones, Vanessa Miller Kaigler, Carolyn Russell, Audrey Singleton, Gwen Smith, Melissa Smith, Dorothy Speed, Marjory Varnedoe, Rena Varnedoe, Denise Williams, Emily C. Williams, Emily Preer-Williams, Wanda Williams, Alvernia Wilson, Dorothy B. Wilson, and Davida Wood. The chapter achieved record attendance (48.8% of membership) at the Regional Conference in 1999 held in Orlando, Florida. The chapter won five Awards for Regional Exhibits. Also, the chapter earned the Master's Degree for contributions to the Educational Advancement Foundation each year.[234]

Members who registered and attended the Regional Conference held in Atlanta, Georgia, April 13-16, 2000 were delegates: Basileus Virginia M. Parham, Vanessa Miller Kaigler, Diane Williams, and Nicole Fields. Others in attendance were Huriyah Al-Batin, Antoinette Barnes, Carolyn Bell, Albertha E. Boston, Patricia Clark, Connie Cooper, Denise Cooper, Jessie DeLoach, Pendar Franklin, Patricia Gardner, Johnye W. Gillans, Sonia R. Grant, Jacqueline Handy, Johnnie Holmes, Ethel Hunter, Annie Jackson, Hope Johnson, Charlene Jones, Carmelita Maynard, Sylvia Perry, I. Denyce Sanders, Audrey Singleton,

Gwendolyn Smith, Melissa Smith, Dorothy Speed, Marjory Varnedoe, Rena Varnedoe, Maureen Maxwell-Walker, Clemontine F. Washington, Emily C. Williams, Dorothy B. Wilson, and Lydia Young. Thirty three and six tenth percent (33.6%) of membership registered at Regional Conference.[235]

The delegates to the Leadership Conference held July 8-11, 1999 in Orlando, Florida were Virginia M. Parham, Clemontine F. Washington, Patricia Clark, and Rebecca Cooper.[236]

Dallas, Texas was a sea of pink and green July 8-14, 2000 as members from all ten regions gathered for the 59th Boule. Chapter delegates were Clemontine F. Washington, Emily C. Williams, Virginia M. Parham, Sonia R. Grant, and Audrey Singleton. Other chapter members attending were Carolyn Bell, Albertha E. Boston, Patricia Clark, Emma Conyers, Connie Cooper, Denise Cooper, Monyca Cundiff, Jessie C. DeLoach, Pendar Franklin, Johnnie Holmes, Ethel Hunter, Ivanette Richardson, Carolyn Russell, Denyce Sanders, Lisa Singleton, Gia Smith, Marjory Varnedoe, Rena Varnedoe, and Lois Vedelle Williams.[237]

Members in attendance at Cluster VI Conference held in Charleston, South Carolina on December 4, 1999 were Basileus Virginia Parham, Clemontine F. Washington, Johnye W. Gillans, Dorothy B. Wilson, Vanessa Miller Kaigler, Charlene Jones, Emma J. Conyers, Maxine Jackson, Diane Williams, Connie Cooper, Brenda Jenkins, Audrey Singleton, Antoinette Barnes, Melinda P. Miller, Lydia Young, Albertha E. Boston, Emily Crawford-Sanders, Emma Preer, Emily Preer-Williams, Maureen Maxwell-Walker, Sharon Savage-Watson, and Annie Jackson. Cluster VI Conference was held December 8-9, 2000 in Vidalia, Georgia. Many chapter members attended, but names were not recorded.[238]

Recognitions

Soror of the Year for 1999 was Johnye W. Gillans. Emily Preer-Williams and Pendar Franklin were recipients of the Basileus Award. Soror of the Year for 2000 was Vanessa Miller Kaigler. Recipients of the Basileus Award were Marjory Varnedoe, I. Denyce Sanders, and Vanessa Miller Kaigler. Clemontine F. Washington received the Scholarship Award.[239] A Special Founders' Recognition was presented to Johnye W. Gillans who proposed the idea of establishing the Tri-Chapter Founders' Day celebration.[240]

2002 Membership Intake

Membership Intake Process was held March 31–April 2, 2002 at the Country Hearth Inn in Pooler, Georgia. The 24 Carats of "Pink Ice" were initiated. They were Janice J. Allen, Queen E. Barnes, Jelana R. Bryan, Lynderia S. Cheevers, Denise M. Cooper, Monyca D. Cundiff, Amy Y. Graham, Eleanor J. Ginn, Ethel Hunter, Shelia B. Hutcherson, Hope Johnson, Alberta E. King, Michelle Mincey-Lee, Carmelita Maynard, Tamika E. Minor, Zenobia L. Mitchell, Lucille C. Reid, Ivanette D. Richardson, April S. Scott, Lisa M. Singleton, Gia S. Smith, Althea M. Thompson, Cerea P. Walker, and Vera C. Young. Connie Cooper was Membership Chairman.[241]

Other Events

Activities aimed at retaining, reclaiming, and recruiting members were continued, including AKA Round-Up and Membership Intake Process in 2000. These activities resulted in the initiation of 24 ladies, 10 members reclaimed, and 5 members transferred into the chapter. Sisterly relation activities were enhanced, including the annual Chapter Planning and Workshop Retreat and fellowship with and support of Gamma Upsilon Chapter's members. Gamma Sigma Omega continued to make annual monetary contributions to civic, social, and educational institutions on the local and national levels.[242]

Vanessa Miller Kaigler, 2001-2002

Celebrate Sisterhood and Prepare Sorors to Lead

Vanessa Miller Kaigler's tenure for two years began with a retreat at her home, affectionately identified as a Planning Celebration. Kaigler's vision for the chapter was to make coalitions with agencies in the Savannah community and to volunteer at agencies that paralleled the Sorority's Program Targets. Her emphasis was to "celebrate sisterhood and to prepare sorors to lead." Her belief, Alpha Kappa Alpha women, college educated professionals, should possess the skills required to lead anyone in any environment.[243] The Jr. Debutantes/Precious Gems Mentoring Program continued to be the local signature program and fundraising arm of Gamma Sigma Omega Chapter.

At her first meeting, Basileus Kaigler announced her theme: "Celebrating Our Sisterhood." She also stated that Gamma Sigma Omega's focus would be on Program Targets with emphasis on the International Signature Program, ON TRACK. She stressed the importance for leaders to be timely. To support the idea of timeliness, Basileus Kaigler encouraged the recommendation to fine members arriving late to meetings. To support the idea of the chapter's security, Kaigler encouraged the recommendation that all members of Alpha Kappa Alpha Sorority, Inc. show identification before entering meetings. At this planning meeting, the Anti-Basileus, Carolyn Bell, presented the Program committees and the Chairmen and Co-Chairmen for implementing the Alpha Kappa Alpha's International Program and Gamma Sigma Omega's Program in meeting the needs of the Savannah community.[244]

ON TRACK Program/Project AKA

Janie B. Bruen followed by Kim Chappell-Stevens chaired the International Signature Program, ON TRACK. The primary planners of activities for 3rd graders at Robert W. Gadsden Elementary School were Ethel Gibbs, Connie Cooper, and Essie Johnson. However, Bell striving to make a greater impact in the community, sought coalition with the school where Gamma Sigma Omega Chapter blazed trails to nurture 3rd, 4th, and 5th graders. Cooper served as the Coordinator to train members to be mentors to work with the students at Gadsden. GSO members volunteered to serve as mentors to the children in the ON TRACK program.

PROJECT AKA, coordinated by Carolyn Bell, established the following mission statement for implementation of the Project: Gamma Sigma Omega Chapter of Alpha Kappa Alpha Sorority is committed to enhancing life skills programs for youth and adults in the Robert W. Gadsden Elementary School neighborhood through the collaborative efforts of Gamma Sigma Omega, Gadsden Elementary School, the Housing Authority of Savannah and other community partners." As a result of this initiative, grants were obtained from the State of Georgia and the "Great Ideas Grant" from United Way.[245]

On February 24, 2001, Gamma Sigma Omega sponsored "AKA Extravaganza" at Gadsden Elementary School. The extravaganza linked Cuyler-Brownville Community and the residents of Kayton and Frazier Homes, public housing units, with community service providers. Wanda Williams and the Black Family Committee served as program coordinators. Members were at Gadsden on Tuesday, May 22, 2001 to participate in the Academic Olympiad by presenting journals to each of the 3rd grade students. The children were encouraged to develop written communication skills by writing about significant events from their summer experiences.[246]

The summer calendar for PROJECT AKA was planned accordingly: June 9, 2001, Pot Luck Social and Etiquette Workshop, Gadsden Elementary, 12:00 noon; June 28, 2001, a visit to the Federal Reserve Bank, Jacksonville, Florida; July 27, 2001, an overnight trip to Atlanta; August 7, 2001, a cultural tour of Savannah; August 9, 2001, a Back to School Extravaganza.[247]

ON TRACK Awards Day was held at Gadsden School in May. The students received certificates, pencils, and medallions from the chapter. In July 2002, the ON TRACK students chaperoned by members of the chapter, toured educational sites in Atlanta, Ga., Chattanooga and Sweetwater, Tennessee. This field trip was an overnight one where children had the opportunity to be exposed to a variety of new experiences.[248]

Collaborations

Emphasizing volunteerism, Kaigler encouraged GSO members to attend "Operation Beating Heart," a joint collaboration with Savannah State University, Candler/St. Joseph's Hospital and Harvard University. Dr. "Butch" Rosser unveiled a revolutionary diagnostic technique to reduce the number of pre-mature deaths in athletics. On Sunday, September 30, 2001, Gamma Sigma Omega partnered with the Junior League of Savannah and other civic organizations in a rally following the "Attack on America." In collaboration with the United Negro College Fund, the chapter was a sponsor of The One Hundred Celebrity Men Who Cook, a fundraising event held December 2001 and December 2002. In celebration of Senior Citizens, members showered Mrs. Addie Reeves, a resident of Frazier Homes, with birthday cards on her 100th birthday and presented gift bags to senior residents of Kayton and Frazier Homes after chapter meeting. In collaboration with the City of Savannah Housing Project, members participated in a home clean-up project along with other members of the Pan-Hellenic Council on August 25, 2001.[249] Continuing to make the net work, Kaigler held a chapter meeting March 9, 2002 at Massie School, a historical educational site and museum in Savannah, one of the institutions to which the chapter contributes financially.[250]

PROJECT AKA and other community service projects were continued. Members volunteered April 14, 2002 to pass out Pin Wheels at the SAND GNATS Baseball Game in remembrance of children who were abused and neglected in Chatham County. Carmelita Maynard chaired this activity. Maynard continued to secure volunteers for the Cancer Relay for Life. There were other Program projects in which the chapter participated. Members collected money for Greenbriar Children's Center. The Black Family Committee collected coats for the needy in the community. Mekta Brown and Janice Allen coordinated

AKA Black Dollar Day, a subsidiary of the Econonmic Development Committee. This Committee distributed AKA dollars to members to use at Black businesses. This Committee also presented a workshop on finances to the Kayton/Frazier Homes residents, May 15, 2001. On behalf of beautifying the Savannah community, the Bus Stop adopted by the chapter, on 52nd Street, was cleaned and decorated for the spring by Eleanor Ginn and Ethel Hunter. The Cultural Arts Committee presented the dramatic oration of Black poetry, "Facing the Rising Sun," performed by children and teens in the Coastal Empire, May 6, 2001, 5:00 p.m., at St. James A.M.E. Church and at Connor's Temple Baptist Church, April 28, 2002, 5:30 p.m., Marjory Varnedoe, Chairman.[251]

Founders' Day

Prior to the 93rd open Founders' Day celebration observed February 11, 2001 at Tremont Temple Baptist Church, 4:00 p.m., members of Gamma Sigma Omega worshiped at St. Philip A.M.E. Church during the 11:00 a.m. worship service. At the open Founders' Day observance, the speaker was Tiffany Cochran, an AKA, the daughter of Attorney Johnnie Cochran. Several members were honored for their hard work and service: Chapter Achievement Award, Virginia Parham; Soror of the Year, I. Dencye Sanders; Basileus Award, Davida Wood; Encouragement Award, Maxine Jackson; and Committee Award, Clemontine Washington.[252]

On January 26, 2002, the Tri-Chapter 94th Founders' Day was hosted by Nu Rho Omega, Hinesville, Georgia, 12:00 noon at the Holiday Inn, Hinesville, Georgia. The members honored for their hard work and service were Patricia Mincey, Soror of the Year; Emma Jean Conyers, Sisterhood; Marjory Varnedoe and Renae Miller, Scholarship; Johnnie Holmes, Maxine Jackson, and Davida Wood, Basileus Awards.[253]

Conferences/Training

The Supreme Basileus, Norma S. White, urged all members to participate in leadership training, especially those who aspire to become officers. Members were encouraged to attend the Leadership Seminar in San Juan, Puerto Rico. The Supreme Basileus outlined a procedure, identified as Leadership Training Modules, for certification of all candidates seeking office in Alpha Kappa Alpha. Each chapter officer had to complete "And Who Shall Lead." Every candidate prior to office had to complete these modules. Leadership Development Training for Gamma Sigma Omega Chapter, chaired by Sylvia Perry, was held May 19, 2001, June 30, 2001, and September 29, 2001, at Savannah State University, School of Business, and on October 8, 2001 at the Board of Education, Room 213. The Standards and Leadership committees presented Gamma Sigma Omega Chapter's Planning Retreat, chaired by Clemontine Washington and Sylvia Perry, Saturday, August 17, 2002, Savannah State University Ballroom. This Retreat was an opportunity for bonding, increasing knowledge about the Sorority and for setting measurable goals that would assure the perpetuity of Gamma Sigma Omega.[254]

The 48th South Atlantic Regional Conference was held in Atlanta, GA, April 5-8, 2001. The delegates for the Conference were Vanessa Kaigler, Clemontine Washington, Diane Williams, Suya Loud, Tamika Minor, Patricia Clark, Hope Johnson, Gia Smith, and Lorna Jackson. Regional Director, Sonja Garcia, made the following regional committee assignments, Conveners, Recorders, Monitors: Ethel Gibbs, Dorothy Wilson, Wanda Jones, and Virginia Parham.[255]

The 49th Regional Conference was held April 4-7, 2002, Tampa, Florida. The delegates selected were Vanessa Kaigler, Clemontine Washington, Carolyn Bell, Janie Bruen, Michelle Mincey-Lee, Emma Conyers, and Jessie Deloach. Johnye Gillans was selected as alternate. Members recognized at the Regional Conference were Carolyn Bell receiving the Lucretia Payton-Stewart Promising Soror Award and Patricia Mincey, being recognized at the Leadership Breakfast as the chapter's Soror of the Year. Marjory Varnedoe presented a workshop during the Cultural Arts session. The following members were certified to be Graduate Advisors: Moncya C. Blanding, Denise Cooper, and Tamika Minor. They completed the Graduate Advisor Institute. Clemontine Washington completed the re-certification process.[256]

Cluster VI, 2001 was held December 7-8, Orangeburg, SC. Members were encouraged to submit exhibits for Program strands. Members serving as workshop monitors, facilitators or recorders were Renae Miller, Denise Cooper, Kimberly Rhodes, and Sonya Sheppard. The following members received awards: Sonya Sheppard received the Irene W. McCollom Under 35 Finer Womanhood Award; Carolyn Bell received both the Dorothy B. Wilson Leadership Award and the Ella S. Jones Outstanding Service Award; Program received the newly created Black Family Award.[257]

The delegates for the 60th Boule, held in Orlando, Florida, were Maxine Jackson, Gwendolyn Johnson, Dorothy Wilson, Johnye Gillans, Renee Miller, Marjory Varnedoe, and Denyce Sanders. The Basileus and the Graduate advisor were included. Dorothy Wilson was selected to serve on a committee to assist with the presentation of Irene McCollom as the 15th Regional Director. Emma Conyers, Albertha E. Boston, and Patricia Clark completed the Leadership Development Institute at the Boule. Linda M. White was elected Supreme Basileus, and her chosen theme was the "SPIRIT of Alpha Kappa Alpha." SPIRIT is an acronym, *S* for sisterhood, scholarship, service; *P* for partnership; *I* for innovation; R for respect; I for involvement; and *T* for technology.[258]

The assignments were made for the 2004 South Atlantic Regional Conference Augusta, GA on March 22-25 with Cluster VI hosting and Ella Jones, Regional Conference Chaiman: Gamma Sigma Omega and Nu Delta Omega Chapters, chaired by Vanessa Kaigler, to plan formal banquet; Clemontine Washington to plan the Undergraduate Luncheon and Step Show. The Steering Committee from Gamma Sigma Omega included Johnye Gillans, Eleanor Ginn, Alvernia Wilson, Dorothy Wilson, Vanessa Kaigler, and Clemontine Washington.[259]

Jr. Debutantes/Precious Gems Mentoring Program

In 2001, the chapter nurtured nine energetic young ladies as Precious Gems/Junior Debs: Ja'Wana K. Baker, Kimberly N. Brown, Whitney C. Scott, Jennifer M. Simmons, Charonnay L. Stewart, Farah

W. Taylor, Jasmine D. Thompson, DeEtte M. Waters and LaTerika K. Young. Each month following chapter meeting, activities were held in hopes of providing or enhancing the lives of the young ladies. The Junior Debutante Cotillion was held June 1, 2001 at Savannah State University, Savannah Room, 7:00 p.m.. Precious Gem Whitney Scott, the daughter of April Scott, was crowned Miss Precious Gem at the Junior Debutante Cotillion. The Precious Gems/Junior Debs participated in the MLK parade; also, they prepared and stuffed gift baskets for the Austin House residents. Johnye Gillans, Gwendolyn Johnson, Lawanda Tillman, and Patricia Mincey spearheaded these events. In 2001-2002, Precious Gems/Junior Debs were JaNae Evonne Swanson, Victoria N. Thorpe, Raven E. Dinsmore, Brittani E. Jarrow, Markia Latrell Leeks, Cierra Jones, Quadeira Lakeisha Sadler, Courtney Katriste Mobley, Brittney C. Wilhite, Nakia Janae Mobley, Tia Marjory Jones, and Arnecia LeShea Newton. The 2002 Precious Gem Tia Marjory Jones was crowned Miss Precious Gem at the Junior Debutante Cotillion, held at Savannah State University Savannah Room.[260]

Other Events

The Connection Committee led the way to the State Capitol, known as AKA Day at the Capitol. Norma White, the Supreme Basileus, met Alpha Kappa Alpha women in Atlanta, February 19, 2001. In 2002, AKAs were back at the Capitol for AKA Day. The chapter participated in the Political Forum on WSOK 1230 Open Line Outreach. The forum included candidates for the First District School Board and presidential candidates for the School Board. Members sold Christmas cards for Greenbriar Children's Center in the Savannah Mall. Selling cards were Eleanor Murdock, Johnnie Holmes, Johnye Gillans, Queen Barnes, Albertha Vaughns, Eudora Allen, Lawanda Tillman, Audrey Singleton, Delorise Wilhite, Carolyn Russell, Albertha Collier, and Emma Conyers, Coordinator.[261]

Book discussions were held at the May Street YMCA and opened to the public. Some of the books discussed: *Think Big* by Dr. Ben Carson; *Race Matters* by Cornell West; *Timeline* by Michael Crichton; *Cradle and All* by James Patterson; *Getting Over It* by Anna Maxted; *Half a Heart* by Rosellen Brown; *White Oleander* by Janet Fitch; *Riptide* by Catherine Coulter; *A Day Late and A Dollar Short* by Terry McMillan; *Prayer of Jabez* by Bruce Wilkerson; *The Wind Done Gone* by Alice Randall; *Sorority Sisters* by Tajuana Butler; *All That Savannah Jazz* by Charles J. Elmore; *Any Way the Wind Blows* by E. Lynn; *The Women*, by Hilton Als.[262]

In order to promote a willingness to serve, Basileus Kaigler honored a member who demonstrated a kind working spirit during the month. The honor was called "Up, Up and Away Trailblazer." The first recipient was Johnnie Holmes. Janie Bruen was the second recipient who worked diligently with the Principal and staff at Gadsden Elementary to enhance the ON TRACK program. The third recipient was Wanda Williams, the Coordinator of the AKA Extravaganza and Chairman of the Black Family Committee. Sonia Renee Grant received the fourth honor for her award winning scrapbooks. Ethel Hunter was honored as the fifth recipient because of her hard work with the Junior Debs Career Fair. Gwendolyn Harris Johnson, Co-Chairman for the Junior Debutante Cotillion, refreshment chairman for Relay for Life, and assistant planner of the Leadership Development, was the sixth recipient, and Queen Barnes received the honor as the seventh recipient.[263]

In celebrating sisterhood, five AKAs transferred from Nu Rho Omega to Gamma Sigma Omega: LaShawna K. Alderman Mullgrav, Kimberly Chappell-Stevens, Annie Chappell, Annie Murray, and Sonya Sheppard. The following AKAs reactivated: Lavinea G. Kennedy, Paprice Roberson, and Vikke Kearse Bargeron. As of April 2001, Gamma Sigma Omega Chapter had 120 active members.[264]

A healthy-food-tasting party was held for members April 14, 2001. The Health Committee, Carmelita Maynard, Chairman, sponsored this event. On May 12, prior to chapter meeting, Dr. James J. Burke, II, M.D., on staff at Memorial Medical Hospital, division of Gynecology Oncology, presented a health forum on women health issues. Mrs. Jane Garrison with Safe Kids spoke to members on children issues in December.[265]

The Archives committee scheduled Gamma Sigma Omega's first "Archives Day," June 2, 2001, initiated by Emma Conyers. The purpose for Archives Day was to move AKA material from homes to Archives for preservation of the chapter's history and artifacts. Following the directives of the National Archives Committee, a one-page history of Gamma Sigma Omega, news clippings of members in the chapter, and a taped oral history of the chapter narrated by Jessie Collier DeLoach, a Golden Soror, and recorded by Conyers, were mailed to the National Archives Office housed at Howard University, Washington, DC. In organizing the chapter's records and documents, they and other storage items were recorded and inventoried. File cabinets were purchased, and the Archives/storage was organized.[266]

Sunday, May 6, 2001, Little Curtis James Richardson was crowned the Pan-Hellenic Council Babes and Tots winner. Members of Gamma Sigma Omega sponsored Master Richardson who is the grandson of member Ivy Richardson and the nephew of member Ivanette Richardson. April Scott served as the chapter's coordinator for this event. Sonia Renee Grant and Gwendolyn Johnson were Pan-Hellenic representatives for the chapter in 2002. These two members were instrumental in soliciting can food for the Pan-Hellenic outreach project.[267]

In recognition of service to mankind, Gamma Sigma Omega received the following awards: United Way Volunteer Recognition Award for work done at Robert W. Gadsden Elementary School and the United Negro College Fund Award. Gamma Sigma Omega Chapter was featured in the *Ivy Leaf*, the Sorority's magazine, page 30, Summer Edition, June 2002.[268]

Gamma Upsilon, under the leadership of Clemontine Washington and Diane Williams, held Membership Intake Process workshops March 27, 2001 and April 1, 2001. The rush was April 2, 2001. Fourteen young ladies were initiated into Gamma Upsilon Chapter. The following members assisted with the MIP process: Vanessa Kaigler, Dorothy Wilson, Albertha E. Boston, Charlene Jones, Patricia Clark, Audrey Singleton, Johnye Gillans, Diane Williams, Virginia Parham, Maxine Jackson, and Patricia Gardner. Gamma Upsilon observed Founders' Day with Johnye Gillans as speaker. The two chapters held a joint meeting

Emma Jean Hawkins Conyers

April 13, 2002.[269]Diane Williams resigned as Assistant Graduate Advisor due to her job's workload. The Nominating Committee submitted Dorothy Speed's name for the office of Anti-Grammateus, but she too resigned. Sheila Hutcherson accepted the position as Anti-Grammateus on the recommendation of the Nominating Committee.[270]

80

Chapter V

PROTE´GE´ES, 2003- 2012

Carolyn Hodges Bell, 2003-2004

CAROLYN H. BELL began her administration under the leadership of Supreme Basileus, Linda M. White. White's theme was "The Spirit of Alpha Kappa Alpha," the flagship for Bell's administration. Bell, using White's SPIRIT acronym and concept, S - Sisterhood, Scholarship and Service; P - Partnership; I - Innovation; R – Respect; I – Involvement; T – Technology, guided Gamma Sigma Omega as a focused and deliberate captain of the ship.

To make certain her sail would overcome rough waters, she began her administration by holding her installation worship service in God's House, December 19, 2002 at First African Baptist Church where Rev. Thurmond Tillman, Pastor, brought the message. Based on the International theme, Bell suggested for her two year tenure, "The Spirit of AKA: Love." Her theme song was "I Need You to Survive" by Hezekiah Walker and The Love Fellowship Choir. Her first meeting was held at Gadsden Elementary School, January 11, 2003.[271]

Education

Anti-Basileus, Patricia Clark, Chairman of Program, reported at the January 11, 2003, chapter meeting that the Ivy Reading AKAdemy will continue to focus on students at Gadsden Elementary and in order to complete the 2002 program project fourteen GSO members were needed to mentor fourteen students for the remaining 4 1/2 months of school.

The Ivy Reading AKAdemy, "How to Become A Millionaire," initiated by Program Chairman, Patricia Clark, focused on grades K-3. Esther F. Garrison Elementary, a school in close proximity to Gadsden Elementary, Kayton and Frazier Homes Public Housing projects, became the second targeted school. Many of Garrison's pupils were from the Yamacraw Village Public Housing project. The goal, for students at Gadsden and Garrison, was to read one million words within one year.[272] The Saturday tutorial became known as the "Third Saturday Tutorial and Nurturing Session," held at Robert W. Gadsden. GSO announced the International signature program, the Ivy Reading AKAdemy (IRA) during April's 2003 sorority meeting. An Education Committee was introduced with Kim Chappell-Stevens serving as Chairman. The two schools, Gadsden (Dr. Delma Pollen, Principal) and Garrison (Dr. Karen Grant, Principal) were the project's sites. Gamma Sigma Omega agreed to move forward by strengthening the legacy of mentoring children. The grades would be K-3. This project was introduced to the Savannah community via the media.

With reading as emphasis and the keeping in touch as mentors with the fourteen students of the ON TRACK Program/Project AKA, March 24, 2003, Annie Jackson and Dr. Freddie Pippen escorted a 5th grade class from Robert W. Gadsden Elementary School to the Live Oak Library.

The IRA conducted a breakfast reception for the teachers of Robert W. Gadsden Elementary School and Esther Garrison Elementary School, Thursday, May 29, 2003 to officially launch the program, K-3 Program, and to enable chapter members to meet the staff of both schools.

Reading, test-taking skills for Criterion-Referenced Competency Test (CRCT), science trivia, practice skills in mathematical problem solving, language arts, and listening comprehension were parts of the tutorial at the Third Saturday Tutorial and Nurturing Session. Ms. Edna Mason served as school liaison. After tutorial session, students were entertained by special guests. These guests incorporated their expertise and expounded on the importance of learning to read to succeed in school and in life, for example, Mrs. Inez Wilkerson, author of *Stella's Daughter* was presented. Ms. Richie Reid from Hardeville,

SC, three members of the Black Cowboys Club with two horses gave demonstrations and presentations.[273]

May 10, 2003, IRA students, including the ON TRACK Program/ Project AKA students joined several other community children and adults at the old airport to listen to billionaire Attorney Willie Gary and to tour his 737 Jet. Attorney Gary shared his rags to riches story with the children and encouraged them to be all they could be. He interacted with the children and adults through conversation, interview, photo shoots and signing autographs.[274]

The ON TRACK Program/Project students were inclusive with other Gadsden students on May 17, 2003, led by Maxine Jackson on a tour of the Mighty Eighth Air Force Heritage Museum. The students toured the facility and listened to a presentation describing the mighty feats of men and women of Air Force. The tour ended with lunch in the museum cafeteria. Members attending were Eleanor Ginn, Ethel Hunter, Johnnie Holmes, and Kimberly Chappell-Stevens.[275]

Remembering the directive from Anti-Basileus Clark to seek volunteers for the fourteen, ON TRACK Program/Project students, Gamma Sigma Omega Update, 2003, a letter to members, reported in the August Happenings and Review of July Events that five GSO members and four parents (guardians) accompanied twenty-three youngsters on a tour of Washington, DC., July 24-26, 2003. Members attending were Basileus Bell, Dorothy Wilson, Emma Conyers, Alvernia Wilson, and Emily Preer Williams.

Gamma Sigma Omega Chapter's impact on children in 2002 and the continued impact reaped the benefits of the service. The United Way recognized and awarded the chapter as Volunteer Group of the Year[276]

Accolades run off the backs of members of Gamma Sigma Omega as water runs off the back of a duck. The chapter knows service must be continued. GSO had promised Gadsden and Garrison students awards for reading during the summer. With the school year beginning, August 2003, the chapter was in the process of collecting reading logs from their students at the same time serving as reading mentors by reading to classes. Those students needing reading assistance were directed to the Third Saturday Tutorial and Nurturing Sessions.[277]

Maxine Jackson will chair the Education Committee reported the Anti-Basileus, Patricia Clark, replacing Kim Chappell-Stevens who began study for her doctorate degree. The goal set for students at Gadsden and Garrison was read 204 by 2004.[278] Essie Johnson was the coordinator for the Ivy Reading AKAdemy.

The chapter initiated reading teams that developed a schedule for GSO members to read to students at Gadsden and Garrison Elementary schools. Robert W. Gadsden, total enrollment, K-3, 442; Emma Conyers (K); Paprice Simmons (1st); Annie Jackson (2nd); LaTasha Thomas (3rd); Esther F. Garrison, total enrollment, K-3, 349; Annie Chappell (K); Brenda Jenkins (1st); Lois V. Williams (2nd); LaShawna Mullgrav (3rd). The reading teams also developed a method to document the reading experience of the Ivy Reading AKAdemy.[279]

Members on the Gadsden Reading team were Virginia M. Parham, Zenobia Mitchell, G.G. White, Sylvia Perry, Eleanor Murdock, Emma J. Conyers, Henrietta Perry, Yolanda L. Fontaine, Paprice Simmons, Johana Johnson, Serdalia Singleton, Tatasha Beckett, Richardine Gresham, Melinda P. Miller, James Riles, Carolyn Russell. Members on the Garrison Reading team were Dr. Albertha E. Boston, Patricia Clark, Carol Bell, Annie Chappell, Johnye Gillans, Charlene Jones, Sal Mullgrav, Corporal Johnson, Carmelita Maynard, Patricia Mincey, Michelle Mincey-Lee.[280]

A Reading Thermometer was placed in front of Gadsden and Garrison Elementary as incentive for students to reach the school's goal and for public observation of the reading progress of the students. The City of Savannah, Michael Brown, City Manager, and the Building and Electrical Maintenance Division provided the thermometers[281]

On Friday, January 30, 2004, Papa John's Pizza provided 150 pizzas for nearly 800 students at Gadsden and Garrison Elementary Schools. Joey Dixon, owner/manager and Richard Cochran, Area Supervisor, sponsored the pizza for the second reading progress celebration at the schools. They were saluted as "204 by 2004" partners. The reading progress as of January 31, 2004: Gadsden's goal was to read 89, 760 books. The students read 55,097, representing 61% of goal. Garrison's goal was to read 69,972 books. The students read 60,435, representing 86% of goal.[282]

GSO members who were not available to visit Gadsden or Garrison were given the opportunity to participate in the 204 x 2004 Reading Program. A special story hour was provided by the Arts Committee during the November Third Saturday Tutorial and Nurturing Session. Members of the Arts/Book Club Committee and all GSO members were asked to participate. Books read to the children during this time were counted toward the children's personal reading goal and the school's reading goal. This reading opportunity supported the initiative 204 x 2004.[283]

In addition to Gamma Sigma Omega members, the chapter solicited other volunteers to help schools reach their reading goals. Some agencies or businesses that volunteered were employees from the City of Savannah, Carver State Bank, Equal Opportunity Authority (EOA), Zeta Phi Beta Sorority, Inc., the National Council of Negro Women, WTOC TV, Savannah Morning News, and Housing Authority of Savannah.[284]

The top readers at Gadsden: grade K, Martin Pounds; 1st grade, Monica Smalls; 2nd grade, Montenise Jackson; 3rd grade, Brandy Brown. Goal, 89,760, Final Count, 104,206. The top readers at Garrison: grade K, Nyjahyia Clark; 1st grade, Kahill Clark; 2nd grade, Tracy Lundy; 3rd grade, Davan Bunch. Goal, 69,676; Final Count, 197,935. Basileus Bell lived up to her word to allow students at both schools to pour water on her if they met school's goal.

A celebration it was! Mr. John Johnson, Jr., General Manager of the Carmike Theater donated the popcorn and the kid's pack containers for the culminating celebration of the 204 x 2004 reading project, May 20, 2004 at Garrison School and May 21, 2004 at Gadsden School.[285]

In addition to GSO's reading initiatives, members participated in other reading programs in the schools. At the March 1, 2004, Dr. Seuss Birthday Celebration, members read to students at Garrison Elementary, Gadsden Elementary, and Tompkins Middle School.[286]

Clark continuing to promote reading with Education Committee as guide, the new slogan for 2004-2005 school year was "Keep Reading Alive in 2005."[287] Third Saturday Tutorial and Nurturing sessions continued.

The Young Authors Program helped to develop minds and writing skills of children. AKAs encouraged youth in various learning exercises.

Improving the reading and writing skills of young children were major goals of the International Program. Annie Jackson and the Young Authors Program committee involved four schools and received sixty entries. Six students placed in first, second, and third places in two separate categories. Participants received trophies and certificates during Awards Day at their schools. The four schools were Gadsden, Garrison, Notre Dame, and Pulaski: 2nd & 3rd graders, 1st place, Tequila Owens, Garrison School, "My New Toys;" 2nd Place, Kadeish Crawford, Garrison School, "The Baby and the Peanut Butter and Jelly Sandwich"; 3rd Place, Cedric Woods, Notre Dame Catholic School, "Spring"; 4th & 5th grades, 1st Place, Martin Terrell (Author), Marcus Youman (Illustrator), Garrison School, "A Walk in the City"; 2nd Place (no name), Garrison School, "Christmas Eve"; 3rd Place, Briana Washington (Author), Shondavia Gibbons (Illustrator), Pulaski School, "Heroes". Committee Members were Annie Jackson, Maxine Jackson, Patricia Clark, Ethel Hunter, Albertha Collier, Hope Johnson, and Davida Wood.[288]

Membership

Chairman, Denyce Sanders, and committee initiated a welcome wagon to acquaint new members to Gamma Sigma Omega Chapter. A "Secret Soror" activity was implemented with 91 members agreeing to participate. Each participant was to purchase a gift valued at $10 for Valentine Day and $20 for Christmas. These gifts would be exchanged during the year and each participant was to purchase two "Thinking of You" cards to be sent to secret soror during the year.[289]

Activities for promoting sisterly relations were directed by Sanders. Members worshiped at Grace Full Gospel, Sunday March 30, 2003 and donated $225 to the church.[290] "Girls Night Out" was held March 28, 2003 at the West Broad Street YMCA. The activity room was transformed to a venue for food, fun, and games. Members delighted in table games, feasting and dancing[291] "Girls Night Out," was held April 2, 2004 at the May Street YMCA for a leisure evening of food, fun, and games. Bingo caller, Johnnie Holmes, kept members in suspense as they tried to be Bingo winners.

At the June 12, 2004 meeting, Kimberly Chappell-Stevens reported a new direction for Membership: "Sorors Caught Doing Good." Each month a box was placed at the sign-in table for members to submit recommendations for this award. The activity's aim was to promote sisterly love and kindness. "Sisters Night Out," was held November 10, 2004 at Notre Dame Academy.

The Membership Retreat was held August 21, 2004, at Con-Ed Family Resource Center. The members decided the program initiatives for 2004-2005. A workshop was presented on Protocol and Bylaw changes. The Nominating Committee detailed how to run for office.[292]

A Reactivation Round-up was held November 14, 2004. Invitations were distributed to inactive AKAs.

Standards Committee

The Standards Committee, Connie Cooper, Chairman, strove to make certain chapter operations were successfully administered. One such activity to secure operations was The Standards/Sisterly Relations Retreat that was held on Saturday, August 23, 2003 at Savannah State University.[293] Members' evaluation of the chapter was a main component of this committee. Committee provided leadership workshops for members.

Connection

The Connection Committee Chairman, Undine Truedell, spearheaded AKA Day at the Capitol, February 17, 2003.On Presidents' Day twenty-three members of GSO boarded a chartered bus and headed for the State Capitol. GSO, at the Awards Luncheon, received five awards, more than any other chapter represented. Three members received the Distinguished Leadership Award in Public Service: Jessie Deloach, Clemontine Washington, and Carolyn Bell. GSO was one of the few chapters recognized for its MLK, Jr. Day of Public Service activity, and finally GSO received an attendance award for having the highest attendance at the Capitol for the past two years. Annie Jackson was identified as the person responsible for promoting Savannah's participation.[294]

Sixteen members attended AKA Day at the Capitol on February 16, 2004. They were Undine Truedell, Carol Bell, Sharon Stallings, Henrietta Perry, Jessie C. Deloach, Emma Preer, Eudora Allen, Albertha E. Boston, Eleanor Murdock, Albertha Collier, Charlene Jones, Clemontine Washington, Lorna Jackson, Connie Cooper, Annie Jackson, and Zenobia Mitchell. Members enjoyed a full day of activities including welcomes from elected officials. Some of whom were AKAs: Rep. Nikki Randall, Rep. Alisha Thomas Morgan, Sen. Horacena Tate, Justice Leah Sears and International Connection Chairman, Ferial Bishop. The members also engaged in Legislative updates, voter empowerment sessions, a photo-op with Governor Sonny Perdue, and attending the opening legislative sessions of both the Georgia House and Senate Chambers. The chapter was recognized for its Martin Luther King, Jr. Day of Public Service.[295]

May 7, 2003, six members attended the Chatham-Savannah Board of Education's regular meeting. Issues discussed were budget constraints; property dispositions and standardized testing. The chapter was acknowledged by Board member, Jessie C. Deloach, Vice President, Pro Tempore of the BOE and an AKA.[296] February 14, 2004 Minutes report that members attended the Chatham-Savannah Board of Education meeting and that Superintendent John O'Sullivan praised chapter's support and efforts.

As Connection Chairman, Truedell sought several ways to implement civic actions for the Savannah community; therefore, she attended the AKA Policy Conference in Washington, DC on September 25-28, 2003.[297] Saturday, September 20, 2003, GSO participated in the NAACP Voter Registration process at Oglethorpe Mall. Members participating were Truedell, Patricia Clark, Hope Johnson and Natatia VanEllison.

September 25, 2003, GSO participated in the Mayoral Aldermanic Debate at St. Paul CME.[298] On October 25, 2003, her committee assisted in hosting the Mayoral Debate at St. Matthews Episcopal Church.[299]

The Committee conducted a Voter Education Drive on May 22, 2004 in Kayton and Frazier Homes. On September 18, 2004, Truedell, Emma Conyers, and Sharon Stallings collaborated with the NAACP and the Omegas. The group canvassed Kayton and Frazier Homes to register individuals. A total of 10 registered that day.[300] GSO members also participated in a collaborative "Get Out to Vote" Rally held at the Pavillion at Daffin Park, sponsored by W.E.A.V.E. (Women Energized to Activate Voter Empowerment). GSO members joined others with a commitment to support on-site voter registration, mobilize volunteers to get voters out on November 2 and energize and influence the community to participate in the Voter Registration Blitz. Members participating were Bell, Connie Cooper, Clemontine Washington, Virginia Edwards, Zena McClain, Sharon Stallings and Truedell. That same day GSO members in partnership with the Links, Inc. canvassed the Ben Van Clark neighborhood to register voters. The Committee co-hosted a political forum/debate with the Savannah Delta Sigma Theta Alumnae Chapter July 13, 2004.

The Committee greeted Eddie Bernice Johnson, an AKA, and Rep. Jesse Jackson, Jr. at a reception at the DeSoto Hilton, October 27, 2004. The members of Congress were in town to energize the community and encourage them to get out to vote on November 2, 2004. GSO members present to welcome the Congresswoman Johnson included Basileus Bell, Patricia Clartk, Albertha Collier, Dothory B. Wlison, Clemontine Washington, Emma Lou Preer, Hope Johnson, Alvernia Wilson, Virginia Edwards, and Truedell.

The Black Family

The Black Family committee members delivered Easter cheer and wishes in the form of Easter baskets to May Street Senior Citizens group and residents of the Savannah Rehabilitation and Nursing Center on 63rd and Paulsen Street, Good Friday, April 18, 2003. The members made the baskets at the YMCA and were assisted by several youth from the center who attended Gadsden Elementary School. Members presenting were Eleanor Ginn, Eudora Allen, Annie Chappell, Kim Chappell-Stevens, Johnnie Holmes, Annie Jackson, Carmelita Maynard, and Eleanor Murdock.[301]

March 4, 2004, the members cooked and served the afternoon meal at the Inner City Night Shelter. The meal consisted of meatloaf, mashed potatoes, lasagna, toss salad, soup, fresh fruit, peach cobbler, and punch. Participating members were Brenda Jenkins, Ethel Hunter, Eleanor Murdock, Emma J. Conyers, Johnnie S. Holmes, Queen Barnes, and Patricia Clark.

Cleaned coats and sweaters were collected by the Black Family/ Clothes Closet and were distributed to Greenbriar Children's Center, Safe Shelter, and Hope House. Members, Maynard and Johnnie Holmes, coordinated this project. During October chapter meeting, Maynard and her committee donated over 200 articles of clothing to the Rape Crisis Center. The donation was received by Marianne Fayhae, Volunteer Coordinator for the Rape Crisis Center.[302] In 2004, 40 coats were donated to Hope House. November 12, 2004, Maynard and Clark presented over 40 outerwear articles of clothing to HOPE house.

"Facing the Rising Sun," the dramatic monologue, presented thirty students reciting by memory writings by African American authors. The event was held at Savannah State University, Sunday, April 27, 2003.[303] The winners were Eric Jones, 1st grade; Angelinicia Coleman, 6th grade; J'Aime Jenkins, 10th grade; Reina Varnedoe, 12th grade; Tina Morrison, 12th grade.

"Facing the Rising Sun," April 25, 2004, was also held at Savannah State University. There were sixteen participants. Each one received a medallion and certificate of participation. The four first place winners received a monetary gift.[304]

Promoting **Black Heritage** through cultural awareness, GSO members escorted thirty two energetic youngsters from Robert W. Gadsden Elementary School to the Black Heritage Festival School Day at Savannah State University, Februray 13, 2003. The escorting members were Annie Jackson, Eudora Allen, Jessie Deloach, Ethel Hunter and Eleanor Murdock.[305]

Greenbriar Children's Center recognized Gamma Sigma Omega as 2003 Donor of the year. The Greenbriar Adhoc Committee in 2004 was chaired by Emma Conyers. The committee solicited donations from several agencies to meet Greenbriar's necessities at that time. Gwendolyn Johnson solicited a donation from Suntrust Bank of $250. Other chapter members also secured donations. Ann Crowder, a community advocate, donated $100, and Weyerhaeuser Company donated $300. The chapter sponsored a Self Esteem Workshop, April 22 for children of Greenbriar, and during Christmas the chapter members donated new Christmas gifts for the children.

Jr. Debutantes/Precious Gems Mentoring Program

The Junior Debutantes experienced a productive retreat at the Riverfront Marriott Hotel Saturday, February 15, 2003. Ethel Hunter coordinated the retreat. Undine Truedell and Gwendolyn Johnson presented icebreakers. Marjory Varnedoe presented the format for the cotillion. Others assisting were Patricia Clark, Virginia Parham, and Johnye Gillans.[306]

The Junior Debs attended the Ebony Fashion Fair at Tiger Stadium, Savannah State University, February 20. The chaperones were Janie Bruen, Natatia VanEllison and Tamika Minor.[307]

The Ninth Annual Junior Debutante Cotillion was held June 6, 2003 where eighteen young ladies were presented before audience of relatives, friends, former debutantes, AKAs and proud parents at the King Frazier Student Center, Savannah State University. "A Touch of Africa: A Homeland Celebration" was the theme.[308] The Precious Gems were Brittany Loretta Carter, Imani Tia Chamberlain, Margaret Latrice Davis, Kiara E. Dorsey, Whitney Marshawn Gamble, Althea Aleese Hall, Jesseca Elizabeth Hendrix, Jasmine Shantel Holmes, Chantrea Noelle Howze, Symon Monique Jackson, Jasmine N. Kirkland, Brittany Oatis, Morgan Oatis, Yeshi Oatis, Aiesha Jamilla Reeves, Manee' T. Stewart, Tatiana Jasmine Tinsley, and Rhashay White. Imani Chamberlain was crowned Miss Precious Gem. Symon Jackson and Brittany Carter were first and second runner-ups. This project generated a net profit of $15,963.59, plus.[309]

The co-chairmen for the Jr. Debutantes/Precious Gems for 2003-2004 were Charlene Jones and Natatia VanEllison.[310] The Tenth Annual Junior Debutante Program, 2003-2004, had the first meeting session for the young girls in November. They attended the coronation of Miss

Savannah State University, and visited and presented useful items to the patients at Tara Thunderbolt Nursing and Rehabilitation Center.[311] The leaders for these activities were Janie Bruen, Gwendolyn Johnson, Charlene Jones, Natatia VanEllison, and Johnye Gilllans.[312]

The Jr. Debutantes experienced a formal luncheon. Janie Bruen coordinated a mother/daughter luncheon in December at the Hilton Hotel, January 10, 2004. Several other activities were introduced to the young girls: February, "Toning our Skills Month"; Ebony Fashion Show, fourteen Gems in attendance; and Public Speaking Workshop, twelve Debs participating, with Tina Tyus Shaw, an AKA, who is WSAV TV news anchor.

The Career Fair promoted for the Jr. Debutantes an awareness of choice. Several professionals explained their professions to the girls. The Career Fair 2004, was coordinated by Ethel Hunter.

The 2004 Cotillion culminated June 4, 2004 at the King Frazier Student Union Building at Savannah State University. Fifteen girls were presented in "Precious Gems of Elegance." They were Justina Lynette Barrett, Ashley Danielle Beach, June Ashley Brown, Ashley Janesse Campbell, Angelinicia Karen Coleman, Shatika Janee'Flowers, Jailyn Kristine Gladney, Ashlea Victoria Gordon, Ashley Renee Hicks, Tiffany Nicole Hicks, Kendra Atecia Johnson, Anisa Ameera Kicklighter, Sheana Contessa Miller, T'Nai Amani Wilkins, and Shakirah Denice Williams. Miss Precious Gem 2004 was Sheana Contessa Miller.

The AKA Spirit, October 2004, reported that twenty girls were to be oriented to the Jr. Debs Program, 2004-2005. The orientation was held at Notre Dame Academy. There were twenty-six Jr. Debutantes/Precious Gems reported at the November chapter meeting. Natatia VanEllison and Charlene Jones were chairmen. The girls' activities focused on "Giving Thanks and Helping Others." Nine Precious Gems worshipped at Greater Gaines Chapel AME Church November 28, 2004. The girls participated in a training session on table etiquette and social graces. The parent/daughter luncheon was held December 18, 2004, DeSoto Hilton, Pulaski Room.

Melissa Ilugbo, the chapter's first Miss Precious Gems/Jr. Deb, passed away in Atlanta. A resolution was presented to her family.[313]

Health

Health/Wellness Committee initiated the "Walk Away the Pounds" that met Thursdays, at the May Street YMCA (West Broad Street YMCA). The Wellness Coordinator, Natatia VanEllison, reported that the "Walk Away the Pounds" program had combined with the Membership Committee, Chairman, Denyce Sanders' church program, at Townsley Chapel A.M.E. Church.[314]

Saturday, September 20, 2003, at Robert W. Gadsden Elementary School, the Health/ Wellness Committee sponsored a cancer awareness seminar, "Breast Care: A Conversation with Dr. John Duttenhaver." He provided information for adults on the most recent medical advancements for early detection of breast cancer.[315]

Chapter members, serving as volunteers to answer telephone calls, participated in the Buddy 3 WSAV TV, a cancer awareness initiative. Virginia Parham was coordinator.[316]

Dr. Wilbur Jenkins, a local family practice physician, discussed the warning signs of cardiovascular disease and stroke prior to chapter meeting on February 14, 2004. The committee distributed "Just Move, A Guide to Physical Activity" and "Easy Food Tips for Heart-Healthy Eating," pamphlets by the American Heart Association.[317]

Chapter members participated in the Child Safety Seat Check-up sponsored by the SAFE Kids of Savannah Coalition, September 25, 2004. This event is a part of the National Program "BUCKLE-UP."

Gamma Upsilon Chapter received support from GSO at Savannah State University in their Breast Cancer Walk-a-Thon.[318]

Relay for Life, sponsored by the American Cancer Society, May 16-17, 2003, was held at Benedictine Military School. Gamma Sigma Omega captains were Clemontine Washington, Natatia VanEllison, Gwendolyn Johnson, Particia Clark, Emily Crawford-Sanders, Virginia Parham, Eudora Allen, Latashia Thomas, Audrey Singleton, Albertha Collier, Carolyn Bell, Maxine Jackson, Ethel Hunter, Michelle Mincey-Lee, Paprice Simmons. The goal was $1500.[319] Chairmen, Virginia Parham and Natatia VanEllison, extended thanks to members for setup, decorations, relay participation, takedown, sleepover and refreshments.

Special thanks were also extended to Honey Dos: Harold Jackson, husband of Maxine Jackson, Wardell Holmes, husband of Johnnie Holmes and Honey Don't: Geoffrey Johnson, son of Gwendolyn Johnson for assisting with transporting equipment and set-up and take-down of tent. Team Captains exceeded the goal by collecting $2,118, with Clemontine Washington and Michelle Lee collecting over $400 each. The grand total reported was $2,318. There were thirty-eight participating members and guests who helped make the event successful.[320]

The Chairmen, continuing to promote Relay for Life, 2004, urged chapter members to attend the event, May 14-15 at Benedictine Military School. The goal was to exceed 2003 year's total of $2,318. The teams for 2004 exceeded previous year's goal by raising $2,926.75. The committee included Patricia Clark, Emily Crawford-Sanders, Audrey Singleton, Gwendolyn Johnson, Johnye Gillans. Team captains were Clemontine Washington, Michelle Mincey-Lee, Connie Cooper, Albertha E. Boston, Carolyn H. Bell, Virginia M. Parham, Emily Crawford-Sanders, Yolanda Jones, Audrey Singleton, Patricia Clark, Annie Chappell, Paprice Simmons, Undine Truedell, Johnnie Holmes.

AKACare

Leona Henley-Williams, chairman, the name, Senior Sorors Outreach, was changed to AKACare.[321] The committee sponsored a lovely luncheon for senior AKAs at Savannah Commons on May 13, 2003. Five seniors were treated to carnations and a delicious lunch. Guests included Bette Milledge, Lola Dixon, Delores Hardwick, Essie Henley, and Agatha Cooper. GSO members included: Carol Bell, Patricia Clark, Albertha Boston, Eleanor Murdock, Margaret Robinson, Eudora Allen, Jessie Deloach, Henrietta Perry, Davida Wood, Annie Jackson, and Henley.[322]

The 2004 AKACare Luncheon was held at Savannah Commons May 18, 2004 to honor senior AKAs. Seniors in attendance were Agatha Cooper, Lola Dixon, Willie Mae Freeman, and Essie Kirkland-Hendley.

Economics

Economics Committee, Gwendolyn Johnson, Chairman, held a Credit and Finance Seminar on April 16, 2003 at the May Street YMCA. The first objective was to make information available to individuals within the community relative to what credit is and what constitutes good credit. The second objective of the seminar was to present information on home ownership and the foundation required to acquire that first dream home. Gwendolyn Johnson and Meketa Brown were presenters for the seminar, and they stressed the importance of how two distinct factors are linked together to accomplish one clear goal-home ownership.[323]

GSO's Economic Committee and Gamma Upsilon jointly sponsored a workshop on the following topics: Protecting Your Credit/ Your Credit Report, Personal Financial Management, and Income Tax preparation. This youth financial workshop was held at Savannah State University in the Freshman Dormitory. Hermise Pierre, Vice President and program Chairman of Gamma Upsilon Chapter was a presenter. Gamma Sigma Omega's presenters were Hope Johnson, Gwendolyn Johnson, and Patricia Clark.

The Committee hosted Tax Freedom Day Saturday, February 21, 2004 at St. Pius Resource Community Center.

Technology Committee

Technology Committee, Sheila Hutcherson, Chairman, launched the GSO website akagso.tripod.com.[324] The website included pages on history of Alpha Kappa Alpha and Gamma Sigma Omega with a message from Basileus, Bell, listed officers, and calendar of activities/programs.[325] Thanks were extended to Ivanette Richardson for her assistance to the site's launching at the September chapter meeting, 2003.

Social Committee

The Social Committee, Maureen Walker, Chairman, presented the "Family and Friends Day," Sunday, June 8, 2003 at Skidaway Island

Park. The attendance was over 90 participants. The theme was centered on countries of the world. Members were divided into teams to prepare dishes that were part of the culture of the country.[326]

Archives Committee

Gamma Sigma Omega Chapter of Alpha Kappa Alpha Sorority, Inc., 1943-2002, the chapter's first history book by committee members, Albertha E. Boston, Emma J. Conyers, and Virginia M. Parham was printed. Conyers served as chairman of the committee. The book was sold to GSO members for $10. Mr. Charlie Hall was the printer.[327] Two hundred books were printed. Books were sent to AKA International Office, community libraries, and the Georgia Historical Society. A press conference was held at Greenbriar Children's Center for the unveiling of the chapter's history book, Saturday, February 21, 2004. As a result of this publication, Gamma Sigma Omega Chapter was recognized at the King Tisdell Cottage Foundation Banquet on October 9, 2004. The chapter received the Leopold Adler Historic Preservation Award.

GSO Uniform Committee

This committee was coordinated by Alvernia Wilson and assisted by Davida Wood. The material selected was a keylime colored buccaneer (crepe). The deadline for the outfits was Thanksgiving, 2003.[328] They were to be ready for chapter members uniformity at the Savannah's 100 Celebrity Men Who Cook, December 14.

Housing Committee

The Housing Committee conducted a survey of sixty-four chapters of similar size to learn about the experience of each chapter in acquiring property to support various chapter programs and activities.[329]

The Housing Committee completed the compilation of housing results survey. Committee planned to meet with an attorney for foundation establishment, i.e. incorporation, bylaws, etc.[330]

GSO Tailgating

Savannah State University' 2003 Homecoming would not go unnoticed. Friends and family attended the AKA tent at Savannah State University Homecoming. The committee included: Undine Truedell, Zenobia Mitchell, Maxine Jackson, Emily Preer Williams, Eudora Allen and Eleanor Murdock.[331] Approximately, thirty-three member participated to the success of this event. The 2004 Tailgating Chairman was Sharon Stallings. The President noted in *The AKA Spirit* November 2004 that the event was truly an experience and a wonderful one.

Founders' Day

February 9, 2003 at Bethel A.M.E. Church, Charletta Jacks, daughter of Dorothy B. Wilson, was speaker. The awardees were the following members: Ethel Hunter, Soror of the Year; Gwendolyn Johnson, Basileus Award Recipient; Patricia Mincey, Basileus Award Recipient; Tamika Minor, Evanel Renfrow Terrell Scholarship Award; Carolyn Bell, Evanel Renfrow Terrell Scholarship Award; Patricia Clark, Evanel Renfrow Terrell Scholarship Award; Clemontine Washington, Basileus Award Recipient.

The 2004 Founders' Day, chairman, Dorothy B. Wilson, was a closed one. Three chapters held the Tri-Chapter Founders' Day, January 24, 2004 at Carey Hilliard's: Nu Delta Omega (Beaufort, SC); Nu Rho Omega (Hinesville, GA); Gamma Sigma Omega (Savannah, GA). GSO's awardees were Soror of the Year, Undine Truedell; Countess Y. Cox Sisterhood Award, Natatia VanEllison; Basileus Awards: Connie Cooper and Wanda Williams.

Conferences

Cluster VI Conference was held December 5-6, 2003. The host chapters were Nu Tau Omega and Eta Nu, in Denmark, SC. Cluster 2005 was held in Savannah, September 23-25, 2005 with Gamma Sigma Omega hosting. The chairmen were Connie Cooper and Carolyn Bell.

South Atlantic Regional Conference, Miami, Florida, April 10-13, 2003, included the following members in addition to the Basileus and Graduate Advisor: April Scott, Sharon Stallings, LaShawna Mullgrav, Nicole Williams, Maureen Walker, and Patricia Clark (alternate). LaShawna Mullgrav, Ericka Coleman and Scrapbook Committee won 1st Place at the Conference for chapter scrapbook; Bell's scrapbook submission, "Savannah's 100 Celebrity Men Who Cook," won 1st Place in the Georgia Schank Innovative Award competition.[332]

The 2004 SARC was in Augusta, Georgia where Gamma Sigma Omega Chapter was one of the host chapters. Vanessa Kaigler served as one of the representatives who reported to the chapter information from the February 22, 2003 meeting held in Orangeburg, SC. Clemontine Washington was Chairman for the undergraduate luncheon.[333] The theme for the conference was "Rolling on the River."[334]

The chapter received a 2nd place trophy for Health entry. The Connection scrapbook won 1st place, The Connection Award; and 1st Place Journalism Award. During the EAF Luncheon, the chapter was recognized as a bronze member for 100% membership and financial contribution. Emma J. Conyers sang a solo part in one of the choir's selections. Members attending were Eudora Allen, Carolyn Bell, Tamika Boone, Tamika Bond-Burnett, Albertha E. Boston, Janie Bruen, Annie Chappell, Patricia Clark, Stacy Clarke, Erica Coleman, Emma Conyers, Connie Cooper, Virginia Edwards, Nicole Fields, Pendar Franklin, Johnye Gillans, Eleanor Ginn, Sonia Renee Grant, Annie Jackson, Maxine Jackson, Brenda Jenkins, Gwendolyn Johnson, Hope Johnson, Charlene Jones, Yolanda Jones, Vanessa Kaigler, Michelle Mincey-Lee, Zenobia Mitchell, LaShawna Mullgrav, Eleanor Murdock, Virginia Parham, Henrietta Perry, Sylvia Perry, Emma Preer, Carolyn Russell, Emily Sanders, Sonya Shepherd, Paprice Simmons, Audrey Singleton, Lisa Singleton, Gwendolyn Smith, Dorothy Speed, Sharon Stallings, Kimberly Stevens, Lawanda Tillman, Undine Truedell, Natatia VanEllison, Marjory Varnedoe, Maureen Washington, Clemontine Washington, Emily Preer-Williams, Leona Williams, Lois Williams, Dorothy Wilson, Doris Wood, Sadie Wright, and Lydia Young. There were five GSO Steppers.[335] The steppers were LaShawna Alderman

Mullgrav, Sharon Stallings, Tamika Boone, Erica Washington, and Stacey Clark.

Eighteen members attended the Leadership Conference in Las Vegas, Nevada. They include Carol Bell, Patricia Clark, Connie Cooper, Emily Crawford Sanders, Vanessa Kaigler, Dorothy Wilson, Clemontine Washington, Johnye Gillans, Dorothy Speed, Virginia Parham, Audrey Singleton, Lisa Singleton, Rena Varnedoe, Patricia Mincey, Charlene Jones, Jackie Handy, Gwendolyn Smith and Carolyn Russell.[336] The delegates were Bell, Washington, and C. Cooper.

The 61st Boule, 2004, was held in Nashville, Tennessee. The nonfunded delegates were Albertha E. Boston, Eudora Allen, Connie Cooper, and Patricia Clark. Members attending were Carolyn Bell, Patricia Clark, Connie Cooper, Denise Cooper, Janese Cooper, Kimberly Chappell-Stevens, Annie Jackson, Emma Conyers, Albertha E. Boston, Maxine Jackson, Eleanor Murdock, and Eudora Allen. The 2003 Connection Report, Undine Truedell, chairman, received International recognition at this Boule.

By attending Regional/Leadership Conferences and Boules, several chapter members became certified to be advisors to the undergraduates. January 10, 2004 Minutes reported fifteen members completed training to become certified Graduate Advisors. The Undergraduate Council met January 7 and proposed a calendar of undergraduate activities.

MIP (Membership Intake Process) at Savannah State University

MIP chapter orientation workshops were held March 18, 22, 23, 2004 for Gamma Upsilon chapter. GSO members were in attendance. Approximately eighty-four young ladies attended the Rush at Savannah State University.[337] MIP took place April 23-24, 2004. There were fifty eight candidates.

Armstrong Atlantic State University Interest Group

Basileus Bell reported at the November chapter meeting, 2003, that students attending Armstrong Atlantic State University had expressed an interest in having an AKA chapter on the campus and she reported that she had been in consultation with the Regional Director, Irene Westbrooks McCollom, on this matter. In the March chapter minutes 2004, it was reported that forty young ladies at Armstrong Atlantic State University had formed an interest group in AKA. At the November 13, 2004, meeting, Basileus Bell announced that AASU interest group, The Pearls of Wisdom, had been officially approved by the Regional Director:

> This energetic and astute group of young women undertook numerous projects throughout the community. Their involvement consisted of donating books and reading to the students at Robert W. Gadsden and Esther F. Garrison Elementary schools and mentoring young girls in Wilson Cottage at Greenbriar Children's Center. In addition they decorated the cottage for Christmas, made Christmas stockings and baked cookies for the residents. They assisted in the American Red Cross Blood Drive, Savannah's 100 Celebrity Men Who Cook (a benefit fundraiser for the United Negro College Fund) and volunteered in the Democratic Congressional Campaign Committee.[338]

Other Events/Activities

Pretty in Pink Lunch: GSO members dazzeled downtown Savannah, Tuesday, April 22, 2003 as forty plus members gathered at First City Club. They were dressed in pink and enjoyed lunch and fellowship.[339]

Donation: The chapter donated from the grant's account $2,500 to the Boy Scouts to support leader Phillip Wright with activities in the Kayton-Frazier Public Housing. Documents were requested from the Boy Scouts for the funded activities.[340]

Also, the **Haitian Relief Project**, Emma Conyers, Chairman and committee members, Albertha Collier, Essie Johnson, Sylvia Perry, Virginia Parham, and Ivy Richardson, directed the chapter's financial donation to the Christian Revival Center's Haitian Program, October 18, 2004. The chapter donated $1,000 to Rev. Freddie L. Hebron of the Christian Revival Center to assist with food and clothing distribution effort in Haiti. Food and water were sent to St. Marks and Gonaive in Haiti. Pastor Hebron and others set up a Hot Meal Program, a mobile kitchen for food preparation and for the distribution of food to those who had cooking appliances. Their objective was to feed 1,000 Haitians a day.

AKAs support **Hurricane victims** GSO donated non-perishables for the victims in Orlando, Florida. After hearing the the Food Bank was low on baby supplies, Basileus Bell appealed to the members to bring items to the September sorority meeting. After the meeting, the items were transported to Florida.

Videography/Photography Camp: The Basileus secured a one-month summer camp grant from the City of Savannah for a videography/ photography camp at Kayton Frazier Center. Maxine Jackson, Martha Hicks, Connie Cooper, Sylvia Perry, and Albertha Collier served as presenters and instructors in the "Introduction to Photography and Videography Camp." This four- week grant funded the collaboration among the AKAs, Deltas, and Omegas ended with an Art Show at the Civic Center.[341]

Book Reviews: *Cycles of Unfinished Business*, by Dr. Bettye Ann Battiste, a Savannahian, May 11, 2004; *Educating at Savannah State College (1890-1990)* by Dr. Clyde Hall, October 20, 2004. Dr. Hall's discussion was hosted by Gamma Upsilon of Savannah State University, Jacqueline Handy, chairman of discussion.

Tenure Ends

Although six months remained for Basileus Bell, Mr. Maurice Jenkins, Vice President of the United Negro College Fund, appeared at the June 12, 2004 chapter meeting, to recognize Bell for her commitment to the education of young people. He presented to her a plaque for her service and the chapter's support to higher education.

The Basileus appointed herself, Dorothy B. Wilson, and Patricia Clark as a committee to close out the grant's account.

At Bell's final meeting in December 2004, she left the chapter with these words: "In closing, I ask that you continue to make a difference by giving of yourselves. Continue to take Gamma Sigma Omega to heights unknown. May God continue to bless and keep each of you and may He shower you with His peace during this holiday season. Be Blessed."[342]

Patricia J. Clark, 2005-2006

Patricia J. Clark as Basileus continued the International Program theme, "The Spirit of Alpha Kappa Alpha" with her mantra, "A Commitment to Serve" ACTS: 2005-2006.

She ensured an effective Chapter Operations and Program success with an inspirational service for chapter members at her church, Second African Baptist Church, Rev. Corey M. Brown, Pastor. She held an Executive Planning Retreat December 30, 2012, at the Club House Inn & Suites. Emma Jean Conyers as Anti-Basileus and Program Chairman proposed the slogan, "No Soror Left Behind" in Program targets: Education, The Black Family, Health, Economics, and the Arts as designed by the International Program.

To improve communication, Clark initiated the Bell South Telephone Message Board Messaging System. This system allowed chapter members to call-in by telephone from anywhere in the world, local or long distance, to receive current chapter information announcements.

However, at the 2006 Boule in July, Clark was under a new Supreme Basileus, Barbara A. McKinzie. McKinzie's program had a new emphasis. At that point, the chapter realized it had to put a spin on targets to incorporate the new program. McKinzie's Program was five platforms that emphasized Economics, Sisterhood, and Partnerships. At the Boule, McKinzie informed the membership: "Sorors, it's a new day. Excellence is our standard, performance is our cloak, and love is our signature. As we embark on this new day, we will see unseen, unimaginable, and unbelievable aspects of sisterhood and service." With these rallying words spoken before the excited assemblage of AKA women at the 2006 Boule, Mckinzie set the tone for her administration and galvanized Alpha Kappa Alpha women with her words of inspiration.[343]

The galvanizing of the membership was the implementation of programs and activities that addressed the **ESP** icon. "The captivating **ESP** icon is a creative symbol that has already energized AKAs to action. Through the Heart of **ESP** an Extraordinary Service Program of Economics, Sisterhood and Partnership, we will spread our service tentacles to tap into the creative and intellectual strengths of our sorors; and then extend our service reach externally to the community."[344]

Basileus Clark held a Planning Retreat, August 12, 2006. After this retreat, she began her leadership under the ESP theme of Supreme Basileus McKinzie. Program Chairman, Conyers, and committees had to strategize ways to implement the new International Program and remain effective serving the Savannah community for the four remaining months under Basileus Clark. Discussions were done, formally and informally, and a survey was taken to meet the challenging time of the period. The results of the survey with twenty-one participants showed the following: (a) an overwhelming vote to continue the local programs (b) 19 votes to continue the community service scholarship [Presidential Freedom Scholarship] (c) 15 votes to seek a partnership with the EOA as the target agency.[345] The results were brought to the September chapter meeting as recommendations from the Executive Committee. The chapter approved the following recommendations: (a) to increase the Presidential Scholarship from $500 to $1000 (b) to merge local programs with the national ESP programs (c) to seek partnership with EOA as a target agency.[346]

Education, Ivy Richardson, Chairman

Ivy Reading AKAdemy: The chapter served as the primary education partners to Robert W. Gadsden and Esther F. Garrison Elementary Schools. The Ivy Reading AKAdemy was held at Gadsden Elementary School every Saturday morning, 10:00 a.m. – 12 noon with the exception of 2nd Saturdays, due to chapter meetings. The school's reading coordinator, Mrs. Edna Mason, recommended students from Kayton and Frazier Homes; after these recommendations, other students in the school were recommended. Students from Esther F. Garrison Elementary school were bused to Gadsden to participate in the Ivy Reading AKAdemy. The targeted community for Garrison students was Yamacraw Village, a housing project. These students were bused to the Ivy Reading AKAdemy at Gadsden. They were selected by school's reading coordinator, Mrs. Deborah Keitt, to attend the AKAdemy. The bus would arrive at the Yamacraw Community Center to pick up students and return them to Center after the session. In partnership with Laidlaw Transportation, Savannah Chatham County Public School System, the Savannah Leisure Services, Bethlehem Baptist Church, Tabernacle Baptist Church, and Connor's Temple Baptist Church, transportation for the Garrison students was provided. The accepted students were tested individually during the month of January to identify the level at which service must be rendered. In additionally, these students were exposed to tutorial and enrichment activities. Siblings and parents of the Ivy Reading AKAdemy's students were given opportunities to attend enrichment activities by paying a nominal fee. At the February chapter meeting, the Program Chairman reported thirty-six students K-3rd grade were registered in addition to five 4th graders. Col. George Bowen, Acting Superintendent of Savannah-Chatham County School System and Mr. Rufus Smith, Branch Manager of Laidlaw transportation were exceptional partners for Gamma Sigma Omega chapter. Transportation was not only provided to the Ivy Reading AKAdemy but to field trip sites as well.

"The Spirit of Alpha Kappa Alpha Sorority, Inc., An Engaging Experience," describes the service given to GSO's Ivy Reading AKAdemy students. Twenty four students from the Ivy Reading AKAdemy along with their parents and siblings experienced the spirit of Alpha Kappa Alpha on the morning of May 31, 2006. The forty eight travelers received tickets to the Georgia Aquarium in Atlanta for a most engaging experience. Seven members chaperoned. They were Basileus Clark, Program chairman, Conyers; Education chairman, Richardson; Queen Bames, Alvernia Wilson-Jackson, Paprice Simmons, and Dorothy B. Wilson. The field trip was the conclusion of the AKAdemy for the 2005-2006 school year.[347]

Also, Ivy Reading AKAdemy students, their siblings, and parents attended the Nutcracker. This Nutcracker performance was very special because it was presented by a young African American man who was the Artistic Director. He was one of the dancers in the performance as well. Clara, the leading star dancer, was performed by a young black dancer.[348]

Finally, December 12, 2006, the Ivy Reading AKAdemy students, their siblings and parents and chapter chaperones attended the Sesame Street Live, Elmo's Coloring Book, one of the most popular children's shows that come alive on stage.[349]

The AKAdemy students, siblings, and parents were very appreciative to Alpha Kappa Alpha Sorority Inc. for the year-long tutorial program, cultural, and nurturing experiences provided by and shared with the members of Gamma Sigma Omega Chapter.

Gamma Upsilon members volunteered tutoring at the AKAdemy. The chapter donated $200 for the purchase of books at the school's book fair. GSO tutors were Queen Barnes, Dorothy Speed, Sheila Hutcherson, Kimberly Chappell-Stevens, Johnye Gillans, Carolyn Russell, Ethel Hunter, Connie Cooper, Maxine Jackson, Albertha E. Boston, Carmelita Maynard, Albertha Collier, Johnnie Holmes, Hope Johnson, Latashia Thomas Stroman, Zena McClain, Virginia Parham, Freddie Pippen, Tiffany Green, April Scott, Paprice Simmons, Sylvia Perry Weston, Carolyn Bell, Clemontine F. Washington, Wanda Williams, Sadie Williams, Annie Jackson, Dorothy Wilson, Danette Boston, Tamika Minor Wright, Sherry Ramsey, Shi Evans, Sadie Wright, Jessie C. DeLoach, Cora Carter, Sonia Renee Grant, Vanessa M. Kaigler, Charlene Jones, Lydia Young, Elza Givens, Angela Grant, LaWanda Tillman, Tammy Barnes Scott, Natatia VanEllison, Audrey Singleton, Pendar Franklin, Henrietta Perry, LaVertta Scott, Leona Henley Williams, Sharon Stallings, Ivanette Richardson, Tuwanna Wilson, Irene Davis, LaShawna Mullgrav, Alvernia Jackson, Mary Coleman, Karla Harper, Janice Bryant, RhaQuay Rucker-Youmans, Shakela Holmes, Krystal Johnson (Sigma Tau), Deidra Stephens (Sigma Tau), Iris Frye (Sigma Tau), Laquita Crawford (Sigma Tau), Quadeira Sadler (volunteer), Alesha R. Sadler, Ingrid Kinlaw (volunteer), JayQuan Turner (volunteer), Richardson, Conyers, and Clark.

The 2005-2006 Ivy Reading AKAdemy was supported by two parent volunteers: Mr. Kim Hunter and Mrs. Ingrid Kinlaw. Also Mrs. Lou Smith, a paraprofessional from Garrison Elementary assisted.[350]

The chapter was informed in January 2006 that Gadsden was implementing a new learning program and would like AKAs to include this program at the Ivy Reading AKAdemy. The program was called Help One Student to Succeed (HOST), a nationally recognized structured mentoring program that matched young students who needed help in learning to read and write with community members who want to make a difference in a child's life. The program was computer oriented. AKA tutors followed the directions given that were included in folders prepared by the coordinators at Gadsden on each child[351]

T-Shirts were provided for the Ivy Reading AKAdemy students. The shirts did not go home with the students. The Program chairman or Education chairman kept them and washed them after each use.

Beginning the new school year, "The Spirit of Alpha Kappa Alpha Sorority, Inc., An Engaging Experience," and Economics, Sisterhood, and Partnerships (**ESP**) must work, for community's sake, to complete school year 2005-2006. Members attended a Volunteer Orientation at Gadsden, September 6, 2006. Members attending were Conyers, Eudora Allen, Mary Coleman, and Annie Jackson.[352]

September 12, 2006, Basileus Clark, Conyers, and Richardson attended PTA at Gadsden. Basileus Clark invited the parents to register their children for the Ivy Reading AKAdemy. The Principal, Mr. Alfred Lincoln, warmly accepted the sorority into the school.[353]

Gadsden started a tutorial for 3rd, 4th, and 5th graders on Saturdays, the same time as the Ivy Reading AKAdemy. The Martin de Porres Society (a charitable organization), and the Food Bank had agreed to feed Gadsden's tutorial students, including the Ivy Reading AKAdemy students. GSO welcomed this partnership. Members present at the first collaborative were Richardson, Conyers, Albertha E. Boston, Shakela Holmes, Johnye Gillans, Carolyn Russell, Kimberly Chappell Stevens, Rhaquay Rucker-Youmans. Two volunteers were Mrs. Yvonne S. Clark and Mrs. Ingrid Kinlaw. At the November 18, 2006 session were Richardson, Janice Bryant, Lakechia Bryant, Laquisha Cokely, Maggie Walker Zeigler, and Lydia Young. Two high school students volunteered: Aiesha Sadler and Olivia Brown.[354]

The AKAdemy students attended the Nutcracker at the Lucas Theater, November 25, 2006. Four parents attended, six siblings, three volunteers and five members. The culminating activity was a field trip to Sesame Street Live that was held at the Civic Center, December 11, 2006.[355]

Keep Reading Alive and Top Reader: "Keep Reading Alive in 2005" was the second component of the Ivy Reading AKAdemy. Members were scheduled with teachers at Garrison and Gadsden to read to students, coordinated by Conyers, Program Chairman. This reading initiative was called "Keep Reading Alive" supplemented with the "Top Reader" initiative. Students in kindergarten, first grade, second, and third grades were challenged to read books. The chapter erected a "Keep Reading Alive in 2005" marquee at Gadsden and Garrison. The student reading the most books in each grade was selected by the teacher. The reading coordinator at Garrison and Gadsden would evaluate the teachers' selections and choose the winner for Kindergarten through Third Grade. "Top Reader" was recognized after each marking period. During the school's assembly or in the student's class, the top reader was presented a plaque with "Top Reader" as title, his/her name, the school and Gamma Sigma Omega Chapter of Alpha Kappa Alpha Sorority, Inc engraved on plaque.

March 2, 2005, members participated in the Dr. Seuss Breakfast. They read books to students and volunteered at the book fair at Gadsden and Garrison Elementary schools.

The Top Readers for the first marking period from Robert W. Gadsden Elementary School and Esther F. Garrison Elementary School respectively: Kindergarten, Romaine Brown; First Grade, Sh'Kila Harris; Second Grade, Thomas Fox; Third Grade, Justin Taylor; Kindergarten, Diamond Gordon; First Grade, Bryant Bigham; Second Grade, Armani Ruth; Third Grade, Taylor Wilson. At this time leading the pack of GSO volunteer readers were the following members: first place, Annie Jackson; second place, Eleanor Murdock, Gadsden Elementary; first place, Ethel Hunter; second place, Eleanor Ginn, Garrison Elementary.[356]

Top Readers for the second marking period were K-3 at Gadsden: Romaine Brown, Darius Green, Nyjawan Howard, and Shontavia Harris; at Garrison: K-3, Janette Nesbitt, Kenneth Rouse, Shantal Benjamin, and Dariauna Williams.[357]

Top Readers at Garrison, first marking period, 2005 -2006 school year were the following student: Kindergarten, Michanda Frazier; 1st Grade, Diamond Gordon; 2nd Grade, Kenneth Rouse; 3rd Grade, Cierra Mobley. The students were judged by the Million Word Campaign.[358] Top Readers at Gadsden were the following students: Kindergarten, Salena DeJesus; First Grade, Tiana Brewington; Second Grade, Milan Kirkland; Third Grade, Tamira Mumford. Top Readers at Garrison the second marking period, 2005-2006 were recognized at Garrison's Honors' Day Program, Tuesday, February 21, 2006: Kindergarten, Cha'kera Bonapart; First Grade, Janette Nesbitt; Second Grade, Katelyn Coaxum; Third Grade, Tykeem Stewart.[359]

Gadsden and Garrison recognized the third and fourth marking period Top Readers at their last Honors' Program for the year. Gadsden's Top Readers, third and fourth marking periods: Kindergarten, Salena DeJesus; first grade, Imani Wilson; second grade, Ty'Mesha Williams; third grade, Eltomisha Hutchinson. Garrison's Top Readers, third and fourth marking periods: Kindergarten, Cha'kera Bonaparte; first grade, Diamond Gordon and Janette Nesbitt; second grade, Katelyn Coaxum; third grade, Cierra Mobley.[360]

In 2006, the theme was no longer "Keep Reading Alive in 2005" but "Keep Reading Alive." Dr. Delma Pollen, Principal of Gadsden requested that GSO members read not only to K-3rd grades but to 4th and 5th graders in preparing Gadsden to make AYP. Members accepted her request.[361]

Robert W. Gadsden Elementary School made AYP (Adequate Yearly Progress). The school and Gamma Sigma Omega Chapter were ecstatic. The school had to make AYP in school year 2005-2006 to be removed from the "needs improvement list." Garrison had made AYP the previous year, and made it again in 2004-2005 school year. Therefore, in 2005, Garrison was removed from the "needs improvement list." According to tests, Lexia and DIBELS, as reported by Garrison and Gadsden respectively, seventeen of the Ivy Reading AKAdemy students in grades 1-3, made remarkable improvements in test scores. All seventeen students scored higher at the post testing.[362]

The week of May 15, 2006 was the last scheduled reading week at the schools for school year, 2005-2006. For school year 2006-2007, members began reading to classes the week of October 2, 2006. They were encouraged to read in Language Arts and Math classes. The readers selected books about problem solving, money, and finances to promote the new International Program, **ESP.** The contacts at Gadsden were Mrs. Edna Mason, Mrs. Kimberly Bell, and Mrs. Dorothy Nisbet, and the contact at Garrison was Mrs. Deborah Keitt.[363]

Completing the last two months of this administration, members continued to read to students at the two schools. Some took their lunch periods to read. Top Readers at Garrison: Kindergarten, Donte Harris; first grade, Latari Brown; second grade, Janette Nesbitt; third grade, Samiya Singleton. The students were recognized at the Honors' Program, Friday, October 20, 2006. Members attending were Basileus Clark, Conyers, Audrey Singleton, and Leona Henley Williams. The Principal of the school was GSO member, Renae Miller McCullough.[364]

Again, the chapter donated $200 to Gadsden's Book Fair, November 16, 2006. The week of December 11, 2006 ended the reading in classes.[365]

Gadsden and Garrison schools were up for review by SACS (Southern Association of Colleges and Schools), the council on accreditation and school improvement in 2006. This accreditation renewal involved a school's self evaluation. To accomplish the passing of this study, all stakeholders in the schools had to get involved. Garrison and Gadsden passed the study. The chapter received commendations for work done at both schools. Albertha E. Boston, Ethel Hunter, and Conyers were the participants in the study on behalf of the chapter.[366]

Presidential Freedom Scholarship, Annie Chappell, coordinator, honored Shazia Ali, a student at H. V. Jenkins High School. She received the honor May 19, 2005 at the school's Honors' program. Ali was a graduating senior. In her letter, she expressed having performed over 230 community service hours. Gamma Sigma Omega Chapter awarded her $500 to be matched by the Federal Government.[367] Therefore, her scholarship was $1,000. Ali was admitted to Emory University.[368]

Chappell reported that the winner for the 2006 Presidential Freedom Scholarship was Christa M. Kahea, a student at Windsor Forest High School. She received the award at the Honors' program at her school

May 10, 2006.[369] Christa was admitted to Georgia College and State University in Milledgeville, Milledgeville, GA.[370]

The Young Authors initiative was coordinated by Paprice Simmons and Ethel Hunter. Letters were sent to the following schools seeking young authors: Gadsden, Garrison, Notre Dame Academy and Tompkins Middle School.[371] Simmons announced the winners: first category, 2nd- 3rd grade, 1st Place: Innocence Boles, Gadsden Elementary; 2nd Place, Camry Joshua, Gadsden Elementary; 3rd Place, Sabria Ford, Gadsden Elementary; second category, 4th -6th grade, 1st Place, Lauren Outler, Gadsden Elementary; 2nd Place, Monet Gardiner, Notre Dame Academy; 3rd Place, Joshlyn Keitt, Garrison Elementary. They were honored and awarded medallions and certificates at "Facing the Rising Sun."[372]

A copy of *The Spirit Within*, Volume 2, was presented to Mrs. Mason (Gadsden) and Mrs. Keitt, (Garrison) for the schools' libraries. This volume was presented at the 2006 Boule and contained the winning international young authors and their writings.[373] Unfortunately, GSO had no young contributors.

CRCT Testing (Criterion-Referenced Competency Tests) was held at Gadsden, April 19-28, 2006. Chapter members served as proctors. Chapter members serving were Margaret B. Johnson, Linda Jordan, Eudora Allen, Carolyn Russell, Pendar S. Franklin, Alvernia Jackson, and Conyers.[374]

The Black Family, Yolanda Jones and Sharon Stallings, Chairmen

The Black Family Committee adopted Safe Shelter. On January 15, 2005, chapter members met at the West Broad Street YMCA, May Street, and prepared baskets of toiletry items, can goods, and other necessities for distribution at Safe Shelter. These items were placed in decorative baskets and boxes adorned with pink and green ribbon for presentation to the Shelter on January 17, 2005 in observance of the Martin Luther King, Jr. Day of Service. The boxes were prepared by the following members: Ethel Hunter, Eleanor Ginn, Clemontine Washington, Conyers, Jones, and Stallings. The baskets and boxes were presented to Ms. Tina Jackson, a representative of the Shelter, by Hunter, Ginn, Conyers, Jones, Stallings, and Clark, Basileus.[375]

"Hand-in-Hand," Guiding and Protecting Children, members assisted the Savannah Chatham Metropolitan Police as they made Photo ID cards of children, February 8, 2005 at Kayton Homes Gymnasium.[376.]

The Black Family Committee promoted the selling of Christmas cards made by the children from Greenbriar Children's Center. The Center engaged in a fundraiser of wrapping Christmas gifts. GSO members continued to volunteer as gift wrappers. The members also purchased gift cards from Wal-Mart for the children.[377]

Sunday, October 23, 2005 and Wednesday, October 26, the committee hosted two spectacular evenings of dining and fellowship with three families at the Faith Lutheran Church on Waters Avenue. Director, Keisha Carter, who is also a member of Alpha Kappa Alpha, directed this family outreach. Alpha Kappa Alpha women displayed their talents in the kitchen by preparing delicious and nutritious full course meals for those families. AKAs who displayed talents in and outside the kitchen were Basileus Clark, chairmen Stallings and Jones, Conyers, Danette H. Boston, Ginn, Hunter, Alvernia Wilson-Jackson, Brenda Jenkins, and Sadie Williams.[378]

National Family Volunteer Day was held November 19, 2005, at West Broad Street YMCA. Chapter members cleaned rooms and did some landscaping.[379]

After celebrating the Rev. Martin Luther King, Jr's Day festivities, January 16, 2006, the committee surprised the children at Greenbriar Children's Center with a pizza party. In addition to Gamma Sigma Omega Chapter, Gamma Upsilon Chapter and other student volunteers from Savannah State University participated. They brought not only food but lots of love and offered tutorial services to the children. Present at the Day of Service were Basileus Clark, Stallings, Jones, Conyers, Janie Bruen, Eleanor Ginn, Lois V. Williams, Eleanor Murdock, Albertha E. Boston, Carolyn H. Russell, Jessie Collier DeLoach, Alvernia Wilson-Jackson, Clemontine F. Washington, Nikki Dorsey, Hermise Pierre, Brittany White, Kim Stephens, Crystal D. Preston, Latrice A. Mack, Nancy C. Williams, April Whitehead, Kennyetta Watkins,

Pendar S. Franklin, Carmelita Maynard, Ivanette Richardson, Undine Truedell-Williams, Leona H. Williams, Annie Chappell, Kimberly Chappell-Stevens[380]

The committee collected coats for the homeless at the December chapter meeting.

Health, Lorna Jackson, Chairman

The Relay for Life orientation was held at Johnnie Harris Restaurant January 6, 2005. Members attending were chairman, Jackson, Janie Bruen, Albertha E. Boston, and Conyers. The general theme for the American Cancer Relay was "Walking Toward Tomorrow's Dream." Gamma Sigma Omega's theme was "The Spirit of AKA Dreams for a Cure." The relay was held May 13, 14, 2005. The team captains were Sheila Hutcherson and Melinda P. Miller; Tiffany Greene; Clemontine Washington and Alvernia Wilson Jackson; Albertha Collier and Janie Bruen; Lorna Jackson and Virginia Parham; Michelle Mincey Lee; Partricia Clark, Emily Sanders, Hope Johnson, and Emma Conyers.[381] The chapter donated over $3,860 to Relay for Life. The grand prize winner was Albertha Collier reporting over $1000.[382]

The Safe Kids "Safety Cruise" Health Fair was held at Gadsden Elementary School Friday, February 4, 2005. Members participating were Lorna Jackson, Annie Jackson, Stacy Clark, Eleanor Murdock, and Jessie C. DeLoach.[383]

"The Importance of Seatbelt Use For High School Students," an essay contest that was sponsored by the Health Committee and coordinated by Johnnie Holmes, was awarded to RaeChelle Miller, a Junior at H.V. Jenkins High School. She was honored at "Facing the Rising Sun" and awarded $50.[384]

In 2006, "The Importance of Seatbelt Use For High School Students," essay winners were in categories: first place, Tiffany Tattnall, $75; second place, Akeem Mitchell, $50; third place, Ashley Heyward, $25. All the winners were students from H.V. Jenkins High School.[385]

The Heritage Nursing Home on White Bluff Road received loving care from committee members: Jackson, Lois Vedell Williams, Virginia

Parham, Leona H. Williams and Basileus Clark. On September 17, 2005, the committee presented the home two beautiful large gift baskets. September 30, 2006, members returned to the facility to present gifts of love (toiletries and other necessities) to the residents. Members attending were Basileus Clark, Conyers, A. Jackson, and Maggie Walker-Zeigler.[386]

A Health Seminar for the parents of the Ivy Reading AKAdemy's students was held October 15, 2005. The health presenters were Registered Nurse, Melinda Lindsay; Registered Dental Hygienist, Andre Young, and Dr. Lorna Jackson, DDS.[387]

Gadsden sponsored a Family Health Workshop, November 30, 2005 with GSO co-sponsoring the event. Mrs. Jane Garrison from the Chatham County Health Department spoke on various areas of seatbelt safety.[388]

The Chain of Life initiative enforced the idea of cancer awareness. The chapter members, divided in group as chain links, had to call the next link within the first five days in each month to remind the other to do a self check breast exam and to have a mammogram check. The initiative culminated in October.[389]

Relay for Life's theme was "Relay Holiday." It was held May 12 and 13, 2006. The chapter's theme was "Lighting the Way to A Cure," in reference to the holiday Kwanzaa, the seven candles. The teams were Albertha Collier and Janie Bruen; Emma Conyers and Alvernia Wilson-Jackson; Johnnie Holmes and Lois Vedelle Williams; Melinda Pippen-Miller and Tiffany Greene; Emma Preer and Annie Chappell; Patricia Clark, Hope Johnson, and Emily Crawford; Brenda Jenkins; Ethel Hunter, Virginia Parham, and Lorna Jackson; Clemontine Washington. The chapter members donated $4,700 to the American Cancer Society. The winning team was Clemontine Washington's.[390]

Cardiovascular Health Day was held at Gadsden Elementary, February 15, 2006, "Jump Rope for Heart." Novelties for the students' contests were provided by the chapter. The chapter also donated $100 to the American Heart Association on behalf of Gadsden's donations.[391] Members attending were Queen Barnes, LaVertta Scott-Perry, Audrey Singleton, and Conyers.[392]

At Gadsden's Fall Festival, November 4, 2006, the Health Committee distributed brochures on cancer awareness to adults. These brochures were donated by the American Cancer Society. GSO member, LaTanya Thompson, Registered Nurse and Mary Lovett, volunteer Registered Nurse, demonstrated how to wash hands properly to the children. The children were informed that colds, flu, diarrhea and other illness may be minimized because of regular washing of hands. The nurses demonstrated the use of hand sanitizers and gave each child who visited the AKA table a bottle. In addition to this gift, each child was given an apple, a granola bar and informative, colorful handouts on the washing of hands.[393]

The Arts, Annie Jackson, Chairman

"AKA Night Out in Pink or Green," February 11, 2005, was the viewing of the film "Body and Soul" and the entertaining music from Lincoln Center's Jazz Band from New York Center. February 4, 2006, the members attended Regina Carter Concert at the Lucas Theatre.[394]

Book Discussions: *The Bond Woman's Narrative* by Henry Louis Gates, Jr. was discussed February 15, 2005 at Jackson's home. The book, *Sweet Bye-Bye,* by an Alpha Kappa Alpha member, Denise Michelle Harris, was discussed Saturday, April 30, 2005, at Barnes Restaurant, Waters Avenue. The discussion was led by Marjory Varnedoe. *Kindred* by Octavia E Butler, who is also an AKA was discussed October 13, 2005 at Barnes Restaurant. The discussion leader was Kimsherion Reid. Sunday, October 1, 2006, at the Public Library, Bull Street, *The Covenant* by Tavis Smiley was discussed. The enthusiastic discussion only permitted three covenants to be discussed: Covenant I, led by Maggie Walker Zeigler; Covenant II, led by Virginia Edwards; and Covenant VII, led by Marjory Varnedoe, who was moderator. The discussion was continued November 5, 2006 at the library. Covenant III, "Correcting the System of Unequal Justice," discussed by member, Zena McClain and visiting AKA, Tadia Kelly; Covenant IV, "Fostering Accountable Community-Centered Policing," discussed by Kimberly Chappell-Stevens; Covenant V, "Ensuring Broad Access to Affordable

Neighborhoods that Connect to Opportunity," discussed by Clemontine F. Washington; and Covenant VI, "Claiming Our Democracy," discussed by Emma Conyers. Jackson, Chairman, presented to Marjory Varnedoe, coordinator of book discussions, a fresh cut floral arrangement for her commitment to the discussions.[395]

Black Heritage Festival: The Heritage Extravaganza Kickoff, sponsored by the City of Savannah and Savannah State University, at Savannah State University was February 10, 2005 where A. Jackson, Eleanor Murdock, and Ivy Richardson assisted Mrs. Sapp and Mrs. Oliver from Gadsden Elementary School transport forty children to the event.[396]

At the Black Heritage Festival in 2006, the Arts Committee, again assisted teachers with chaperoning children from Gadsden to the festival at SSU. Chapter members also volunteered to monitor children at a jewelry making workshop sponsored by the festival.[397]

"Facing the Rising Sun," coordinator, Eudora Allen, was held April 24, 2005 at Tompkins Middle School. The winners were the following: the first category, Eric Marcell Jones; the second category, Alexis Myers; the third category, Michelle Mobley; the fourth category, Shanell Hills. The first category and second category first place winners were honored with medallions, certificates, and received $25 each. The third category and fourth category first place winners were honored with medallions, certificates and received $50 each.[398]

The winners for the 2006 "Facing the Rising Sun" were the following young people: First Category, Zion A. Williams, $25; Second Category, Raquel Monet Tucker, $25; Third Category, Brian Allen, $50, and Fourth Category, Arkeem Manigo, $50.[399]

During National Library Week, chairman Annie Jackson, chaperoned 2nd graders from Gadsden Elementary to the Bull Street Library, April 29, 2005. The purpose of the field trip was to promote reading as a hobby, "Keep Reading Alive in 2005." The students acquired information about computers and about ways to check out materials. Each child was given a book mark and an application to apply for a library card. The highlight of the trip was the Storyteller. The children were amused and interested.[400]

AKA Honors the Arts was celebrated Friday, May 27, 2005 at Tompkins Middle School. At this gala event, AKAs demonstrated talent: vocal, instrumental, arts and crafts, writings, dramatic readings, paintings, drawings, sewing/tailoring, etc.[401] The special guest was Walter Simmons, Jr., saxophonist, senior at Johnson High School.[402]

The committee presented AKA Honors the Arts May 5, 2006 at Shuman Middle School. Showcasing the arts were members of the community and sorority members. The audience was amused, delighted, and receptive to expressions of creativity. The following members demonstrated talent: Elza Givens, vocal; LaVertta Scott-Perry, visual; Albertha Collier, visual. The guest soloist, Juanita Tucker, who is a member of Alpha Kappa Alpha, performed.[403]

Economics, Zena McClain, Chairman

Tax Freedom Day at Liberty Tax Service, March 24, 2005, the Economics Committee in partnership with Liberty Tax Service provided free tax preparation for the residents of Frazier Homes, Kayton Homes, and Yamacraw Village where many of the participants in the Ivy Reading Academy live. However, there was a charge for the Bank Product Refund Anticipation Loan. Hosting members were Zena McClain, Melinda Pippen Miller, Sylvia Perry, Carolyn Russell, and Patricia Clark. The committee worked with Dana Skiljan and Richard K. Cheong, Owner/Manager of Liberty Tax Service. The theme was "We're Dancing in the Streets." Food and music were provided by the partners. Connor's Temple Baptist Church, Pastor Bennie R. Mitchell, Jr., provided church bus for transporting residents and Mrs. Margie Williams, a church member, was driver.[404]

February 25, 2006, Tax Freedom Day was observed, Connor's Temple Baptist Church again provided transportation for the residents.[405]

The Committee conducted two seminars under the national approved curriculum, Youth Financial Literacy Program, Investing Pays Off. The seminars were conducted Monday, May 16, 2005, Wednesday, May 18, 2005 at Tompkins Middle School, beginning at 2:45 p.m. The guest presenter was Richard Cheong, a local businessman and owner of Libery Tax Service.[406]

The Youth Financial Literacy program was held March 3, 2006 at Tompkins Middle School. The curriculum for study was Merrill Lynch.[407]

Black Dollar Month was celebrated in April. Members were encouraged to patronize Black business and bring receipts to May chapter meeting to verify purchases.[408] The first place winner who purchased $19,891 from Black merchants was Virginia Parham; the second place winner who purchased $3,958 from Black merchants was Sylathea Hutchins; and the third place winner who purchased $1,295 from Black merchants was Albertha E. Boston. The first and second place winners received gifts.[409] Total spent with Black businesses in April was $27,023.50.[410]

ESP International Program

The Heart of ESP: An **Extraordinary Service Program** included five platforms. Platform #1, Non-Traditional Entrepreneur, promoted entrepreneurship among women. Platform #2, Economic Keys to Success, promoted economic education for life's sustenance and global competition. Platform #3, The Economic Growth of the Black Family, promoted strengthening the Black community. Platform #4, Undergraduate Signature Program: Economic Educational Advancement Through Technology, promoted Undergraduate successes. Graduate chapter were not assigned this platform. Platform #5, Health Resource Management and Economics, promoted being physical and mentally fit for all people. For the chapter at that time, Platform 3 and 5 were easiest to implement because of the chapter's tutoring and Black family and health initiatives.

Platform 3: The Economic Growth of the Black Family

Chapter members sought books at Gadsden and Garrison that placed emphasis on problem solving and money to read to students. At the Ivy Reading AKAdemy more emphasis was placed on Math and Language Arts. Parents were invited to attend field trips. The book discussion of *The Covenant* by Tavis Smiley made aware the role of Blacks in society. The chapter initiated a partnership with ConEd Family Resource Center of Connor's Temple Baptist Church that had a program that presented strategies for working with males. The program was connected with the Criminal Justice System.[411] Bettina Tate coordinated the efforts for a partnership with ConEd Center.[412] The coat collection for distribution to the homeless supported this Platform.

Platform 5: Health Resource Management and Economics

The Chain of Life (buddy system) was immediately integrated in this ESP Platform. To promote physical and emotional health is emphasized in this initiative. Each member in a group as links in a chain called a member to make her aware of the importance of self breast checks and mammograms. Each called once a month, the first five days. Attending worship services on 5th Sundays promotes spiritually health that contributes to emotional wellness. Participation in the Fall Festival at Gadsden and other health seminars were demonstrative of this Platform. GSO did find ways to implement **ESP:** Every Student Participates; Every Soror Participates; Each Student Is Prepared; Encourage Students to Plan for Success; Energizing Sisterly Programs. An **ESP** inspires AKAs to service.

Connection, Melinda Pippen-Miller, Chairman

The Committee's selected acronym was PACK (Political Awareness, Analyzing Call to Action and Knowledge Management). The 12th Annual AKA Day at the Capitol was held February 21, 2005. A photo shot was taken with Governor Sonny Perdue. Legislative concerns by the following AKA Legislators: Senator Horacena Tate, Representative Nikki Randall, Representative Alisha Morgan, and Representative Carolyn F. Hugley. Members attending were Eudora Allen, Jessie C. DeLoach, Henrietta Perry, Emma Conyers, Freddie Pippen,

Zena McClain, Patricia Clark, Connie Cooper, Carolyn Bell, Lorna Jackson, Clemontine F. Washington, Albertha E. Boston, and Miller.[413] At the luncheon, DeLoach received the Outstanding Service Award for Vice President Pro-tempore, 8th District School Board Member, and Washington received the Outstanding Service Award for City Councilman Midway, Georgia.

AKA Day at the Capitol was February 20, 2006. Some of the issues discussed were voter registration drives, having the right to vote without a photo ID, absentee ballots, discrepancies between requirements for absentee ballot voting, and voting in person. Three members attended: Conyers, Albertha E. Boston, and Clemontine Washington.

The Committee celebrated the Month of the Military Child on April 4, 2005 and the Army Community Services Center Block Party was held April 29. Chapter members participating were Conyers, Shi Evans, Elza Givens, Yolanda Jones, Paprice Simmons, Sherry Ramsey, Freddie Pippen, Maxine Jackson and Miller.[414]

Ladies in Pink and Green attended the Savannah Chatham County Board of Education meeting, November 2, 2005. Members in attendance were Audrey Singleton, Jessie C. DeLoach, Henrietta Perry, Freddie Pippen, Emma Conyers, Sherry Ramsey, Johnye Gillans, Eudora Allen, Melinda P. Miller, and Ericka Washington. Board President, Hugh Golson, and Superintendent, Dr. Thomas B. Lockamy, Jr., welcomed the sorority's support. Retired AKAs were present, and our member, Patricia Mincey, accepted the proclamation for Retired Educators.[415] On November 1, 2006, members attended Board of Education meeting. The chapter was recognized for the dedication and hard work at Gadsden and Garrison. Miller spoke on behalf of the Basileus in her absence. Dr. Lockamy and Mr. Golson acknowledged the group by standing and thanking the sorority for service to young people.[416]

The committee completed a political directory, AKA Connections Directory, that was issued to all members. To be included were Clemontine F. Washington and Kimberly Chappell-Stevens.[417]

The Youth Registration Drive on October 16, 2006 at Beach High School was successful. The students were very interested and concerned about issues facing young people. The total number of students registered was thirty-five. Members present were Clark, Irene Davis, Eleanor Murdock, Deonn Stone, Conyers, and Miller.[418]

Membership, Kimberly Chappell-Stevens, Chairman

Former chapter Basilei were recognized and given a book of poems at the chapter meeting, January 8, 2005. Members with perfect attendance in 2004 were recognized: Albertha E. Boston, Patricia Clark, Johnye Gillans, Eleanor Murdock, Undine Truedell, Kimberly Chappell-Stevens, Natatia VanEllison, and Albertha Collier.[419]

Orientation workshops in preparation for the Membership Intake Process for "The Pearls of Wisdom," the interest group at Armstrong Atlantic State University, were held April 5, 2005 and April 14, 2005.

March 10, 2005, members attended Nu Delta Omega's Pink Ice Ball in anticipation for Gamma Sigma Omega's first Pink Ice Ball. GSO members who attended the event were Chappell-Stevens, Basileus Patricia Clark, Hope Johnson, Emma Conyers, Carol Bell, Connie Cooper, Clemontine Washington, and Annie Chappell.[420]

The chapter hosted a Sisterly Relations Dinner at 514 West Restaurant, "Celebrating Our Sisterhood With A Dinner Fit for AKA Queens." The event was held July 26, 2005.

The Christmas social was held December 9, 2005 at Notre Dame Academy where secret sorors exchanged gifts.[421]

The committee sponsored a bag swap. Members were asked to bring to the March chapter meeting new or gently used sorority bags from previous Alpha Kappa Alpha conferences for purchasing at $5.00 or less.[422]

2006 Membership Intake

The 2006 Membership Intake Initiates into Gamma Sigma Omega Chapter were thirty ladies: Patrice Boston, Harriette Brinson-Johnson, Tara Scott Brown, Margaret Burney Johnson, Janice Bryant, Lakechia Bryant, Mary Coleman, Amy Conyers, Jacquelyn Gilbert-Grant, Karla Harper, LaKyah Hatcher, Shakela Holmes, Terri Hurst, Kimberly Knowles, Alexia Luten, Nicole A. Maske, Dawlyn Myles-Buckles, Eddie

LaWanda Ransom, RhaQuay Rucker-Youmans, Deonn Stone, Bettina Tate, LaTanya Thompson, Gloria Thompson-Johnson, Lucille Tyson Brown, Natosha Watson, Betty Williams, Janine Williams, Linda Williams, Linda Wright Jordan.[442]

The Membership Intake extended from March 24-26, 2006 at Wingate Inn, Port Wentworth, GA. The closing luncheon was held at the Mighty 8th Museum in Pooler, GA. Membership Chairman, Stevens, and Basileus Clark prepared for a smooth/successful intake of new members.

Standards Committee, Johnye Gillans, Chairman

The committee conducted a Leadership Retreat August 20, 2005 at the West Broad Street YMCA. On November 10, 2005, a Leadership Workshop was held at Notre Dame Academy. There was a Leadership Training Workshop held May 18, 2006 at Butler Memorial Presbyterian Church.

AKACare, Lois Vedelle Williams, Chairman

Observance of "Older American Month" was May 19, 2005 at the EOA Savannah Boardroom. Lunch was provided by Mrs. Linda Fields, Project Director of Faith in Action and Project Coordinator of Retired Senior Volunteers and Foster Grandparents. She was also the speaker.[423]

A Celebration for "Older American Month" was held at the Carnegie Library, May 17, 2006. The seminar was "An Awareness Seminar on Breast and Cervical Cancer." This seminar was conducted by Mrs. Martina Correia, RN, BSN, an Executive Director of the National Black Leadership Initiative on Cancer.[424]

Jr. Debutantes/Precious Gems, Charlene Jones, Chairman; Sharon Stallings, Co-Chairman

The Jr. Debutantes/Precious Gems Mentoring Program continued to be the local signature program and fundraising arm of Gamma Sigma Omega Chapter in 2005 and 2006.

At the February 2005 meeting, the Junior Debs/Precious Gems received a lecture on Health and Proper Nutrition from Alvernia Wilson-Jackson and Martha Hicks. Tiffany Greene conducted the Public Speaking Workshop in March.[425] They participated in many community service projects, received information on developing self-esteem and confidence, and attended many field trips. In 2006, the Jr. Debs continued a program of worth.

The Precious Gems included the following girls: Marisa Arnold, Charmaine Andrea Crumbley, Demika Dempsey, Taylor Danielle Grant, Brittany A. Grimes, Shanequa Harris, Cheria Hawkins, Chelcee Jenkins, Fabrielle Breana Lowe, Morgan May, Jamila Mitchell, Olivia Phillips-Brown, Latessa Rivers, Whitney K. Robinson, Aiesha Sadler, Anna Maria Santos, NaTashia Alexis Small, ShaTerrilyn Thomas, Rachel Williams. Miss Precious Gem 2005 was Whitney K. Robinson. Basileus Clark extended special thanks to Johnye Gillans and Dorothy Wilson.[426]

In 2006 Basileus Clark met with the Executive Director of Greenbriar's Children's Center, Ms. Gina Taylor, to discuss including in the mentoring program middle school aged girls who reside at Greenbriar Children's Center. The discussions resulted in three (3) girls participating in the Jr. Debutantes/Precious Gems Mentoring Program

The 2005-2006 Precious Gems included the following girls: Aljunese Gaston, Hailey King, Alexis Myers, DiAsia Rogers, Brittani Truell, Nzinga Washington, Kea'erra Wilson, Kennisha Wilson, and Samira Young. Miss Precious Gem 2006 was Samira Young.[427]

Some of the programs and events in which the Jr. Debutantes/Precious Gems participated in 2005-2006: appearance on float in MLK parade, a tour of Old Savannah City Mission, table etiquette, test taking skills, and many other field trips and self-esteem activities. The Mother/Daughter Luncheon was held May 21, 2006 at the DeSoto Hilton's Pulaski Room.

The Chartering of Sigma Tau

The article, "Sigma Tau Chartered in South Atlantic Region," presents the chartering of Sigma Tau Chapter supervised by Gamma

Sigma Omega Chapter, Patricia Clark, Basileus, Audrey B. Singleton, Graduate Advisor, and Clemontine F. Washington, Membership Intake Chairman.[428]

Sunday, April 24, 2005, Irene Westbrooks McCollom, South Atlantic Regional Director, conducted the chartering ceremony at the Comfort Inn and Suites in Pooler, GA. The chartering members were Brianna Bellamy, Dekira Bowe, Andrea Carter, Rena Dixon, Carnika Donald, Misty Ellison, Iris Frye, Albertina Ivy, Krystle Johnson, Tonetta Ray, Amanda Robinson, Tameka Rucks, Salaia Sifford, Janice Smith and Deidra Stephens.[429]

2005 Cluster VI in Savannah

Gamma Sigma Omega Chapter hosted the 2005 Cluster VI Meeting at Tompkins Middle School, Savannah, Georgia, September 23-24, 2005. The theme was "Spirit of AKA." The Chairmen were Carolyn Bell and Connie Cooper. Constance Gardner was Cluster VI Coordinator and Irene W. McCollom was Regional Director. The undergraduate chapters, Gamma Upsilon and Sigma Tau, were also hostesses. As a part of the chapter's exhibit, flags were prepared by Henrietta Perry and Albertha Collier.

Other Conferences

The 2005 Regional Conference was held in Jacksonville, Fl., April 6-10. Delegates funded for 2005 Regional Conference were Patricia J. Clark, Clemontine F. Washington, Undine Truedell, Zenobia Mitchell, Hope Johnson, and Yolanda Jones. The alternates were Gwendolyn Harris Johnson and Melinda Pippen-Miller. Forty-three known chapter members attended the Regional Conference.[430]

The 2005 Leadership Seminar was held August 4-7, 2005 in Paradise Island, Bahamas at the Atlantis Hotel and Resort. Leadership Seminar attendees were Basileus Clark, Marjory Varnedoe, Clemontine Washington, Emma J. Conyers, Lorna Jackson, Kimberly Chappell-Stevens, and Zena McClain.[431] The delegates were Basileus Clark,

Clemontine Washington, Connie Cooper, Lorna Jackson, Zena McClain and Marjory Varnedoe.[432]

Members registered for the 2006 Regional Conference: Eudora Allen, Carolyn Bell, Brianna Bellamy, Albertha E. Boston, Annie Chappell, Kimberly Chappell-Stevens, Patricia Clark, Albertha Collier, Emma Conyers, Connie Cooper, Irene Davis, Jessie C. DeLoach, Nikki Dorsey, Pendar Franklin, Johnye Gillans, Angela Grant, Lorna Jackson, Annie Jackson, Hope Johnson, Charlene Jones, Yolanda Jones, Carmelita Maynard, Zena McClain, Eleanor Murdock, Virginia Parham, Henrietta Perry, Emma Preer, Emily Preer Williams, April Scott, LaVertta Scott Perry, Audrey Singleton, Gwendolyn Smith, Dorothy Speed, Sharon Stallings, Lawanda Tillman, Undine Truedell, Marjory Varnedoe, Clemontine Washington, Nicole Williams, Dorothy Wilson, Alvernia Jackson, Lydia Young, Terri Hurst, Natosha Watson, Kimberly Knowles.[433]

Delegates funded for 2006 Regional Conference in Charlotte, NC were Patricia J. Clark, Clemontine F. Washington, Audrey B. Singleton, Nicole Williams, Sharon Stallings, Lorna C. Jackson, and April Scott. Alternates were Carolyn Bell, Johnye Gillans, and Marjorie Varnedoe. The Conference was held April 19-23, 2006. The chapter was presented an "Ivy Level" award. This award means the chapter retained 75% of its 2005 membership.[434]

Gamma Sigma Omega Chapter was selected as the South Atlantic Region's *Exemplary Ivy Reading AKAdemy Program* winner for the 2005-2006 year. The chapter entered into the competition for the National Exemplary Program Award that was presented at the Detroit Boule in 2006. Gamma Sigma Omega Chapter received a $1,000 award for being selected the Regional winner and a Certificate of Recognition at the Detroit Boule.

Also, the Connection Committee was recognized at 2006 Regional Conference for AKA Day at the Capitol, Voter Registration Drives, attendance at the Board Meetings of the Chatham County Schools Board of Education, Connection Activity with military families, and Youth Voter Registration Drive. Connection received *Certificate of Recognition* at the 2006 Regional Conference and *Certificate of Recognition at the* 2006 Boule in Detroit, MI.[435]

Delegates funded for 2006 Boule Conference in Detroit, MI were Patricia J. Clark, Clemontine F. Washington, Audrey B. Singleton, Emma J. Conyers, Zena McClain, Albertha E. Boston, Dorothy B. Wilson, Virginia Parham, Kimberly Chappell-Stevens, Pendar Franklin, and Eudora Allen. Alternates were Queen Barnes and Eleanor Murdock. Patricia Clark received the Homie Regulus Basileus Award, 3rd Place.[436] Basileus Clark and Conyers prepared the chapter's exhibit for the Boule. Program Chairman, Conyers, set up the exhibit at the Boule. The Basileus presented the chapter's program at Boule Program Workshop.[437]

The chapter mailed boxes of books for the children in Detroit. These books from chapters throughout the nation were mailed to be distributed to the school children.[438]

At the 2006 Cluster in Georgetown, SC, the chapter received the following program 2006 Cluster Awards: *The Constance S. Gardner Graduate Polished Pearls Award* and *The Helen F. McKune Innovative Black Family Award*.

Founders' Day

The 2005 Founders' Day was held at First African Baptist Church, February 13. The speaker was the Honorable Carolyn F. Hugley, Georgia House of Representatives, District 133.

Essie Stewart Johnson was General Chairman, Wanda Williams, General Co-Chairman, and Carolyn Bell, Chairman of Program.[439] Winners of the Evanel Renfrow Terrell Scholarship Award were LaShawna Mullgrav, Kimberly Chappell Stevens, and Michelle Mincey-Lee. Winner of the Countess Y. Cox Sisterhood Award was Albertha Collier. Winner of Soror of the Year Award was Carolyn Bell.

Tri-Chapter Founders' Day was held February 18, 2006 in Hardeeville, South Carolina at Argent Square. The representatives on the Tri-Chapter Founders' Day committee were Johnye Gillans and Ivy Richardson.[440] Gamma Sigma Omega Chapter, Nu Delta Omega Chapter, and Nu Rho Omega Chapter celebrated with a luncheon. The theme was "Honoring Our Past, Fulfilling Our Present, and Preparing for Our Future." Chapter awards were presented to the following members: Sharon Stallings, Evanel Renfrow Terrell Scholarship Award and the Soror of the Year Award; Hope Johnson and Nicole Williams, the Countess Y. Cox Sisterhood Award.[441]

Donations/Greenbriar

Clemontine Washington, Emma Conyers, and Patricia Clark attended the Greenbriar Children's Center Volunteer/Donor Appreciation Luncheon, March 10, 2005.

The following organizations or charitable causes received donations: $1,001 Louisiana citizens affected by Hurrican Katrina; $2,000, West Broad Street YMCA; $200, Savannah Federation of the Blind; $500, Economic Opportunity Authority of Savannah Head Start Program; Membership in the Parent Teacher Association (PTA) of Gadsden Elementary and Garrison Elementary schools. The December 9, 2006 chapter minutes indicate that $4,000 was given to Greenbriar above the chapter's annual contribution during Clark's tenure. Gamma Sigma Omega Chapter supported Greenbriar Children's Center by volunteering during the Month of December for the Center's Annual Holiday Gift Wrapping Fundraiser. Chapter members wrapped gifts for the cause.[443] The gift wrappers were Queen Barnes, Patricia Clark, Emma Conyers, Carmelita Maynard, Alvernia Wilson-Jackson, Lawanda Tillman, Debbie Hagins, Clemontine Washington, Teresa Middleton, Sharon Stallings. In 2006, members wrapped gifts for the Center and purchased gift certificates for the children as Christmas gifts.[444]

Graduate Advisors/Undergrades

Graduate certification ensures a member's ability to advise undergraduates:

> The Graduate Advisor Certification Program: The program
> is coordinated to train graduate members of the sorority to
> serve as advisors to undergraduate members of the sorority
> and to supervise the activities of undergraduate chapters

of the sorority. The program is offered annually at each regional conference and/or the Leadership Seminar or Boule. To be admitted to the program, a soror must not have been suspended for hazing and must be at least a five year post graduate from an undergraduate college or university education program.[445]

Basileus Clark announced the following members had received Graduate Advisors certificates for completing Graduate Advisor's Training: Tamika Bond-Burnette, Stacy Clarke, Johnye Gillans, Hope Johnson, Dorothy Wilson, Albertha Boston, Emma Conyers, Sharon Stallings, Nicole Williams, Ericka Washington, Michelle Mincey-Lee, and LaShawna Mullgrav.[446] In 2006, the following members received Graduate Advisor's Certification: Eudora Allen, April Scott, and Annie Jackson.[447]

In addition, the following members completed Graduate Advisor's training for certification: Carolyn Bell, Connie Cooper, Charlene Jones, Zena McClain, Virginia Parham, Audrey Singleton, Clemontine Washington, and Patricia Clark.[448]

Joint chapter meetings, Gamma Sigma Omega, Gamma Upsilon, and Sigma Tau, were held Saturday November 12, 2005 and October 14, 2006.

Pan-Hellenic, Savannah Chapter, Angela Grant, Chairman

Little Miss Tanea Johnson, daughter of Hope Johnson, won the Annual Babes and Tots Contest sponsored by the Savannah Chapter, Pan-Hellenic. Tanea represented the Alpha Kappa Alpha baby. The AKAs won with a total of $1,430 collected for Tanea.[449]

The Annual Babes and Tots Contest in 2006 was February 19, at Butler Memorial Presbyterian Church. Gamma Sigma Omega Chapter's baby, Little Miss Trinity Perry was first runner up, the daughter of member, LaVertta Scott-Perry. Little Miss Perry represented AKA with $1,040.[450]

AKAs won the attendance award at the Pan-Hellenic annual Greek Picnic, May 20, 2006 at Skidaway Island Park.[451]

SSU Tailgating

GSO chapter members support SSU Tailgating at Savannah State University for alumni and friends to reunite. The chairman for the October 29, 2005 tailgating was LaVertta Scott-Perry and Hope Johnson, assistant chairman. The 2006 SSU Tailgating was chaired by Glenda James, Hodegos, and Membership Committee Chairman, Kimberly Chappel-Stevens. The tailgating booth was decorated and manned by LaVertta Scott-Perry and Hope Johnson.[452]

Other Events

In 2005 and 2006, chapter members worshipped together each fifth Sunday and made a financial contribution to the church's education program. The following churches were visited: Overcoming By Faith Church, Jonesville Baptist Church, St. Philip A.M.E. Church, The Temple of Glory Church, and St. Philip Monumental A.M.E. Church, and Butler Memorial Presbyterian Church.

The following honors were bestowed upon members. Janie Bruen and Gwendolyn Smith received Silver Star status, 2005. Pendar Franklin, Annie Jackson, and Carolyn Russell received Golden Soror status, 2005.

Continuing to promote sisterhood, In 2006, Gamma Sigma Omega Chapter hosted a picnic for Alpha Kappa Alpha members of Gamma Xi Omega Chapter, Charleston, SC after their fall retreat held in Savannah. The picnic was held at the Mutual's house.

In 2006, Gamma Sigma Omega Chapter was nominated to receive a United Way Community Service Program Award.

Chapter Blazers were ordered for chapter members to dress uniformly at some events. Many members ordered blazers in 2005.

Ivies Beyond the Wall

There were four Ivies Beyond the Wall ceremonies. They were Jacqueline A. Handy and Henrietta Perry, chapter members. Basileus Clark also presided for Hortense Wiley and Pamela McClary Williams.[453]

The Establishment of M.A.R.T.H.A., Inc.

Basileus Patricia Clark led a team consisting of Emma Conyers (Anti-Basileus) and Lydia Young, former chapter Tamiouchos, in the creation of the chapter's Georgia Non-Profit Corporation, 501 (c) (3), public foundation, M.A.R.T.H.A., Inc., Moving All Races To Higher Achievement, Inc.[454] M.A.R.T.H.A was incorporated September 15, 2005 and received tax exempt status as a 501(c) (3) August 25, 2006. This organization is structured, with the exception of financial officers, where the officers of Gamma Sigma Omega Chapter are the same officers of M.A.R.T.H.A., Inc.

In planning to meet the challenges of the 21st Century, the implementation of M.A.R.T.H.A., Inc. (Moving All Races To Higher Achievement), the 501 (c) (3) nonprofit foundation was created for Gamma Sigma Omega to be of greater service in the community. This nonprofit foundation was named after Gamma Sigma Omega's first President, Mrs. Martha Wright Wilson.

The resource contact for the structuring and implementation of the entity was the law firm of Hunter Maclean, Savannah, GA.; Attorney Frank S. Macgill was direct contact resource for Anti-Basileus, Conyers. The Articles of Incorporation, Article 5 reads:

...the Corporation shall support the charitable, educational and community programs andinitiatives of Gamma Sigma Omega Chapter of Alpha Kappa Alpha Sorority, ChathamCounty, Georgia, including: the organization's educational initiatives for at-risk childrenand their parents, in the organization's mentoring of Middle School Girls, theorganization's health, economics, and arts initiatives, and the organization's procurementof property for literacy and educational programs.[455]

December 9, 2006, the Basileus presented to the Board of Directors and officers (Lydia Young, Clemontine Washington, Albertha E. Boston, Emma Conyers, Zena McClain) of M.A.R.T.H.A., Inc. a check for $9,929.28. A letter designating how the funds would be spent was given to them at a later date. However, $8,000 was designated for Program of GSO.[456]

The Closing of a Tenure

Awards were given to Patricia Clark, the 2006 Soror of the Year Award and the Basileus Appreciation Award; and to Hope Johnson, the 2006 Evanel Renfrow Terrell Scholarship Award.[457] The Basileus also presented the Countess Y. Cox Sisterhood Award to Kimberly Chappell-Stevens and Hope Johnson.[458]

Basileus Clark's tenure was celebrated December 16, 2006. Chapter member roasted her with a luncheon. Glenda James, Hodegos, and Emma Preer were contacts for the Pink and Green Celebration.

Gamma Sigma Omega Chapter, circa 1950 – 1952, standing left to right: Stella Jones Reeves, Jane Parker Starr, Marion Priester Roberts, Eleanor Bryant Williams, Dr. Mary Williams, President Kathryn Bogan Johnson, Jean Warrick, Shirley Pike, Dorothy Jamerson, Quida Fraizer Thompson, Martha Wright Wilson; seated, left to right: Johnnie Locket Fluker, Agatha Curley Morris, Mary B. McDew, Lois Wilson Conyers, Winona Carter, Edwina Ford, Ernestine Bertrand, Violet Singleton

The Afro-American March 1, 1952

Savannah Sorors Celebrate Founders' Day

Shown in receiving line, circa 1950 – 1952, at the reception which was a part of the celebration of Founders' Day by Gamma Upsilon and the Savannah (GA) graduate chapter of Alpha Kappa Alpha Sorority, Inc. are left to right: Miss Jimmie Colley, Epistoleus of the Gamma Upsilon Chapter; Miss Dorothy McIver, Basileus, Gamma Upsilon; Mrs. W. K. Payne wife of President W. K. Payne and member of the Savannah Graduate Chapter of AKA; Mrs. Edna O. Gray of Baltimore, Md, and past national Basileus who delivered the Founders' Day address; President W. K. Payne, Savannah State College; Miss Kathryn Bogan, Basileus, Savannah Graduate Chapter; Dr. Mary Williams, member of Savannah Graduate Chapter.

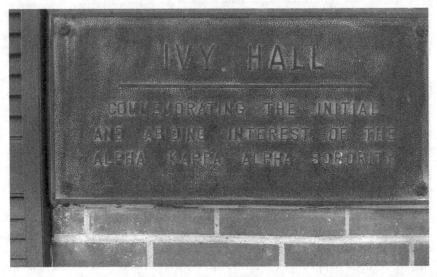

Ivy Hall is a building on the campus of Greenbriar Children's Center. "Ivy" is a symbol of Alpha Kappa Alpha that represents strength and endurance. This building was named in honor of the sorority.

1976 South Atlantic Regional Conference, downtown Savannah

Gamma Sigma Omega Chapter led by Dorothy B. Wilson, 1985-1986; left to Wilson is Martha Wright Wilson, Charter President.

1998 South Atlantic Regional Conference, Savannah Civic Center

Gamma Sigma Omega Chapter led by Charlene E. Jones, 1993-1994

AKA Day at the Capitol in Atlanta, GA

GSO members strategize means for service projects.

GSO members make decisions about short story and
poetry contest entries submitted by students.

GSO member reads to class

GSO presents financial workshop to middle school students.

"Facing the Rising Sun" particpants at AKA Honors the Arts

GSO in retreat

GSO in retreat

Ivy Reading AKAdemy at the Ralph Mark Gilbert
Civil Rights Museum, Savannah, GA

Ivy Reading AKAdemy

Junior Debutante Cotillion, featuring Precious Gems

Junior Debutante Cotillion, featuring Precious Gems

Junior Debutante Cotillion, featuring Precious Gems

Golden Sorors honored at chapter meeting

Alpha Kappa Alpha Sorority celebrates 100 years in 2008

Emma Jean Conyers, 2007 - 2008

The International Driving Force

Emma Jean Conyers, affectionately known as "the Centennial Chapter Basileus," coined from the phrase "the Centennial Supreme Basileus," Barbara A. McKinzie, was excited about plans for the centennial celebration of Alpha Kappa Alpha Sorority in 2008. She and her team with Clemontine F. Washington as Program chairman set out to complete the mission of the Supreme Basileus by developing ideas and strategies that Gamma Sigma Omega Chapter would pursue for the celebration. The blessing for her administration was held at Connor's Temple Baptist Church. A Basileus' Retreat was held December 30, 2006, at the DoubleTree Hotel in Historic Savannah, for chapter members to plan how to meet the challenges of McKinzie. Continuing the International theme: Economics, Sisterhood, and Partnerships, Conyers showed McKinzie's video that had been debuted at the 2006 Boule in Detroit. Conyers sought the expertise of Dr. Cherry A Collier, People Psychologist and Attitude Improvement Expert who is viewed on TV and heard on radio, to help inspire and motivate Gamma Sigma Omega (GSO) members at the retreat. Dr. Collier is a member of Alpha Kappa Alpha Sorority (AKA), the author of several positive mental attitude books, the niece of chapter members Jessie Collier DeLoach, Albertha Collier, and the late Henrietta Collier Perry. Collier discussed "Three Magic Keys for Keeping you Moving: (1) Know your intentions (2) Break the Pattern. (3) Do something."

Conyers' mission was two-fold: (1) to continue the successful operational program of Gamma Sigma Omega and (2) to meet the challenges of a centennial celebration for Alpha Kappa Alpha Sorority. The Jr. Debutants/Precious Gems Mentoring Program continued to be the local signature program and fundraising arm of Gamma Sigma Omega Chapter.

Conyers was ready for work. Her theme for 2007-2008 was "Study to Show Thyself Approved in Documents, Sisterly Relations, Technology, Partnerships to Produce the Heart of ESP: An Exemplary Service Program." In her plans to meet the challenges of the 21st Century, she formulated a Technology Committee, Ivanette Richardson and Sharon Stallings, Chairmen. This Committee updated the chapter's website: www.akagso.com. Reports were downloaded from the site, saving the chapter money and conserving the environment. She continued to improve the procedures for obtaining grants from M.A.R.T.H.A., Inc.

On August 18, 2007, the chapter's retreat was held at the Con-Ed Family Resource Center. The retreat's theme was **ESP**: Essential Vigilant Study for Progress. Vanessa Kaigler, Membership Chairman, presented a sisterly relation activity. The undergraduate chapters, Gamma Upsilon and Sigma Tau, supervised by Gamma Sigma Omega, presented to GSO chapter their joint service project. Zena McClain coordinated the discussion on the proposed amendments to Chapter Bylaws, and Carolyn Bell entertained questions and comments on the proposed Chapter Campaign Guidelines. GSO members who were entrepreneurs sold their products. Lunch was held at Mom & Nikki's Soul Food, a black owned restaurant located in the Con-Ed building.

The Standing Committees ensured a successful infrastructure program of service for Gamma Sigma Omega Chapter. One requirement to be an officer in GSO Chapter is to attend one of the last two Standards workshops.

Standards Committee

The Standards Committee, Virginia Parham, Chairman, presented the Standards Workshop, "Duties and Responsibilities of All Elected Officers," March 22, 2007, 6:00 p.m., West Broad Street YMCA, Childcare Building. It was presented as "Amended AKA Feud" in an altered format of "Family Feud" with Clemontine Washington as the game-show Hostess. Members of the chapter made up the feuding families.

For year 2008, the Standards Workshop was held Thursday, March 27, 2008, at the Westbroad Street YMCA on May Street. GSO members: Janie B. Bruen, Jessie DeLoach, Joyce G. Dingle, Johnye W. Gillans, Henrietta Gray, Zena McClain, Patricia Mincey, Audrey Singleton, Kimberly Chappell Stevens, Marjory Varnedoe, and Clemontine Washington, implemented the workshop sessions. The presenters were

Audrey Singleton and Johnye Gillans, Rituals and Chapter Courtesies/ Protocol; Joyce Dingle and Kimberly Chappell Stevens, How to be a Sisterly Soror; Charlene Jones, So You Want to Be a Delegate; Dorothy B. Wilson, Fiscal Tidbits; and Zena McClain, So You Want to Run for Office — Campaigning GSO Style.[459]

Membership Committee

The Membership Committee, Vanessa Kaigler, Chairman, initiated the Energetic Soror Passport, **ESP**. Members were encouraged to have their chapter passport signed by a Membership Committee member when attending events or activities sponsored by the chapter, 2007-2008. A Telephone Blitz on February 16, 2007 was conducted to reclaim and reactivate AKAs. The Membership Committee recommended to the chapter to waive local dues and chapter assessments for any inactive AKA with a minimum of three years of inactivity. The chapter approved the recommendation.

At the October Meeting, 2007, Kaigler asked members to bring an AKA keepsake, especially a centennial memorabilia, to be placed in a Time Capsule that would be sealed and opened in ten years. The Capsule was sealed in 2009 under the administration of Clemontine Washington.

At the 54th South Atlantic Regional Conference in Atlanta, GA, the Membership Committee, with the assistance of Patricia Mincey and Basileus Conyers hosted the first Regional Conference fellowship in Conyers' suite. The GSO members gave donations for the refreshments. The camaraderie made a joyous sisterly relations event.

In response to the Membership Roundup, Every Soror is a Pearl, **ESP**, an International Initiative, the Committee held a "Welcome Home" fellowship on Sunday afternoon, October 28, 2007. The chapter reclaimed two AKAs in October: Sonya Jackson and Nicole Fields. Newly activated and inactive AKAs were invited to attend the session. The Membership Committee discussed the financial obligations associated with membership and the requirements to take advantage of the "2007" reactivation drive. One AKA reactivated during the fellowship, two additional AKAs who were unable to attend made contact to obtain information related to reactivating. The Committee reclaimed 22 AKAs in 2007.[460]

"Are You Ready for Boule?" Sisters Helping Sisters: The Membership Committee held a navigation session at the Economic Opportunity Authority (EOA), building, Thursday, February 28, 2008, from 5:00–7:00 p.m. The session assisted AKAs with navigating through the registration process to include the taking of photographs and the uploading of them to Alpha Kappa Alpha's corporate web page.[461]

At the 55th South Atlantic Regional Conference, the Membership Committee received 4 Star Recognition, the 2nd highest recognition: 10% reactivation and 85% retention of members.[462]

Gamma Sigma Omega Chapter's Countdown to Centennial Boule was a component of the Membership Committee and the mission of the Centennial Committee. These committees ignited excitement among the chapter members with exceptional events that led to AKAs' departure from Savannah to Washington, D.C. for Alpha Kappa Alpha's International Conference's 100 Year Celebration and the Post Boule trip, the South Africa Pilgrimage.

The Boule Launch scheduled for the end of the chapter's countdown generated energy and excitement by all chapter members. The enthusiasm was contagious. To include the Community in the celebration, on Thursday, July 10, 2008, 6:00 p.m., the eve of the GSO Connection's (bus) departure to Washington, D.C., the Boule Launch was held at the Economic Opportunity Authority of Savannah Chatham County, Inc in the Multipurpose Room, Mr. John Finney, Executive Director. City and County politicians, religious leaders, and the Savannah public at large were in attendance. The public's appearance confirmed for Gamma Sigma Omega Chapter the love and support by the community for the chapter. At the Launch, the chapter donated a total of $11,000 to various service and charitable organizations in the community.[463]

Other Membership activities included: "Sorors Night Out," at the Mavis Staples Concert, Lucas Theater, February 2, 2008; Tea Party, honoring Mothers and celebrating sisterhood, after May 2008 Chapter meeting; **ESP**, Enjoying Sorors Personally (Sorors in My Circle), a method of keeping in touch on a sisterly basis.

Centennial Committee and Activities to Spotlight Centennial

The Centennial Celebration of Alpha Kappa Alpha Sorority, Inc. implemented the 365-Day Countdown for The Centennial Celebration beginning January 1, 2007 to promote Regional Centennial Celebrations. The International Centennial Chairman was Norma S. White, 25th Supreme Basileus. South Atlantic Centennial Regional Chairman was Lucretia Payton Stewart, 13th Regional Director. Each Region was assigned a month to celebrate sorority's history. February was the South Atlantic's month to hold the Regional Conference and Founders' Day celebration that were held in Atlanta, GA.[464]

Gamma Sigma Omega Chapter's Centennial Committee scheduled events and activities. The members were Chairmen, Lakechia Bryant and Elza Givens; Carolyn Bell, Albertha E. Boston, Patricia Clark, Albertha Collier, Jacquelyn Gibert-Grant, Alvernia W. Jackson, Vanessa M. Kaigler, Carmelita Maynard, Zena McClain, Sharon Stallings, and Kimberly Chappell-Stevens.

AKAs were encouraged to purchase the Ethel Hedgeman Lyle South Atlantic Centennial Pin[465] and to wear it each day in February to promote unity and sisterhood to commemorate the centennial.

During the month of February, Golden Sorors and former Basilei (Presidents) were honored. GSO's Golden Sorors were given the title "Achievers" by Centennial Commitee. They were highlighted in local newspapers. Pendar Franklin, Annie Jackson, Carolyn Russell, Jessie C. DeLoach, Eudora Allen, Janie B. Bruen, Eleanor Murdock, and Margaret Robinson.[466]

Golden Sorors Pendar Franklin, Annie C. Jackson, Carolyn Russell, Jessie C. DeLoach, and Eudora Allen gave oral interviews, Elza Givens, interviewer and Sharon Stallings, video technician.[467]

Mayor of Savannah, Otis S. Johnson, Ph.D. sent a letter of commendation to the chapter for 100 years of service, January 31, 2007. He writes, "We are proud of the service that you have rendered in this city, most notably the founding of the Greenbriar Children's Center. This institution, established for orphaned and destitute Negro children, was founded on June 8, 1944."

WTOC Television (CBS), Sonny and Jody Morning Show featured Emma Conyers, Basileus and Clemontine F. Washington, Anti-Basileus, as guests to discuss Alpha Kappa Alpha Sorority's 100 years of service and Gamma Sigma Omega Chapter's activities during the month of February to highlight the sorority's celebration.

February 3, 2007-GSO Centennial Walk and Weight Loss:

ESP, Enthusiastically Shedding Pounds, an International initiative by Alpha Kappa Alpha Sorority for members to lose a million pounds by centennial celebration in 2008 in support of the "ESP 1908 Centennial Walk" by committing to walk 1,908 miles in 18 months or commit to exercise a minimum of 19.08 minutes/seconds per day. To address this initiative, Gamma Sigma Omega Chapter and Nu Rho Omega Chapter, Hinesville, GA, Beverly L. Pitts, Basileus, in collaboration with the American Heart Association, held their 1908 Centennial Walk Kick-off in Savannah, GA at Lake Mayer, emphasizing their **ESP**, Each Soror Physically Fit, from 9:00 a.m.-11:00 a.m. The Mayor of Savannah, Otis Johnson, walked with the sorority. GSO members were to keep record of exercise time, weight loss, and miles walked. According to *The Centennial*, Platform V, Chairman and Co-chairman, Debbie Hagins and LaTanya Thompson, respectively, in preparation for the 1908 Centennial Walk in July 2008 and in promoting the sorority's emphasis on wellness and the fight against obesity, GSO was committed to walk 2,200 miles and to lose 500 pounds by July 2008.[468]

February 5, 2007- The Ralph Mark Gilbert Civil Rights Museum, Alpha Kappa Alpha Display

The Museum hosted Gamma Sigma Omega Chapter's historical display in honor of the Centennial. AKAs and guests were encouraged to leave a financial donation to the Museum. The exhibit was on display February 5 through the end of the month.

February 9, 2007

GSO members showcased pink and green attire in the workplace.

Proclamation: The Chatham County Commission issued a proclamation proclaiming February as Alpha Kappa Alpha Month.

February 10, 2007

GSO members enjoyed family fun at the Black Heritage Grand Festival, Savannah Civic Center.

February 11, 2007

South Atlantic Day of Worship, St. Philip Monumental Church, 1112 Jefferson Street (wearing Ethel Hedgeman Lyle pin, 4:00 pm; black attire)

February 14, 2007

AKA Pink Valentine's Day, honored Senior AKAs and sick and shut-in AKAs with gift bags

October 2007 Chapter Meeting

The Chapter observed Rededication, long form, led by Basileus Conyers

June 28, 2008

Alpha Kappa Alpha Sorority, Inc. held an "ESP 1908 Global Centennial Walk" for Emotional, Spiritual, and Physical Health. The walk occurred simultaneously around the world wherever a chapter of Alpha Kappa Alpha Sorority was located. Two of the local chapters, Gamma Sigma Omega and Gamma Upsilon of Savannah State University, participated in the walk. From Forsyth Park to Johnson Square, in historic downtown Savannah, the streets and parks were adorned with shades of pink and green as GSO members, their families, friends, visiting AKAs, and supporters took part in the walk. This culmination of the ESP 1908 Centennial Walk initiative concluded with a symbolic walk at the Sorority's 2008 National Convention in Washington, D.C. on Sunday, July 13, 2008, in the celebration of one hundred years of service to all mankind.

The local walk, led by officers of Gamma Sigma Omega Chapter, began at Forsyth Park at 11:00 a.m. at the corner of Gaston and Whitaker streets and moved south to circle the park before proceeding north on Bull to Johnson Square. The large oak trees that lined the route formed a continuous natural umbrella that provided the more than seventy walkers a cool breeze and shade from the scorching sun. As the group moved through downtown Savannah, they received astonishing glares, waves, and congratulatory remarks from bystanders and tourists in trolleys and other tour vehicles. The walkers were greeted in Johnson Square by other sorority and family members. The walkers were served cold water, and souvenirs were distributed to all participants: a water bottle, adorned with a pink ribbon, with the inscription of Global Centennial Walk, Alpha Kappa Alpha Celebrates 100 Years, 1908-2008, and the chapter's name. The walk culminated in front of Savannah City Hall with a reception. The local Centennial Walk was coordinated by Program Chairman, Washington.[469]

Sunday, July 6, chapter members invoked the presence of God by worshipping at First African Baptist Church, Franklin Square, "The Oldest Black Church in North America," Rev. Thurmond N. Tillman, Pastor. His text was "Where Are You Going?" Mark 8:34. Rev. Tillman prayed for Alpha Kappa Alpha's continued success and traveling mercies for members journeying to Washington, D.C and South Africa with a safe return home. The Pastor's Support Ministry and Lawanda Tillman, the first lady of First African Baptist Church and GSO member, provided an elaborate reception for AKAs, their families, and friends immediately after worship service.

Monday, July 7, the chapter presented Greenbriar Children's Center over 200 pairs of socks in response to a request to donate 100 pairs. The Program Chairman, Clemontine Washington, made the presentation.

The gift was warmly received by the Executive Director, Mrs. Gena P. Taylor, as television media recorded the presentation.

Tuesday, July 8, a Unity Rally, at Savannah State University, AKA Park, was held. Members thanked God for His blessings, embraced each other in fellowship before returning to work, and concluded with the Sorority's hymn. The Lord's presence was obvious with His sending of light kisses of rain drops.

Wednesday, July 9, the Day of Reflection was set aside for packing or doing whatever needed to be done for departure as well as remembering the Founders. GSO members placed pink and or green balloons or ribbons on their door or mail box.

Connection Committee

The Connection Committee's **ESP,** Energizing, Strategizing, Politically, the goal of the committee, Ivy Richardson, Chairman, was to register 19 persons by 2008. In her October 4, 2007 chapter meeting report, she said that in partnership with the NAACP, Pendar Franklin and Carolyn Russell registered eleven students at Johnson High School during the month of September. The Committee distributed flyers to local churches announcing Gamma Sigma Omega Chapter's declaration of October 2007 as Voter Preparation Month. The Committee requested churches, family members, and friends to join the AKA Car-A-Van in transporting individuals to obtain picture IDs. The Committee reported that as of Saturday October 27, 2007, the goal was exceeded by eleven. Annie Jackson, Conyers, Melinda Pippen-Miller, Franklin, and Richardson registered seventeen individuals at Savannah State University's Homecoming tailgating activity.

The second phase of the Voter Registering Preparation Drive resulted in four individuals getting a Voter Identification Card and one individual registering for the 2008 Absentee Ballots. The last phase of the Voter Preparation Drive was to assist individuals in the application process for the Official Absentee Ballot for the 2008 elections. Six GSO members were trained to be Voter Registration Deputies on May 7, 2008.

Voter Registration Drive Partners: St. Matthew's Episcopal Church, NAACP, and Delta Sigma Theta Sorority. Chapter members participating as registrars were Irene Davis, Elza Givens, Sylvia Perry-Weston, Russell, and Conyers. Seven were registered at St. Matthew's Episcopal Church community carnival on September 20 and 35 registered, 22 change of address, and 1 absentee ballot for a total of 58 registration documents processed at Savannah Technical College on September 29.[470]

Alpha Kappa Alpha Voter Registration Blitz continued. In the October 30, 2008 report, Richardson reported that the Connection Committee held a Voter Registration Drive at the Super Walmart off Montgomery Cross Roads. The Supervising Manager, Lee Stacey, granted permission for the Drive to be held. The Voter Registration Drive was to be a partnership with the local members of Omega Psi Phi Fraternity, Inc., Gamma Upsilon, and Gamma Sigma Omega. Twelve people registered as first time voters, and three had change of address. Members serving as registrars were Davis, Perry-Weston, Michelle Mincey-Gwyn, LaShawna Mullgrav, and Conyers. Other voter registration drives were held at Kroger's store in McAlpine Square on June 12, 2008 and Ridgeland Middle School Star Academy where Richardson and GSO member, Carolyn Mayes, distributed twenty-four registration forms; twelve were returned. These drives helped to secure the first African American, Barack Obama, to the position of President of the United States of America.

The Connection Committee spearheaded AKA Day at the Capitol. The 14th Annual AKA Day at the Capitol was held March 6, 2007. Richardson reported in April 14, 2007, chapter minutes that Clemontine F. Washington was recognized as a politician. The 15th Annual AKA Day at the Capitol was February 18, 2008. AKAs were informed on the major legislative issues for 2008: the 2008 budget; property taxes; lower taxes, better schools, the Democratic plan; water; transportation; education charter school; expanding Pre-K; health care; trauma care; and working families. GSO members in attendance were Conyers, Irene Davis, Annie Jackson, and Zena McClain. Washington registered but couldn't attend.[471]

A Political Forum was sponsored by the NAACP, October 20, 2008. The panelists included Basileus Conyers, Sondra Barnes (an NAACP volunteer), and Elijah West (Beta Phi Lambda Chapter of Alpha Phi Alpha Fraternity, Inc.).

Social Committee

ESP, an "Elegant "Sweetthang Production"-- A Family Affair" sponsored by the Social Committee was held at the University Village on Savannah State University campus, Friday, October 24. This event was a pre festivity to SSU 2008 Homecoming. Unbelievable tasty desserts with tea, coffee, and other beverages and creative performances by GSO members who represented the decade of their year of initiation into Alpha Kappa Alpha, created a genuine fellowship and entertainment for members, their families, and friends. Can goods were collected as admission to be delivered to the Second Harvest Food Bank.[472]

The Social Committee, Irene Davis and Hope Johnson, Chairmen, welcomed AKAs, their families, and friends to Homecoming Tailgating at Savannah State University, Saturday, October 27, 2007. A total of 156 AKAs inclusive of GSO members and visiting AKAs signed attendance list. Fifty guests and friends were also recorded. Special thanks were extended to the following: members of the committee and other GSO members who contributed in various ways to the success of the event, to Mrs. Deborah Enoch of the West Broad Street YMCA for allowing the use of tables and chairs, Mr. Chris Holland, Mr. Sean Holland, and Mr. Alex Cooper for the delivery of the tables and chairs, and for their assistance in assembling the tailgating tent.[473]

The Social Committee again welcomed SSU 2008 Homecoming celebration with tailgating. In honor of the 100th year birthday of Alpha Kappa Alpha Sorority, members wore T-Shirts that depicted 100 years and gave gifts to those who visited the AKA tent. The food was very palatable and the fellowship was good. Each AKA received a birthday cup and pink and green pompoms. It was very rewarding to have AKAs in fellowship who had celebrated 50 years and more, the "Golden Sorors."[474]

Other Committees

The AKAcare Committee, Patricia Mincey, Chairman and Lois Vedelle Williams, Coordinator, for senior members' issues presented a seminar in partnership with First Mount Bethel Baptist Church's senior ministry, February 14, 2008, 10:00 AM. The guest speaker was Terry Clark from United Healthcare. He explained Medicare.

The Mentoring Committee, Lawanda Tillman, Chairman, held the first social meeting for mentoring reactivating and transferring AKAs, Saturday, April 12, 2008, at Geneva's Restaurant. The Heritage Committee, June 2007, in its evaluation of Gamma Sigma Omega Chapter recommended the chapter formulate a Mentoring Committee.

Educational Advancement Foundation, Inc (EAF), Alvernia Jackson, Representative. In 2007, GSO received recognition in giving on the Silver level and a certificate. In 2008, a $400 donation was made, Silver Level.

International Program

Clemontine F. Washington led the direction for Program of Gamma Sigma Omega Chapter in the vision of McKinzie by implementing the Platforms of Alpha Kappa Alpha Sorority, Inc. and the local service programs of the chapter.

Platform I-The Non-Traditional Entrepreneur

This Platform was chaired by Dorothy B. Wilson, Janie B. Bruen, and Natosha Watson. These members and the Committee implemented the Survey, the Entrepreneurial Spirit and Passion. **ESP.** There were 56 surveys returned: 9 interested in becoming entrepreneurs, 25 not interested, 1 franchise, 15 home base businesses, 1 corporation, and 5 others, reported in the March 10, 2007, *The Centennial.*

In 2007 Janie B. Bruen, co-owner of Artistic Impressions, Inc., presented an informative session on her home business. Bruen and husband, Joe, are independent Art Consultants. She listed the steps involved in starting the business, keeping it going, and the financial and personal rewards of being entrepreneurs.

The publication of "Entrepreneurial Spirit and Passion," Director of Soror Entrepreneurs, January 2008, Volume I, Issue I; *Sisters Helping Sisters*, entrepreneurs displayed wares for sale prior to and after the

June chapter meeting and extended the invitation to mentor interested members.

In 2008, Wilson presented a copy of the chapter's Entrepreneurial Directory to each member. Marjory Varnedoe, a non-traditional entrepreneur, discussed publishing one's own written work. During the June chapter meeting, Sisters Helping Sisters, entrepreneurs displayed and discussed their businesses. Interested members signed up to be mentored by the experienced member. Entrepreneurs were Janie B. Bruen–Artistic Impression; Patricia Clark–Avon; Lorna Jackson-Dentistry; Tara Scott Brown–Title Search; Marjory Varnedoe–Publishing.

Committee members: Carol Bell, Janese Cooper, Sharonda Johnson, Annette Mitchell, Emily Sanders, Sharon Stallings, Natosha Watson, Tamika Bond-Burnett, Jane Gates, Nicole Mask, Virginia Parham, Gwendolyn Smith, Joi Stevens, April Whitehead, Harriett Brinson, Glenda James, Maureen Maxwell, Kimberly Rhodes, Dorothy Speed, Gloria Thompson, and Nicole Williams.

Platform II-Economic Keys to Success

Economic Keys to Success, **ESP,** the Committee presented the **AKA-nomics Checkbook** for GSO members to record monthly financial concepts to improve their financial literacy. At the December 2007 chapter meeting, Economic Keys to Success--Economic Literacy Assessment Quiz for Sorors was administered to each GSO member to assess the knowledge learned from the AKA-nomics presentations.

Earn-Save-Prosper (ESP Kids Club), Mary Coleman and Sonia Renee W. Grant, Chairmen, the ESP Kids Club summer session was held at Hubert Middle School during the month of June 2007, in partnership with 21st Century. There were 22 participants and the project was chaired by LaWanda Ransom. Gifts and prizes were awarded during each session. Four workshop sessions were conducted on Tuesdays beginning at 1:00 p.m. and ending at 2:00 p.m. The workshops and consultants were Making Money - Clemontine Washington and Grant; Managing Money - Coleman and Kimberly Chappell-Stevens; Spending Smarts - Grant and Shelia Hutcherson;

and Planning a Business - Washington and Conyers. At the completion of the project, each participant received a certificate of participation, a money bookmarker and a pencil.

Gamma Sigma Omega Chapter of Alpha Kappa Alpha Sorority, Incorporated and St. Matthew's Episcopal Church formed a partnership to organize an Earn-Save Prosper (ESP) Kids Investment Club. The Kids Club at St. Matthew's Episcopal Church, including children from the community, held its initial meeting on Wednesday, November 7, 2007 at 5:00 p.m. in the social hall of the church. Parents and children were presented the ESP Kids Club Rules along with a permission slip. They participated in discussing the rules and ESP projects.

The goals of the club: (1) to increase economic literacy of youth in the 4th through 9th grades before they reach the age of employability; (2) to help young people understand to earn and save; and (3) to provide children the opportunity to have a financial head start in today's fast paced economic society.

Fifteen young people signed up for the club. Of this number the sponsors had assisted five of them in opening savings accounts at Capitol City Bank.[475]

The ESP Kids Kamp was held Saturday, February 16, 2008 from 10:00 a.m. to 12:00 noon at the Con-Ed Building. The twelve attendees were members of the ESP Club and Junior Debs/Precious Gems. Topics discussed were "Making Money, Managing Money and Spending Smart." The participants were engaged in learning activities, discussion session, and a question and answer summary. All attendees completed an evaluation form. Coleman, Grant, and Washington served as presenters. Ms. Chiriga Gordon represented Con-Ed Center.

ESP Kids Club bank accounts were opened at Capitol City Bank and an ESP Kids Club budget planning workshop was May 28, 2008, at St. Matthew's Episcopal Church.

Economic Smart Fair, Wanda Williams and Sylvia Perry-Weston, Chairmen, flyers distributed in Savannah read: "Alpha Kappa Alpha Sorority and the City of Savannah sponsor The Economic Smart Fair." The Economic Smart Fair was organized to increase economic literacy in the greater community by providing a "one stop shop" for information, workshops and technical assistance. This Fair provided the community with options for financial education, entrepreneurial lessons, wealth building, and opportunities for enhancement of assets. The Fair was held on Saturday, September 29, 2007 at the Savannah Civic Center. Participants had the opportunity to attend two workshops of their choice and participate in the opening and closing general session.[476]

Ten exhibitors participated in the Fair, including Platform V (Health Resource Management and Economics). Members Debbie Hagins and LaTanya Stringer of The Health Committee, Platform V, collaborated with the Economic Smart Fair by providing free blood pressure checks, blood sugar testing, cancer information, and body mass index calculations to participants. Appropriate health related literature was distributed.

Other workshops: Your Economic Lifestyle; Building Your Investment Portfolio; How to Start and Grow a Business; Loans, Interest Rates, and Credit Scores; How to Help Children Earn, Save and Prosper, ESP-Kids Club; and Don't Sabotage Your Retirement. The Community partners exhibitors were City of Savannah, Housing Department; City of Savannah, Economic Development Department; BOAN Consults, LLC; Capitol City Bank & Trust; Carver State Bank; Savannah-Chatham Economic Opportunity Authority; Dollar Wise Program, Savannah Business Assistance Corporation; and Social Security Administration. Numerous door prizes were given. The top prize was a laptop computer.

The evaluative data for the Economic Smart Fair: Savannah Civic Center, overall rating 87% Excellent; 13% Average; 97% of the respondents had never attended an Economic Smart Fair; 4.0% had attended an Economic Smart Fair; 100.0% of respondents found the Economic Smart Fair beneficial; 3.0% of respondents were 10 to 15 years old; 51.0% of respondents were 16 to 21 years old; 6.0% of respondents were 22 to 35 years old; 34.0% of respondents were 35 to 55 years old; and 6.0% of respondents were over 55 years old.[477]

Committee members: Tarangula Barnes Scott, Patrice Boston, Amy Conyers, Tiffany Green, Terri Hurst, Janice Johnson, Yolanda Jones, Sylvia Perry-Weston, Tammy Cox Stokes, Janine Williams,

Lydia Young, Brianna Bellamy, Tara Scott-Brown, Nikki Dorsey, Karla Harper, Sheila Hutcherson, Vanessa Kaigler, Carolyn Mays, Eddie L. Ransom, Natatia VanEllison, Undine Williams, Albertha Boston, Dawlyn Buckles, Deonn S. Ellison, Alice Harvey, Gwendolyn Johnson, Kimberly Knowles, Zena McClain, Kimberly Chappell-Stevens, Yvette Wells, and Wanda Williams.

Platform III-Economic Growth of the Black Family

Partnerships, Bettina Tate, Chairman. On February 17, 2007, Sylvia Perry-Weston and Gwendolyn Harris Johnson, members of Platform II, presented a financial workshop at Community Works, a program that targets at-risk students.

Greenbriar Connection, Johnye Gillans, Eleanor Ginn, Lois Vedelle Williams, Chairmen. Ms. Gena Taylor, Executive Director of Greenbriar Children's Center, requested that Gamma Sigma Omega chair (plan and organize) Greenbriar's 60th Anniversary to be celebrated in July 2009. The Committee Chairs coordinated the members to support the events sponsored by the Greenbriar Children's Center, 2007: Fundraising, Cooking for Charity at the New South Café; Fundraising Luncheon at Bonefish Grill, June 24; Ribbon Cutting Ceremony for Jack Jones Cottage, May 11, special guest, Victoria Rowell (Young and the Restless and Diagnosis Murder); the furnishing of beddings and other furnishing for eight rooms in one of the cottages in addition to giving a $1500 donation, budgeted item; the volunteering of members to do Christmas gift wrapping at Savannah Mall, giving proceeds to Greenbriar. The Committee Chairs coordinated the members to support the events sponsored by the Greenbriar Children's Center, 2008: attendance at organizational meeting for the 60th Anniversary Celebration; attendance at the 59th Anniversary Kick-off Brunch at Bonefish Grill, June 29; Christmas gift wrapping at Savannah Mall with proceeds to Greenbriar in addition to giving a $2000 donation, budgeted item. The Epistoleus recorded in her report, February 2009, an acknowledgment from Greenbriar Children's Center for the Chapter's donation in 2008 of $3,045.

The Arts –Marjory Varnedoe, Chairman. "Facing the Rising Sun," was held April 29, 2007 at 4:00 p.m. at Butler Elementary School. Students demonstrated oratorical skills by reciting poems written by African American Authors. The winners were Category I - First Place, Ashli Smith; Category II - First Place, Jazmin Smith; and Category III - First Place was Whitney Robinson.[478] In 2008, Sunday, April 13, 4:00 p.m. at St. Matthew's Episcopal Church, young people ages 7-18, demonstrated their oratorical talent by reciting poetry from memory in a "Celebration of Black Poets." The judges for the contest were Mrs. Paulette Sanders, Ms. Myra Lynda White, and Mrs. Inez Bennett. The contestants were judged by categories: Category 1, Ages 7– 9, Briana M. Robinson, Bless Loadholt, Ashli Smith, Saral Rhett, and Jessica Hill; Category 2, Ages 10-12, Kaitlyn Louise Walker, Khaleed D. Barrett, Jazmin Smith, Victoria Smith, Ayanna Cobb, Willie Robinson, Timryl Rhett; Category 3, Ages 13-15, Jasmine Williams, Lee Alice Brown, Cianna Hill, Jordan Feggins, Whitney Robinson; and Category 4, Ages 16-18, Latoria Paige Scott.[479]

"Facing the Rising Sun" committee members: Eudora Allen, Cora Carter, Albertha Collier, Jessie C. DeLoach, Joyce Dingle, Maxine Jackson, Margaret Johnson, Carmelita Maynard, Emma Preer, Maggie Walker-Zeigler, Doris D. Wood, and Rhaquay Rucker-Youmans.

Tutorial/Reading, Queen Barnes, Ethel Hunter, Pendar Franklin, Carolyn Russell, and Washington expressed in February's newsletter, *The Centennial,* that tutorial began February 3, 2007 at Gadsden Elementary School, sessions 10:00 a.m.– 12:00 noon. The sessions included reading and math with emphasis on test taking skills. Students in grades 1 through 3 were invited but kindergarten students were not refused. The Saturday tutorial session ended on April 17 with special events for the participants. The closing session was held Saturday, April 21 at Gadsden Elementary School. The children and parents were entertained by Mr. Magic. Refreshments were served by members in attendance.

Top Readers, **ESP,** (Excellence in Student Performance) at Robert W. Gadsden and Esther F. Garrison Elementary Schools were presented plaques on Friday, January 26, 2007. Gadsden's readers were recognized during the Awards Program. Garrison's awards were presented to the students in their classes.[480]

AYP (Average Yearly Progress) for Gadsden and Garrison/ Transition to new reading program

In September 2007, Average Yearly Progress (AYP), the Chapter reported in *The Centennial*, that Robert W. Gadsden and Esther F. Garrison schools met AYP benchmarks, state-mandated achievement goals. The two schools where members of Gamma Sigma Omega Chapter had volunteered, Gadsden for eight years, and Garrison for four years, were no longer on the Needs Improvement list. Gadsden passed for the second consecutive year, thereby being moved from the Needs Improvement list.

After closing the Saturday Tutorial Session, the chapter restructured its Tutorial Program to include only Robert W. Gadsden Elementary School. The school's program was called Academic Character Educational Services (ACES Extended Services Program). Gamma Sigma Omega tutored a select group of first grade students in reading and math, every Monday and Wednesday from 4:00 p.m.–5:30 p.m. Language Arts was on Mondays and Math on Wednesdays. Program Chairman, Washington, and GSO volunteers were highlighted in the March 8, 2008 newsletter, *The Centennial*. The article says The ACES Tutorial Program is in full swing at Robert W. Gadsden Elementary School under the direction of Clemontine Washington, Anti-Basileus. Thanks to volunteers: Conyers, Washington, Lucille Brown, Janice Bryant, Cora Carter, Patricia Clark, Mary Coleman, Irene Davis, Juanita Denson, Patricia Devoe, Joyce Dingle, Virginia Edwards, Pendar Franklin, Johnye Gillans, Elza Givens, Margaret Johnson, Linda Jordan, Ivy Richardson, Carolyn Russell, Faria Singleton, Dorothy Speed, Betty Williams, Lois Vedelle Williams, Marjory Varnedoe, Dorothy Wilson, Dorothy Worthy, and Lydia Young.

In 2008, due to conflicting schedules, the Top Readers at Esther F. Garrison Elementary, GSO member, Renae McCollough, Principal, were recognized May 14. The students were Kindergarten, Khaild Thomas; First grade, Adasiha Taylor; Second grade, Franeska Payton; Third grade, Kelsey Bryan.

Committee members: Eudora Allen, Janice Bryant, Annie Chappell, Juanita Denson, Virginia Edwards, Wanda Hopkins, Essie Johnson,

Alexia Luten, Michelle Mincey-Gwyn, Freddie Pippen, Danette Boston, Lakechia Bryant, Albertha Collier, Patricia Devoe, Misty Dawn Ellison, Sylathea Hutchins, Margaret Johnson, Anne Mahone, LaShawna Mullgrav, Emma J. Preer, Ethel G. Bradshaw, Cora Carter, Jessie C. DeLoach, Joyce Dingle, Henrietta Gray, Maxine Jackson, Charlene Jones, Renae McCullough, Princetta Quarterman-Bacon, and Ivy Richardson.

Platform IV- Undergraduates Platform

Alpha Kappa Alpha Sorority, Inc. assigned this Platform to undergraduate chapters not graduate chapters.

Platform V- Health Resource Management and Economics

Debbie Hagins and LaTanya Thompson, Chairmen of committee that presented
Emotional Health Issues and AKA-nomics announcements. Issues and announcements were presented at each chapter meeting. GSO members evaluated each Emotional Health Issue presentation in 2007 and 2008.

Relay for Life

Relay for Life, 2007, was chaired by Patricia Mincey and Lorna Jackson. In support of the American Cancer Society, the chapter was divided into teams. Each Team captain was asked to be responsible for $1,000 to reach a goal of $10,000. The event was May 11 - May 12 at Benedictine Military Academy. Team Captains were Emma Conyers/ Alvernia Wilson-Jackson, Clemontine Washington, Debbie Hagins, Lorna Jackson, Patricia Clark, Michelle Mincey-Lee(Gwyn)/Patricia Mincey, Connie Cooper, Melinda Pippen-Miller, Jackie Gilbert-Grant, and the undergraduate chapters. Thanks were extended to members, Irene Davis, Paprice Simmons, Lawanda Tillman, and Shakela Holmes for coordinating the decorations and food. The amount donated to the American Cancer Society was $4,840.

The American Cancer Society's Relay-for-life, 2008, Exceptional Service Project's goal for GSO was $10,000. Each team was asked to raise a minimum of $1,000. Team captains: Alvernia Jackson (Emma Conyers), Audrey Singleton, LaTanya Thompson, Kimberly Chappell Stevens, Michelle Mincey-Gwyn, Clemontine Washington. Members labored with love to put up tent and decorations, to haul food and drink through the hustle and bustle of crowds, to walk the tracks, and to donate funds. This service, a public awareness event, demonstrated love for cancer survivors and victims, family and friends, and to provide hope for a cure. GSO contributed $3,520.

In March 2008 in recognition of National Nutrition Month, Alvernia Wilson-Jackson, a Dietician for the Savannah Chatham Public Schools, set up a very informative display on nutrition. Topics displayed were salt, sugar, and fats in food and good nutrition. Wilson-Jackson was on hand to answer questions. Members took advantage of the opportunity by reading information on improving nutritional habits.

Enthusiastically Shedding Pounds (ESP)

The *Centennial*, June 14, 2008, reported that the Chairmen of Platform V, Hagins and Thompson, gave a summary of the Enthusiastically Shedding Pounds, Million Pound Challenges, log of exercise time and weight loss, 2007-08, GSO AKA Centennial Walk and Weight Loss. Eleven members submitted exercise logs: Emma Conyers, Charlene Jones, Elza Givens, Patricia Clark, Freddie Pippen, Melinda Pippen-Miller, Virginia Parham, Kim Chappell-Stevens, Debbie Hagins, Tara Scott-Brown, and Johnny Gillans. KUDOS to Givens with 1200 miles!!! The walks included the Centennial Walk 2008, the Dorchester Run 2008, Relay for Life 2008, and the Heart Walk 2007 for a grand total of 2,091.5 miles walked by GSO members. Seven members submitted weight loss of 76 pounds, total. There were many members who exercised and walked but did not submit any documentation. For members who submitted only time, minutes exercises were converted into miles based upon the formula of 20 minutes/mile.[481]

At the October 2008 chapter meeting, Platform V Committee members directed the observance of Breast Cancer Awareness Month.

Four breast cancer survivors within the sisterhood were recognized with gift bags, and applaused for their courage and strength: Eudora Allen, Janie B. Bruen, and Lawanda Tillman, Mildred Mobley, in absentia.

2008 Women Health Symposium

The 2008 Savannah Women's Health Symposium, October 18, 2008, was recognized as the day for Remembering Our [Women] Health, 7:00 a.m.—5:00 p.m. In the words of Lynda M. Dorman, Executive Director and Vice President of BET Foundation, "This special day is our sincere way to show African-American women in Savannah and surrounding metropolitan area that health is top priority." Prior to the Symposium, the Basileus and Program Chairman attended several planning sessions. The Symposium was held at Savannah State University, and the gym was packed with over 700 women in attendance. The Symposium was organized by the BET Foundation, and title sponsors were General Mills, Honey Nut Cheerios, and St. Joseph's/Candler Hospitals. Local sponsor recognitions were Savannah State University, Nancy N. and J. C. Lewis Cancer Research Center, go for BP GOAL, Coca Cola, WellCare of Georgia, The Links Incorporated, SBG (Savannah Business Group), Gamma Sigma Omega Chapter of Alpha Kappa Alpha Sorority, Inc., Delta Sigma Theta Sorority, Inc., Savannah Alumnae Chapter.

Debbie P. Hagins, M.D., Chronic Disease Expert, Co-Chairman of Platform V, was a panelist. Dr. Hagins is the Clinical Director of the largest HIV services provider in the coastal region. Workshop topics were Obesity and Cardiovascular Diseases, Reproductive Health, Mental Health and Eating Disorders, Blood Pressure and Hypertension, Fitness, Nutrition and Digestive Health Care, Women & Clinical Trials and Diabetes, Health Aging and Fitness, Living With a Chronic Disease (HIV/AIDS, Lupus, Diabetes), Interactive Approaches to Health, and Health and Disability. At the end of the Symposium, 4:00 p.m.—5:00 p.m., the Grammy Nominated songstress, Kelly Price, performed.

GSO members volunteered in several capacities: Registration Table, Health Fair, Exercise, Breakfast, Lunch, Workshop, Collecting Evaluations, Directing participants to building and meeting rooms, and in other needed ways. Members in attendance: Debbie Hagins, LaTanya T. Stringer, Sylvia P. Weston, Emma Conyers, Tamika Burnett, Renee Grant, Charlene Jones, Emily Crawford Sanders, Vanessa Kaigler, LaShawna Mullgrav, Geraldine Mack, Hope Johnson, Lawanda Tillman, LaWanda Ransom, Gwendolyn H. Johnson, Alvernia W. Jackson, Lydia Young, Lavinea Kennedy, Alucia Walton, Bonny LaPread, Ethel Hunter, and Annie Mahone.[482] The Chapter was one of the sponsors of the Savannah Women's Health Symposium with a $1.500 donation.

Other Health Resource Management and Economics activities included: (1) The chapter's donation of $200 in 2007 to the American Diabetes Association; (2) A presentation on Foot Wear, in anticipation of the walking exercises for The Centennial Celebration, was done by Mr. Tony Cooper, owner of The Athlete's Foot. He gave a demonstration and discussion on proper shoe fitting for athletic/walking shoes. Mr. Cooper used a model of a foot to demonstrate the different "healthy foot" services that includes FitPrint Analysis.

Committee members: Lucille Brown, Connie Cooper, Elza Givens, Johnnie Holmes, Brenda Jenkins, Carmelita Maynard, Mildred Mobley, Cathy Reynolds, Audrey Singleton, Leona H. Williams, Doris Davida Wood, Patricia Clark, Irene Davis, Lakyah Hatcher, Shakela Holmes, Hope Johnson, Melinda Pippen-Miller, Eleanor Murdock, Sharon Savage Watson, Lawanda Tillman, Alvernia Wilson-Jackson, LaQuisha Coakley, Jackie Gilbert-Grant, Martha Hicks, Lorna Jackson, Linda Jordan, Patricia Mincey, LaVertta Scott-Perry, April Scott, Emily P. Williams, and Tuwanna Wilson.

Other Service Projects

1. Jr. Debuntantes/Precious Gems and Fundraising

The 2006-2007 Junior Debutante Mentoring Program/Precious Gems: Whitney C. Campbell, Carrie Elizabeth Coppock, Davida B. Daniels, Cianna Latrelle Hill, Erica E. Humes, Shaniqua Maxwell, Jelanni A. Jones, Alonda J. Miller, Roneishia Shateama Jones; Chairman, Charlene Jones. Contestant Winners: Miss Precious Gem 2007, Cianna Latrelle Hill; Carrie Elizabeth Coppock, Runner Up.

The Chairman for the Mentoring Program, 2007-2008 was Charlene Jones. The Junior Debutante Mentoring Program/Precious Gems were Courtney S.N. Brown, Ambreana D. Clark, JaBria A. Cooper, Jasmine L. Ellison, Gabrielle J. Gardner, Ashley N. Haley, Raven S. Hall, DaNajah M. Johnson, Shantel M. Johnson, Emani J. Mitchell, Akua A. Agyemang, Dana B. Outing, TaDazsia A. Patterson-Brown, Destiney C. Roberts, Kaleeuh Steele, and Charvian K. Williams.

Contestant Winners: Miss Precious Gem 2008, Gabrielle Gardner; 1st Runner Up, Shantel Johnson; 2nd Runner Up, TaDazsia Patterson-Brown; 3rd Runner Up, Da'Najah Johnson.

The 2008-2009 Junior Debutante Mentoring Program/Precious Gems: Nine young ladies present at Orientation, October 5, 2008, at Con-Ed Family Resource Center, Chairman, Gwendolyn Johnson.

The Mentoring Program included the following activities: Black Heritage Tour, 2007; Mother/Daughter Luncheon at Desoto Hilton, 2007; Precious Gems and parents met sorority members after April Chapter meeting, 2007; Junior Debutante Cotillion, June 2, 2007; Nutcracker Ballet Performance, Civic Center, November 24, 2007; Sounds of Winter, musical, Savannah Arts Academy, December 13, 2007; Precious Gems and parents met sorority members after November Chapter, meeting 2007; *Annie,* Broadway play, January 17, 2008, Johnny Mercer Theater; thirteen Precious Gems riding on float in MLK Parade. Food and nutrition workshop, City Hall: Precious Gems sat in chairs of Mayor and City Councilmen followed by etiquette lesson on dining procedures and later dinner, January 25, 2008; February 4, 2008, attendance at the Rebecca Padgett School of Dance, salute to Black History through music and dance; February 9, 2008, the Black Heritage Tour; Financial workshop, February 16, 2008, Con-Ed Resource Center; Career Fair, after March Chapter meeting; Parents met sorority members after the April Chapter meeting 2008; Mother/Daughter Luncheon, Geneva's Restaurant, May 31, 2008.

Contributing members directly involved in the success of the Mentoring Program: Alvernia Jackson; Gloria Thompson-Johnson, Janie B. Bruen, Patricia Clark, Elza Givens, Eleanor Murdock, Albertha Collier, Emma Conyers, Charlene Jones, Carolyn Bell, Wanda Williams, Carliss

Bates, Rochelle Small-Toney, Hope Johnson, Dorothy Wilson, Ethel Hunter, Brenda Jenkins, Eleanor Ginn, Queen Barnes, Serdelia Singleton, Sheila Hutcherson, S. Renee' Grant, Lydia Young, Vanessa Kaigler, Cora Carter, Gwendolyn Johnson, LaWanda Ransom, Ivanette Richardson, Johnye Gillans, Glenda James, Lolita Hickman, and Annette Mitchell.

2. 100 Celebrity Men Who Cook

The local fundraiser for the United Negro College Fund was the 100 Celebrity Men Who Cook, Carolyn Bell, Chairman. The event was a partnership with the local chapters of Alpha Kappa Alpha, Delta Sigma Theta, Sigma Gamma Rho, and Zeta Phi Beta sororities. GSO members participated on different committees to make this fundraiser a community success. Gamma Sigma Omega Chapter contributed $1000 and more.

3. Fifth Sunday Worship Services

April 29, 2007, with the Pan Hellenic Council, First Union Missionary Baptist Church, Rev. Matthew Southall Brown, Jr., Pastor, on behalf of the West Broad Street YMCA. Gamma Sigma Omega's donation was $359; September 30, 2007, St. Matthew's Episcopal Church, Rev. Cheryl Parris, Rector, approximately $200 donated; St. Philip A.M. E. Church, Rev. John Foster, Pastor, donation $245; November 30, 2008, Connor's Temple Baptist Church, Rev. Bennie R. Mitchell, Jr., Pastor, approximately $300 donated.

4. Book Discussions

GSO discussed the following books: *The Audacity of Hope*, by Barack Obama, February 24, 2008, public library, Bull Street, discussion leader, Marjory Varnedoe; Citywide Book Discussion, *Their Eyes Were Watching God*, by Zora Neale Hurston, sponsored by the Public Library and Zeta Phi Beta local chapter on behalf of Daffin Park's Centennial Celebration; Book review, *Developing the Leader Within You*, November 19, 2008, Con-Ed Family Resource Center, Coordinator, Carolyn Bell.

5. Other: 2007 Services

Black Heritage Festival, jewelry making, $500 donation; Beta Phi Lambda Chapter of Alpha Phi Alpha Fraternity, Inc., MEGAGENESIS, registration; Savannah Music Festival, featuring trumpeter, Wynton Marsalis, usher, $500 donation; Butler Elementary School Chorus, $450 donation; Crowns on Parade, fundraiser, Savannah State University, $100 donation; West Broad Street YMCA, fundraiser, Comedy Show, $412 donation; Con-Ed Resource Center, fundraiser, $300 donation; Alpha Phi Alpha and Omega Psi Phi, local chapters, Blood Drive, tied in number of donors, Gamma Sigma Omega and the Deltas.

6. Other 2008 Services

Black Heritage Festival; Blood Drive sponsored by Alpha Kappa Alpha, Zeta Phi Beta, Alpha Phi Alpha, Omega Psi Phi, Phi Beta Sigma at the American Red Cross Donor Center, February 19-21 on behalf of fire victims from the Savannah Sugar Refinery Explosion; Diabetes University, January 19, 2008; Kappa Omega Foundation: donated $100; Homage to Founders at Regional Director's request: March 15 chapter prayed for the sisterhood; Black Business Awareness, April 15, the purchase of gas from black owned stations: Jackson's Brothers and Sheppard's Po Boy; the purchase of gas from Jackson's Brothers and Sheppard's Po Boy, June 1 – 15. Letter sent to the US House of Representatives supporting a bill to make July "Bebe Moore Campbell National Minority Mental Health Month"; Prayer for the renewed health of Regional Director, Ella Springs Jones, after heart complications.

Founders' Day /Centennial Celebration, Every Soror Participates (ESP)

National Founders' Day

Washington, D. C., January 12-15, 2008, GSO mailed twenty books to Alpha Chapter to distribute to an elementary school in

Washington, D. C. Three GSO members attended the 100th Founders' Day celebration, January 12-15, 2008, on the campus of Howard University in Washington, D. C. They were Emma Conyers, Clemontine Washington, and Patricia Clark. It was a nostalgic event for Alpha Kappa Alpha women.

Tri-Chapter Founders' Day

Tri Chapters observed Founders' Day (closed) on January 26, 2008, 11:00 a.m., Club Stewart, Fort Stewart, GA. Chapters participating were Gamma Sigma Omega, Nu Delta Omega, Nu Rho Omega, and Sigma Tau. Gamma Sigma Omega Chorus sang.

Founders' Day with the Supreme Basileus

Gamma Sigma Omega Chapter members spent an evening of celebrating the birthday of Alpha Kappa Alpha Sorority with neighboring chapters: Berkeley, Charleston, and Dorchester and with the Centennial Supreme Basileus, Barbara A. McKinzie, along with the South Atlantic Centennial Regional Director, Ella Springs Jones, Sunday, February 10, 2008, 4:00 p.m. at the Morris Street Baptist Church in Charleston, SC. GSO members in attendance were Eudora Allen, Albertha E. Boston, Mary Coleman, Albertha Collier, Emma Conyers, Irene Davis, Jessie DeLoach, Joyce Dingle, Pendar Franklin, Johnye Gillans, Maxine Jackson, Glenda James, Hope Johnson, Charlene Jones, Annie Mahone, Patricia Mincey, Carolyn Russell, Dorothy D. Speed, Maggie Walker-Zeigler, Clemontine F. Washington, Leona Henley Williams, Dorothy B. Wilson, and Dorothy Worthy.

International Appeal

Alpha Kappa Alpha Sorority, Inc. made an international appeal to AKAs to participate in the Centennial Celebration Appeal: **ESP** (Every Soror Participates), Graduate Sorors (active, inactive, general, life)--$190 and Graduate Chapters--$1,908. Contributions were sent to the

Corporate Office specified as anniversary gift. Gifts were sent between January 1, 2007 – January 15, 2008. All AKAs who participated in this project received special recognition. Gamma Sigma Omega donated the gift of $1,908, and the following GSO members made individual gift donations: Albertha E. Boston, Emma Jean Conyers, Jessie Collier DeLoach, Joyce Griffin Dingle, Pendar S. Franklin, Carolyn H. Russell, and Clemontine F. Washington.[483]

February 22-25, 2007, 54th South Atlantic Regional Conference, Atlanta, GA

The Centennial reports that with a membership of 140 members, 57 members attended the Conference. It was an "Oscar" winning evening for the Savannah chapter. "Gamma Sigma Omega" resonated in the conference room of the Marriott Hotel as the Chapter received five awards: the A Cathryn Johnson Alumna Reading Award, 2nd Place (The Ivy Reading AKAdemy, Keep Reading Alive, Top Reader), Ivy Richardson, Chairman, 2006; Ella Springs Jones AKA Connection Innovative Award, 3rd Place (Martin Luther King Day of Service, voter registration, AKA Day at the Capitol), Melinda Pippen Miller, Chairman, 2006; Chapter Achievement, 3rd Place (Education, the Black Family, Health, Economics, the Arts), Emma J. Conyers, Chairman, 2006; the Odessa S. Nelson Graduate Advisor Award, 2nd Place (Gamma Upsilon, Savannah State University), Dr. Clemontine F. Washington, Advisor, 2006; and the Homie Regulus Basileus Award, 3rd Place (President Award), Patricia Clark, 2006. "Congratulations! Impressive!" AKAs commented throughout the assembly.

Under the chapter's supervision, Gamma Upsilon at Savannah State University and Sigma Tau at Armstrong Atlantic State University were also a part of the "Oscars." These young college women made Savannah proud. Gamma Upsilon received the following awards: 1st Place, the Margaret B. Roach Health Award; 2nd Place, Chapter Achievement Award; and 2nd Place, the Georgia Schank Innovative Award. Sigma Tau, Audrey Singleton, Advisor, 2006, received the following awards: 3rd Place, Chapter Program Exhibit; and 3rd Place, Attendance Award.

GSO members in attendance at 54th Regional Conference: Eudora Allen, Carolyn Bell, Albertha E. Boston, Patrice Boston, Harriette Johnson, Tara Scott Brown, Janie Bruen, Dawlyn Myles-Buckles, Patricia Clark, Mary Coleman, Albertha Collier, Emma Jean Conyers, Connie Cooper, Irene Davis, Juanita Denson, Patricia DeVoe, Nikki Dorsey, Pendar Franklin, Johnye Gillans, Elza Givens, Henrietta Gray, Zena McClain, Terri Hurst, Sheila Hutcherson, Alvernia W. Jackson, Annie Jackson, Glenda James, Brenda Jenkins, Hope Johnson, Charlene Jones, Yolanda Jones, Linda Wright Jordan, Vanessa Kaigler, Kimberly Knowles, Michelle Mincey Lee Gwyn, Nicole Maske, Carmelita Maynard, Patricia Mincey, Annette Mitchell, LaShawna Mullgrav, Eleanor Murdock, Virginia Parham, Emma Preer, Ivanette Richardson, Ivy Richardson, Carolyn Russell, April Scott, Paprice Simmons, Audrey Singleton, Dorothy Speed, Sharon Stallings, Kimberly Chappell Stevens, LaTanya Thompson, Maggie Walker-Zeigler, Maureen Maxwell Walker, Clemontine F. Washington, Ericka Coleman Washington, Natosha Watson, Sylvia Perry-Weston, Nicole Williams, Dorothy B. Wilson, Sadie Wright.

Congratulations were also extended to Patricia Mincey, Annie Jackson, Carolyn Bell, and Albertha Collier. Mincey submitted a scrapbook for the Emory O. Jackson Journalism Award, Annie Jackson submitted a scrapbook for the Freddie L. Groomes-McLendon Caring Award, Carolyn Bell submitted a scrapbook for the Deloris H. Oliver Service To Mankind Award, and Albertha Collier entered the Individual Arts and Crafts exhibit. They all had been previous winners at conferences.

Silver Star honors (twenty-five years in Alpha Kappa Alpha) at the Conference was bestowed upon Vanessa Miller Kaigler.[484]

April 23-25, 2008, 55th South Atlantic Regional Conference, Tampa, FL

"In praise of our founders, we celebrate 100 Years of Service, 1908-2008," expressed by our South Atlantic Regional Director, Ella Springs Jones. Thirty-two members of Gamma Sigma Omega Chapter attended the 55th South Atlantic Regional Conference, April 23-27, 2008, in

Tampa, Florida. The theme for the conference was E.S.P.[2] Empowering Sorors: Our Potential…Our Passion. AKAs geared up to learn strategic methods of service, to network, and to learn ways for effective chapter operations. Nearly 2,500 AKAs were in attendance.

Gamma Sigma Omega received the following recognition at the 55th South Atlantic Regional Conference: Membership Committee, Vanessa Kaigler, Chairman, retention of members, 4 Hearts, (recognition at Boule); Technology Committee, Ivanette Richardson and Sharon Stallings, Chairmen, Website compliance; Connection Committee, Ivy Richardson, Chairman and Standards Committee, Virginia Parham, Chairman, annual reports; and the EAF 2008 Silver Level Award, Alvernia Jackson, Chairman, (money over and above membership dues based on chapter size). Congratulations were extended to Emma Preer Golden Star; Zena McClain and Emma Conyers, Leadership recognition. Platform II, Economic Keys to Success, in the Scrapbook Award competition received first place and Platform V -- Health, received honorable recognition by Regional Program. Congratulations were extended to Clemontine F. Washington, Program Chairman; Mary Coleman and Sonia Renee W. Grant, Platform II Chairmen; and Debbie Hagins and LaTanya Thompson Stringer, Platform V, Chairmen.

Delegates were Emma Conyers, Kimberly Chappell Stevens, Audrey Singleton, Henrietta Gray, Hope Johnson, and LaVertta Scott-Perry. The unfunded delegates in attendance were Zena McClain, Patricia Clark, Dorothy B. Wilson, Clemontine F. Washington, and Johnye Gillans. The unfunded alternate delegates in attendance were Carolyn Bell and Annie Jackson.

Regional Committee members were Connection, Clemontine F. Washington; Constitution, Dorothy B. Wilson; Program, Patricia Clark; South Atlantic Regional Leadership Team, Hospitality, Annie Jackson.

The following members served as Conveners, Recorders, Monitors for workshops. Conveners: Carolyn Bell and Marjory Varnedoe; Recorders: Patricia Clark, Emma J. Conyers, and Sharon Stallings; Monitor: Virginia M. Parham.

GSO members who attended the Regional Conference were Eudora Allen, Carol Bell, Kimberly Chappell Stevens, Patricia Clark, Albertha

Collier, Emma Conyers, Irene Davis, Jessie Deloach, Juanita Denson, Nikki Dorsey, Johnye Gillans, Henrietta Gray, Alvernia Jackson, Annie Jackson, Hope Johnson, Annie Mahone, Zena McClain, Michelle Mincey Gwyn, Eleanor Murdock, Virginia Parham, Melinda Pippen-Miller, Emma Preer, Tara Scott-Brown, LaVertta Scott-Perry, Audrey B. Singleton, Dorothy Speed, Sharon Stallings, Marjory Varnedoe, Clemontine F. Washington, Nicole Williams, Dorothy B. Wilson, Dorothy Worthy.

At the Ivy Beyond the Wall Service, Shirley McGee Brown was recognized as an Ivy Beyond the Wall.[485]

GSO at Centennial Boule 2008

Attendance: Eudora Allen, Queen Barnes, Tarangula Barnes-Scott, Carol Bell, Albertha E. Boston, Janie B. Bruen, Lakechia Bryant, Thelma T. Bryant, Annie Chappell, Kimberly Chappell-Stevens, Patricia J. Clark, Mary Coleman, Albertha Collier, Emma Conyers, Connie Cooper, Irene Davis, Jessie C. DeLoach, Patricia Devoe, Joyce Dingle, Pendar Franklin, Jane Gates, Johnye Gillans, Eleanor Ginn, Elza Givens, Sonia Renee W. Grant, Johnnie Holmes, Ethel Hunter, Annie Jackson, Maxine Jackson, Brenda Jenkins, Sharonda Johnson, Harriette Johnson-Brinson, Charlene Jones, Vanessa Kaigler, Lavinea Kennedy, Bonnie LaPread, Nicole Maske, Carmelita Maynard, Patricia Mincey, LaShawna Mullgrav, Virginia Parham, Margaret A. R. Pearson, Sylvia Perry, Shawnta C. Pitts, Emma Preer, Emily Preer-Williams, Kathy Reynolds, Carolyn Russell, Tara Scott-Brown, LaVertta Scott-Perry, Paprice Simmons, Audrey B. Singleton, Dorothy D. Speed, Sharon Stallings, LaTanya Thompson, Lawanda Tillman, Undine Truedell-Williams, Marjory Varnedoe, Maggie Walker-Zeigler, Clemontine Washington, Natosha Watson, Yvette Wells, Leona B. Henley Williams, Lois Vedelle Williams, Nicole M. Williams, Dorothy B. Wilson, Alvernia Wilson-Jackson, Doris Davida Wood, and Lydia Young.

Funded Delegates: Emma Conyers, Audrey Singleton, Kimberly Chappell-Stevens, Emma Preer, and Tarangula Barnes-Scott. Non

Funded Delegates: Charlene Jones, Johnye Gillans, Marjory Varnedoe, Patricia Clark, Virginia Parham, Elza Givens, and Lakechia Bryant. Alternate Delegates: Clemontine F. Washington and Jessie C. DeLoach.

4 Star Recognition, 2nd highest recognition: Membership Committee, Vanessa Kaigler, Chairman (10% reactivation and 85% retention of members).

GSO members who served at Boule: Centennial Boule Choir, Emma Jean Conyers;

Committee Recognition as printed in the Centennial Boule Agenda: Diamond and Golden Soror Monitors-- Eudora Allen, Jessie C. DeLoach, Dorothy Speed, Dorothy Wilson; Resolution Committee-- Emma Jean Conyers; Tellers-- Albertha E. Boston, Kimberly Chappell Stevens; Philacters-- Charlene Jones; Hostesses South Atlantic Centennial Regional Luncheon: Eudora Allen, Queen Barnes, Lakechia Bryant, Jessie C. DeLoach, Johnye Gillans, Ethel Hunter, Annie Jackson, Nicole Maske, Tarangula B. Scott, and Kimberly Chappell-Stevens.

The following GSO members appeared in the news: *The Washington Post:* Unity March, Carolyn Bell made the following comments, reported by Sindya N. Bhanoo and Keith L. Alexander in the article "Sorority Leads March for Change," Friday, July 18, 2008: "Our work is not in a vacuum, but felt by the world and heard in the halls of Congress." She said that she was inspired to continue her pledge of service through her sorority when she returns home. CNN Website: CNN's Jill Dougherty reports, "Sisterhood Turns 100," July 20, 2008, The following GSO members were featured Harriett Brinson, Patricia DeVoe, Johnnie Holmes and Margaret A. Pearson.

We Got There! Sixty-nine GSO members strong, (167 on roster)! GSO Connection transported twenty-two members, Dorothy B. Wilson, Chairman, others by air, train, car, or rail, "We Got There!"

South Africa Pilgrimage, Post Boule Trip: Emma Jean Conyers

Conyers writes in *The Savannah Tribune* that words could not express the experiences learned and the acquired deeper faith in Christ as a result of her trip to Africa. Pertinent to Alpha Kappa Alpha were ten AKA schools in South Africa began under the leadership of former Supreme Basileus, Norma S. White. At dinner, in Cape Town, the sorority members were informed by the Principal the conditions of their schools. His statement to Alpha Kappa Alpha was "the hands that have given the poor, blessings upon you." However, he described the very, very poor conditions of the schools, yet in comparison to other schools in the rural areas, he said, AKA schools were the best. It was appalling to hear in some rural areas that there were no buildings for children. They held school outside in the dirt. Unfortunately, the members did not have the opportunity to visit the schools.

Visiting a preschool in Cape Town, AKAs saw children's faces, eyes, and smiles that looked like ordinary African American children. However, they were crowded in very small rooms with teachers whose appearances were not representative of the professional ones in the United States. Many sorority members' hearts went out to these children and teachers, so they gave money freely to the teachers.

Conyers reflects, "Wouldn't it be great if a team of retired professionals and others volunteered to teach during the summer months in some rural area."[486]

Undergraduates/Joint Chapter Meetings

April 10, 2007, Gamma Sigma Omega and Sigma Tau held a Joint Meeting. At the time, Gamma Upsilon was being represented by Graduate Advisor, Kimberly Chappell Stevens, who registered to attend the Undergraduate Luncheon at the Regional Conference, and stated in her report, February 1, 2007, that she will attend meetings for undergraduates. She indicated in the January 4, 2007 minutes that there were no active members on Savannah State University's campus and that Membership Intake Process Date was set tentatively for March 30, 2007.

Joint Membership Intake Process

The first Joint Membership Intake Process inducted 82 candidates into Alpha Kappa Alpha Sorority, Inc., April 22, 2007. Seventy three of the candidates were from Gamma Upsilon Chapter, Savannah State University, and nine of the candidates were from Sigma Tau Chapter, Armstrong Atlantic State University, both chapters supervised by Gamma Sigma Omega Chapter. Thanks to Graduate Advisors: Savannah State University, Kimberly Chappell- Stevens; Armstrong Atlantic State University, Audrey B. Singleton, and Graduate Council: Chappell-Stevens and Singleton, Co–Chairmen; Carolyn Bell, Albertha E. Boston, Patricia Clark, Emma Conyers, Connie Cooper, Annie C. Jackson, Charlene Jones, Zena McClain, Virginia Parham, April Scott, Sharon Stallings (Assistant Graduate Advisor, AASU), Clemontine F. Washington, Ericka Coleman Washington (Assistant Graduate Advisors, SSU), Nicole Williams, workshop presenters, and helpers, especially, Deana Cross, an Alpha Kappa Alpha member and the on-campus advisor at Armstrong. A magical celebration luncheon was held at the historic downtown Desoto Hilton Hotel with over 260 guests.

Undergraduate Roundup

Undergraduate members of Alpha Kappa Alpha Sorority are those who are pursuing a course of study leading to a baccalaureate (bachelor's) degree in an accredited two, three or four-year senior college or university. The Undergraduate Roundup is a conference of these members from their respective institutions. Each undergraduate chapter is sponsored by a graduate chapter. The Roundup in the South Atlantic Region includes chapters in Georgia, South Carolina, and Florida.

The Basileus wrote in newsletter "Ensuring Sorority Prominence," Gamma Upsilon and Sigma Tau are precious to Gamma Sigma Omega Chapter. The Chapter is committed to providing opportunities for these undergraduates to continue the legacy of the Founders. Saturday, September 15, 2007, the wish of the Basileus and Graduate Advisors, Kimberly Chappell-Stevens and Audrey B. Singleton, respectively, was to provide a safe arrival to the Undergraduate Roundup in Atlanta and a safe return to Savannah. Therefore, a bus was chartered for this purpose and a total of 53 undergrads from Gamma Upsilon and 10 from Sigma Tau attended the Roundup. With God's help the mission was accomplished.

The 2007 Undergraduate Roundup and Leadership Retreat was held at Georgia State University. The Centennial Regional Director, Ella Springs Jones, and the Centennial Supreme Basileus, Barbara A. McKinzie, were present for guidance and to ensure perpetuity the Alpha Kappa Alpha way. The undergraduates attended the following workshops: Constitution, Protocol, Rituals, and Standards.[487]

September 5-7, 2008, the Undergraduate Roundup was held at the Hyatt Regency Jacksonville, Florida. The following members were in attendance: Emma Conyers, Clemontine F. Washington, Kimberly Chappell Stevens, Patricia Clark, Audrey Singleton, and Zena McClain. The undergrads from Gamma Upsilon and Sigma Tau were in attendance. The Regional Director, Ella Springs Jones applauded Graduate Chapters for sponsoring undergraduate chapters.[488]

Gamma Sigma Omega and Sigma Tau

October 13, 2007 minutes report that Kimberly Chappell Stevens discussed the list of activities of Gamma Upsilon Chapter and that the chapter had the largest attendance at the Undergraduate Roundup. However, on October 6, 2007, a meeting was held with the undergraduates to inform them of alleged hazing. Therefore, the chapter was temporarily deactivated and an investigation was conducted by the Heritage Team.

A Joint Chapter meeting of Gamma Sigma Omega and Sigma Tau was held November 10, 2007, in Adams Hall on the historical campus of Savannah State University, founded in 1890. The young ladies of Sigma Tau explained their implementation of Platform IV. They served at Moses Jackson Center where they taught senior adults computer skills. They enthusiastically explained many of their service projects. Gamma Sigma Omega Chapter was impressed by their work.

April 6, 2008, Stevens, Graduate Advisor of Gamma Upsilon reported that The Heritage Team's investigation was completed and that Gamma Upsilon had been reactivated on campus. The Regional Director, Ella

Springs Jones, had given the chapter certain requirements to complete in order for the status to remain active. There were 31 financial members.

Sisterly Relations: Gamma Upsilon and Sigma Tau

In celebration of one year of sisterhood, April 22, 2008, at the Con-Ed Family Resource Center, members who were initiated in the last MIP, April 22, 2007, from Gamma Upsilon, Savannah State University and Sigma Tau, Armstrong Atlantic State University, gathered again in unity and love for Alpha Kappa Alpha. These young women warmed the hearts of the Graduate Advisors, Stevens, and Singleton, and Basileus Conyers. Also present was Assistant Graduate Advisor, Patricia Clark. It was the prayer of the Basileus that love will continue to abound between these two chapters.[489]

Joint Chapter Meeting

Joint Chapter Meeting was held October 4, 2008: Gamma Sigma Omega, Gamma Upsilon, and Sigma Tau, at EOA Building.

Cluster VI Conference, December 5-6, 2008, Swainsboro, GA; Rowena Loadholt, Cluster VI Coordinator

Attendance: Eudora Allen, Queen Barnes, Albertha E. Boston, Renee D. Buckles, Tamika Burnett, Annie Chappell, Kimberly Chappell-Stevens, Patricia J. Clark, Mary C. Coleman, Albertha Collier, Emma J. Conyers, Irene Davis, Jessie C. Deloach, Joyce G. Dingle, Emma J. Preer, Latondia Gadson, Johnye Gillans, Eleanor J. Ginn, Elza L. Givens, Sonia Renee Grant, Henrietta Gray, Ethel H. Hunter, Sheila B. Hutcherson, Annie C. Jackson, Lorna C. Jackson, Maxine Jackson, Sonya Jackson, Glenda James, Gwendolyn H. Johnson, Hope Johnson, Charlene E. Jones, Linda Jordan, Carolyn Mayes, Carmelita S. Maynard, Zena McClain, Michelle Mincey-Gwynn, Eleanor Murdock, Virginia Parham, Margaret A. R. Pearson, Sylvia Perry-Weston, Carolyn H. Russell, Taqwaa Saleem, Tarangula B. Scott, Tara Scott Brown,

Audrey B. Singleton, LaTanya Thompson Stringer, Marjory Varnedoe, Clemontine F. Washington, Ericka Washington, Lois Vedelle Williams, Dorothy B. Wilson, Lydia Young.[490]

EmmaLue Jordan Preer

Gamma Sigma Omega Chapter, Johnye Gillans and Melinda Pippen-Miller, Protocol Chairmen, spearheaded the program and reception to honor EmmaLue Jordan Preer with a public reception, A Celebration of 50 Years of Service, Sunday, August 24, 2008, 5:00 PM, at St. Benedict the Moor Catholic Church, Rev. Christian A. Alimaji, M.S.P., Pastor. The reception was well attended by her family, friends, and AKAs. The Supreme Basileus, Barbara A. McKinzie, honored Preer with a letter of recognition. Preer is a Life Member of Alpha Kappa Alpha Sorority and has served Gamma Sigma Omega Chapter as Basileus, Hodegos, Archives Chairman, and Member-at-Large. She has been continuously active since initiation.

The Centennial Supreme Basileus in Savannah

Anxious with over anticipation after hearing a rumor that the Centennial Supreme Basileus, McKinzie, was coming to town, yet with no confirmation from the International Office after repeated calls and emails, Conyers was eventually officially notified that indeed McKinzie would be in Savannah but as the guest of Top Ladies of Distinction, Inc. Conyers immediately contacted chapter members. Jessie C. DeLoach expressed the overall sentiment in an article that she wrote in the chapter's newsletter, September 8, 2007, "Basileus Visits Savannah." She wrote there was an aura of excitement and inspiration surrounding the presence of Dr. Barbara A. McKinzie, the International President of Alpha Kappa Alpha Sorority, who was in Savannah recently. Several members of Gamma Sigma Omega Chapter and Gamma Upsilon Chapter, Savannah State University, were present at the banquet honoring Dr. McKinzie by the Top Ladies of Distinction, Inc. Gamma Sigma Omega Chapter members, Emma Jean Conyers, President, presented to Dr. McKinzie: (1) The Medallion and Paper Weight from the Chatham County Commission, Pete Liakakis, Chairman; (2) The book, *The Black American Series, Savannah, Georgia* by Dr. Charles Elmore; (3) a beautiful corsage; (4) an embroidery of the Savannah Riverfront etched on a picture frame; and (5) other trinkets and gifts of love. The Undergraduate Chapter from Savannah State University, Gamma Upsilon, Katie Dixon, President, also showered her with gifts.

Although Dr. McKinzie's stay was short, it was a delightful experience for persons in Savannah to meet such an international officer, to chat with her, and to take pictures. It was a very memorable occasion. It was obvious that she did not want the AKAs to disrespect Top Ladies of Distinction, Inc. Quietly she came, and quietly she left.

Heritage Committee and Gamma Sigma Omega

Gamma Sigma Omega Chapter was evaluated by the Heritage Committee, June 1-3, 2007. The Evaluation Team was Gladys Brown Davis, Team Leader, Laurel Howell and Irene Jones, from the South Eastern Regional Heritage Committee of Alpha Kappa Alpha Sorority. They conducted the investigation and presented the preliminary on-site evaluation. The official findings of the chapter evaluation and any recommendation for corrective action were submitted to the Chapter, Regional Director and the Regional Representative to the International Standards Committee as part of the final report.

The preliminary On-Site Review covered the following three categories with two ratings, "meets requirements" or "not satisfactory/needs improvement": The chapter met requirements in Logistics (i.e. housing, transportation, meeting location, etc.) of the Chapter Visit; Records in order and Accessible; Sorority Documents in Files – International and Local.

Concerns and recommendations of the Heritage Committee: 1. When Gamma Sigma Omega has financial records audited, consider having the undergraduate chapters' financial records audited at the same time. 2. Implement "Leadership Modules". 3. Invite undergraduates to workshops sponsored by Gamma Sigma Omega. 4. Implement a continuous mentoring program: undergraduates, new sorors, reactivating sorors, transferring sorors. 5. Consider the bonding of Undergraduate Advisor and those in undergraduate chapter (Sigma Tau [small chapter]) who handle money. 6. Secure a copy of the bonding papers of Gamma Upsilon. 7. Improve Joint Meetings: one agenda, discuss common issues (sisterhood, finances, etc.). 8. Provide a chapter handbook to each soror: Basileus speech, history of sorority, history of chapter, chapter bylaws, directory, etc. 9. Finances: a. cash disbursement journal; b. computerized "quick book" (a kind of spread sheet); c. expenditures of officers should be indicated; d. external audit whenever the Tamiouchos changes. e. increase bonding insurance coverage. f. Pecunious Grammateus records information in a numerically numbered duplicate receipt book. g. Pecunious Grammateus maintains a cash receipt journal. h. Pecunious Grammateus maintains a transmittal of funds report given to Tamiouchos. i. Tamiouchos maintains a cash disbursement journal. j. Tamiouchos does not collect money; any bonded soror may collect money in the absence of the Pecunious Grammateus with the bonded soror issuing a temporary receipt. k. Put in writing in the chapter bylaws reference to cash disbursements and cash receipts. 10. Hold a transitional meeting of outgoing officers to turn over material to the incoming officers. 11. Establish a Basileus Council to support the Basileus, not to police the Basileus; this council serves at the wishes of the Basileus. 12. Graduate Advisors sign all undergraduate chapter checks. 13. At the end of the school year, the Graduate Advisor should secure all undergraduate records during the summer. 14. Anti-Grammateus records minutes at Executive Committee meetings. 15. M.A.R.T.H.A., Inc.: a. Put in the bylaws of M.A.R.T.H.A., Inc that an audit should be done when treasurer changes to a new one. b. Introduce M.A.R.T.H.A. to the public. c. All Gamma Sigma Omega Chapter members should be a member of M.A.R.T.H.A.; place such ruling in Gamma Sigma Omega's bylaws; the membership fee for M.A.R.T.H.A should be assessed in Gamma Sigma Omega Chapter dues. Think beyond the present to the future of having a sorority house (save money and rent out house).

Changes in Governance Documents

The Regional Parliamentarian, Carol Johnson Davis, reviewed Chapter's Bylaws dated September 2007. She made recommendations including creating a Policy and Procedure Manual. Several provisions that were in the Chapter Bylaws were recommended to be placed in the Policy and Procedure Manual. The Regional Director gave the chapter sixty days to bring Chapter Bylaws into compliance. The Bylaws Committee of Gamma Sigma Omega Chapter met to discuss her recommendations. After this meeting, the necessary changes were made, and the Bylaws were mailed to the Regional Director and to Davis on April 18, 2008, Zena McClain, Chairman of Bylaws Committee. A *Campaign Guidelines* document based on the *So You Want to Run for Office* was also established to make the election process as fair and transparent as possible, Carolyn Bell, Chairman of Campaign Guidelines.

Pan-Hellenic Council, Savannah Chapter

In 2007 Gamma Sigma Omega Chapter, with other Greek fraternities and sororities, planned a special event with the Greenbriar Children's Center to take 20 students to a Savannah State University football game. The Pan-Hellenic Council members brought toys to their Christmas party. These toys were given to hospitalized and underprivileged children. Alpha Kappa Alpha, Delta Sigma Theta, Zeta Phi Beta, and Sigma Gamma Rho Sororities collaboratively sponsored the 100 Celebrity Men Who Cook, raising over $30,000 for the United Negro College Fund. Thanks to the leadership of Carolyn Bell, Chairman, UNCF, and Tuwanna Wilson, Pan Hellenic Representative.[491]

God blessed May 26, 2008 for a beautiful fellowship among the Greek fraternities and sororities, their families, and friends. The weather was absolutely perfect. The picnic was held at Hunter Army Airfield's Lotts Island Recreational Facility. The food was absolutely sumptuous, including the macaroni dish, prepared and donated by GSO representative, Irene Davis. Alpha Kappa Alpha won the attendance award.

The 2008 Babes and Tots Contest was held Sunday, October 26, 2008, 5:00 p.m. at Butler Presbyterian Church, Rev. Desmond Walker, Pastor. Mrs. Patricia M. Henderson, member of Alpha Theta Zeta Chapter, Zeta Phi Beta Sorority, President. The Council had three contestants: Little Miss Mina Iona Smith, sponsored by Phi Beta Sigma Fraternity, Inc; Little Miss Gabrielle Naomi Trappio, sponsored by Zeta Phi Beta Sorority, Inc.; and Little Miss Nia Ayanna Brown, sponsored by Gamma Sigma Omega Chapter. Little Miss Nia Ayanna is the daughter of GSO member, Tara Scott Brown, and Mr. Jerome Brown and little sister to Taylor Imani Brown. The amount donated on behalf of the chapter was $2,200. Gamma Sigma Omega was one of the recipients for a Service Award. Irene Davis was the Pan-Hellenic Representative for chapter.[492]

Featured Honey Dos

There is so much work to be done in Alpha Kappa Alpha and spouses and significant others make some of the work easier. The following spouses were featured in chapter newsletter. Gamma Sigma Omega thanks these men and others for helping GSO women excel: Representative Lester G. Jackson, District 124, The Georgia General Assembly; Bernard Y. Conyers, Sr., Retired Director of Auxiliary Services, Savannah State University; Joseph N. Bell, Jr., Executive Director, Chatham Association of Educators; Richard Washington, Jr., Retired Teacher/Coach; Michael Kaigler, Director of Human Resources and Services for Chatham County Government.[493]

Ivies Beyond the Wall

There were three Ivies Beyond the Wall rituals performed: Sadie Williams, March 20, 2007; Mary McDew, March 22, 2007; and Shirley McGee Brown, January 17, 2008.

MARTHA, Inc.

The year 2007 was the second year of implementation of M.A.R.T.H.A. Conyers and Charlene Jones submitted to the United Way of the Coastal Empire an application for a grant to support the Mentoring Program. Their panel presentation was October 6, 2008; however, the Mentoring Program did not receive funding. Nevertheless, donations were received from J. C. Lewis, III and Chatham Steel.

To secure the Alpha Kappa Alpha way of implementing a chapter's foundation, several GSO members traveled to Atlanta to meet with chapters there that had foundations. In a forum August 11, 2007, members from Kappa Omega, Nu Lambda Omega, and Pi Alpha Omega met with Gamma Sigma Omega chapter members. GSO's members learned ways to implement their nonprofit, M.A.R.T.H.A., Inc. Gamma Sigma Omega members in attendance were Albertha E. Boston, Hope Johnson, Charlene Jones, Zena McClain, Virginia M. Parham, Yvette Wells, Lydia Young, and Emma Conyers.

Deborah Sims, Basileus of Kappa Omega, graciously welcomed GSO's members to their sorority house where the meeting was held. Elegant, comfortable, clean, spacious, describes the facility with plentiful parking spaces. Eloise Roberts from Nu Lambda Omega, Melanie Bales, Basileus, and Francine Greer from Pi Alpha Omega, and several other AKAs participated in the forum discussion.

Retiring Reception for Centennial Chapter Basileus

The Protocol Committee, Johnye Gillans and Melinda Pippen-Miller, Chairmen, planned and organized the reception for retiring Basileus. The event was held at the Con-Ed Family Resource Center, December 11, 2008, 7:00 p.m. Conyers ended her tenure with the following quote: "Finally, brethren, whatsoever things are true, whatsoever things are honest, whatsoever things are just, whatsoever things are pure, whatsoever things are lovely, whatsoever things are of good report; if there be any virtue, and if there be any praise, think on these things, Philippians 4:8."[494]

Dr. Clemontine F. Washington, 2009-2010

Preparing Sorors to Lead

Clemontine F. Washington demonstrated how to "Enthusiastically Serve while Preparing Sorors to Lead" ESP, which was the theme of her administration by her personal sharings with chapter members. Continuing the national focus of Barbara A. McKinzie, the Heart of ESP: An Extraordinary Service Program, Washington worked to its success by enforcing the four platforms.

To ensure that all officers and members were prepared to lead, the first chapter meeting of each year of her tenure was a joint Standards Retreat for the three chapters (Gamma Sigma Omega, Gamma Upsilon, and Sigma Tau) with all officers and committee chairmen participating. Certificates were presented to each member attending the entire meeting. The second joint chapter meeting was held in September of each year. Summer Conference reports were presented, the nomination process was reviewed, and year end reminders were emphasized. Most importantly, Washington made certain that joint chapter meetings were fun, fun, fun.[495]

Also, during the first chapter meeting of each year of her tenure, she promoted socialization among the three chapters by hosting an annual "Leadership Luncheon" at the end of the meeting.[496]

Providing an opportunity for all members to participate in the singing of the Sorority's Hymn and the reciting of the Pledge in the event members had to leave before adjournment, Washington initiated placing Hymn and Pledge at beginning of meeting as opposed to end of meeting.[497]

Washington supported sisterhood by recognizing members who rendered service to the chapter but may have never been recognized. Each Christmas, she presented members with a card and a gift. She assured attendance at conferences by sharing her delegate stipend with members. She acknowledged breast cancer survivors by recognizing them during the month of October with special words of inspirations and a personal gift, and she placed reports and other bits of information on chapter's website for members to retrieve information.[498]

The 64th Boule was held in St. Louis, Missouri, July 9-16, 2010 where Carolyn House Stewart was elected Supreme Basileus. She reaffirmed the Sorority's commitment to service:

> The 2010-2014 administration continues fulfilling the service imperative of our Founders. Committed leadership is necessary to address issues related to social justice, human rights, health, poverty, economic security, environmental sustainability and maintaining a viable sisterhood. "Global Leadership Through Timeless Service."
>
> In our second century of service, Alpha Kappa Alpha's Global Leadership Through Timeless Service Initiatives will help meet the needs of our communities. Members will continue to unleash our unlimited potential to significantly empower citizens and promote peace in the global community. Our 2010-2014 programs require Alpha Kappa Alpha to work "**SMART.**" Each initiative is **S**trategic, **M**easurable, **A**ttainable, **R**elevant and **T**ransferable for enhanced impact.[499]

After this Boule, Washington was challenged to integrate ESP programs with Global Leadership Through Timeless Service. She and Program Chairman, Zena McClain, welcomed the mission.

To ensure appropriate directions for undergraduate chapters, on September 12, 2009, the undergrads worked with their mentors and fellowshipped with chapter members.[500] Joint Chapter meetings were held January 9, 2010 and September 18, 2010. Annually, one young lady from each school receives a $1000 scholarship.

Founders' Day

Gamma Sigma Omega Chapter's Founders' Day Observance – Celebrating the One Hundredth and one year of Alpha Kappa Alpha Sorority was held March 1, 2009, at 4:00 p.m., at St. Matthew's Episcopal

Church. The theme was Alpha Kappa Alpha Sorority, Incorporated -
"Leading the Way Toward Economic Sustainable Prosperity." Henrietta
S. Gray, a member of the chapter was speaker. The following members
were chapter award recipients: Emma Conyers, Soror of the Year; Glenda
S. James, Countess Y. Cox Sisterhood Award; Tarangula Barnes Scott
and Kimberly Chappell-Stevens, Evanel Renfroe Terrell Scholarship
Award.[501]

Mr. Arnold Jackson, a community volunteer, received the Mozella
Gaither Collier Volunteer Award for outstanding service contribution
to Greenbriar Children's Center, Incorporated. A highlight of the
Founders' Day Observance was "A Tribute to Greenbriar Children's
Center, Incorporated. Basileus Washington, who was also serving as
President of the Board of Directors of Greenbriar, presented Certificates
of Appreciation to Board Members, the Director and Assistant Director
of Greenbriar. Connie Cooper and Glenda S. James served as Chairman
and Co-Chairman respectively of Founders' Day.[502]

The 2010 Founders' Day Observance, The Seventh Tri-Chapter
Founders' Day, was hosted by Gamma Sigma Omega Chapter,
including Gamma Upsilon and Sigma Tau chapters, more than
100 AKAs attended. Connie Cooper and Glenda P. James served as
Gamma Sigma Omega's Founders' Day Chairman and Co-chairman
respectively. The Observance was held Saturday, February 29, 2010,
at 11:00 a.m. at the Woodville-Tompkins Technical and Career
Center, in Savannah, Georgia. The theme, 102 Years of Service To
All Mankind-"Esteemed Past ~ Significant Present ~ Precious Future,"
captivated the chapter's presentations: "The Way We Were" (Gamma
Sigma Omega), "The Way We Are" (Nu Delta Omega), and "The Way
We Will Be" (Nu Rho Omega). Service and sisterhood initiatives were
highlighted in the presentations. Each chapter recognized individual
members with awards for service, Sisterhood, Scholarship, and Soror
of the Year. Gamma Sigma Omega Chapter award recipients were
Johnye P. Gillans, Basileus Award for Exemplary Service; Patricia
Clark, Basileus Award for Exemplary Support; Audrey Singleton,
Soror of the Year; Clemontine F. Washington, Countess Y. Cox
Sisterhood Award.[503]

Remembering GSO's Chartering

June 25, 2009, the 66th anniversary of the chapter's chartering was highlighted. Washington charged the membership with the task of planning an event for members. The celebration was held in the social hall of Central Baptist Church in Thunderbolt, Georgia. Members highlighted important aspects of each decade of the chapter's existence.[504]

Program Committees, Zena McClain, Chairman

AKA-nomics_ This national initiative was done monthly at chapter meetings. For example, Patricia Clark discussed "what entails a healthy credit and how one's credit can become healthy."[505] At the October chapter meeting, Glenda James discussed "How to Grocery Shop on a Budget."[506] Vanessa Kaigler did a presentation on preparing Thanksgiving Dinner under $60.[507] "How to Live Well With the Money You Have" was discussed by Denise Weems.[508]

Platform I_ Saturday, November 21, 2009, the chapted hosted "Taste of Soul." Over a hundred people from the community came to taste food cooked by some of Savannah's best women caterers and restaurant owners. GSO members wore AKA paraphernalia. The following caterers/restaurant owners participated: Cakes Couture, Eat Smart Deli, Gladis Catering, One Love Jamaican Restaurant, Savannah Pie Lady, the Last Biscuit, Waldburg's Catering, De'Bella's Catering & Event Planning, Geneva's Home Plate, Rosie Glo's Catering, Simply Delightful, The Milk and Honey House Catering Co., and Well Done. The vendors wore chef hats and aprons printed with "Taste of Soul." Visitors were treated to an array of foods: cakes, pies, breads, Jamaican food, turkey, roast beef and more. The Program Chairman expressed appreciation to Alvernia Wilson-Jackson, Annette Mitchell, Janie B. Bruen, Lydia Young, Patricia Clark, Latondia Gadson, Ericka Benjamin, Denise Weems, and Emily Crawford-Sanders.[509]

Platform II – Saturday, October 24, eight members of the ESP Kids Club toured Capitol City Bank. Sonya Miller, Customer Service Representative, served as tour guide. She discussed the banking process and answered questions before and after the tour. Mary Coleman, Sonia Renee Grant and Basileus Washington were chaperons.[510]

Mary Coleman presented a workshop for the ESP Kids Club, March 24, 2010. Members attending were Basileus Washington, Charlene Jones, and McClain.[511]

Denise Weems–White presented a workshop for twenty-eight high school seniors. The workshop was based on Platform II's Economic theme: "Informative Seminar Series." Her topic was "Can I Get A Loan? Making an Informed Decision." The following members were present to support her: Charlene Jones, Linda Jordan, Mary Coleman, Bettina Tate, and McClain.[512]

Platform III- The Tutorial sessions at Gadsden Elementary School continued. However, tutoring took place Mondays and Wednesdays, 4:00 p.m.-5:00 p.m. Volunteers for March were Queen Barnes, Ethel Hunter, Irene Davis, Deonne Stone, and Washington. The last week of tutorial for school year was April 20, 2009.[513]

In keeping with the mandate of International Program, the chapter adopted two families.[514]

A meeting was held March 2009 at the Clara Barton Library of the Unitarian Universalist Church of Savannah on plans to implement the First Responder Training.[515]

The first GSO First Responder Training for Black males was a partnership with Sankofa Male Chorale, Inc. The Chorale was comprised of approximately 30 at-risk males between the ages of 13-20 years of age.[516]

The first Responder Training for the young men of the Sankofa Male Chorale took place Saturday, November 7, 2009 at Memorial Medical Educational Building. The young men participated in a workshop which encompassed the following topics: understanding specific types of disasters, how to make a disaster plan, how to make a disaster kit, how to be informed, and how to apply training. This workshop was conducted in partnership with the Savannah Red Cross. Members attending were Emma J. Conyers, Charlene Jones, Latondia Gadson, Particia Clark, McClain and Washington.[517]

The chapter donated 85 pounds of can goods to the Second Harvest Food Bank, November 24, 2009.[518]

AKA-MLK Day of Service, Monday, January 18, 2010, nineteen graduate members, eleven undergraduate AKAs from Gamma Upsilon Chapter at Savannah State University and five undergraduate AKAs from Sigma Tau Chapter at Armstrong Atlantic State University volunteered their time to help renovate three homes in the Tremont Park Neighborhood. This joint community service in collaboration with the Economic Opportunity Authority made a difference in the community. AKAs painted the exterior of three homes and assisted with the removal of debris, and they did some landscaping. The three renovated homes belonged to low-income seniors. This project was part of an ongoing effort of EOA to help reduce blight in the community. The following members participated: Maxine Jackson, S.Renee Grant, Elza Givens, Ashle´ King, Erica Benjamin, Vanessa Kaigler, Lakyah Hatcher, Audrey Singleton, Tara Scott-Brown, Eleanor Murdock, Patricia Clark, Tammy Barnes Scott, Latondia Gadson, Dorothy Speed, Emma J. Preer, Annette Mitchell, Joyce Dingle, and McClain.[519]

Continuing the Support for Global Leadership Through Timeless Service, chapter members shared Christmas joy with three very needy families. Each family was headed by a single mother. A total of six children was assisted, 3 boys and 3 girls; 2 (4 year old males); 1 male (3 years old); 1 female (7 years old), 1 female (2 years old) and 1 female (1 year old). Members contributed wrapped gifts.[520]

Platform V – Chairmen: LaTanya Thompson-Stringer and LaTondia Gadson. To assure full participation from the chapter, Program Chairman, McClain, attended the Relay for Life Team Captains' meeting March 23, 2009. The Relay plans were for May 8-9, 2009. The chapter's goal was set at $3500.[521] Relay for Life in 2010 was May 14-15. June chapter minutes reported $1800 donated for the 2010 Relay.[522]

The Emotional Health Issue - How to Have a Healthy Emotional Relationship with Men, was discussed by Latondia Gadson.[523] At the October chapter meeting, Emma J. Conyers and other members gave a presentation on the H1N1 Virus.[524] March 13, 2010, Patricia Clark's presentation was Having Hope. Chapter minutes, April 10, 2010, reported that Latondia Gadson did a presentation on Chronic Fatigue Syndrome.

The "Go Healthy" Challenge between Gamma Sigma Omega Chapter of Alpha Kappa Alpha Sorority, Inc and Delta Sigma Theta Sorority, Inc., Savannah Chapter, began with a media event. Over thirty-five AKAs registered, weighted in and were measured. The event took place at the West Broad Street YMCA, May Street. The ladies had their "before" pictures taken and had their blood pressure checked. They were asked to exercise, eat healthy, and weigh in every Monday at the West Broad Street YMCA.[525] The challenge extended from June 1– August 8.[526] Carolyn Bell reported at the October chapter meeting that Latondia Gadson won the AKA challenge with the most weight lost.[527]

Saturday, November 14, 2009, after chapter meeting, the committee hosted a guest speaker, Ms. Roland Milton, who spoke on "Seasonal Depression." Members received a wealth of information on Seasonal Depression and how to recognize the warning signs.[528]

Jr. Debutantes/Precious Gems Mentoring Program, Structural Changes

In 2009, the Jr. Debutantes/Precious Gems Mentoring Program incurred changes in its structure and operation. M.A.R.T.H.A., Inc. became the fundraising arm for the Program, and Gamma Sigma Omega Chapter became the mentors for the Program. For example, Saturday, February 14, 2009, the Precious Gems assembled "Bags of Love" for Ronald McDonald House.[529] At the April 11, 2009 meeting, a Career Fair was held, coordinated by Ethel Hunter. Women from a variety of careers served as presenters at the Fair. The presenters engaged the Precious Gems in conversation relative to career interest and shared information about what educational paths to pursue based on that interest. This Fair allowed for a Precious Gem to invite a friend. This procedure for inviting others was a first for the Career Fair committee.[530]

The inaugural year for joint sponsorship of the AKA's Precious Gems 14th Annual Junior Debutante Cotillion, presented by Alpha Kappa Alpha Sorority, Inc., Gamma Sigma Omega Chapter and M.A.R.T.H.A., Inc., was June 6, 2009, 7:00 p.m. in the Savannah

Ballroom, King Frazier Student Center at Savannah State University, the oldest historically Black State institution in Georgia.[531]

Gwendolyn Harris Johnson served as chairman of the 2009 Mentoring Program. The mentored girls were Rhonda Bryant, Jana Carpenter, Iyana M. Crawford, DaNasia DeVore, Jaylah Diggs, Nekiria West and Raymonia Hall. Jana M. Carpenter, a 7th grade student at Oglethorpe Charter School, Savannah, Georgia, was crowned "Miss Precious Gem" June 6, 2009. The Cotillion's theme was "Cultured Pearls: Precious and Rare."[532]

The 2010 Jr. Debutante/Precious Gem Mentoring Program was chaired by Dorothy B. Wilson and Johnye W. Gillans, the co-founders of the Jr. Debutante/Precious Gem Mentoring Program. The mentored girls were Aissa Bowers, Victoria Brown, Bhrea Dobson, Da'Najah Johnson, Sarai Rhett, Makeila Richardson. Da'Najah Johnson, an 8th grade student at DeRenne Middle School, Savannah, Georgia, was crowned "Miss Precious Gem" 2010. The Cotillion's theme was "A Vision of Beauty and Elegance From the Inside Out". It was also held on the campus of Savannah State University.[533]

Precious Gems Mentoring reported by Johnye Gillans indicated that the Gems engaged in techniques for effective public speaking, coordinated by Charlene Jones and Emma Conyers; The Gems participated in the MLK parade.[534] Tammy Barnes-Scott did a presentation on Social Graces for the girls at the February 13, 2010 meeting.[535] March 13, 2010, Erica Benjamin and Ashle' King presented the workshop "Precious Gems from the Outside In." This workshop involved techniques for developing self-esteem and keeping a positive attitude. Michelle Mincey-Lee presented samples of lip gloss and noted that clean skin and a mild cream were only needed for girls their age.[536]

Career Fair 2010 was chaired by Ethel Hunter. Committee members were Queen Barnes, Brenda Jenkins, Eleanor Ginn, Connie Cooper and Ethel Bradshaw. The Fair's vendors included AKAs and guests. "Precious Gems Doing Special Things," chaired by Carolyn Bell, gave Gems an opportunity to tour City Hall, April 29, 2010.[537]

The orientation for mentoring a new set of girls for 2010- 2011 was August 29, 2010 in Toomer-Walker Social Hall at St. Matthew's

Episcopal Church, Chairman Johnye Gillans and Co-Chairmen, Charlene Jones and Emma Conyers.

Mrs. Connie Morgan, Retired Instructor, Savannah State University, presented an informative educational enrichment workshop on "Developing and Maintaining Good Study Skills" at the October Precious Gems meeting. Also, Kimberly Chappell-Stevens presented a mini leadership workshop on Confidence, A character Trait Essential to Leadership at this meeting.

Greenbriar Children's Center

Johnye Gillans and Charlene Jones served as chairmen of the Greenbriar Connection. The chapter provided service to Greenbriar by selling tickets for the annual anniversary kick-off luncheon, volunteering at the Christmas Gift Wrap Center, donating needy items, and attending events.

Members supported the Greenbriar Children's fundraiser at CiCi's: Mary Coleman, Ericka Coleman Washington, Latondia Gadson, Michelle Mincey-Gwyn, LaShawna Mullgrav, Taqwaa Saleem and Basileus Washington.[538]

The chapter purchased a $200 full page ad in the Greenbriar Children's Center 60th Anniversay Program Book and donated $1000 from the operation budget toward the 60th Anniversary Kick-Off Reception.[539]

During 2009, Greenbriar celebrated its 60th Anniversary. The chapter supported the event by attending the anniversary kickoff reception on the campus of Greenbriar, attending the Anniversary Brunch, selling tickets, serving on planning committees, serving as a sponsor for the banquet and attending the banquet. During this 60th Anniversary celebration, Washington served as president of the Board of Directors. AKAs serving on the anniversary committee were Johnye Gillans, Charlene Jones, Emma Conyers, Virginia Parham, Virginia Edwards, Lolita Hickman, Ethel Hunter, Lakechia Bryant, and Annette Mitchell.

December 13, 2010, the chapter celebrated AKA Day at Greenbriar by visiting the center and donating 300 rolls of paper towels.

Greenbriar Children's Center bestowed the honor to Gamma Sigma Omega Chapter as 2009 Donor of the Year.[540]

Other Committees

Standards Committee was chaired by Sonia Renee Grant. January 8, 2009, Grant presided over workshop sessions. Gamma Sigma Omega, Gamma Upsilon, and Sigma Tau participated. The emphasis was placed on Duties and Responsibilities of Officers. Seventeen presentations were made. The presenters were applauded by Basileus Washington for their creativity.[541] Grant reported at the February chapter meeting that six GSO committees presented: Bylaws, Tammy Barnes Scott; Connection, Carolyn Russell; Technology, Sharon Stallings; Social, Lakyah Hatcher; AKACare, Johnye Gillans; Awards & Recognition, LaShawna Mullgrav.[542]

The Standards Retreat was held again, September 26, 2009 at Central Baptist Church, Banquet Hall. Chapter operations were discussed and Program committees made plans for 2010.[543] The theme was "Standards: A Day at the SPA" (Sorors Planning Annually). During the retreat, each Standing Committee met in groups to develop goals for 2010.

Membership Committee was chaired by Vanessa Kaigler. She reported at chapter meeting that the Time Capsule initiated by committee under former Basileus, Conyers, would be sealed under Washington's administration. Washington added to the Capsule a gavel used and purchased by her in 1975.[544]

Bylaws Committee, chaired by Tarangula Barnes-Scott, worked tenaciously to develop and write the criteria for an "active member." At the November 14, 2009 chapter meeting, the proposal was presented to the chapter. Members in attendance at the writing were Emma J. Conyers, Courtney Eaton, Zena McClain, Virginia Parham, Audrey Singleton, Washington, and Barnes-Scott.[545]

Hospitality Committee, chaired by Hodegos, Maxine Jackson and Assistant, Alvernia Jackson, presented creative ways with the **ESP** icon to feed chapter members and visiting AKAs. For example, the May chapter meeting celebrated mothers. The theme for that meeting was "Recognition of Extraordinary, Spectacular and Phenomenal Soror Mothers." June's theme was "Encouraging Social and Physical

Activities During the Summer Break." Expressions of thanks were given to chapter members for using their culinary skills. September's ESP was Enthusiastic Sisters Planning and Gearing UP After the Summer Break."[546] ESP themes for October, November, and December respectively: "Energetic Sorors Prepared to Move Forward"; "Efficient Service Programs Under Very Capable Leadership"; and "Eventful Serious Progression." In 2010, the committee continued the monthly ESP themes.

Mentoring Committee, chaired by Marjory Varnedoe and Joyce Dingle, welcomed transferring, recently activated, and members needing sisterly support to request committee's assistance. The committee emphasized the importance of having a thorough understanding of Chapter By-Laws. They provided a list of Mentees and Mentors.[547]

Social Committee, Lakyah Hatcher, Chairman, held its annual Tailgating event October 31, 2009 at Savannah State University. Committee members who served were Hatcher, April Scott, and Hope Johnson. Non committee members who served were Maxine Jackson, LaTanya Stringer, Zena McClain, and Mary Coleman. Honey-dos who worked were the husband of LaTanya Stringer and the husband of Maxine Jackson. These Honey-dos constructed the tent. Mary Coleman's nephew delivered tables and chairs. Special donations were received from Basileus, Washington, and Michelle Mincey.[548]

Hatcher expressed in her report at the May 2010 meeting that the Mother's Day Luncheon included the collaboration with the Hospitality and Membership committees.[549]

Pan-Hellenic Council Representative was Latondia Gadson. She was elected Recording Secretary in 2009, and Jacklyn Minimah was elected Chaplain in 2009.[550] GSO supported the council's social activities, annual Christmas party and summer cookout by attendance and donations requested.

Conferences

The 56th Regional Conference_ Delegates: Clemontine F. Washington, Audrey Singleton, Kimberly Chappell-Stevens, Mary

Coleman, LaTanya Thompson-Stringer, Joyce Dingle, Sonia Renee Grant, Hope Johnson, Dorothy B. Wilson, and Zena McClain; Alternates: Connie Cooper and Maxine Jackson.[551] The following members were recognized at the 56th Regional Conference: Golden Sorors, Virginia Parham, Patricia Mincey, Joyce Dingle, and Bettie Milledge. The Silver Star Sorors honored were Sonia Renee Grant and Henrietta Gray. Basileus Washington reported forty-two members were seen at the conference: Eudora Allen, Queen Barnes, Tarangula Barnes-Scott, Harriett Brinson, Janie Bruen, Albertha E. Boston, Kimberly Chappell-Stevens, Emma J. Conyers, Connie Cooper, Rebecca Cooper, Jessie C. DeLoach, Joyce Dingle, Latondia Gadson, Patricia Gardner, Jackie Gilbert-Grant, Johnye Gillans, Sonia Renee Grant, Henrietta Gray, Ethel Hunter, Sheila Hutcherson, Maxine Jackson, Hope Johnson, Charlene Jones, Vanessa Kaigler, Zena McClain, Michelle Mincey-Gwyn, LaShawna Mullgrav, Eleanor Murdock, Virginia Parham, Sylvia Perry-Weston, Carolyn Russell, Tara Scott-Brown, Audrey Singleton, Gwendolyn Smith, Dorothy Speed, Sharon Stallings, LaTanya Thompson-Stringer, Clemontine F. Washington, Nicole Williams, Dorothy Worthy, Alvernia Wilson-Jackson, Dorothy B. Wilson.[552]

Emma J. Conyers served as conference workshop recorder. Patricia Clark, Cluster VI Representative to the Regional Program Committee, assisted in one of the Program Workshops. The chapter received certificates for Membership, Educational Advancement Foundation, and Technology.[553]

The 2009 Leadership Seminar - The Seminar was held in Anchorage, Alaska. The delegates were Clemontine F. Washington, Basileus; Kimberly Chappell-Stevens, Graduate Advisor, Gamma Upsilon; Audrey Singleton, Graduate Advisor, Sigma Tau. Other members attending were Zena McClain, Anti-Basileus, and Maggie Walker-Zeigler, member. Vernetta Epps, Basileus of Gamma Upsilon and Whitney Richardson of Sigma Tau, the undergraduates, attended. Basileus Washington shared her registration fee with McClain and Maggie Walker- Zeigler to assist with their attendance at Leadership Seminiar 2009.[554]

The 57th South Atlantic Regional Conference - The Conference was held in Atlanta, GA, April 22-25, 2010. The delegates were

Clemontine F. Washington, Basileus; Zena McClain, Anti-Basileus; Kimberly Chappell Stevens, Graduate Advisor, Gamma Upsilon; Audrey Singleton, Graduate Advisor, Sigma Tau; Latondia Gadson, Nicole Williams, Chaplain; Tara Scott Brown, Anti-Tamiochos; Alvernia Jackson, Co-Hodegos. Awards received at the Conference were Membership, ESP Club, Platform I for a Taste of Soul and Health Management for the Health Challenge with Delta Sigma Theta Sorority.[555]

The 64th Boule - The Boule was held in St. Louis, Missouri, July 2010. The delegates were Clemontine F. Washington, Basileus; Zena McClain, Anti-Basileus; Patricia J. Clark, Assistant Graduate Advisor, Gamma Upsilon; Audrey Singleton, Graduate Advisor, Sigma Tau; Lolita Hickman, Sharon Stallings, Assistant Graduate Advisor, Sigma Tau; Johnye Gillans, Tarangular B. Scott, Parliamentarian; Latondia Gadson, Alternate.[556]

2010 Undergraduate Roundup in Savannah - Gamma Sigma Omega Chapter assisted Gamma Upsilon Chapter of Savannah State University and Sigma Tau Chapter of Armstrong Atlantic State University in hosting the 2010 Undergraduate Roundup. The Roundup was held at the Marriott River Front, Savannah, Georgia on August 28-30, 2010.[557]

AKA Day at the Capitol_ The 16th AKA Day At the Capitol (2009) was coordinated by Connection Chairman, Carolyn Russell. Attendance: Basileus Clemontine F. Washington, Audrey Singleton, Zena Mcclain, and Russell.

The 17th Annual AKA Day at the Capitol (2010) was attended by Clemontine F. Washington, Basileus; Mary Coleman, Philacter; Carolyn Russell, Chapter Connection Chairman, and Connie Cooper. AKAs from throughout the state of Georgia gathered at the State Capitol on February 15, 2010 to visit with legislators and receive directions for the 2010 Connection activities. Major emphasis was placed on the 2010 Census. During the luncheon, Basileus Washington was recognized as a newly elected official. Representative Craig Gordon greeted the Gamma Sigma Omega members and posed for a photo.[558]

Top Readers

As a result of International Program changes, June 5, 2009 was the last report of Top Readers. Robert W. Gadsden: 1st grade, Kayla Jones; 2nd grade, Aaliyah Burgest and Camron Bryant; 3rd grade, Shelby Thomas, top point earner, Accelerator and Symarieona Williams, top point earner, Star Reader; 4th grade, Elizabeth Shields and Robert Lamar; 5th grade, Ahkeem McClinton and Tymesha Williams.[559]

Golden Sorors

Joyce Dingle, Bettie J.C Milledge, Patricia Mincey, and Virginia M. Parham became Golden Sorors in 2009. According to Chapter By-Bylaws only Virginia Parham met the qualification for a public reception.[560]

Therefore, Gamma Sigma Omega Chapter hosted a 50th Anniversary Reception in honor of Virginia M. Parham. The reception was held July 19, 2009 at 4:00 p.m. at Connor's Temple Baptist Church in Savannah, Georgia.

Ivies Beyond the Wall

Ivy Beyond the Wall Ceremony was performed for Marion Priester Roberts. Roberts was inactive at the time of her demise but had been a dedicated member of Gamma Sigma Omega chapter for a number of years.[561]

On November 13, 2010 an Ivy Beyond the Wall Ceremony was held for Martha Wilson, Gamma Sigma Omega Chapter's first Basileus. The Ceremony was held at St. Matthew's Episcopal Church, Savannah, Georgia. At the time of her demise, Wilson was residing with her daughter in Cincinnati, Ohio.[562]

Zena E. McClain, Esq., 2011-2012

Zena E. McClain, Esq., the Basileus, 2011-2012, held an inspirational worship service for her administration, December 17, 2010 at Bethel A.M.E. Church, Rev. Charles W. Purnell, Pastor. The planning retreat for her tenure was held December 18, 2010. She served under Supreme Basileus, Carolyn House Stewart, Esq., whose international theme was "Global Leadership Through Timeless Service." Therefore, McClain was mandated to bring to full fruition Stewart's service initiatives: Emerging Young Leaders, impacting the lives of girls grades six through eight; Health initiatives: (a) Asthma Prevention and Management Initiatives (b) Environmental Stewardship and Sustainability; Global Poverty; Economic Security Initiative; Social Justice and Human Rights Initiative; and Internal Leadership Training for External Service Initiative.

McClain wanted chapter meetings to run efficiently with paper free reports. She desired that members bring laptops, smart phones, computers, to meeting and read reports by these technical means to promote the Environmental Stewardship and Sustainability initiative.[563] Her first newsletter, *The Vintage Pearl* was published January 3, 2011. She invited members to submit article to the publication, sought an editorial board, proof readers and a layout designer. She held officers' transitional meeting December 27, 2010. In spite of the challenge for paperless meetings, she provided for members who were technologically challenged copies of minutes and reports.[564]

Committees

Hospitality Committee, Denise Weems-White, Hodegos, began the new year by emphasizing that the Hospitality Committee will work SMART (**S**isters **M**aking **A**ppetizing **R**ecipes **T**ogether). The membership was divided into SMART caterers by being assigned a month to produce a 5-star breakfast. Each month was assigned a theme, for example: January, Go Green; February, Black History Month; March, American Diabetes Alert; April, Earth Day; May, Happy Mother's

Day; June, Pink Picnic.[565] Due to more demanding responsibilities for Weems-White, Taqwaa Saleem was appointed Interim Hodegos.[566]

The 2012 Sisterly Chefs Calendar indicating which members assigned to prepare breakfast was distributed to members in December 2011. Saleem reported that LaTanya Thompson had been appointed Social Chairman and Co-Hodegos by Basileus McClain.[567]

Membership committee, Carolyn H. Bell, Chairman, organized a sisterly relations activity at the House of Pancakes. Chapter members ate, laughed, talked, joked and took lots of pictures. After the meal, members attended a movie at Carmike Cinemas. Members attending this sisterly event were Basileus McClain, Bell, Ashle' King, Deonne Stone, Latondia Gadson, Joyce Dingle, Margaret Pearson, Albertha Collier, Emma Conyers, Diann Scott, Eleanor Murdock, Mary Coleman, Lolita Hickman, and Annie Mahone.[568]

The Committee presented a survey to indicate preferences for specific membership activities during 2011. Regarding educational membership activities 52.8% of members said they would participate in book reviews, 63.9% of members said that they would participate in cooking classes, and 50% said they would participate in chapter sponsored Bible Study. Other activities receiving the most votes were a daytime movie, a day at the spa, game night, "Pretty-In-Pink," a formal affair, a bowling league, feeding the hungry, a clothing drive and Soror Pals.[569]

"A Day at the Spa," was held February 19, 2011 at Vanity Day Spa. On March 28, 2011, a sisterly relations activity was a dinner and Bible Study led by Chaplain, Lolita Hickman.[570]

"Pretty-in-Pink" Luncheon was held at the Hilton Savannah Desoto Hotel Restaurant. Seeking to reclaim inactive Alpha Kappa Alpha women, each GSO member was asked to invite an inactive AKA.

"Progressive Dinner" Party, a reclaiming of inactive Alpha Kappa Alpha women, also, was one purpose for party. The other purpose was fellowship for members. The party was an afternoon of drinks, appetizers, entrees, desserts, and after dinner cocktails. This event was held June 9, 2012 in Historic Savannah/Victorian District. The coordinators were Alvernia Jackson and Wanda Williams.[571]

Connection Committee, Lorna Jackson, Chairman, led a delegation of GSO members to AKA Day at the Capitol, February 20, 2011. Pyllis T. Blake, Georgia Connection Coordinator, assigned GSO the task of conducting the Connection Symposium, "A Call to Action Through Timeless Service." The members were assigned time keeper, hostesses, and an introducer for speaker.[572]

Jackson presided at the afternoon connection symposium. Members attending were Jackson, McClain, Melinda Pippen-Miller, Kimberly Chappell-Stevens, Annie Chappell, and Maxine Jackson. Honey Do, State Senator Lester Jackson, organized the overnight trip and secured a driver for chapter members. Other members in attendance were Patricia Clark, Audrey Singleton, Sharon Stallings, and Clemontine F. Washington.[573] Jackson reported a wealth of information was received. Some of the presenters were Attorney Ryan Haygood Co-Director of the Voter Protection Group at the NAACP Legal Defense and Education Fund, Inc., Jeanetta Braytboy-Alexander, a parent trainer and education advocate for 27 years, and Kirk Clay who led the NAACP political work as the National Civic engagement Director.[574]

Standards Committee, Emma Jean Conyers, Chairman, under the guidance of the initiative, "Internal Leadership Training for External Service," provided opportunities for GSO members to lead with more proficiency. The committee held an emergency Duties and Responsibilities of All Officers workshop, Friday, January 6, 2011, 6:00 p.m. at the ConEd Resource Center. The workshop was conducted by Conyers and the Parliamentarian, Charlene Jones. The theme was "Standards! Meeting the Expedient Needs of the Chapter" There were twenty-three members in attendance.[575]

Standards held the Duties and Responsibilities of All Officers Workshop, Thursday, March 24, 2011, 6:00 p.m. at the ConEd Resource Center. The theme was "Standards Check-up." The workshop presenters were Virginia Parham, Medical Moments, You Make the Call (Chapter Self-Assessment Form); Denise Weems-White, Healthy Members' Participation in Chapter Activities; Charlene Jones, Amending Chapter Bylaws & the Alpha Kappa Alpha Sorority, Inc. Constitution and Bylaws. There were 22 members in training.[576]

The last Standards workshop for 2011 was August 13, a part of the chapter's retreat. The theme was "Catch the Wave: Worthwhile Information, Awesome Presenters, Versatile Topics, and Excellent Instruction." The presenters were Conyers, Lydia Young, Tamika Minor-Wright, and Virginia Parham. There were 41 members in attendance.[577]

Ninety-one Chapter Self-Assessment Forms were completed.[578] The Duties and Responsibilities of All Officers Workshop was held March 22, 2012 at West Broad Street YMCA. The theme was "Spring Into Action with Two Peas in a Pod." The worshop's presenters were Connie Cooper, Protocol; and Charlene Jones, Parliamentary Procedures. There were thirty-seven members present. Assignments for the workshop were Lolita Hickman, Evaluation; Dorothy Wilson, Sign-in; Sonia Renee Grant and Charlene Jones, Theme; and Taqwaa Saleem and Terri Lewis, Repast.[579]

August 30, 2012, 6:45 p.m. at the Aaron L. Buchsbaum Learning Center, the Duties and Responsibilities of All Officers workshop was held. The theme was "Back to Basics." The workshop presenters were Taqwaa Saleem who presented Officers and Tara Scott-Brown who presented Finances. There were twenty-three members attending.[580] Workshop assignments were Evaluation, Hickman; Sign-in, Parham; theme, Grant and Jones; Repast, Maxine Jackson and Lewis.

Protocol Committee, Connie Cooper, Chairman, met March 2, 2011 and began a review of the Committee's general responsibilities for ensuring the courtesies to include in chapter's Standing Rules and/or Bylaws; and the logistics for chapter events.[581]

Archives Committee, Sheila Hutcherson, Chairman, invested in the importance of historical upkeep of the Archives storage area, recommended a larger unit for storage. The chapter agreed to rent a larger unit, 10x18, instead of the 10x10. January 28, 2012, the committee met to officially relocate. All items were organized and inventoried by Historian, Hutcherson. The items that were purged were given to Standards Chairman, Emma Conyers. Members who assisted in the relocation process were Tara Scott-Brown, Conyers, Jessie C. DeLoach, and Audrey Singleton.[582]

Pan-Hellenic, Courtney Eaton, Representative, reported that Alpha Kappa Alpha and Phi Beta Sigma were the victors in the Greek's basketball game.[583] Basileus McClain indicated in *The Vintage Pearl* that the basketball competition was between AKAs, 16 points and Deltas, 10 points, and game occurred March 26, 2011. The Greeks participated in "Hoopin For A Cure" campaign to raise awareness and money for Sickle Cell disease. The chapter was presented a plaque and trophy.[584]

Program, Tarangula (Tammy) Barnes Scott, Anti-Basileus/ General Program Chairman

Emerging Young Leaders (EYL), Kenisha Brown and Ashle′ King, Chairmen, the initial meeting for the year was January 26, 2011. Members present were Ashle′ King, Kenisha Brown, McClain and Scott. King and Brown served as Chairmen.[585] February 16, 2011, members in attendance at the meeting were Kenisha Brown, Ashley Renfro, Carol Bell, McClain, and Scott. At the April 11, 2011 meeting Kenisha Brown, Ashley Renfro, Ashle′ King, Emma Conyers, Charlene Jones, Denise Cooper, McClain, and Scott attended.[586] Kenisha Brown, Ashley Renfro, Ashle′ King, Emma Conyers, Charlene Jones, Courtney Eaton, and Scott met May 17, 2011. Scott reported that 22 applications were received and 21 were approved for the 2011-2012 EYL. There was a parent informational meeting May 31, 2011.[587]

June 25, 2011 was the inaugural session for EYL in the AKAdemy. Twenty-three girls were in attendance, but nineteen met eligibility. The program began with an introduction to the EYL expectations and outcomes. Charlene Jones conducted the Goal-setting, and the girls made EYL t-shirts. The following members attended: Brown, King, Jones, Conyers, Audrey Singleton, and Scott.[588] The young ladies who qualified for the inaugural Emerging Young Leaders were Ayanna Robinson, Brittany Hayes, Chantel Lewis-Cummings, Christina Moore, Imani McFadden, Jarkaylah Kelly, JonNashia Gaddis, Kai Wade, Kayla Harmon, Leslie Weeks, Miracle Reeves, Raven Wilson, Shakema McNeil, Shalaila Duke, Sydney Grant, Tianna Irwin, Tiffany Campbell, Tyelor Moore, and Vanessa Glover.[589]

July 9, twenty-seven Emerging Young Leaders participated in the Freedom Trail Tour. This two-hour tour was narrated and made stops at historic sites important in the experiences and contributions of African Americans to the city and region. Members chaperoning were Brown, King, Renfro, Jones, Singleton, and Scott.[590]

August 20, 2011, the Emerging Young Leaders session was conducted by Deonn B. Stone discussing Back-to-School Tips for Success. Melinda P. Miller did a presentation on character education and the importance of good skin and body care. Her presentation was called "Beauty is Only Skin Deep." Members in attendance were Brown, Renfro, Sonia. Renee Grant, Stone, Miller, Singleton, Conyers, and Scott.[591]

The September 10, 2011 meeting's "AKAdemy" character education focus was Values, Trust, and Friendship. After discussiong the importance of each topic and how it was related to middle-school aged girls, the girls made friendship boxes. Members supervising were Brown, Grant, Connie Cooper, and McClain.[592]

The "AKAdemy" character education focus on October 8, 2011 was Financial Literacy. The presentation was on the importance of checking and savings accounts, the use of credit and credit cards. The girls divided into teams "Avoiding Financial Traps" game. The presentation was facilitated by Brown and King. Nineteen girls were present. Chapter members present were King, Brown, Grant, Conyers, Singleton, C. Cooper, Lavinea Kennedy, Jones, Courtney Eaton, Terri Lewis, Lakyah Hatcher, Jessie C. DeLoach, McClain, and Scott.[593].

Seventeen Emerging Young Leaders on November 22, 2011 attended the Federal Reserve Bank of Atlanta Tour in Jacksonville, FL. The girls discovered the fascinating story of money from barter to modern times. The chaperones were King, Eaton, and Scott.[594]

At the December 10, 2011 "AKAdemy," with the guidance of King, the girls completed and discussed the Federal Reserve Bank Post Test. Members attending this session were Basileus McClain, Conyers, and Jones. EYL donated forty-one toys for the Holiday Hope Toy Campaign. Emerging Young Leaders: Sydney Grant, Raven Wilson and Chantel Lewis Cummings, with chaperones, Grant and Scott presented the toys to the WSAV Toy Collection Event, Thursday, December 15, 2011 at

Grayson Stadium. The girls were featured in the "WSAV Thank You" commercial.[595]

At the January 14, 2012 meeting, ten EYL girls attended. "The AKAdemy's" focus was writing skills. To assist the 8th graders as they prepared to take the Georgia 8th Grade Writing Assessment on January 18, 2012. Members attending this session were Grant, Eudora Alllen, Lewis, King, and Scott. According to the February 11, 2012 Program Report, Ashle' King was listed as the only Chairman for Emerging Young Leaders. The report stated that EYL attended a musical concert sponsored by SONATA and Still Waters Sinfo-Nia Orchestra at St. John Baptist Church, The Mighty Fortress, to fulfill the AKAdemy Character Building Benchmark.[596] Eleven girls attended the concert which was a Musical Symposium/Concert for Orchestra, Band and Piano students. Chapter members in attendance were King, Conyers, Lewis, Grant, Eudora Allen, and Scott.[597]

March 10, 2012, the EYL "AKAdemy's" focus was leadership skills and public speaking. The girls learned and practiced the skill of public speaking in conjunction with their Black History research project. The chapter members present were Conyers, Jones, Lewis, Sharon Savage-Watson, Queen Barnes, Kimberly Nixon, and McClain.[598]

The EYL "AKAdemy's" focus was a Career and Leadership Seminar, April 21, 2012. The twelve EYL participants were informed of varies career choices, involvement in the community and the importance of leadership from chapter members in careers as elected officials, education, nutrition, and law enforcement. The speakers were Clemontine F. Washington, Taqwaa Saleem, Terri Lewis, LaSonya Stovall, Erica Benjamin, and Dabrina Moore.[599]

"Pearls and Purses," an etiquette and manners workshop facilitated by Grant was held at the May 12, 2012 EYL "AKAdemy." Members present were King, Conyers, Jones, Singleton, Clemontine Washington, Denise Cooper, Patricia Clark, and Scott.[600].

The EYL Closing Celebration Luncheon was held at Carey Hilliards Restaurant on Abercorn, June 23, 2012. Denise Cooper was speaker. She encouraged the girls to think positively and not to give up on their dreams. The highlight of the program was the Spotlight of the

2011-2012 Emerging Young Leaders. Chapter members in attendance were Emma Preer, Virginia Parham, Albertha Collier, Charlene Jones, Queen Barnes, Audrey Singleton, Connie Copper, Terri Lewis, Courtney Eaton, Melinda Pippen-Miller, Freddie Pippen, Amber Brown (Sigma Tau), McClain, Barnes-Scott, and King.[601]

At the September 9, 2012 EYL meeting, fourteen girls and their parent/guardian attended. King and Tara Scott-Brown reviewed the curriculm and expectations for the 2012-2013 EYL sessions. Chapter members in attendance were Grant, Hope Johnson, McClain, Brown-Scott, and King.[602]

The EYL focus October 13, 2012 was Leadership Development. Alexis Parker, a member of the Chatham County Youth Commission, spoke to EYL about the Youth Commission process, leadership potential/skills, and dedication to education. Also, King and Erica Benjamin presented an interactive workshop on goal setting and responsibility. Chapter members present were Eaton, Lewis, D. Cooper, Grant, Benjamin, Brown-Scott, and King.[603]

Courtney Eaton became Co-Chairman with Ashle' King. According to the January 11, 2013 Program report, the Emerging Young Leaders participated in WSAV Holiday Hope Campaign (Toys for Tots), December 2012. The report continued with the Emerging Young Leaders participating: Dae'Kyla Stewart, Grace Albright, Jarkaylah Kelly, Kal Wade, Raven Wilson, Sydney Grant, Tanea Johnson, Tiffany Campbell, and Tyra Johnson. GSO members present were Scott, Eaton, King, and Sonia Renee Grant.

Also, the report stated that a character building event was held. The Emerging Young Leaders were taken to see "The Chocolate Nutcracker" in Jacksonville, FL. Those present were Grace Albright, Raven Wilson, ShaKayla King, Tanea Johnson, Tiffany Campbell, and Tyra Johnson. Taneya Johson, one of the mothers, and GSO members chapteroned: King, Eaton and Taqwaa Saleem.

Health Initiatives, LaTanya Thompson and Lorna Jackson, Chairmen, the initial meeting for the year was January 24, 2011. Members present were Eleanor Ginn, Ethel Hunter, Queen Barnes, Sonia Renee Grant, Thompson, McClain, and Scott.[604]

At March 2011 chapter meeting, the committee provided an exhibit containing a wealth of information regarding Diabetes, its detection and prevention.[605]

GSO participated in EOA Head Start/Early Head Start Annual Health, Nutrition & Prenatal Fair on April 13, 2011 with an Asthma Prevention and Diabetes Booth. The following members attended: Ethel Hunter, Sonia Renee Grant, Queen Barnes, Emma J. Preer, and McClain. Eleanor Ginn and Scott helped with set-up and information for booth.

Relay for Life, May 13-14, 2011, was held at Armstrong Atlantic State University. Chapter members participating in relay were Thompson, Margaret Pearson, Terri Lewis, Carmelita Maynard, Queen Barnes, Patricia Clark, S. Renee Grant, Denise Cooper, Connie Cooper, Sharon Stallings, Audrey Singleton, Scott.[606]

GSO participated with the West Chatham Relay for Life March 30, 2012. Team Captains were Clemontine Washington, Margaret Pearson, and Thompson. The goal was set for $6,000. The following members participated Margaret Pearson, Tara Scott-Brown, Sheila Hutcherson, Lorna Jackson, Emma Conyers, Queen Barnes, Clemontine Washington, Ethel Hunter, Terri Lewis, Audrey Singleton, Patricia Clark, Sharon Savage-Watson, Nicole Williams, Ashle' King, Erica Benjamin, Lorna Jackson, Thompson, and Scott.[607]

April 18, 2011, GSO participated in the Susan G. Komen Race for the Cure: Queen Barnes, Emma Conyers, Virginia Parham, Sheila Hutcherson, Tara Scott-Brown, LaTanya Thompson, Melinda P. Miller, McClain and Scott.[608]

At the May chapter meeting, National High Blood Pressure Month, was recognized by members taking blood pressure screenings before sorority meeting.[609]

St. Jude's 5K Walk held November 19, 2011 had chapter members participating: Taqwaa Saleem, Courtney Eaton, Ashle' King, and Erica Benjamin.[610]

The Health Initiative Committee sponsored a "Pink Goes Red for a Day" Education Seminar on heart disease at the West Broad Street YMCA. The program consisted of a panelist of four speakers affected by the disease and speaker, Alpha Kappa Alpha member, Dr. Debbie Hagins. Chapter members participating were Thompson, Jackson, Diann Scott, Charlene Jones, Alvernia Jackson, Wanda Williams, Tara Scott-Brown, Taqwaa Saleem, Terri Lewis, Virginia Parham, Emma Conyers, Basileus McClain, and Scott.[611]

On October 28, 2012, Tarangula Barnes Scott (GSO) and Amber Brown from Sigma Tau conducted a Breast Cancer Awareness Seminar for Sigma Tau's MIP. Chapter members present were Audrey Singleton and Sharon Stallings.[612]

Global Poverty Initiative, Taqwaa Saleem and Terri Lewis, Chairmen, the initial meeting for the year was January 25, 2011. Members present were Joyce Dingle, Denise Weems-White, McClain and Scott.[613] The chapter, in partnership with the EOA (Equal Opportunity Authority), had thirteen members, including thirty other volunteer organizations, restore the homes of three families. Each family was headed by a single parent with 4 or 5 children. Members spent the day doing yard work, painting and removing debris. They were Sonia Renee Grant, Patricia Clark, Audrey Singleton, Vanessa Kaigler, Eleanor Ginn, Connie Cooper, Denise Cooper, Ethel Hunter, Eleanor Murdock, Deonne Stone, Alvernia Jackson, Lakyah Hatcher, and Sharon Stallings.[614]

Chapter members were challenged by Scott to end hunger. Beginning March 2011 through December, members, coordinated by this committee, served dinner at Old Savannah City Mission: Kimberly Nixon, Dorothy B. Wilson, Emma Conyers, Audrey B. Singleton, Queen Barnes, Charlene E. Jones, Dorothy Speed, Johnye Gillans, Lolita Hickman, Melinda P. Miller, Freddie Pippen, Virginia Parham, Lakechia Bryant, Terri Lewis, Sharon Stallings, Eleanor Ginn, Margaret Pearson, Eleanor Murdock, and Barnes-Scott. Guest helpers were Deja Gillans; Sigma Tau: Amber Brown, Tanesha Sloan, Nicole Neal, Jontavia Branson, Alicia Fultz, LeKara Simmons, and Sydnei Bacon.

Chapter members donated can goods to Wesley Community Center March 2, 2011. Members delivering the can goods were Scott, Queen Barnes, and Charlene Jones.[615]

Alpha Kappa Alpha Sorority selected Heifer International as one of its charities of choice during the term of International President, Carolyn House Stewart. Supporting the platform of "Global Leadership Through Timeless Service," Stewart rallied AKAs, 260,000 members, in the effort to raise awareness of and funds for the work of Heifer International in Kenya and Ecuador. Heifer International is a global nonprofit with a proven solution to ending hunger and poverty in a sustainable way. Heifer helps empower millions of families to lift them out of poverty and hunger to self-reliance through gifts of livestock, seeds and trees and extensive training, which provide a multiplying source of food and income.[616]

June 3, 2011, a Bowl-AKA-Thon was hosted by chapter to raise funds for Heifer International. The chapter was recognized at the Public Meeting for its donation of $500 to Heifer International.[617] In 2012, Scott was challenged to fundraise March through May for this cause.[618] Her April report indicated that the Global Poverty Fundraiser was a raffle for an iPad, and tickets were $10 each and that the drawing would take place during the May meeting. The committee commenced the selling of tickets March 22, 2012 at the Standard's workshop.[619] Mrs. Sharon Benjamin won the iPad. The fundraiser's total was $1230. The following members were acknowledged for participating as of June 9, 2012: Alvernia Jackson, Ashle' King, Charlene Jones, Connie Cooper, Denise Cooper, Diann Scott, Emma Conyers, Erica Benjamin, Joyce Dingle, Juanita Denson, Kimberly Nixon, Mary Coleman, Maxine Jackson, Monifa Johnson, Queen Barnes, Renee Grant, Sheila Hutcherson, Tara Scott-Brown, Tarangula Barnes-Scott, Teri Lewis, Virginia Parham, and Taqwaa Saleem.[620]

For the November Service Project, 81 pairs of shoes were donated to Soles4souls.[621]

The chapter, in partnership with the Wesley Community Center, adopted three families during the holidays: Octavia and Family, two members; Terry and Family, three members; Yvonne and Family four members.[622]

The Global Poverty Committee thanked members for donations to the Center. The presentation was made December 15, 2011. The children of the Center made Christmas cards for AKAs. Members present during the presentation were McClain, Saleem, Lewis, and Tara Scott-Brown. Sonia Renee Grant was acknowledged for pre delivery of donations.[623]

The January 11, 2013 Program reports that Gamma Sigma Omega provided Christmas gifts for twelve CASA (Court Appointed Special Advocates for Children) children, December 13, 2012. Members presenting the donations for the chapter were Terri Lewis, Virginia Parham, and Emma J. Conyers. The report said members making donations to CASA were Tarangula Barnes Scott, Erica Benjamin, Mary Coleman, Emma Conyers, Henrietta Gray, Johnye W. Gillans, Eleanor Ginn, Lolita hickman, Ethel Hunter, Alvernia Jackson, Julie Jackson, Monifah Johnson, Charlene E. Jones, Terri Lewis, Melinda Pippen-Miller, Virginia M. Parham, Freddie Pippen, Emma J. Preer, Carolyn H. Russell, Diann B. Scott, Serdalia Singleton, Dorothy Speed, and Dorothy B. Wilson.

Economic Security Initiative, Denise Cooper, Chairman, met February 22, 2011. Chapter members attending were Audrey Singleton, Connie Cooper, Ann Chappell, Patricia Clark, Ashley Renfro, Johnye Gillans, Clemontine Washington, McClain and Scott.[624] D. Cooper advised chapter to document patronage in minority owned businesses in support of "Power Dollar Days."[625]

The Economic Security Initiative in partnership with Gamma Upsilon of Savannah State University hosted a financial workshop: Creating a Spending Plan. The speaker was Mr. Richard Reeve from Consumer Credit Counseling. Over forty guests were present. Members attending were Patricia Clark, Connie Cooper, Nicole Fields, Terri Lewis, Elisia Rooks, Basileus McClain and D. Cooper.[626] There was a follow-up workshop sponsored by GSO, Gamma Upsilon (Savannah State University) and Sigma Tau (Armstrong Atlantic State University), April 4, 2012 with Mr. Reeve as speaker. There were over fifty guests in attendance. Gamma Sigma Omega members present were Denise Cooper, Patricia Clark, Audrey Singleton, Taqwaa Saleem, Connie

Cooper, Latondia Gadson, Sharon Savage-Watson, Courtney Eaton and Scott.[627]

Social Justice and Human Rights Initiative, Clemontine F. Washington, Chairman, the initial meeting was January 27, 2011. Members attending were Audrey Singleton, Charlene Jones and Scott. Clemontine F. Washington chaired this committee.[628]

In support of the "Arts," "Facing the Rising Sun," the annual oratorical contest celebrating original poetry by African Americans, was held March 27, 2011.[629] This event was held at St. Matthew's Episcopal Church. The students participating were Franklin Steven, ages 5-9, Category 1; Amber Baker, Ariona Elaine Campbell, Tiffany Campbell, Tannia Drayton, Traleah Eady, Aneia Ferguson, Jauquica Khabryl Jackson, Cateria McBean, ages 10-12, Category II; and NaKeOra Bryant, Tamara Cooper, Da'Najah Johnson, ages 13-15, Category III. The judges were Mrs. Mildred Hall, Ms. Sametria McFall, Mrs. Barbara L. McGhee, and Ms. Louise Owens [Alpha Kappa Alpha], Marjory Varnedoe was Chairman.[630]

In conjunction with the Connection Committee, September 22, 2011, the Social Justice and Human Rights Committee sponsored a Voter Registration Training at the NAACP office. The training was conducted by Mr. Earl Shinholster. The following members were in training: Connie Cooper, Denise Cooper, Johnye Gillans, Maxine Jackson, Terri Lewis, Virginia Parham, Diann Scott (coordinator), Patricia Clark, Emma Conyers, LaTanya Thompson-Stringer, Charlene Jones, Basileus McClain, and Washington. Donisha Rowe attended from Gamma Upsilon.[631]

October was Domestic Violence Awareness Month. Twenty used cell phones were donated to the National Coalition against Domestic Violence Campaign.[632]

A partnership of Gamma Sigma Omega Chapter and Gamma Upsilon Chapter sponsored a forum on Domestic Violence, October 31, 2011. Denise Cooper was the speaker. Members attending were Connie Cooper, Patricia Clark, Mary Coleman, Johnye Gillans, Charlene Jones, Linda Jordan, and Washington.[633]

Greenbriar Children's Center, a component of Social Justice and the Human Rights Initiative, observed the Center's 62nd Anniversary with a luncheon at Belford's. Members purchased $40 tickets to attend.[634].

The Greenbriar Children's Center Family Day was held July 19, 2012. This committee coordinated the donation of Tide detergent in recognition of the Center's 63rd Anniversary. Chapter members were encouraged to purchase a box of Tide.[635]

December 17-18, 2011 members of Gamma Sigma Omega participated in the Greenbriar Children's Center Holiday Gift Wrapping project at Oglethorpe Mall. Members gift wrapping were Charlene Jones, Audrey Singleton, Lakyah Hatcher, Annette Mitchell, Jessie C. DeLoach, Margaret Pearson, Patricia Clark, Carmelita Maynard, Diann Scott, Melinda Pippen-Miller, and Washington.[536]

In December, 2012 members participating in the Greenbriar Children's gift wrapping were Charlene Jones, Diann Scott, Alvernia Jackson, Lakyah Hatcher, Margaret Anne Pearson, Clemontine F. Washington, Tara Scott-Brown, Emma J. Conyers, Amy Conyers, Annette Mitchell, Patricia Clark, Audrey Singleton, and Sigma Tau Chapter members.

Jr. Debutantes/Precious Gems, Johnye Gillans, Charlene Jones, and Emma Conyers, Chairmen

The Precious Gems, on parade float, represented the chapter in the Martin Luther King, Jr. Parade, January 17, 2011 on a cold and rainy day.[637] In February, in preparation for Mother/Daughter Luncheon, the Gems prepared speeches for their moms. Also in February, the Gems, supervised by chapter members, participated in the Savannah Black Heritage Tour, coordinated by Eleanor Murdock. The chaperones were Murdock, Gillans, Jones and Conyers. The photographer was Patricia Clark.[638] Registered Dietician, Sharon Weeks, conducted an engaging one hour session on good nutrition at the March 12, 2011 meeting. At the April 9, 2011 meeting, Donisha Rowe and Anastasia Oshunlalu from Gamma Upsilon led the monthly leadership discussion.[639]

The 16th Annual Junior Debutante Cotillion presented by Gamma Sigma Omega and M.A.R.T.H.A., Inc. was held June 11, 2011, 7:00

p.m. in the Savannah Ballroom/King Frazier Student Center, Savannah State University. The Precious Gems were Helena Armanie-Brazelton, Johnnise Jabre' Dickerson, Jermaya Patterson, Callie Elizabeth Washington, Silviller Asha-Omari Watson, Chrysta Nicholle Williams, and Sierra Ashley Williams. Miss Precious Gem 2011 was Callie Elizabeth Washington.[640]

Johnye Gillans expressed appreciation for Gamma Sigma Omega Chapter's support for the 2010-2011 Precious Gems and the 16th Annual Junior Debutante Cotillion. The chapter's last duty to perform for Jr.Debutante/Precious Gems was to secure a spot in the Savannah State University Homecoming parade, October 29, 2011 for Miss Precious Gem 2011, Ms. Callie Washington.[641]

Mentoring/Name Change

The mentoring program of middle school girls for Gamma Sigma Omega was no longer called Jr. Debutantes/Precious Gems under the leadership of Supreme Basileus Carolyn House Stewart. Gamma Sigma Omega's mentoring program's name was changed to Emerging Young Leaders. The motion was made by Emma Conyers and seconded by Scott at the September 1, 2011 Executive meeting.[642] The recommendation passed at chapter meeting.[643]

Founders' Day, Alvernia Jackson, Chairman

Founders' Day Luncheon was held March 19, 2011 at the Savannah Marriott Riverfront Hotel. The Chairman was Alvernia Jackson. The committee included Connie Cooper, Lolita Hickman, Denise Weems-White, Annette Mitchell, Carolyn H. Bell, Taqwaa F. Saleem, Johnnie Holmes, Eudora Allen, Kimberly Chappell-Stevens, Clemontine Washington, Deonn Stone, and Basileus McClain. The theme was "103 Years Later - Reflections on the Power of Sisterhood & Timeless Service." Members were encouraged to purchase at least two tickets. The guest speaker was Alpha Kappa Alpha, Alisha Morgan Thomas, Georgia State House of Representatives, who also held a book signing.[644] Jackson reported that 145 meals were served.[645] The April 9, 2011 minutes indicated that 159 tickets were sold, and Representative Thomas sold 30 books. Members receiving chapter awards were Charlene Jones, the Soror of the Year Award, Clemontine F. Washington, the Countess Y. Cox Sisterhood Award, and Taqwaa F. Saleem, the Evanel Renfroe Terrell Scholarship Award.

Joint Founders' Day, Nu Delta Omega, Gamma Sigma Omega, Nu Rho Omega, Sigma Tau, and Gamma Upsilon, was held at Hampton Hall Country Club in Bluffton, SC., January 21, 2012. Nu Delta Omega, Beaufort, SC, was hostess. The theme was "Look Back And See How Far We've Come."[646] The award recipients were Clemontine F. Washington, Soror of the Year; and Tara Scott-Brown, Countess Cox Sisterhood Award.[647] Jackson reported sixty-one GSO members attended.[648]

Conferences

The 58th South Atlantic Regional Conference was in Hollywood, FL. Delegates elected were Taqwaa Saleem, Denise Weems-White, Queen Barnes, Henrietta Gray, Melinda Pippen-Miller.[649] The chapter donated 39 pairs of socks to Soles4Souls at the Regional Conference. The chapter was recognized at the Public Meeting for its donation of $500 to Heifer International.[650]

The 59th South Atlantic Regional Conference was held in Greenville, SC: Delegates elected were Mary Coleman, LaTanya Thompson, Ashle' King, Sonia Renee Grant, Johnye Gillans, Emma Preer, Tarangula Barnes-Scott. Alternates were Denise Cooper and Nicole Williams.[651] Members attending were Harriett Brinson, Gwendolyn Smith, Carolyn Russell, Ashle' King, Taqwaa Saleem, Charlene Jones, Emma Conyers, Joyce Dingle, Maxine Jackson, Audrey Singleton, Renee Grant, Lois Vedell Williams, Eleanor Murdock, Eudora Allen, Jessie DeLoach, Margaret Pearson, Albertha Collier, Henrietta Gray, Dorothy Wilson, Janie B. Bruen, Virginia Parham, Dorothy Speed, Nicole Williams, Clemontine Washington, Alvernia Wilson-Jackson, Carol Bell, Erica Washington, Michelle Mincey-Gwyn,

Connie Cooper, Denise Cooper, Erica Benjamin, LaTanya Thompson, Patricia Clark, and Zena McClain.[652]

Boule 2012 was held in San Francisco, California. The funded delegates were Basileus Zena McClain, Anti-Basileus Tarangula B. Scott, Audrey Singleton, and Patricia Clark, Graduate Advisors. The non-funded delegates were Clemontine Washington, Charlene Jones, Emma Conyers, Johnye Gillans, Rebecca Cooper, and Terri Lewis. Chapter members donated items to the "Youth Leadership Summit, Back to School Drive."[653] At this conference, Conyers attended the Timeless History Workshop and reported to chapter that all chapters were mandated to complete a history book by January 2014.

Cluster VI meeting was held September 16-17, 2011 in Statesboro, GA. Members attending were Carol Bell, Alvernia Wilson-Jackson, Dorothy Wilson, Clemontine Washington, Queen Barnes, Ethel Hunter, Taqwaa Saleem, Sheila Hutcherson, Nicole Williams, Tara Scott-Brown, Terri Lewis, Tarangula Barnes Scott, Charlene Jones, Virginia Parham, Lydia Young, Maxine Jackson, Melinda P. Miller, Freddie Pippen, Henrietta Gray, LaVerta Scott Perry, Audrey Singleton, Patricia Clark, Diann Scott, Annie Mahone and Joyce Dingle.[654] The following members announced at the October chapter meeting that they were in attendance: LaTanya Thompson, Kimberly Nixon, Elza Givens, Sharon Stallings, Hope Johnson, and Latondia Gadson.

Cluster VI in 2012 was held in Charleston, SC. Thirty-one members registered for the conference, and twenty-eight attended: Basileus, McClain, Emma Conyers, Charlene Jones, Connie Cooper, Denise Cooper, Taqwaa Saleem, LaShawna Mullgrav, Michelle Mincey -Gwyn, Patricia Clark, Sheila Hutcherson, Tara Scott-Brown, Sonia Renee Grant, Lois Vedelle Williams, Kimberly Nixon, Audrey Singleton, Sharon Stallings, Virginia Parham, Jackie Tomlin, Jessie C. DeLoach, Eudora Allen, Henrietta Gray, Eleanor Murdock, Ericka Washington, Mary Coleman, Tarangula Barnes Scott, Nicole Williams, Queen Barnes, and LaTanya Thompson.[655]

Basileus McClain announced that Cluster VI would host the 60th South Atlantic Regional Conference in Charleston, SC., 2013.[656] She also stated that GSO will be responsible for three committees and that the Regional Conference assessment per member would be $200.[657]

GSO was assigned the Conference Gala and Transportation committees for the 60th South Atlantic Regional Conference reported the Basileus.[658] McClain appointed Jacqueline Tomlin Chairman of the Gala and Johnye Gillans Assistant Chairman. McClain appointed herself Chairman of Transportation and Dorothy B. Wilson Assistant Chairman of Transportation.

Patricia Clark served as Regional Conference Co-Chairman of the 60th South Atlantic Regional Conference.

The 2011 AKA Public Policy Conference in Washington, D.C. was attended by Basileus McClain. She indicated the agenda was full with briefings, workshops and forums that educated, stimulated and motivated Alpha Kappa Alpha Sorority members to implement the C.A.R.E.S. (Collaborate, Advocate, Register, Educate, and Stimulate) initiative in their communities. C.A.R.E.S. is an initiative through the Connection Committee to energize and mobilize voters. Included in the activities were a Welcome Reception, White House Briefing, Voter Empowerment and Civic Engagement Workshops, Congressional Briefings, Town Hall Meeting at Howard University moderated by Donna Brazile, U.S. Capitol photo and reception for the newly elected Alpha Kappa Alpha women to the U.S. House of Representatives.[659]

Undergrades

A joint chapter meeting of Gamma Sigma Omega, Gamma Upsilon, and Sigma Tau was held March 12, 2011.[660] Joint chapter meeting, Gamma Sigma Omega, Gamma Upsilon and Sigma Tau, was held September 10, 2011.[661] In 2012, the Joint Chapter meeting was April 21, 2012 and September 8, 2012.

GSO welcomed new members into Alpha Kappa Alpha Sorority: fifteen undergraduates into Sigma Tau and forty-nine undergraduates into Gamma Upsilon. The Membership-Intake-Process (MIP) Celebration Luncheon for Sigma Tau was held November 11, 2012, and Luncheon for Gamma Upsilon was held November 19, 2012.

The Graduate Advisory Committee included the following members: Graduate Advisors, Patricia Clark (Gamma Upsilon), Audrey Singleton (Sigma Tau); Assistant Graduate Advisors, Clemontine F. Washington (Gamma Upsilon), Sharon Stallings (Sigma Tau); Tara Scott-Brown, Emma Conyers, Johnye Gillans, Hope Johnson, Charlene Jones, Virginia Parham, Tarangula Barnes-Scott, and Nicole Williams.

Silver Stars

Annie Mahone and Annette Mitchell received Silver Star recognition, 25 years, in 2011.

Golden Soror

Johnye W. Gillans celebrated 50 years in Alpha Kappa Alpha Sorority June 10, 2012 at Butler Memorial Presbyterian Church, Savannah, GA. This event was sponsored by Gamma Sigma Omega Chapter.[662]

Ivy Beyond the Wall

Ivies Beyond the Wall ceremonies were conducted for Gwendolyn Harris Johnson in 2011 and for Agatha Anderson Cooper and Albertha E. Boston in 2012.

SSU Tailgating

GSO observed Savannah State University's Homecoming Tailgating celebration in 2011 and 2012, led by the Social Committee, Taqwaa Saleem, Chairman, and LaTanya Thompson, Chairman, respectively.

United Negro College Fund

100 Celebrity Men Who Cook was Sunday, December 11, 2011. Members were asked to purchase at least two tickets at $25 each.

Alvernia Jackson, Carol Bell, Jessie C. DeLoach, and McClain were the contacts.[663]

Nominating

Chairman, Clemontine F. Washington presented the slate of officers for 2013 -2014. The officers were approved: Basileus, Tarangula Barnes Scott; Anti-Basileus, Sonia Renee Grant; Grammateus, Mary Coleman; Anti-Grammateus, Virginia Parham; Tamiouchos, Emma Jean Conyers; Anti-Tamiouchos, Charlene Jones; Philacter, Melinda Pippen-Miller; Graduate Advisor, Patricia Clark, Savannah State University (Gamma Upsilon); Audrey Singleton, Armstrong Atlantic State University (Sigma Tau).[664] The other officers continuing or appointed were Parliamentarian, Johnye Gillans; Epistoleus, Diann Scott; Pecunious Grammateus, Sheila Hutcherson; Member-at-Large, Annie Mahone; Ivy Leaf Reporter, Eudora Allen; Hodegos, Tara Scott-Brown; Historian, Nicole Williams; Chaplain, Henrietta Gray; Assistant Graduate Advisor, Savannah State University (Gamma Upsilon), Clemontine F. Washington; Assistant Graduate Advisor, Armstrong Atlantic State University (Sigma Tau), Sharon Stallings; Pan-Hellenic Representatives, Hope Johnson and Courtney Eaton; EAF Representative, Charlene Jones.

Retiring Basileus

Saturday, December 8, 2012 Zena McClain retired as Basileus. At McClain's retiring celebration, December 8, 2012, she requested an unselfish act through the chapter's Chairmen of Protocol and Hospitality: "Sorors interested in sharing a personal gift with Soror Zena should please consider making a donation on her behalf to the Leukemia & Lymphoma Society. In April 2013, Soror Zena will run the Nike Marathon, raising funds for the worthy charitable agency." The contacts for this celebration and donation were Connie Cooper, Protocol Chairman, and Taqwaa Saleem, Hodegos.[665]

Epilogue

A TRAVELOGUE OF experiences is provided in this book to ensure that those who sojourn through its pages will come to know Gamma Sigma Omega Chapter in Savannah, Georgia.

A spirit of unity, sisterhood, service, and conferences for learning strategic ways to impact residents of the city is chronicled beginning with the first service project, a home for orphaned Negro children.

Having been inspired by seven women, this chapter celebrates in 2013 the Diamond Year. Times have not been easy in 70 years, for the chapter has had to strategize ways and means to secure funding for many service projects, beginning with the initial service project, a home for Negro orphans which eventually became Greenbriar Children's Center. The commitment to service has not wavered through the years. With today's membership of one hundred and eighteen members, Gamma Sigma Omega provides services in many capacities, financially and physically. Notably, in 1949, the chapter made a $5000 contribution to a $35,000 project, the renovation of WAC (Women Army Corp) Headquarters, to accommodate eleven girls and nine boys. This energy for service inspired other citizens to serve and support worthy causes in the Savannah community. For example, Chatham County and the United Community Services became supporters of Greenbriar Children's Center. Later, this center became supported by State and Federal governments. Thereafter, the chapter sought other charitable causes to support while continuing to support Greenbriar Children's Center.

Knowing the struggle for funds, members decided to organize a separate organization to assist them with charitable causes. The idea of a foundation had been considered for many years and came into fruition August 25, 2006. M.A.R.T.H.A., Inc., (Moving All Races To Higher

Achievement), became a 501(c)(3), organized to support the charitable, educational and community programs and initiatives of the chapter.

The outstanding projects have been many for this community: (1) The founding of the Greenbriar Children's Center, Inc., 1944 (2) The establishment of the Savannah Chapter of the National Pan-Hellenic Council (3) Fashionetta, a fundraising project (4) Project SEARCH (Service through Emulation, Action, Resources, Counseling, and Humanity), a project that provided services in Ogeecheeton, a deprived community for which Gamma Sigma Omega was recipient of the 1977 Top Chatham Savannah Volunteer Award and honored by Governor George Busbee for volunteer service in Ogeecheeton (5) "Facing the Rising Sun," a contest of students doing dramatic monologues of Black poetry (6) Junior Debutante/Precious Gems Mentoring Program, fundraising and mentoring (7) American Cancer Society Relay for Life, the first African American team to participate, 1994 (8) Ivy Reading AKAdemy, Robert W. Gadsden Elementary School and Esther F. Garrison Elementary School, AYP (Adequate Yearly Progress, 2004-2005, 2005-2006) (9) The Mozella Gaither Collier Community Volunteer Service Award: awarded to a local citizen (10) A sponsor of 100 Celebrity Men Who Cook: United Negro College Fund, a community fundraiser (11) A sponsor of the 60th Anniversary of Greenbriar Children's Center, 2009.

Today, in addition to several of the above charitable causes that GSO still supports, there are additional ones: Emerging Young Leaders, Health Initiatives, Economic Security Initiative, Social Justice and Human Rights Initiative, and Global Poverty Initiative. These service projects are directed by the chapter's Vice President, Sonia Renee Grant who becomes President of chapter in 2015.

Initially, Gamma Sigma Omega Chapter was a part of the Southeastern Region, but in 1953, the chapter became a part of the South Atlantic Region as a result of realignment. GSO has been recognized regionally and internationally: (1) Twenty-Seventh Annual Boule, 1947: Recognition for outstanding civic service to the community (2) Twenty-Ninth Annual Boule, 1949: Recognition for community and interracial interest (3) South Atlantic Regional Conference, 1977: Recognition for

Tutorial Reading Program (4) South Atlantic Region's Exemplary Ivy Reading AKAdemy Program winner, 2005 -2006 (4) Boule, 2006: Ivy Reading AKAdemy Program Certificate of Recognition; Connection, Certificate of Recognition (5) Host for South Atlantic Regional Conference in Savannah: 1959, 1976, 1989, and 1998 (6) The Mozella Gaither Collier Community Volunteer Service Award, established at the 1985 South Atlantic Regional Conference (7) Co-Host for South Atlantic Regional Conference outside of Savannah: Augusta, GA, 2004 and Charleston, SC, 2013 (8) 60th South Atlantic Regional Conference Leadership, 2013: Patricia J. Clark, Conference Co-Chairman; Dorothy B. Wilson, Transportation, Co-Chairman; Johnye W. Gillans, Gala, Chairman, and Charlene Jones, Gala, Co-Chairman; Henrietta Gray, Ecumenical speaker.

Gamma Sigma Omega supervises two undergraduate chapters: Gamma Upsilon Chapter, chartered November 26, 1949, Savannah State University and Sigma Tau Chapter, chartered April 24, 2005, Armstrong Atlantic State University.

Alpha Kappa Alpha Sorority has provided administrative services to Gamma Sigma Omega Chapter since 1943 through the present. The chapter has had thirty-four presidents with three of them serving two terms, non-consecutive terms; a term is two years.

Each year the chapter honors the Founders of the Sorority with a program where sisterhood is uplifted and service is recognized. In celebrating 105 years of Alpha Kappa Alpha Sorority, Gamma Sigma Omega Chapter salutes the current leaders of this sisterhood: chapter President, Tarangula Barnes Scott; Cluster VI Coordinator, Thuane B. Fielding; Regional Director, Marsha Lewis Brown; and International President, Carolyn House Stewart.

Appendix A

Profiles of Membership
Submitted by Members

Name: Eudora Pearl Moore Allen
Undergraduate College/University: Savannah State University
Chapter initiated: Gamma Upsilon
Year initiated: 1956
Profession: Educator
Position in profession: Teacher of English Literature
Community Service: Butler Presbyterian Church, organist/pianist; Moderator
    of Worship Ministry

Name: Valencia R. Thomas Austin
Undergraduate College/University: Savannah State University
Chapter initiated: Gamma Upsilon
Year initiated: 1991
Profession: Chemist
Position in profession: Quality Control Manager at EM Industries
Community Service: Marathon Runner; Public School Volunteer

Name: Geraldine J Mack Baker
Undergraduate College/University: Savannah State University
Chapter initiated: Gamma Sigma Omega
Year initiated: 1980
Profession: Retired from the City Of Savannah after 35 Years
Position in profession: Management Analysis
Community Service: Youth advisor at Tremont Temple Missionary Baptist
    Church

Name: Queen E. Barnes
Undergraduate College/University: Savannah State College/University
Chapter initiated: Gamma Sigma Omega
Year initiated: 2000
Profession: Retired Teacher
Position in profession: Teacher
Community Service: Cloverdale Community Improvement Association; Chatham Retired Educators Association; Volunteer Reading Tutorial Program, SSU Alumni Association; Old City Savannah Mission (serving meals)

Name: Carolyn Evelyn Hodges Bell
Undergraduate College/University: Shaw University – Raleigh, NC
Chapter initiated: Beta Rho
Year initiated: 1968
Profession: Retired Public Administrator / City Council Member/Executive Leadership Coach
Community Service: Junior League, University of Georgia Graduate School Board, Horizons of Savannah Summer Enrichment Program, Savannah Chapter of the Links, Leadership Savannah Board

Name: Erica Benjamin
Undergraduate College/University: Georgia Southern University
Chapter initiated: Lambda Kappa
Year initiated: 2007
Profession: Teacher (Middle School)
Position in profession: 7th Grade Science Teacher
Community Service: Volunteering at Relay for Life; working summers at Old Savannah City Mission; Coaching sports; Recycling

Name: Lucille T. Brown
Undergraduate College/University: Savannah State College
Chapter initiated: Gamma Sigma Omega
Year initiated: 2006
Profession: Education
Position in profession: Special Education Department Head
Community Service: Feed the Hungry Can Drive, Community Blanket Drive

Name: Janie B. Bruen
Undergraduate College/University: Savannah State College
Chapter initiated: Gamma Upsilon
Year initiated: 1956
Profession: Reading Specialist/Administrative Coordinator of Reading/ Chapter 1 Coordinator
Position in profession: Retired Educator (1995)
Community Service: Top Ladies of Distinction, Incorporated-1st Vice President; Soignee' Civic and Social Club – Reporter; Life Member and Golden Soror in Alpha Kappa Alpha Sorority

Name: Lakechia Bryant
Undergraduate College/University: Fort Valley State University
Chapter initiated: Gamma Sigma Omega
Year initiated: 2006
Profession: Education
Position in profession: Third Grade Teacher
Community Service: National Council of Negro Women, Vacation Bible School, Celestine Guild, 21st Century Community Learning Centers

Name: Annie Chappell
Undergraduate College/University: Savannah State University
Chapter initiated: Nu Rho Omega
Year initiated: 1987
Profession: Education
Position in profession: Retired Teacher
Community Service: Volunteer in schools, choir member of St. Benedict the Moor Church, member of Thunderbolt Community Improvement Association

Name: Kimberly Chappell-Stevens
Undergraduate College/University: University of Georgia
Chapter initiated: Nu Rho Omega
Year initiated: 1989
Profession: Education
Position in profession: Assistant Principal at East Broad Street School
Community Service: Thunderbolt Alderman, President- Thunderbolt Community Improvement Association, Lector and Choir Member of St. Benedict the Moor

Name: Patricia Johnson Clark
Undergraduate College: Savannah State University
Chapter Initiated: Gamma Upsilon
Year Initiated: 1975
Profession: State of Georgia/Department of Revenue
Position in Profession: Legal Analysis Specialist
Community Service: Citizen Advocate, International Program of Alpha
    Kappa Alpha, Toastmasters International, Graduate Advisor, Alpha
    Kappa Alpha Gamma Upsilon Chapter

Name: Mary C. Coleman
Undergraduate College/University: St. Leo University
Chapter initiated: Gamma Sigma Omega
Year initiated: 2006
Profession: Retired Banker
Position in profession: Financial Service Representative
Community Service: Volunteer Boy Scout of America, Junior Achievement of
    Georgia, American Cancer Society, Port Wentworth Elementary School,
    Gadsden Elementary School and Jacob G. Smith Elementary School

Name: Albertha W. Collier
Undergraduate College/University: Savannah State College/University
Chapter initiated: Gamma Sigma Omega
Year initiated: 1970
Profession: Education-Teacher/Retired
Position in profession: Teacher

Name: Amy Conyers
Undergraduate College/University: Skidmore College
Chapter initiated: Gamma Sigma Omega
Year initiated: 2006
Profession: Marketing Manager
Position in profession: Direct Mail Marketing Manager
Community Service: Cellist: Marylhurst Symphony Orchestra, Portland, Oregon

Name: Emma Jean Conyers
Undergraduate College/University: Savannah State College
Chapter initiated: Gamma Upsilon

Year initiated: 1968

Profession: Retired Teacher of English and Spanish

Position in profession: High School English Teach and Spanish Teacher, 1970-2006; Adjunct professor of Freshman English, Savannah State University, 1999-2011; SEARCH Facilitator and Lead Teacher of 9th grade Academy; Teacher Support Specialist

Community Service: Voter Registrar; BRAVO Board Member; SONATA Board Member; Friends of Music; Connor's Temple Baptist Church mission outreach

Name: Connie S. Cooper

Undergraduate College/University: Benedict College

Chapter initiated: Psi Chapter

Year initiated: 1966

Profession: Social Work & Education

Position in profession: Retired Educational Administrator/Social Worker

Community Service: Chair of Hodge Memorial Day Care Center Board; Chair of Board of Education's Audit Committee; Board Member of Youth Futures Authority; President of Savannah Chapter of The Links, Inc.; St. Paul CME Church – Christian Education Ministry

Name: Denise M. Cooper, Esq.

Undergraduate College/University: Spelman College

Chapter initiated: Gamma Sigma Omega

Year initiated: 2000

Profession: Attorney – Legal Services

Position in profession: Attorney

Community Service: Georgia Association of Black Women Attorneys; The Links, Inc.; High School Mock Trial Coach; St. Paul CME Church

Name: Rebecca R. Cooper

Undergraduate College/University: Savannah State College/University

Chapter initiated: Gamma Upsilon

Year initiated: 1968

Profession: Education/Administration (Retired)

Position in profession: Assistant Superintendent

Community Service: AAUW; Links, Inc.; former Board Member of American Red Cross; YMCA; Board Member, King-Tisdell Cottage Foundation

Name: Brittany Davis
Undergraduate College/University: Savannah State University
Chapter initiated: Gamma Upsilon
Year initiated: 2009
Profession: Behavior Specialist/Mental Health Counselor
Position in profession: Behavior Specialist/Mental Health Counselor
Community Service: Big Brother, Big Sister, Salvation Army; Light the
    Night; March of Dimes; Camp Unity; Hands on Atlanta; Inner City
    Night Shelter

Name: Jessie Collier DeLoach
Undergraduate College/University: Savannah State College/University
Chapter initiated: Gamma Upsilon
Year initiated: 1949
Profession: Teacher of Mathmatics
Position in profession: Teacher/Supervisor
Community Service: Elected School Board Member; Cloverdale Community
    Organization, treasurer; CHARMS, Inc., member/officer; King-Tisdell
    Cottage Foundation Board, member; former Rape Crisis Center Board,
    member; Chancel Choir member, Butler Memorial Presbyterian Church;
    member, several Socio-Civic clubs

Name: Juanita Walker Denson
Undergraduate College/University: Albany State University
Chapter initiated: Kappa Gamma Omega
Year initiated: 1977
Profession: Education
Position in profession: Instructor
Community Service: United Way; Unwed mothers

Name: Joyce Griffin Dingle
Undergraduate College/University: Savannah State College/University
Chapter initiated: Gamma Upsilon
Year initiated: 1959
Profession: Retired Educator
Position in profession: Secondary History Teacher
Community Service: United Way, Hospice Savannah, Savannah Mission

Name: Tenay Drayton
Undergraduate College/University: Savannah State University
Chapter initiated: Gamma Upsilon
Year initiated: 2009
Profession: Social Services
Position in profession: Family Service Specialist

Name: Courtney Eaton
Undergraduate College/University: Armstrong Atlantic State University
Chapter initiated: Sigma Tau
Year initiated: 2008
Profession: Master of Public Administration Grad Candidate
Position in profession: Intern, Savannah Airport Commission (Airport Administration)/Administrative Assistant, Cooper Law, LLC
Community Service: Old Savannah City Mission; City of Savannah neighborhood Leadership Academy; Volunteer Mentor, Windsor Forest Elementary School; Light the Night Walk; St. Jude Walk

Name: Ellen Evans
Undergraduate College/University: Armstrong Atlantic State University
Chapter initiated: Sigma Tau
Year initiated: 2010
Profession: Educator
Position in profession: 2nd Grade Teacher
Community Service: Light the Night; Greenbriar; Diabetes, Hooping for Pearls basketball tournament for Diabetes; school supplies, food drive, blood drives, recycling initiative, mentor/mentee and more

Name: Nicole Simone Fields
Undergraduate College/University: Savannah State University
Chapter initiated: Gamma Upsilon
Year initiated: 1993
Profession: Social Worker/Master in Public Administration
Position in profession: Utilization Manager at Georgia Regional Hospital of Savannah
Community Service: NAADAC the Association for Addiction Professionals

Name: Latondia Gadson
Undergraduate College/University: Savannah State University
Chapter initiated: Gamma Upsilon
Year initiated: 2007
Profession: Hospitality
Position in profession: Manager
Community Service: Voter registration; Spoken Word - arts and technology
    education for at-risk youth (AWOL) All Walks of Life

Name: Carol R. Gamble
Undergraduate College/University: Tuskegee University
Chapter initiated: Gamma Kappa
Year initiated: 1975
Profession: Educator
Position in profession: Director of School Improvement, Beach High School
Community Service: served on Board of Directors of the Frank Callen Boys
    & Girls Club

Name: Marquitha Gibson
Undergraduate College/University: Savannah State University
Chapter initiated: Gamma Upsilon
Year initiated: 2009
Profession: Computer Information Systems/Air Force Reservist
Position in profession: IT Specialist/Personnel Specialist
Community Service: Inner City Youth Recreational and Salvation Army

Name: Jacquelyn Gilbert-Grant
Undergraduate College/University: Savannah State University
Chapter initiated: Gamma Sigma Omega
Year initiated: 2005
Profession: Ordained Apostle
Position in profession: Pastor of the Sanctuary of Praise Christian Assembly
Community Service: Member of the Pentecostal Ministerial Alliance; Newly
    formed Community Collaborative against Crime

Name: Johnye W. Gillans
Undergraduate College/University: Savannah State University
Chapter Initiated: Gamma Upsilon
Year Initiated: 1962
Profession: Teacher (Math)
Position in Profession: Teacher
Community Service: AARP-GA, Savannah Sickle Cell Association, BRAVO
    Music Company, Inc.

Name: Eleanor J. Ginn
Undergraduate College/University: Savannah State University
Chapter initiated: Gamma Sigma Omega Chapter
Year initiated: 2000
Profession: Sales, Customer Service Representative
Position in profession: Customer Service Representative
Community Service: Hospice of Savannah, United Way Volunteer, MLK Day
    of Service Project, YMCA Miracle on May Street, Greenbriar Children
    Center, Senior Citizens and Second Harvest Food Bank

Name: Elza L. Givens
Undergraduate College/University: GA Southern University
Chapter initiated: Lambda Kappa
Year initiated: 1992
Profession: Laboratory Science
Position in profession: Medical Technologist II
Community Service: Savannah Blood Alliance, committee member

Name: Sonia Renee Grant
Undergraduate College/University: Savannah State University
Chapter initiated: Gamma Upsilon Chapter
Year initiated: 1984
Profession: Chemist and Personnel Officer
Position in profession: Personnel Officer
Community Service: United Way Volunteer, MLK Day of Service Project,
    Thomas Austin, YMCA Miracle on May Street, Rock and Roll Marathon,
    and Second Harvest Food Bank

Name: Dr. Henrietta Sloan Gray
Undergraduate College/University: Florida A&M University
Chapter initiated: Beta Alpha
Year initiated: 1965
Profession: Education
Position in profession: Teacher/Trainer
Community Service: Living Hope Community Church Ministerial Alliance,
    Chatham County Democratic Committee, Chatham Retired Educator
    Association, Georgia Retired Educators Association

Name: Lakyah Johnson-Hatcher
Undergraduate College/University: Savannah State University
Chapter initiated: Gamma Sigma Omega
Year initiated: 2006
Profession: Social Worker, BSW, MA
Position in profession: Social Services Case Manager, Advance
Community Service: 100 Black Men Volunteer; Greenbriar Volunteer; Foster
    Care Association Volunteer; Relay for Life Volunteer

Name: Lolita L. Hickman
Undergraduate College/University: Southern Illinois University (Edwardsville)
Chapter initiated: Epsilon Iota
Year initiated: 1968
Profession/Position: Organizational Development/Management Consultant;
    and Minister of the Gospel
Community Service: Conducted "Yes, I Can: Goals for Growth Project" for
    Kayton-Frazier Boys and Girls Club of Savannah; support educational,
    and anti-violence projects with Interdenominational Ministerial Alliance;
    support Greenbriar Children's Center; serve meals and contribute to Old
    Savannah City Mission

Name: Johnnie Louise Sanders Holmes
Undergraduate College/University: Savannah State College
Chapter initiated: Gamma Sigma Omega
Year initiated: 1997
Profession: Educator
Position in profession: Guidance Counselor/Teacher
Community Service: Top Ladies of Distinction, Inc.; NAACP

Name: Ethel Hunter
Undergraduate College/University: Southern University, Baton Rouge, Louisiana
Chapter initiated: Gamma Sigma Omega
Year initiated: 2000
Profession: Education
Position in profession: Teacher
Community Service: Serve food to homeless people; Tutor children below
    grade level; Confirmation Class, Butler Memorial Presbyterian Church;
    member, Neighborhood Watch Committee

Name: Sheila Burton Hutcherson
Undergraduate College/University: Savannah State University
Chapter initiated: Gamma Sigma Omega
Year initiated: 2000
Profession: Computer Information
Position in profession: Data Analyst/Data Processes Coordinator
Community Service: Member of Jonesville Baptist Church of The PAW;
    volunteer of various charity events

Name: Alvernia Smith Jackson
Undergraduate College/University: Savannah State University
Chapter initiated: Gamma Sigma Omega
Profession: Retired Nutritionist (Public School Nutrition Program Coordinator)
Community Service: The Mediation Center Board Member, Salvation Army
    Board Member, Savannah State University National Alumni Association,
    SSUNAA Savannah Chapter member, former board member "Interfaith
    Hospitality" Board

Name: Annie C. Jackson
Undergraduate College/University: Albany State College/University
Chapter initiated: Gamma Sigma
Year initiated: 1955
Profession: Education/Teacher
Position in profession: Teacher
Community Service: Volunteer worker, Greenbriar Children's Center; Bethel
    A.M.E. Church volunteer

Name: Julie Jackson
Undergraduate College/University: Spelman College
Chapter initiated: Mu Pi
Year initiated: 2000
Profession: Registered Nurse
Position in profession: Certified Registered Nurse Anesthetist

Name: Maxine E. Jones Jackson
Undergraduate College/University: Savannah State College (University)
Chapter initiated: Gamma Sigma Omega
Year initiated: 1997
Profession: Secretarial Employment/Account Clerk Paymaster/Elementary
    School Teacher
Position in profession: Classroom teacher; Grade Group Chairperson; Lead
    Teacher in Special Instructional Assistance Program SSIA; twice Teacher
    of the Year 1983 and 1993 at Eli Whitney Elementary School
Community Service: Church-wide organizations: Christian Growth and
    Nurture – working with the Youth and adults in the Community, Usher
    Board, Presbyterian Women Association, Pickens Circle, Fiscal Affairs
    Ministry, Church Treasurer, Member of the Session, Stated Meeting
    Commissioner; volunteer at Savannah Special Care Center

Name: Brenda M. Jenkins
Undergraduate College/University: Savannah State College/University
Chapter initiated: Gamma Sigma Omega
Year initiated: 1997
Profession: Media Specialist
Position in profession: Retired

Name: Hope Johnson
Undergraduate College/University: Savannah State College
Chapter initiated: Gamma Sigma Omega
Year initiated: 2000
Profession: Law Enforcement
Position in profession: Deputy Marshal
Community Service: Voters registration, Cancer Society, Girl Scouts, Red Cross,
    Green Brier Parent Volunteer (Daughters School), Alpha Kappa Alpha Sorority,
    Inc. Emerging Young Leaders and Church Volunteer Outreach program

Name: Margaret Burney Johnson
Undergraduate College/University: Savannah State College/University
Chapter initiated: Gamma Sigma Omega
Year initiated: 2006
Profession: Education
Position in profession: Retired Teacher, Curriculum Specialist, Principal, Human Resource Coordinator
Community Service: Soignee' Civic/Social Organization; Board of Directors Learning Center, Tremont Temple Baptist Church; volunteering in Chatham County Public Schools System

Name: Monifa Johnson
Undergraduate College/University: Tulane University
Chapter initiated: Omicron Psi
Year initiated: 1990
Profession: Nonprofit Management
Community Service: Chatham County Board of Elections; NAACP; Holy Spirit Lutheran Church

Name: Harriette Johnson-Brinson
Undergraduate College/University: Edward Waters College
Chapter initiated: Gamma Sigma Omega
Year initiated: 2006
Profession: Record & Information/Library Archive Science
Position in profession: Records & Information Manager, CSX Transportation
Community Service: Duval County Schools tutor; City of Jacksonville "Paint the Town" Community project; Juvenile Diabetes Volunteer and United Way services

Name: Charlene E. Jones
Undergraduate College/University: University of Pittsburgh, Pittsburgh, Pennsylvania
Chapter initiated: Iota Chapter
Year initiated: 1975
Profession: Public School Educator/Administrator
Position in profession: Retired School District Administrator
Community Service: Voter Registrar, Community/Church Tutor, Greenbriar Children's Center Marketing Committee Voluntee

Name: Vanessa Miller-Kaigler
Undergraduate College/University: Savannah State College/University
Chapter initiated: Gamma Upsilon
Year initiated: 1981
Profession: Public Administration
Position in profession: Director of Purchasing
Community Service: Voter Registration, Youth Mentor

Name: Ashle' King
Undergraduate College/University: Georgia Southern University
Chapter initiated: Lambda Kappa
Year initiated: 2007
Profession: Healthcare Administration
Position in profession: Secretary

Name: Kayla R. Knight
Undergraduate College/University: Armstrong Atlantic State University
Chapter initiated: Sigma Tau Chapter
Year initiated: 2008
Profession: Public Health
Position in profession: Student: Master of Public Health candidate (May 2013)

Name: Tanesha D. Sloan Lester
Undergraduate College/University: Armstrong Atlantic State University
Chapter initiated: Sigma Tau
Year initiated: 2010
Profession: Graduate Student
Community Service: Public Health Ambassador for the Coastal Health
    District, Volunteer Coordinator for Girls on the Run of Coastal Georgia,
    Youth Advocate for the Great American Condom Campaign, Campus
    Liaison for the American Public Health Association

Name: Terri E. Lewis
Undergraduate College/University: South Carolina State University
Chapter initiated: Alpha Alpha Omega Chapter
Year initiated: 2007
Profession: Law Enforcement (Retired)
Position in profession: Police Officer (Retired)
Community Service: Connor's Temple Baptist Church Food Bank & Senior
    Mission Ministry; Savannah Technical College, Peace Officer Academy

Name: Annie L. Mahone
Undergraduate College/University: Albany State University
Chapter initiated: Kappa Gamma Omega
Year initiated: 1986
Profession: Educator (Retired)
Position in profession: Classroom Teacher/Summer School Principal
Community Service: Gamma Sigma Omega service projects; community
    advocate for American Heart and Lung Associations and AARP

Name: Carmelita S. Maynard
Undergraduate College/University: St. Augustine's College (Raleigh, NC)
Chapter initiated: Gamma Sigma Omega
Year initiated: 2000
Profession: Social Worker
Position in profession: Community Relations Social Worker; Recruiter for
    Foster Care and Adoption
Community Service: Life line for Children; Company & Kids; One Church,
    One Child

Name: Zena E. McClain, esq.
Undergraduate College/University: Howard University
Chapter initiated: Omicron Theta Omega
Year initiated: 1994
Profession: Attorney and Counselor at Law
Position in profession: Owner, The McClain Law Firm, LLC
Community Service: Historic Savannah Review Board; Chatham County's
    Personnel Advisory Board; The Links Incorporated; Jack and Jill of
    America, Inc.; Trustee, Bethel A.M.E. Church

Name: Bette C. Milledge
Undergraduate College/University: West Virginia State College/University
Chapter initiated: Nu
Year initiated: 1951
Profession: Home Economist (Classroom Teacher)
Position in profession: Teacher
Community Service: Brought CHEC Program to Savannah; Taught at
    Myers Middle School and Savannah State College/University; Taught
    parents in all Savannah's projects

Name: Patricia Jenkins Mincey
Undergraduate College/University: Morris Brown College
Chapter initiated: Gamma Gamma
Year initiated: 1959
Profession: Education
Position in profession: Retired Educator
Community Service: Lamarville Community Association; SALT Council; Vacation Bible School; Pickens Circle and Moderator of Presbyterian Women; Ivy Leaf Reporter; Worked with Retired Sorors; Pan Hellenic Baby Contest

Name: Michelle Mincey-Gwyn
Undergraduate College/University: Savannah State College/Armstrong State College
Chapter initiated: Gamma Sigma Omega
Year initiated: 2000
Profession: Education
Position in profession: Teacher
Community Service: Church and organizations in church; Mentoring

Name: Annette S. Mitchell
Undergraduate College/University: Savannah State College
Chapter initiated: Gamma Sigma Omega
Year initiated: 1980
Profession: Retire Educator
Position in profession: Teacher/Media Specialist
Community Service: Feed and Clothe the Homeless; Sojourner Savannah Project, Hospice Savannah; March of Dimes; Susan G. Komen Race for Cure; Cancer Society; Sickle Cell Foundation; Relay for Life; West Broad Street YMCA; Boys Booked on Barber Shops; Girls Booked on Beauty Shops; Savannah Black Heritage Festival; Martin Luther King, Jr. Day Observance Committee; United Negro College Fund; NAACP

Name: LaShawna K. Alderman-Mullgrav
Undergraduate College/University: South Carolina State University
Chapter initiated: Beta Sigma
Year initiated: 1991
Profession: Education

Position in profession: Program Manager for Exceptional Children

Community Service: Resurrection of Our Lord Catholic Church – Eucharistic Minister; St. Martin DePorres Society; South Carolina State University National Alumni Association, Savannah Chapter – Charter Member, Life member, former chapter president

Name: Eleanor W. Murdock

Undergraduate College/University: South Carolina State College

Chapter initiated: 1947

Year initiated: Beta Sigma

Profession: Rehabilitation Services of Illinois

Position in profession: Associate Director of the Illinois Department of Rehabilitation Services (Retired)

Community Service: Voter Registration, providing clothes for needy children and adults, reading to 2nd and 3rd graders in the public school system, assisting with feeding the homeless, taking food to and visiting the homebound

Name: Nicole A. Neal

Undergraduate College/University: Armstrong Atlantic State University

Chapter initiated: Sigma Tau

Year initiated: 2010

Profession: Student/Doctor's Technician

Position in profession: Graduate Student

Community Service: volunteer at Memorial Health, Light the Night Walk, Old Savannah City Mission, Breast Cancer Walk

Name: Kimberly Nixon

Undergraduate College/University: Florida Memorial University

Chapter initiated: Delta Eta

Year initiated: 2000

Profession: Information Technology

Position in profession: Adjunct Instructor

Community Service: Old Savannah City Mission; HAAF Youth Center; 4 H; Boys & Girls Club; Torch Club, Keystone Club; Girls Scouts

Name: Virginia Annette Mercer Parham
Undergraduate College/University: Savannah State College (now University)
Chapter initiated: Gamma Upsilon
Year initiated: 1959
Profession: Employee Benefits
Position in profession: Trust Fund Administrator/Manager, Retired
Community Service: Greenbriar Children's Center Board of Directors; West Broad Street YMCA Board of Directors; Connor's Temple Baptist Church Board of Christian Education (Youth Activities)

Name: Margaret Anne Roberts Pearson
Undergraduate College/University: Savannah State University
Chapter initiated: Gamma Upsilon
Year initiated: 1974
Profession: Educator
Position in profession: Teacher
Community Service: American Cancer Society; Tutoring; Quilts for Senior Citizens; Leukemia and Lymphoma, Old Savannah City Mission

Name: Dr. Freddie L. Pippen
Undergraduate College/University: Savannah State College/University; Atlanta University; Jacksonville Theology Seminary
Chapter initiated: Gamma Sigma Omega
Year initiated: 1970
Profession: Retired Teacher/Professor, Savannah State University
Position in profession: Teacher
Community Service: Feeding Homeless; Tutoring; Voter Registration

Name: Melinda Pippen-Miller
Undergraduate College/University: Tuskegee University
Chapter initiated: Gamma Kappa
Year initiated: 1989
Profession: School Social Worker
Position in profession: School Social Worker
Community Service: Old Savannah City Mission, Voter Registration; Formal Cheerleader Coach, Savannah Pals; Character Counts, committee, Board of Education; assisting needy school kids with clothing; gift wrapping with Greenbriar Children's Center

Name: Carolyne Powers
Undergraduate College/University: Tuskegee University/Albany State University/ Nova Southeastern University
Chapter initiated: Lambda Xi Omega
Year initiated: 1997
Profession: Education
Position in profession: Retired Assistant Principal
Community Service: Member of Jonesville Baptist Church; King Tisdell Cottage Foundation

Name: Cherée Powers
Undergraduate College/University: Armstrong Atlantic State University
Chapter initiated: Sigma Tau
Year initiated: Fall 2008
Profession: Department of Justice/U.S. Attorney's Office
Position in profession: Executive Assistant to the U.S. Attorney

Name: Emma Lue Jordan Preer
Undergraduate College/University: Savannah State College/University
Chapter initiated: Gamma Upsilon
Year initiated: 1958
Profession: Education
Position in profession: Elementary Education/Retired Title 1 Family Advocate
Community Service: Cloverdale Improvement Association; Life Member of the NAACP and Savannah State University National Alumni Association; Benedict Council of Catholic Women; Social Apostolate of Savannah Advisory Board

Name: Ivy Richardson
Undergraduate College/University: Savannah State College/University
Chapter initiated: Gamma Upsilon
Year initiated: 1973
Profession: Education
Position in profession: Director of Alternative Program
Community Service: Tutoring in math and reading; serving the homeless

Name: Carolyn H. Russell
Undergraduate College/University: Savannah State College/University
Chapter initiated: Gamma Upsilon
Year initiated: 1955
Profession: Education
Position in profession: Retired Teacher
Community Service: Volunteer AARP Tax preparer

Name: Taqwaa Falaq Saleem
Undergraduate College: Savannah State University
Chapter Initiated: Gamma Upsilon
Year Initiated: 2007
Profession: Higher Education and Consulting
Position in Profession: College Professor, Department of Liberal Arts at Savannah
    State University; Legal Assistant - Law Offices of Lester B. Johnson, III;
    Professional Consultant and Event Planner - Simply Splendid Events
Community Service: Co-Founder and Administrator - The #BlockParty Movement;
    National Council of Negro Women, Inc.; Primary Advisor - Savannah State
    University Collegiate Section of National Council of Negro Women, Inc.;
    Member - Telfair Museums of Art; Membership Council (Strategic Planning)
    - Junior League of Savannah; Pastor's Armor Bearers, Hospitality, Embrace the
    Vision Team Ministries - Living Hope Community Fellowship

Name: Dr. Emily Crawford Sanders
Undergraduate College/University: Savannah State University
Chapter initiated: Gamma Upsilon
Year initiated: 1974
Profession: Online Professor and Curriculum Writer Designer
Position in profession: College Professor
Community Service: Minister of Music and Video Production Grant Chapel
    Presbyterian Church, American Marketing Association, Presbyterian
    Deacon; Board of Directors Raising Consciousness

Name: Diann B. Scott
Undergraduate College/University: Fort Valley State College
Chapter initiated: Alpha Beta
Year initiated: 1971
Profession: Retail Management
Position in profession: Corporate Buyer, Systems Trainer, Store Manager
Community Service: NAACP, NCNW, Gadsden Elementary School Volunteer

Name: Tarangula "Tammy" Barnes Scott
Undergraduate College/University: Tuskegee University
Chapter initiated: Gamma Kappa
Year initiated: 1987
Profession: Educator
Position in profession: Teacher/Instructional Coach
Community Service: Old Savannah City Mission; Beta Club; Summit
    Gymnastics Parent Advisory Student Leadership Program

Name: Tara Scott-Brown
Undergraduate College/University: Savannah State University
Chapter initiated: Gamma Sigma Omega
Year initiated: 2006
Profession: Paralegal/Law
Position in profession: Paralegal
Community Service: Member of Top Ladies of Distinction, Inc, a community
    service organization

Name: Audrey Barnes Singleton
Undergraduate College/University: Savannah State College/University
Chapter initiated: Gamma Upsilon
Year initiated: 1969
Profession: Retired Educator
Position in profession: 2nd grade Gifted Teacher/Facilitator
Community Service: Old Savannah City Mission, Tom Austin's House, 2nd
    Harvest American Food Bank, Greenbriar Children's Center, Light the
    Night Walk, Relay for Life, Ronald McDonald House, American Cancer
    Society, Bartlett Middle School

Name: Gwendolyn J. Smith
Undergraduate College/University: Savannah State University
Chapter initiated: Gamma Sigma Omega
Year initiated: 1980
Profession: Educator Administrator
Position in profession: Deputy Superintendent of Schools
Community Service: Vice Chairman Low Country Council of Government
    of Ridgeland, SC; Low Country Foundation Board – Jasper County
    Community

Name: Dorothy D. Speed
Undergraduate College/University: Tuskegee (Institute) University
Chapter initiated: Gamma Sigma Omega
Year initiated: 1992
Profession: Education
Position in profession: Teacher/Assistant Principal
Community Service: Curtis V. Cooper Primary Health Care Center Board;
    Advisor for Bethel Missionary Baptist Church Women's Ministry; Block
    Volunteer for March of Dimes; Artistic Society and Easter Seal

Name: Sharon Brown-Stallings
Undergraduate College/University: Savannah State University
Chapter initiated: Gamma Upsilon
Year initiated: 2001
Profession: Education
Position in profession: Teacher
Community Service: FBLA Advisor, Assistant Graduate Advisor, Sigma Tau

Name: Regina R. Thomas-Williams
Undergraduate College/University: Albany State University
Chapter initiated: Gamma Sigma
Year initiated: 1986
Profession: Registrar, Accountant
Position in profession: Savannah Technical College Registrar
Community Service: Church Treasurer, Berean Bible Chapel; Volunteer,
    Girl Scouts of the USA; Sol C. Johnson High School Varsity Cheerleader
    Team Co-Advisor

Name: LaTanya Thompson
Undergraduate College/University: Georgia Southern University/Armstrong
    State College
Chapter initiated: Gamma Sigma Omega
Year initiated: 2006
Profession: Professional Registered Nurse
Position in profession: Registered Nurse
Community Service: NAACP, Savannah Black Nurses Association; National
    Black Nurses Association

Name: Marjory Varnedoe
Undergraduate College/University: Hampton Institute/University
Chapter initiated: Gamma Theta
Year initiated: 1969
Profession: Education
Position in profession: Retired English Teacher, Retired Guidance Counselor
Community Service: Hi-Fidelity Civic Club; Stewardess and Missionary President at St. Peter's A.M.E. Church, Midway, GA

Name: Dr. Clemontine F. Washington
Undergraduate College: Savannah State University
Chapter Initiated: Gamma Upsilon
Year Initiated: 1965
Profession: Education
Position in Profession: Teacher and Administrator
Community Service: Greenbriar Children's Center Board of Director; Hodge Memorial Day Care Center Board of Directors; Dorchester Improvement Association Board of Directors; Advisory Board Member Liberty County-United Way of the Coastal Empire; member, St. Matthews Episcopal Church; Mayor, City of Midway; member, Georgia Municipal Association

Name: Ericka Coleman Washington
Undergraduate College/University: South Carolina State University
Chapter initiated: Beta Zeta Omega
Year initiated: 1996
Profession: Education
Position in profession: Assistant Principal, Savannah High School
Community Service: Cheerleader Advisor; volunteer with Savannah G.I.R.L.S.; Rock; Volunteer with Miss Black Savannah Pageant; volunteer with Hodge Memorial Daycare and Hodge Memorial PTA

Name: Emily Preer-Williams
Undergraduate College/University: Savannah State University
Chapter initiated: Gamma Sigma Omega
Year initiated: 1997
Profession: N/A
Position in profession: N/A

Name: Lois Vedelle Williams
Undergraduate College/University: Savannah State University
Chapter initiated: Gamma Sigma Omega Chapter
Year initiated: 1997
Profession: Elementary School Teacher
Position in profession: Retired Educator
Community Service: United Way Volunteer, MLK Day of Service Project,
   Thomas Austin House, Senior Citizens of Savannah and Second Harvest
   Food Bank

Name: Nicole Michelle Williams
Undergraduate College/University: Savannah State University
Chapter initiated: Gamma Upsilon
Year initiated: 2002
Profession: United States Army Corps of Engineers
Position in profession: Budget Technician
Community Service: Electa Chapter #1-Order of Eastern Star; Savannah
   Chapter Top Ladies of Distinction; Omar Court #91-Daughters of Isis;
   Castle Club Toastmasters; Coastal Georgia Chapter American Society
   of Military Comptrollers; American Cancer Society Chatham County
   and West Chatham County Relay for Life; Tremont Temple Missionary
   Baptist Church

Name: Wanda L. Williams
Undergraduate College/University: Georgia College
Chapter initiated: Kappa Eta
Year initiated: 1976
Profession: Local Municipal Government
Position in profession: (Retired) Public Administrator, Research and Budget
   Director
Community Service: American Cancer Society, United Way

Name: Dorothy Boston Wilson
Undergraduate College/University: Savannah State College
Chapter initiated: Gamma Sigma Omega
Year initiated: 1975
Profession: Educator
Position in profession: Retired Vocational Office Training Coordinator

Community Service: Board of Directors, Greenbriar Children's Center; Savannah Schools Credit Union Supervisory Committee; President, Chatham County Retired Educators; President of Georgia Retired Educators Association Foundation, Inc.; President of the Georgia Retired Educators Association; Chairperson of the Independent Resource Committee for the Department of Family and Children Services; Member of NAACP; St. James A.M.E. Church Trustee Board Emeritus; Diamond Life Member, Savannah State University Alumni Association

Name: Doris D. Wood
Undergraduate College/University: South Carolina State/University
Chapter initiated: Gamma Sigma Omega
Year initiated: 1992
Profession: Education
Position in profession: High School Social Studies Teacher
Community Service: Church Service; Food Bank

Name: Dr. Tamika M. Wright
Undergraduate College/University: Georgia Southern University
Chapter initiated: Gamma Sigma Omega
Year initiated: 2000
Profession: Educator
Position in profession: Assistant Principal
Community Service: Tutorial at Townsley Chapel AME, mentoring the youth

Name: Lydia Smith Young
Undergraduate College/University: Savannah State College
Chapter initiated: Gamma Upsilon
Year initiated: 1965
Profession: Chemist; Accountant
Position in profession: Analytical Lab Manager; Office Manager
Community Service: Butler Presbyterian Church Witness Ministry, Elder, Moderator Fiscal Affairs; BRAVO Music Company, Treasurer; MARTHA, Inc., Treasurer; Board Member, Hodge Day Care Center; Beach High School Class of 1964 Treasurer

Appendix B

Former Basilei

Zena McClain	2011-2012
Clemontine F. Washington	2009-2010
Emma Jean Conyers	2007-2008
Patricia J. Clark	2005-2006
Carolyn H. Bell	2003-2004
Vanessa M. Kaigler	2001-2002
Virginia M. Parham	1999-2000
Johnye W. Gillans	1997-1998
Emily C. Williams	1995-1996
Charlene Jones	1993-1994
Marilyn Taylor	1991-1992
Albertha E. Boston (deceased)	1989-1990
Marjory Varnedoe	1987-1988
Dorothy B. Wilson	1985-1986
Rebecca J. Cooper	1983-1984
Johnye W. Gillans	1981-1982
Jessie C. DeLoach	1979-1980
Lydia S. Young	1977-1978
Clemontine F. Washington	1975-1976
Margaret C. Robinson	1972-1974
Carolyn Gantt	1971-1972
Mozella G. Collier (deceased)	1969-1970
Eudora Allen	1967-1968
Emma L. Preer	1965-1966
Virginia Parham	1963-1964
Hettie Copeland	1961-1963
Leila Braithwaite (deceased)	1959-1961
Ouida Thompson	1958-1959

Violet Singleton (deceased)	1956-1957
Inez B. Williams (deceased)	1954-1956
Mary McDew (deceased)	1953-1954
Jane Parker (deceased)	1952-1953
Kathryn Bogan Johnson	1950-1952
Mary McDew (deceased)	1949-1950
Mattie B. Payne (deceased)	1946-1949
Dorothy B. Jamerson (deceased)	1945-1946
Martha W. Wilson (Charter Basileus, deceased)	1943-1945

Appendix C

Ivies Beyond the Wall

Sylvia E. Bowen

Leila Braithwaite

Mozella G. Collier

Countess Verdelle Young Cox

Beatrice Doe

Dorothy C. Hamilton

Dorothy Jamerson

Mattie Leftwich

Nadine C. Lewis

Ethel J. Miller

Linda A. Owens

Violet A. Singleton

Bernyce S. Smith

Evanel R. Terrell

Eleanor B. Williams

Inez B. Williams

Ellen W. Wilson

Mattie B. Payne

Jacqueline A. Handy

Henrietta Collier Perry

Brenda Stevens

Sadie Bryant Williams

Mary McDew

Shirley A. McGee Brown

Marion Priester Roberts

Martha W. Wilson

Gwendolyn Johnson

Agatha Anderson Cooper

Albertha E. Boston

Appendix D

Explanation of Terms

AKA	Alpha Kappa Alpha
Anti-Basileus	Vice President
Anti-Grammateus	Assistant Secretary
Anti-Tamiouchos	Assistant Treasurer
Basilei	Presidents
Basileus	President
Boule Launch	Activities that led up to the 100th birthday celebration at the Boule
Boule	International Conference; constitutional decision making body of the Sorority
Cluster VI	The Cluster in which Gamma Sigma Omega is located
Cluster	A group of chapters in a Region
EAF	The Alpha Kappa Alpha Educational Advancement Foundation that promotes lifelong learning by securing charitable contributions, gifts and endowed fund to award scholarships, fellowships and grants
Epistoleus	Corresponding Secretary
Founders' Day	A day within January – March to honor the founding members of Alpha Kappa Alpha Sorority, Inc.
Golden Soror	A woman who has been an Alpha Kappa Alpha woman for 50 years through 74 years
Grammateus	Secretary
Greek Medley	The playing of the hymns of sororities and fraternities that are a part of the National Pan-Hellenic Council, Inc

GSO	Gamma Sigma Omega
Hodegos	Hostess
Honey Do	A husband or significant other who assists an AKA when requested
Honey Don't	A child of an AKA
Ivies Beyond the Wall	Deceased sorors
Life Member	A soror who has been a member for at least 25 years and meets the financial and active membership requirements of the Sorority
MIP	Membership Intake Process, the procedure to become an Alpha Kappa Alpha member
Pan-Hellenic Council	A collaborative decision making body on services and social issues for the following sororities and fraternities: Alpha Phi Alpa Fraternity, Alpha Kappa Alpha Sorority, Kappa Alpha Psi Fraternity, Omega Psi Phi Fraternity, Delta Sigma Theta Sorority, Phi Beta Sigma Fraternity, Zeta Phi Beta Sorority, Sigma Gamma Rho Sorority, and Iota Phi Theta Fraternity
Pecunious Grammateus	Financial Secretary
Philacter	Sergeant-At-Arms
Program	International, National, and Local Service and Social Initiatives established by the Sorority
Regional Conference	An annual conference held in each region hosted by the chapters within that region
Regions	Chapters grouped by the Boule according to geographical location and density of population
Silver Soror	A woman who has been an Alpha Kappa Alpha woman for 25 years through 49 years
Soror of the Year	Member honored as best all around for the year
Soror	Sister
Sorority	Sisterhood
South Atlantic Region	Gamma Sigma Omega's region: Florida, Georgia, South Carolina
Supreme	International Officer
Tamiouchos	Treasurer

Appendix E

Life Members
Eudora Allen
Carol Bell
+Albertha Boston
Janie Bruen
Patricia Clark
Emma Conyers
Connie Cooper
Jessie Deloach
*Pendar Franklin
Johnye Gillans
Sonia R. Grant
Annie Jackson
Charlene Jones
+Merdis Lyons
Betty Milledge

Patricia Mincey
Eleanor Murdock
Virginia Parham
Emma Preer
Margaret Robinson
Carolyn Russell
Emily Crawford Sanders
Audrey Singleton
Rochelle D. Small-Toney
Gwendolyn Smith
Marjory Varnedoe
*Albertha Vaughn
Clemontine Washington
*Leona Williams
Dorothy Wilson
Lydia Young

+deceased

*inactive in Gamma Sigma Omega Chapter

Appendix F

Gamma Sigma Omega Chapter
Names as appeared on December Roster 2012

Eudora M. Allen
Valencia R. Thomas Austin
Geraldine Baker
Queen Barnes
Carol Bell
Erica Benjamin
Albertha E. Boston
Lucille Tyson Brown
Janie B. Bruen
Janice M. Kennedy Bryant
Lakechia Bryant
Annie Coleman Chappell
Kimberly Chappell-Stevens
Patricia J. Clark
Mary Coleman
Albertha Collier
Amy Conyers
Emma J. Conyers
Connie Cooper
Denise Cooper
Rebecca Cooper
Brittany Davis
Irene Davis
Jessie Collier DeLoach
Juanita Denson
Joyce Griffin Dingle
Carolyn S. Drayton

Tenay Drayton
Courtney Eaton
Ellen V. Evans
Laveda D. Farrior
Nicole Fields
Neldra Jewel Flint
Latondia Gadson
Carol Gamble
Ethel Gibbs
Marquitha Gibson
Jacquelyn Gilbert-Grant
Johnye W. Gillans
Eleanor J. Ginn
Elza L. Givens
Christian B. Goodman
Sonia Renee Grant
Henrietta S. Gray
Lakyah Hatcher
Anna Henderson
Lolita Hickman
Johnnie Holmes
Ethel Hunter
Sheila Hutcherson
Alvernia Jackson
Annie C. Jackson
Julie Latrace Jackson
Lorna C. Jackson

Maxine E. Jackson
Glenda S. James
Brenda Jenkins
Andrea L. Johnson
Hope Johnson
Janice Johnson
Margaret Burney Johnson
Monifa I. Johnson
Harriette Johnson-Brinson
Charlene E. Jones
Linda Wright Jordan
Vanessa Kaigler
Lavinea G. Kennedy
Ashle' S. King
Kayla R. Knight
Tanesha D. Sloan Lester
Terri Lewis
Annie Mahone
Shakela Martin
Carmelita Maynard
Zena E. McClain
Renae M. McCollough
Betty J. Milledge
Patricia J. Mincey
Michelle Mincey-Gwyn
Annette Mitchell
LaShawna K. Mullgrav
Eleanor Murdock
Nicole A. Neal
Kimberly Nixon
Virginia M. Parham
Margaret A.R.Pearson
Freddie L. Pippen
Melinda Pippen-Miller
Cheree M. Powers
Emma Lue Preer
Kathy Reynolds
Ivy Richardson
Margaret Robinson

Elisia A. Rooks
Carolyn H. Russell
Taqwaa F. Saleem
Emily Crawford Sanders
Sharon Savage-Watson
April Scott
Diann Scott
Tarangula Barnes Scott
Tara M. Scott-Brown
Lavertta Scott-Perry
LeKara Simmons
Audrey B. Signleton
Serdalia Singleton
Rochelle D. Small-Toney
Ellisha M. Smith
Gwendolyn Smith
Dorothy D. Speed
Sharon Stallings
Deonn Stone
Regina R. Thomas-Williams
Kia W. Thompson
LaTanya Thompson
Jacqueline P. Tomlin
Natatia VanEllison
Marjory Varnedoe
Clemontine F. Washington
Ericka Coleman Washington
Denise Weems-White
Delores Wilhite
Andrea Bowers Williams
Emily Preer Williams
Janine Williams
Lois Vedelle Williams
Nicole M. Williams
Wanda Williams
Dorothy B. Wilson
Doris D. Wood
Tamika Minor Wright
Lydia S. Young

APPENDIX G

Officers and Committee Chairmen, 1983-2012

Rebecca R. Cooper, 1983-1984

Basileus	Rebecca R. Cooper
Anti-Basileus	Dorothy B. Wilson
Grammateus	Henrietta C. Perry
Anti-Grammateus	Virginia Parham
Epistoleus	Brenda T. Stevens
Tamiouchos	Marilyn Taylor
Anti-Tamiouchos	Eunice Washington
Hodegos	Nadine C. Lewis
Philacter	Winifred Badger
Ivy Leaf Reporter	Quay Hurt
Membership Chairman	Albertha E. Boston
Parliamentarian	Dora Myles
Undergraduate Advisor	Clemontine F. Washington
Assistant Undergraduate Advisor	Charlene Jones
Member-at-Large	Rena Varnedoe

Committee Chairmen

Audit	Jessie C. DeLoach
Hodegos	Nadine C. Lewis
Music	Jane Parker
Constitution	Dora S. Myles
Convention Transportation	Emily Williams
Hardship	Audrey B. Singleton
Housing	Mozella G. Collier

1984 Officers filling the following offices:

Anti-Grammateus	Marian Wiles
Epistoleus	Mildred J. Mobley
Tamiouchos	Eunice Washington
Anti-Tamiouchos	Ivy Richardson
Ivy Leaf Reporter	Marjory Varnedoe
Assistant Membership Chairman	Linda Alston
Undergraduate Advisor	Charlene Jones
Assistant Undergraduate Advisor	Clemontine F. Washington

Dorothy Boston Wilson, 1985-1986

Basileus	Dorothy B. Wilson
Anti-Basileus	Marjory Varnedoe
Grammateus	Jeraldine W. Coleman
Anti-Grammateus	Marian Wiles
Tamiouchos	Eunice Washington
Anti-Tamiouchos	Ivy Richardson
Epistoleus	Mildred J. Mobley
Parliamentarian	Albertha Collier
Member-at-Large	Emma L. Preer
Ivy Leaf Reporter	Theresa White
Graduate Advisor	Charlene Jones
Assistant Graduate Advisor	Anne Lipsey
Membership Chairman	Countess Y. Cox
Assistant Membership Chairman	Linda Alston
Hodegos	Annie Jackson
Philacter	Carolyn Russell
Historian	Evanel Terrell

Committee Chairmen

Program	Marjory Varnedoe
Basileus Council	Carolyn Gantt
Inspiration	Emily Williams
Retreat/Grievance	Carolyn Bell
Membership	Countess Y. Cox
Constitution and By-Laws	Albertha Collier
Graduate Advisor Council	Charlene Jones
Foundation	Lydia Young
Founders' Day	Freddie Pippen
Hardship	Agatha Cooper
Hospitality	Annie Jackson
Budget	Eunice Washington
Awards	Emma Preer

Audit	Virginia Parham
Transportation	Johnye Gilllans
Fundraising	Clemontine F. Washington
Regional Scrapbook	Bette Milledge
Music	Jane Parker
Mozella G. Collier Memorial Award	Onnye J. Sears
Connection	Jessie C. DeLoach
YMCA	Emma Preer
TRI-HI-Y	Ivy Richardson

Marjory Varnedoe, 1987-1988

Basileus	Marjory Varnedoe
Anti-Basileus	Carolyn Bell
Grammateus	Inez Williams
Anti-Grammateus	Audrey Singleton
Tamiouchos	Albertha E. Boston
Anti-Tamiouchos	Lydia Young
Epistoleus	Onnye Jean Sears
Graduate Advisor	Charlene Jones
Assistant Graduate Advisor	Linda Alston
Ivy Leaf Reporter	Theresa White
Parliamentarian	Rebecca Cooper
Philacter	Barbara Wilborn
Historian	Evanel Terrell
Member-at-Large	Carolyn Russell
Membership Chairman	Leona Henley
Hodegos	Johnye Gillans

Albertha E. Boston, 1989-1990

Basileus	Albertha E. Boston
Anti-Basileus	Marilyn S. Taylor
Grammateus	Renee' Williams
Anti-Grammateus	Emily Williams
Tamiouchos	Merdis Lyons
Anti-Tamiouchos	Rena Varnedoe
Epistoleus	Emma Jean Conyers
Graduate Advisor	Charlene Jones
Assistant Graduate Advisor	Gwendolyn Cummings
Ivy Leaf Reporter	Linda Alston
Parliamentarian	Ivy Richardson
Philacters	Theresa Hudson and Tarangula D. Barnes
Historian	Shirley M. Brown
Member-at-Large	Willie Mae Freeman
Hodegos	Virginia M. Parham and Rosa L. Pringle
Membership Chairman	Jeraldine C. Patterson
Assistant Membership Chairman	Clemontine F. Washington

1990 Officers filling the following offices:

Grammateus	Charlene Jones
Anti-Grammateus	Carolyn Russell
Epistoleus	Mildred J. Mobley
Graduate Advisor	Renee' Williams
Ivy Leaf Reporter	Marjory Varnedoe
Philacter	Audrey B. Singleton
Membership Chairman	Clemontine F. Washington
Assistant Membership Chairman	Emily Williams

Marilyn Taylor, 1991-1992

Basileus	Marilyn S. Taylor
Anti-Basileus	Charlene Jones
Grammateus	Deanna Cross
Anti-Grammateus	Karen Clark
Tamiouchos	Dorothy B. Wilson
Anti-Tamiouchos	Carolyn Russell
Epistoleus	Mildred J. Mobley
Graduate Advisor	Renee' Williams
Assistant Graduate Advisor	Gwendolyn Cummings
Ivy Leaf Reporter	Marjory Varnedoe
Parliamentarian	Patricia Mincey
Philacter	Linda Alston-Owens
Hodegos	Albertha W. Collier and Nettie M. Levett
Member-at-Large	Willie Mae Freeman
Historian	Albertha E. Boston
Membership Chairman	Clemontine F. Washington
Assistant Membership Chairman	Emily Williams

1992 Officers filling the following offices:

Epistoleus	Johnye W. Gillans
Graduate Advisor	Audrey Singleton
Ivy Leaf Reporter	Vernice C. Whitfield
Member-at-Large	Lydia Young
Assistant Membership Chairman	Virginia Parham

1991-1992 Committee Chairmen

Archives	Albertha E. Boston
Audit	Lydia Young
Budget/Finance	Dorothy B. Wilson
EAF	Virginia Parham

AKA-Christmas Savings	Virginia M. Parham/Emma J. Conyers
Constitution	Patricia Mincey
Founders' Day	Johnye Gillans
Founders' Day Awards	Lydia Young
Fundraising	Carolyn Bell/Dorothy Gardner
Hospitality/Social	Nettie Levette/Albertha Collier
Membership	Clemontine F. Washington/Emily Williams
Music	Jane Parker
Pan-Hellenic	Karen Clark/Ellen Wilson
Photography	Freddie Pippen
Program	Charlene Jones/Clemontine F. Washington
Protocol	Shirley Brown
Public Relations/Newsletter	Marjory Varnedoe
Standards/Retreat	Virginia Parham

Charlene E. Jones, 1993-1994

Basileus	Charlene E. Jones
Anti-Basileus	Emily Williams
Grammateus	Ivy Richardson
Anti-Grammateus	Martha Hicks
Tamiouchos	Carolyn Russell
Anti-Tamiouchos	Vanessa Miller
Pecunious Grammateus	Dorothy B. Wilson
Hodegos	Ellen Wilson
Philacter	Andrea Williams
Parlimentarian	Patricia Mincey
Ivy Leaf Reporter	Vernice Whitfield
Membership Chairman	Clemontine F. Washington
Assistant Membership Chairman	Virginia Parham
Graduate Advisor	Audrey Singleton
Assistant Graduate Advisor	Marilyn Taylor and Vicky Jackson
Historian	Albertha E. Boston
Member-at-Large	Lydia Young

1994 Officers filling the following offices:

Epistoleus	Cora Thompson
Member-at-Large	Virginia James
Ivy Leaf Reporter	Vernice C. Whitfield (2nd two year term)
Graduate Advisor	Audrey Singleton (1st full two year term)
Assistant Graduate Advisor	Vicky Sutton Jackson (1st full two year term)
Pecunious Grammateus	Dorothy B. Wilson (1st full two year term)

Committee Chairmen

Archives	Albertha E. Boston
Audit	Lydia Young

Budget/Finance	Carolyn Russell
EAF	Natasha Haggins
AKA-Christmas Savings	Carolyn Russell
Constitution/Bylaws	Patricia Mincey
Founders' Day	Ellen Wilson
Founders' Day Awards	Emma Preer
Fundraising	Marjory Varnedoe
Hospitality/Social	Ellen Wilson
Membership	Clemontine F. Washington
Music	Vernice Whitfield
Pan-Hellenic	Dorothy Williams
Photography	Vernice Whitfield
Program	Emily Williams
Protocol	Shirley Brown
Public Relations/Newsletter	Vernice Whitfield
Regional Scrapbooks	Renee' Grant
Standards/Retreat	Virginia Parham
Inspiration	Freddie Pippen
Newsletter	Dorothy B. Wilson
Connection	Virginia James
COIP	Linda Owens

1994 Program Chairmen

Education	Vernice Whitfield/Emily Williams
Black Family	Dorothy Williams
Health	Alvernia Wilson
Economics	Dorothy Wilson
Cultural Arts	Carolyn Bell; Renee' Grant/ Gwendolyn Moore, Co-Chairs
World Family	Freddie Pippen

Assignments for the coverage of Program activities:

February	Charlene Jones, Water Day
	Dorothy Wilson, Cluster Luncheon

March	Vicky Sutton-Jackson/Charlene Jones, Regional Conference
April	Vicky Sutton-Jackson, Black Dollar Day and Media Appreciation Day
May	Dorothy Williams, Black Family
June	Gwendolyn Moore, Performing Arts Vernice Whitfield, Boule
August	Dorothy Wilson/Vernice Whitfield, Child Wellness Month
September	Renee' Williams Grant, Senior Citizens Day
October	Emily Williams, World Hunger Day
November-December	Freddie Pippen, International Adoption Month

Emma C. Williams (Emily), 1995-1996

Basileus	Emma C. Williams
Anti-Basileus	Vernice P. Whitfield
Grammateus	Martha Hicks
Anti-Grammateus	Dorothy Williams
Tamiouchos	Vanessa M. Kaigler
Pecunious Grammateus	Dorothy B. Wilson
Epistoleus	Bernyce Smith
Hodegos	Melinda Pippen Miller
Philacter	Pendar Franklin
Ivy Leaf Reporter	Carolyn Bell
Membership Chairman	Annie Jackson
Assistant Membership Chairman	Linda Owens
Graduate Advisor	Audrey Singleton
Assistant Graduate Advisor	Vicky Sutton-Jackson
On-Campus Advisor	Emily Crawford-Sanders
Historian	Lydia Young
Member-at-Large	Virginia James

1996 Officers filling the following offices:

Anti-Basileus	Johnye W. Gillans
Anti-Tamiouchos	Doris D. Wood
Pecunious Grammateus	Merdis J. Lyons
Hodegos	Natasha Harris-Haggan
Ivy Leaf Reporter	Stephanie Grantham
Graduate Advisor	Emily Crawford-Sanders
Member-at-large	Sonia Renee' Williams Grant

Committee Chairmen

Mathematics and Science Literacy	Pendar Franklin and Davida Wood
American Red Cross/Health	Sylvia Perry and Alvernia Wilson
Business Round Table	Dorothy B. Wilson

Black Family   Dorothy Williams Speed
Senior Citizens   Patricia Clark
Cleveland Job Corp   Emily Sanders
Cultural Arts   Carolyn Bell

Johnye W. Gillans, 1997-1998

Basileus	Johnye W. Gillans
Anti-Basileus	Virginia Parham
Grammateus	Dorothy D. Speed
Anti-Grammateus	Denyce Sanders
Epistoleus	Bernyce S. Smith
Tamiouchos	Doris D. Wood
Anti-Tamiouchos	Nicole Fields
Pecunious Grammateus	Merdis J. Lyons
Hodegos	Alvernia Wilson
Philacter	Kimberly David
Parliamentarian	Connie Cooper
Ivy Leaf Reporter	Patricia Mincey
Membership Chairman	Patricia Clark
Assistant Membership Chairman	Albertha E. Boston
Graduate Advisor	Emily Crawford-Sanders
Assistant Graduate Advisor	Clemontine F. Washington
Historian	Rena Varnedoe
Member-at-Large	Sonia Renee' Grant

Committee Chairmen

Archives/Historian	Rena Varnedoe
	Sadie Williams, Co-Chairman
Audit	Lydia Young
	Carolyn Russell /Albertha Vaughns, Co-Chairmen
Awards	Audrey Singleton
	Gwendolyn Smith, Co-Chairman
Budget and Finance	Doris Davida Wood
	Nicole Fields, Co-Chairman
Connection	Jacqueline Hand
	Chandra Haines, Co-Chairman

Constitution/Bylaws	Connie Cooper
	Emma Jean Conyers, Co-Chairman
Founders' Day	Clemontine F. Washington
	Marjory Varnedoe, Co-Chairman
Fundraising/Junior Debs	Dorothy Wilson
	Andrea Williams/Simikia Young,
	Co-Chairmen
Graduate Council	Emily Crawford-Sanders
	Clemontine F. Washington,
	Co-Chairman
Hospitality	Alvernia Wilson
	LeRon McKendricks, Co-Chairman
Membership	Patricia Clark
	Alberha E. Boston, Co-Chairman
Public Relations	Patricia Mincey
	Melissa Smith, Co-Chairman
Standards and Retreat	Charlene Jones, Denise Williams,
	Co-Chairman

1998 Officers filling the following offices:

Epistoleus	Marjory Varnedoe
Pecunious Grammateus	Regina Williams
Ivy Leaf Reporter	Patricia Mincey
Member-at-Large	Chandra Haines
Chaplain	Maureen Maxwell

Virginia Mercer Parham, 1999-2000

Basileus	Virginia M. Parham
Anti-Basileus	Vanessa M. Kaigler
Grammateus	I. Denyce Sanders
Anti-Grammateus	Maureen Maxwell
Tamiouchos	Doris Davida Wood
Hodegos	Emily Williams
Parliamentarian	Lydia Young
Philacter	Melissa Smith Miller (resigned June 2000)
Huriyah Al-Batin	
Historian	Emma J. Preer
Chaplain	Emily Preer-Williams
Graduate Advisor	Emily Crawford-Sanders (resigned January 2000)
Assistant Graduate Advisor	Clemontine F. Washington
Member-at-Large	Chandra Haines (resigned in June)

Other officers elected or appointed

Epistoleus	Marjory Varnedoe, 1999
	Brenda Jenkins, 2000
Anti-Tamiouchos	Diane Williams, 1999
	Patricia Clark, 2000
Pecunious Grammateus	Regina Williams, 1999
	Albertha E. Boston, 2000
Member-at-Large	Antoinette Barnes (resigned in June)
	Patricia Mincey
Ivy Leaf Reporter	Patricia Mincey
	Charlene Jones, 2000
Graduate Advisor	Clemontine Washington, 2000
Assistant Graduate Advisor	Diane Williams, 2000

Vanessa Miller Kaigler, 2001-2002

Basileus	Vaness Miller Kaigler
Anti-Basileus	Carolyn H. Bell
Grammateus	Maureen Maxwell Walker
Anti-Grammateus	Alvernia S. Wilson
Epistoleus	Brenda Jenkins
Tamiouchos	Patricia Clark
Anti-Tamiouchos	Dorothy B. Wilson
Pecunious Grammateus	Albertha E. Boston
Parliamentarian	Essie S. Johnson
Member-at-Large	Patricia Mincey
Philacter	Maxine Jackson
Ivy Leaf Reporter	Charlene Jones
Hodegos	Johnnie S. Holmes
Historian	Emma J. Conyers
Chaplain	Mildred Mobley
Graduate Advisor	Clemontine F. Washington
Assistant Graduate Advisor	Dianne F. Williams

2002 Officers filling the following offices:

Epistoleus	Patricia Mincey
Pecunious Grammateus	Renae Miller
Ivy Leaf Reporter	Annie Jackson
Member-at-Large	Johnye W. Gillans

Committee Chairmen

Archives	Emma J. Conyers
Budget/Finance	Patricia Clark
Constitution and Bylaws	Essie S. Johnson
Hospitality/Social/Protocol	Johnnie Holmes
Membership	Marjory Varnedoe, Denyce Sanders, Co-Chairman
Public Relations	Charlene Jones

276

Founders' Day	Carolyn H. Bell, Dorothy B. Wilson, Co-Chairman
Junior Deb/Fundraising	Gwendolyn Johnson, LaWanda Tillman, Co-Chairmen
EAF	Carolyn Russell

Carolyn H. Bell, 2003-2004

Basileus	Carolyn H. Bell
Anti-Basileus	Patricia J. Clark
Grammateus	Alvernia Wilson
Anti-Grammateus	Sheila Hutcherson
Tamiouchos	Dorothy B. Wilson
Anti-Tamiouchos	Gwen Johnson
Pecunious Grammateus	Renae M. Miller
Epistoleus	Patricia Mincey
Graduate Advisor	Clemontine Washington
Assistant Graduate Advisor	Michelle Mincey-Lee
On Campus Advisor	Emily Crawford
Ivy Leaf Reporter	Annie Jackson
Parliamentarian	Charlene Jones
Philacter	Natatia VanEllison
Historian	Emma J. Conyers
Member-at-Large	Johnye Gillans
Hodegos	Albertha Collier
Chaplain	Virginia Parham
Pan Hellenic Council Rep	Zenobia Mitchell
Leadership	Sylvia Perry

Committee Chairmen

Audit	Ivy Richardson
Awards	Tamika Minor
Black Family	Johnnie Holmes
Clothes Closet	Carmelita Maynard
Connection	Undine Truedell
Cultural Arts	Jacquelyn Handy/Annie Jackson
Economics	Gwen Johnson
Education	Kim Chappell Stevens
Fundraising	Johnye Gillans
Grants Oversight	Latashia Stroman

GSO Chorale	Johnnie Holmes
Health	Virginia M. Parham
Housing	Wanda Williams
Membership	Denyce Sanders
Scrapbook	LaShawna Mulgrav/Ericka Hayes
Senior Soror Outreach	Leona Williams
Social	Maureen Walker
Standards	Connie Cooper
Technology	Sheila Hutcherson
Uniform	Alvernia Wilson
Wellness	Natatia VanEllison

2004 Officers filling the following offices:

Epistoleus	Sharon Stallings
Pecunious Grammateus	Nicole Williams
Assistant Graduate Advisor	Connie Cooper
Member-at-Large	Sylvia Perry
Ivy Leaf Reporter	Eudora Allen

Patricia J. Clark, 2005-2006

Basileus	Patricia J. Clark
Anti-Basileus	Emma Conyers
Grammateus	Sheila B. Hutcherson
Anti-Grammateus	Undine V. Truedell-Williams
Epistoleus	Shi Evans
Tamiouchos	Gwendolyn Harris Johnson
Anti-Tamiouchos	Ivy P. Richardson
Pecunious Grammateus	Nicole M. Williams
Parliamentarian	Virginia M. Parham
Member-at-Large	Sylvia B. Perry
Philacter	Hope Johnson
Ivy Leaf Reporter	Eudora M. Allen
Hodegos	Michelle Mincey-Lee
Historians	Johnnie S. Holmes & Doris Davida Wood
Chaplain	Patricia Mincey
Graduate Advisor SSU	Dr. Clemontine F. Washington
Assistant Graduate Advisor SSU	Dr. Connie Cooper
On Campus Advisor	Dr. Emily C. Sanders
Graduate Advisor AASU	Audrey B. Singleton
Educational Advancement Foundation	Yolanda Jones
Pan-Hellenic Representative	Zenobia Mitchell/Angela Grant

2006 Officers filling the following offices:

Anti-Tamiouchos	Nicole Williams
Pecunious Grammateus	April S. Scott
Member-at-Large	Pendar Franklin
Hodegos	Glenda James
Assistant Graduate Advisor SSU	Ericka Coleman-Washington
Assistant Graduate Advisor AASU	Michelle Mincey-Lee

Emma Jean Conyers, 2007-2008

Basileus	Emma Jean Conyers
Anti-Basileus	Clemontine F. Washington
Grammateus	LaShawna K. Mullgrav
Anti-Grammateus	Elza Givens
Tamiouchos	Nicole Williams
Anti-Tamiouchos	Sylvia Perry Weston
Pecunious Grammateus	April Scott
Epistoleus	Shi Evans
Member-at-Large	Pendar Franklin
Parliamentarian	Zena McClain Haymon
Philacter	Paprice Gresham Simmons
Ivy Leaf Reporter	Jessie Collier DeLoach
Hodegos	Glenda James
Historian	Dorothy B. Wilson
Chaplain	Albertha E. Boston
Assistant Public Relations Chairman	Nikki Dorsey
Graduate Advisor SSU	Kimberly Chappell Stevens
Assistant Graduate Advisor SSU	Ericka Coleman Washington
Graduate Advisor AASU	Audrey B. Singleton
Assistant Graduate Advisor AASU	Sharon Stallings

2007 Committee Chairman:

AKACare	Patricia Mincey
Archives	Dorothy B. Wilson
Audit	Ivy Richardson
Awards & Recognitions:	Lorna Jackson/LaVertta Scott Perry
Centennial/Founders' Day	Elza Givens/Lakechia Bryant
Connection	Ivy Richardson
EAF Representative	Alvernia Wilson Jackson
Graduate Advisors	Audrey B. Singleton/Kimberly C. Stevens

281

GSO Chorale	Eudora Allen/Johnnie Holmes
Hardship	Queen Barnes/Lois Vedelle Williams
Hospitality	Glenda James
Junior Debutantes/Fundraising	Charlene Jones
Membership	Vanessa Miller Kaigler
Nominating	Carolyn Bell
Pan-Hellenic Representative	Tuwanna Wilson
Program Scrapbook, 2008	Clemontine F. Washington
Protocol	Johnye Gilllans/Melinda Pippen Miller
Social	Irene Davis/Hope Johnson
Standards	Virginia Parham
Technology	Ivanette Richardson/Sharon Stallings

2008 Officers filling the following offices:

Pecunious Grammateus	Dorothy B. Wilson
Epistoleus	Charlene E. Jones
Member-at-Large	Virginia Parham
Ivy Leaf Reporter	Carolyn H. Bell
Assistant Graduate Advisor, SSU	Patricia J. Clark
Assistant Graduate Advisor AASU	Zena McClain

2008 Committee Chairmen filling Committee

Junior Debutantes Mentoring Director	Charlene Jones/Gwendolyn H. Johnson
Nominating Committee	Mary Coleman
Pan-Hellenic Representative	Irene Davis

Clemontine F. Washington, 2009-2010

Basileus	Clemontine F. Washington
Anti-Basileus	Zena McClain Haymon
Grammateus	Elza Givens
Anti-Grammateus	Janie Bruen
Tamiouchos	Sylvia Weston-Perry
Anti-Tamiouchos	Tara Scott Brown
Pecunious Grammateus	Dorothy B. Wilson
Epistoleus	Charlene Jones
Member-at-Large	Virginia M. Parham
Parliamentarian	Tarangula Barnes Scott
Philacter	Mary Coleman
Ivy Leaf Reporter	Carolyn Bell
Hodegos	Maxine Jackson & Alvernia Wilson
Historian	Dorothy B. Speed
Chaplain	Nicole Williams
Graduate Advisor SSU	Kimberly Chappell Stevens
Assistant Graduate Advisor SSU	Patricia Clark
Graduate Advisor AASU	Audrey B. Singleton
Assistant Graduate Advisor AASU	Sharon Stallings

2009 Committee Chairman:

Archives	Dorothy Speed
Budget/Finance	Sylvia Perry
Connection	Carolyn Russell
Bylaws	Tarangula Barnes Scott
Graduate Advisors	Audrey B. Singleton/Kimberly C. Stevens
Executive	Clemontine F. Washington
Hospitality	Alvernia Jackson/Maxine Jackson
Social	Lakyah Hatcher
Public Relations	Carolyn Bell
Protocol	Irene Davis/Juanita Denson

Mentoring	Joyce Dingle/Marjory Varnedoe
Standards	Sonia Renee' Grant
Technology	Sharon Stallings
EAF	April Scott
Membership	Vanessa M. Kaigler
Program	Zena McClain
AKACare	Johnye Gillans
Awards & Recognition	LaShawna Mullgrav
Audit	Diann Scott
Founders' Day	Connie Cooper
Greenbriar Connection	Johnye Gillans
Hardship	Lois Vedelle Williams
Precious Gems Mentoring	Gwendolyn H. Johnson/Johnye Gillans/Dorothy B. Wilson
Pan-Hellenic Representatives	Latondia Gadson, Hope Johnson, Courtney Eaton

2010 Officers filling the following offices:

Pecunious Grammateus	Lucille Brown
Epistoleus	LaTanya Thompson-Stringer
Member-at-Large	Eleanor Murdock
Ivy Leaf Reporter	Taqwaa Saleem

2010 Committee Chairmen filling Committee

Precious Gems Mentoring	Johnye Gillans/Dorothy B. Wilson
Pan-Hellenic Representatives	Latondia Gadson, Hope Johnson, Courtney Eaton

Zena E. McClain, 2011-2012

Basileus	Zena E. McClain
Anti-Basileus	Tarangula Barnes-Scott
Grammateus	Latondia Gadson
Anti-Grammateus	Mary Coleman
Tamiouchos	Tara Scott-Brown
Anti-Tamiouchos	Sonia Renee' Grant
Pecunious Grammateus	Lucille T. Brown
Epistoleus	LaTanya Thompson
Member-at-Large	Eleanor Murdock
Parliamentarian	Charlene Jones
Philacter	Joyce Dingle
Ivy Leaf Reporter	Taqwaa F. Saleem
Hodegos	Denise Weems-White
Historian	Sheila Hutcherson
Chaplain	Lolita L. Hickman
Graduate Advisor SSU	Patricia J. Clark
Assistant Graduate Advisor SSU	Nicole Williams
Graduate Advisor AASU	Audrey B. Singleton
Assistant Graduate Advisor AASU	Sharon Stallings

2011 Committee Chairman:

Archives	Sheila Hutcherson
Budget/Finance	Tara Scott-Brown
Connection	Lorna Jackson
Membership	Carolyn Bell
Bylaws	Charlene Jones
Graduate Advisors	Audrey B. Singleton/Patricia J. Clark
Executive	Zena E. McClain
Hospitality	Denise Weems-White/Taqwaa F. Saleem
Public Relations	Taqwaa F. Saleem

Protocol	Connie Cooper
Standards	Emma Jean Conyers
Technology	Denise Cooper
Precious Gems Mentoring	Johnye Gillans
Founders' Day	Alvernia Wilson-Jackson
Audit	Ivy Richardson
Awards & Recognition	Kimberly Chappell-Stevens
Pan-Hellenic Representative	Courtney Eaton
Nominating	Dorothy B. Wilson

2012 Officers filling the following offices:

Pecunious Grammateus	Sheila Hutcherson
Epistoleus	Diann Scott
Member-at-Large	Annie Mahone
Ivy Leaf Reporter	Eudora Allen

2012 Committee Chairmen filling Committee

Mentoring	Dorothy B. Wilson
Nominating	Clemontine F. Washington
Social	LaTanya Thompson
Timeless History	Emma Jean Conyers

Appendix H

Honors and Accomplishments as Documented

Adams, Dorothy U.
   Chatham County as the "Teacher of the Year," *Ivy Leaf* June 1957
Allen, Eudora
   Life Member of Alpha Kappa Alpha Sorority, Inc.
Anderson, Anika Blackwell
   Senior Investigator with the Equal Employment Opportunity
      Commission

Barnes, Queen
   Retirement, 2005
Bell, Carolyn H.
   May 22, 1978 named Central Services Director, a department
      head, for the city of Savannah, the first Black to hold
      this position "Outstanding Jaycette of Savannah" and
      "Outstanding Jaycette of Georgia"
   Production Assistant for the syndicated cable show Bobby Jones
   Vice President of Management Analyhsts in State and Local
      Government (MASLIG)
   Citizen of the Year, honored by Mu Phi Chapter of Omega Psi Phi
      Fraternity, Inc., November 17, 2001
   Co-Chairman of Membership Campaign, West Broad
      Street YMCA
   2002 Scholarship Award
   2003 Grand Marshall, Martin Luther King Observance Day
      Association Parade
   Platinum Hood Award Finalist – Community Leader
   President of the Women's Auxiliary of the Gospel Music
      Workshop of America

Life Member of Alpha Kappa Alpha Sorority, Inc.

The Mankind Assisting Students Kindle Educational Dreams (MASKED) Award for her twenty years of service to United Negro College Fund, helping to raise over one million dollars

2004 Soror of the Year

2005 Regional Appointment: Resolution Committee

2007 Evanel Renfroe Terrell Scholarship Award

2010 Management Service Director, City of Savannah

2011 Retirement, City of Savannah, 38 years

2011 Elected Alderman-at-Large, City of Savannah

Boston, Albertha E.

Doctor's Degree, Temple University, Philadelphia, Pennsylvania

Life Member of Alpha Kappa Alpha Sorority, Inc.

Scott-Brown, Tara

2011 Countess Cox Sisterhood Award

Bruen, Janie B.

Administrative Coordinator of Reading, Savannah Chatham Public Schools

2005 Silver Star

Life Member of Alpha Kappa Alpha Sorority, Inc.

2009 Vice President, Local Chapter of Top Ladies of Distinction

Bryant, Janice

2011 Jasper County School District's Teacher of the Year

Clark, Patricia

Phi Alpha Alpha Honor Society

Master's Degree in Public Administration

Life Member of Alpha Kappa Alpha Sorority, Inc.

2002 Scholarship Award

2005 Regional Appointment: Program Committee

2006 Soror of the Year

Collier, Albertha

WTOC, Top Teacher

2004 Countess Cox Sisterhood Award

2005 Winner (sold most tickets), 100 Celebrity Men Who Cook

2012 Retirement: Savannah Chatham County Public Schools

Collier, Mozella

Full-time volunteer worker

Heart fund, March of Dimes and Cancer Drive

Honored by Jack and Jill of America, Inc., 1982

Jack and Jill Charter Member; president of Jack and Jill, 1967-69

"Heart Volunteer of the Year" for the State of Georgia, presented by Governor Busbee in Atlanta

"Chatham County Volunteer of the Year" by Chatham County Voluntary Action Center

Coleman, Ericka

Charter member, Savannah Chapter of South Carolina State University National Alumni Association

Coleman, Mary

2009 Honoree, General Missionary Baptist Convention of GA, 1st District Woman's President at Second St. John Baptist Church, Golden Street

Coleman, Jeraldine

Assistant Principal, Hinesville Middle School, Hinesville, Georgia

Conyers, Emma Jean

"Messiah," Savannah Symphony Chorale

Soloist, The National Anthem, Relay for Life, American Cancer Society

Contributor, *Pearls of Service, The Legacy of America's First Black Sorority, Alpha Kappa Alpha, 2006,* by Earnestine Green McNealey, 2006 Articles: Soror Portrait, "Positively AKA, Virginia Mercer Parham"; Soror Portrait, "Sisters-Friends," Albertha E. Boston; and Soror Portrait, "Sister of Service, Clemontine F. Washington"

Photo in *Ivy Leaf,* Fall 2007, page 19 and *Ivy Leaf,* Spring 2008, page 8

2008 Soror of the Year

Life Member of Alpha Kappa Alpha Sorority, Inc.

Cooper, Agatha

Full-time volunteer worker

Chairman of the Economic Opportunity Authority (EOA) Board of Directors

In charge of honoring women Elders, Butler Presbyterian Church

Cooper, Connie

Platinum Hood Award – Woman of Courage

Appointment: Public Safety Task Force

Life Member of Alpha Kappa Alpha Sorority, Inc.

Cooper, Denise
    2010 Sworn into the Georgia State Bar

Cooper, Rebecca
    Administrative Coordinator of Elementary Education for Savannah Chatham Public Schools
    Director of Human Resources for Glynn County School
    Honored by YMCA of Brunswick for outstanding leadership and community service
    Life Member of Alpha Kappa Alpha Sorority, Inc.

Cox, Countess Y.
    A charter member of Chatham Association of Principals (CAP), treasurer and member of the steering committee
    Life Member of Alpha Kappa Alpha Sorority, Inc.

Cox-Stokes, Tammy
    1st Black woman appointed judge in Chatham County

DeLoach, Jessie Collier
    "Messiah," Savannah Symphony Chorale
    Life Member of Alpha Kappa Alpha Sorority, Inc.
    8th District School Board Representative, Savannah Chatham County Public School System
    Honored January 5, 2005, Retirement: Savannah Chatham County School Board
    Vice-President Pro-Tem of the Savannah/Chatham Board of Education
    50th Wedding Anniversary
    2005 Honored: The Naming of Board Room in her honor, Savannah Chatham County Public School System
    Recipient: 2005 King-Tisdell Cottage Foundation Annual Award, the Rev. James M. Simms Public Service Award

Dingle, Joyce
    2009 Golden Soror

Drayton, Tenay
    2012 Master's Degree, Savannah State University

Edwards, Virginia
    Superintendent of Chatham County Public Schools
    State Department of Education, First Congressional District, appointee

"Spirit Award" in Education, Public Meeting, SARC 2004
Unveiling of portrait at Ralph Mark Gilbert Museum

Franklin, Pendar
    2005 Golden Soror
    Life Member of Alpha Kappa Alpha Sorority, Inc.
Freeman, Willie Mae
    Life Member of Alpha Kappa Alpha Sorority, Inc.

Gates, Jane
    2011 Appointed Provost and Vice President of Academic Affairs at
        Western Connecticut State University.
Gibbs, Ethel
    Principal, Barnard Elementary School
Gillans, Johnye
    Professional Practices Commission for Elementary Classroom
        Teachers, member
    Life Member of Alpha Kappa Alpha Sorority, Inc.
    Regional Membership Committee, 2003
Grant, Sonia Renee
    South Atlantic Region Odessa S. Nelson Graduate Advisor Award,
        April 13, 1991
    Life Member of Alpha Kappa Alpha Sorority, Inc.
    2009 Silver Star
Gilbert-Grant, Jackie
    Coastal Christian Magazine, article inclusion
Gray, Henrietta
    2009 Silver Star
    2012 Retirement: Savannah Chatham County Public Schools

Hickman, Lolita L.
    2009 Speaker, Butler Presbyterian Church, Second St. John
        Baptist Church, First Evergreen Baptist Church
    2011 Interim Pastor, Connor's Temple Baptist Church
Hunter, Ethel
    2002 Soror of the Year

Jackson, Annie
  Judge for the Southeastern Regional Jack and Jill Teens
    Conference
  2005 Golden Soror
  Life Member of Alpha Kappa Alpha Sorority, Inc.
  Appointment: Tax Assessors Board
Jackson, Lorna
  Medical College of Georgia, teeth implant
  The Opening of Southside Dental Office
  2007 Countess Y. Cox Sisterhood Award
  Winner of the Savannah A.M.E. Churches Queen Contest
Jackson, Maxine
  2009 Retirement, Savannah Chatham County Public School
    System
James, Glenda
  2008 Countess Y. Cox Sisterhood Award
  Life Member of Alpha Kappa Alpha Sorority, Inc.
Johnson, Gwendolyn Harris
  Trainer for Sun Trust Bank.
Johnson, Hope
  2005 Countess Y. Cox Sisterhood Award
  2006 Countess Y. Cox Sisterhood Award
Jones, Charlene
  Assistant Principal, Esther Garrison Elementary School
  Who's Who in American Education
  Director of Professional Development, Savannah Chatham
    County Public School System
  2008 Basileus Award
  Life Member of Alpha Kappa Alpha Sorority, Inc.

Kaigler, Vanessa Miller
  2007 Silver Star

Loud, Suyah
  M.D. in Pediatrics, Memorial Health University Medical Center,
    June 20, 2003
Lyons, Merdis J.
  Life Member of Alpha Kappa Alpha Sorority, Inc.

Mahone, Annie
> 2011 Silver Star

Maynard, Carmelita
> IMPACT Trainer (for all prospective foster parents)

Mincey-Lee, Michelle
> Facilitator at Haven Elementary School.
> Education Specialist Degree, Cambridge College, Augusta
> 2004 Evanel Renfroe Terrell Scholarship Award

McClain, Zena
> 2004 Candidate for State Court Judge of Chatham County
> 2007 Soror of the Year
> 2011 Appointment: Historic Savannah Review Board

Milledge, Bettie J.C.
> Life Member of Alpha Kappa Alpha Sorority, Inc.
> 2009 Golden Soror

Miller, Renae
> Assistant Principal at Pooler Elementary School and received the
> Ed.S. Degree.

Mincey, Patricia
> Life Member of Alpha Kappa Alpha Sorority, Inc.
> 2009 Golden Soror

Minor, Tamika
> 2002 Scholarship Award

Mitchell, Annette
> 2009 President, Local Chapter, Top Ladies of Distinction
> 2011 Top Lady of the Year, Top Ladies of Distinction
> 2011 Silver Star

Mullgrav, LaShawna Alderman
> 2004 Evanel Renfroe Terrell Scholarship Award
> 2008 Basileus Award
> Charter member, Savannah Chapter, South Carolina State
> University National Alumni Association, elected President
> Education Specialist Degree, Cambridge College, Augusta

Murdock, Eleanor W.
> 2004 Golden Soror
> Recipient of proclamation for forty-one years of stellar service
> from Governor Jim Edgar, Illinois; the naming of a conference
> room, Eleanor W. Murdock Conference Room, a state agency
> building, Chicago, Illinois

Parham, Virginia M.
    Manager of the International Longshoremen Association Welfare
        and Pension Fund (ILAWP).
    "1992 Woman of Achievement Award," Port City Business and
        Professional Women's Organization
    50 years of employment with the International Longshoremen's
        Association (ILA).
    Life Member of Alpha Kappa Alpha Sorority, Inc.
    SSU Wall of Scholars, $5,000 + contributors
    2009 Golden Soror
Parker, Jane J.
    Life Member of Alpha Kappa Alpha Sorority, Inc.
    Golden Soror
Perry, Henrietta
    Life Member of Alpha Kappa Alpha Sorority, Inc.
Pippen-Miller, Melinda
    Social Worker of the Year for the 1st School District
Preer, Emma Lue Jordan
    2008 Golden Soror
    Life Member of Alpha Kappa Alpha Sorority, Inc.

Richardson, Ivy
    Retired High School Assistant Principal, 2004
Riley, Sandra
    "Messiah," Savannah Symphony Chorale
Robinson, Margaret C.
    Ph.D. degree from Washington University Graduate School of
        Arts and Sciences, field of study, Botany with a speciality in
        plant physiology; Ph.D. research work titled, "Inheritable
        Changes in Euglena Graclis Induced by Ultracentrifugation"
    Undergraduate advisor to Gamma Upsilon Chapter, 1962-64
    Savannah State University Magazine, Fall 2002, featured
    Life Member of Alpha Kappa Alpha Sorority, Inc.
    Scholarship at Savannah State University, in her honor
    SSU Wall of Scholars, $5,000 + contributors
Russell, Carolyn
    2005 Golden Soror
    Life Member of Alpha Kappa Alpha Sorority, Inc.

Sanders, Emily Crawford

>Life Member of Alpha Kappa Alpha Sorority, Inc.
>
>National Urban League recognition, bridging the "digital divide" at Historical Black Colleges and Universities
>
>Good Service Exhibit at Savannah Entrepreneurial Center
>
>Mattie B. Payne Volunteer Award

Sears, Onnye Jean

>President, Savannah Branch of American Association of University Women (AAUW)
>
>Columnist, "Community News and Views," *The Savannah Tribune*

Scott, April

>Director of Mental Health for the Chatham County Jail

Scott, Tarangula Barnes

>2006 Promotion: Coordinator of Academic Excellence Magnet Academy
>
>2008 Evanel Renfroe Terrell Scholarship Award

Sheppard, Sonya

>Promotion: Assistant Professor to Associate Professor, Georgia Southern University

Singleton, Audrey B.

>Life Member of Alpha Kappa Alpha Sorority, Inc.
>
>Retired School Teacher, 2004

Smith, Gwendolyn

>Deputy Superintendent of the Jasper County School District, to the South Carolina State Library Board, appointed by Governor Jim Hodges
>
>"Milestones in Education," featured in *Jasper County Sun*, February 4, 2009
>
>2005 Silver Star
>
>Life Member of Alpha Kappa Alpha Sorority, Inc.

Stallings, Sharon

>2005 Masters Degree
>
>2005 Soror of the Year
>
>2005 Evanel Renfroe Terrell Scholarship Award
>
>2010-2011 Teacher of the Year
>
>2012 Top Teacher of the Week, Woodville/Tompkins Technical School

Stevens, Kimberly Chappell
  2004, 2008 Evanel Renfroe Terrell Scholarship Award
  Appointment: State Board of Education Title I Committee
  Ed.S Degree, Education Administration, May 1, 2004, Georgia
    Southern University
  2006 Countess Y. Cox Sisterhood Award

Tate, Bettina
  2010-2011 Teacher of the Year
  2010-2011 District Teacher of the Year
Terrell, Evanel
  Representative from the Georgia Dietetic Association in
    Washington, DC.
  State Legislative Chairman for the Dietetic Association
  Golden Soror
  Life Member of Alpha Kappa Alpha Sorority, Inc.
Tillman, LaWanda
  PBS broadcast of the Tillman Family
Thompson, LaTanya
  2011 Head Start/Early Head Start Health Advisory Committee
Truedell, Undine
  Miss Omega Mardi Gras
  City of Savannah's Employee Advisory Council, at-large
    representative for employees
  2003 Soror of the Year
  Appointment: City of Savannah's 2004 Loan Executive for the
    United Way of the Coastal Empire

VanEllison, Natatia
  2003 Countess Y. Cox Sisterhood Award
  2010-2011 Teacher of the Year
Varnedoe, Marjory
  Ed.S. Degree
  Life Member of Alpha Kappa Alpha Sorority, Inc.
Vaughn, Albertha
  Life Member of Alpha Kappa Alpha Sorority, Inc.

Walker, Maureen
    2004 Attendance at the Grammy's, Staple Center, Los Angeles,
        California
Washington, Clemontine
    Winner, first-place plaque, Undergraduate Advisor
    Chairman of St. Mary's Guild of St. Matthew's Episcopal Church
    Life Member of Alpha Kappa Alpha Sorority, Inc.
    Assistant Principal, Liberty Elementary School
    Midway City Councilwoman
    2003, retirement, Liberty County High School System
    Mayor Pro Tem: 2006-2009, Midway, GA
    Leadership Certificate, the Georgia Municipal Association
    SSU Wall of Scholars, $5,000 + contributors
    2009, Mayoral Candidate, Midway, GA
    2010 – 2012, Mayor, Midway, GA
    2006 President Greenbriar Children's Center 2nd term completion
    2011and 2012 Rock and Roll Marathon, walked 13 miles for
        Greenbriar Children's Center
    2011 Soror of the Year
    2012 Greenbriar Children's Center Board
Weems-White, Denise
    2011 Promoted to the rank of Associate Professor and tenure at
        Georgia Southern University
Williams, Dianne
    Appointment, Affirmative Action Officer at Savannah State
        University
Williams, Emily
    Master's Degree
Williams, Leona Henley
    Moderator of Deacon Board, Butler Presbyterian Church
    Life Member of Alpha Kappa Alpha Sorority, Inc.
Williams, Nicole
    2005 Countess Y. Cox Sisterhood Award
    2007 Evanel Terrell Scholarship Award
    First Place Winner: Miss Mardi Gras, Savannah Alumni Chapter
        Omega Psi Phi Fraternity, Inc.
Williams, Wanda
    2011 Retirement, City of Savannah, 28 years

Jackson-Wilson, Alvernia
> State Health Committee appointee
> 2009 Retirement, Savannah Chatham County Public School
> System

Wilson, Dororthy Boston
> "Teacher of the Year," Tompkins High School
> Appointment: Retired State Educator's Governing Board
> Director VI for the Georgia Retired Educator's Association
> Life Member of Alpha Kappa Alpha Sorority, Inc.
> SSU Wall of Scholars, $5,000 + contributors
> 13th President of the Georgia Retired Education Association,
> Installed 5-6-10
> 2010 Honoree, Mothers' Brunch, sponsored by Men's Ministry, St.
> James A.M.E.

Henley-Williams, Leona
> Moderator of Deacon Board, Butler Presbyterian Church
> Life Member of Alpha Kappa Alpha Sorority, Inc.
> President, The Charms

Wright, Tamika
> 2010 Assistant Principal, Jacob G. Smith Elementary School
> 2012 Interim Principal, Port Wentworth Elementary School

Young, Lydia S.
> Life Member of Alpha Kappa Alpha Sorority, Inc.

Notes

1. Martha Wilson. Obituary. November 13, 2010.

2. Alpha Kappa Alpha Sorority, Inc. *Constitution and Bylaws 2010.*

3. Cathy Cox. Certificate of Incorporation. September 15, 2005.

4. "WWII and Roosevelt's Last Days." Franklin D. Roosevelt. http://www. sparknotes.com/biography/fdr/section12.rhtml.

5. Ibid.

6. Angelo Patri. "Our Children." *Savannah Morning News.* January 1, 1943, 4.

7. Marjorie H. Parker. *Alpha Kappa Alpha Sorority 1908 – 1958.* Alpha Kappa Alpha Sorority, Inc. 1958. 71.

8. Ibid.

9. Ibid.

10. Collye Lee Riley. "Report of the Southeastern Region." Minutes presented at the Twenty-Fifth Annual Boule of Alpha Kappa Alpha Sorority. Feb. 18-20, 1944. Chicago, Illinois. http://www.aka1908.com.

11. Irma F. Clarke. "Report of the Supreme Grammateus." Minutes presented at the Twenty Fifth Annual Boule of Alpha Kappa Alpha Sorority. Feb. 18-20, 1944. Chicago, Illinois. http://www.aka1908.com.

12. "Gamma Sigma Omega." *Ivy Leaf,* September 1943. http://www.aka1908.com.

13. Dr. Albertha E. Boston, Emma J. Conyers, and Virginia M. Parham. *Gamma Sigma Omega Chapter of Alpha Kappa Alpha Sorority, Inc..* Savannah, GA: Gamma Sigma Omega Chapter, 2003.

14. Wilson, Obituary.

15. Boston and others, 1.

16. Riley, 21-23.

17. Norman E. Boyd. "Report of National Non-Partisan Council on Public Affairs." Minutes presented at the Twenty-Fifth Annual Boule of Alpha

Kappa Alpha Sorority, Inc. Chicago, Illinois. Feb. 18-20, 1944, 50. http://www.aka1908.com.

18. Ida L. Jackson. "Report of the Mississippi Health Project." Minutes presented at the Twenty-Fifth Annual Boule of Alpha Kappa Alpha Sorority, Inc. Chicago, Illinois. Feb. 18-20, 1944, 55. http://www.aka1908.com.

19. Ida L. Jackson, 55-58.

20. "Gamma Sigma Omega." *Ivy Leaf,* March 1944, 26. http://www.aka1908.com.

21. "Negro Children's Need is Shown." Verticlal Files. November 5, 1947. The Live Oak Public Library. Savannah, GA.

22. Frank Rossiter. "Neglected Negro Children May Get Overdue 'Break'. "Verticlal Files. November 27, 1947. The Live Oak Public Library. Savannah, GA.

23. Boston and others, 1.

24. Wilson. Obituary.

25. Boston and others, 1-2.

26. Wilson. Obituary.

27. Minutes presented at the Twenty-Seventh Annual Boule of Alpha Kappa Alpha Sorority, Inc. August 18-23, 1947. Cleveland, Ohio. http://www.aka1908.com.

28. "Greenbriar Children's Center Orphanage Built by Sorority Dedicated." Ivy Leaf, September 1949, 24. http://www.aka1908.com.

29. Minutes presented at the Twenty-Ninth Annual Boule of Alpha Kappa Alpha Sorority, Inc. December 27-30, 1949. Houston, Texas, 11. http://www.aka1908.com.

30. "Gamma Sigma Omega Notes." Ivy Leaf, September – December 1950, 47. http://www.aka1908.com.

31. "Gamma Sigma Omega." *Ivy Leaf,* March 1944, 26. http://www.aka1908.com.

32. "Gamma Sigma Omega Chapter, Savannah, Georgia." *Ivy Leaf,* June 1946, 23. http://www.aka1908.com.

33. Ibid.

34. Ibid.

35. "Gamma Sigma Omega." *Ivy Leaf,* March 1944, 22. http://www.aka1908.com.

36. "Gamma Sigma Omega Chapter Initiates Two." *Ivy Leaf,* March 1948. http://www.aka1908.com.

37. National Pan-Hellenic Council, Incorporated. Mission. http://www. nphchq.org/mission.htm.

38. "Report of the Supreme Basileus." Minutes presented at the Thirteenth Annual Boule of Alpha Kappa Alpha Sorority, Inc. Marshall, Texas. Dec. 28-31, 1930, 47. http://www.aka1908.com.

39. "Gamma Sigma Omega in Pan-Hellenic Organization." *Ivy Leaf*, June 1947, 21. http://www.aka1908.com.

40. "Gamma Sigma Omega Notes." Ivy Leaf, September – December 1950, 47. http://www.aka1908.com.

41. "Gamma Sigma Omega in Pan-Hellenic Organization," 21.

42. "Greenbriar Children's Center Orphanage Built by Sorority Dedicated," 24.

43. "Gamma Sigma Omega Notes," 47.

44. Boston and others, Appendix H.

45. Ibid.

46. Ibid.

47. Ibid.

48. Ibid.

49. Ibid.

50. "Gamma Upsilon Set up at Savannah State College." *Ivy Leaf*, March 1950, 48. http://www.aka1908.com.

51. "Gamma Sigma Omega Planning to Present Fashionetta." *Ivy Leaf*, December 1951, 25. http://www.aka1908.com.

52. "Fashionetta Held at Savannah, GA." *Ivy Leaf*, March 1952, 45. http:// www.aka1908.com.

53. Ibid.

54. "Gamma Sigma Omega Gives $500 to Charity." *Ivy Leaf*, March 1953, 36. http://www.aka1908.com/

55. "Gamma Sigma Omega and Gamma Upsilon Give Resume of Activites." *Ivy Leaf*, June 1957, 19. http://www.aka1908.com.

56. Boston and others, 2.

57. A. Cathryn Johnson. "South Eastern Region." Minutes presented at the Thirty-Third Annual Boule of Alpha Kappa Alpha Sorority, Inc. St. Louis, Missouri. Dec. 26-30, 1953, 32.

58. A. Cathryn Johnson. Thirty-fourth Boule, 1954, 12-13.

59. Minutes presented at the Thirty-Six Boule of Alpha Kappa Alpha Sorority, Inc. Atlanta, GA. Dec. 28-31,1956, 23-24. http://www.aka1908.com.

60. "Health News." *Ivy Leaf*, March 1956, 10. http://www.aka1908.com.

61. Tiggett, Jimmie C. "Gamma Sigma Omega." *Ivy Leaf*, March 1960, 18. http://www.aka1908.com.

62. Minutes presented at the Thirty-Eight Boule of Alpha Kappa Alpha Sorority, Inc., Cincinnati, Ohio.Dec. 26-30, 1959, 90. http://www.aka1908.com.

63. Wilson, Obituary.

64. "Greenbriar Foundation is Organized." Verticlal Files. April 3, 1961. The Live Oak Public Library. Savannah, GA.

65. "Gamma Sigma Omega." *Ivy Leaf*, February 1961, 26. http://www.aka1908.com.

66. Mercer, Virginia. "Gamma Sigma Omega." *Ivy Leaf*, March 1963, 25. http://www.aka1908.com.

67. Boston and others, 2.

68. Ibid.

69. Ibid.

70. Ibid., 3.

71. Ibid.

72. Ibid.

73. "Chapter News Highlights." *Ivy Leaf*, Spring 1974, 13. http://www.aka1908.com.

74. Boston and others, 4-5.

75. Ibid.

76. Ibid, 5-6.

77. "[Twenty-Third] 23rd South Atlantic Regional Conference." *Ivy Leaf*, Fall 1976, 54-55. http://www.aka1908.com.

78. Boston and others, 5.

79. "Gamma Sigma Omega: Sisterhood at Work." *Ivy Leaf*, Spring 1977, 13. http://www.aka1908.com

80. Boston and others, 6.

81. "Gamma Sigma Omega Tutorial Reading Program." *Ivy Leaf,* Fall 1977, 61. http://www.aka1908.com.

82. "Gamma Sigma Omega and Gamma Upsilon Host Neighborhood Meeting." *Ivy Leaf,* Spring 1978, 41. http://www.aka1908.com.

83. Boston and others, 8.

84. Ibid., 9.

85. Ibid.

86. "Gamma Sigma Omega." *Ivy Leaf,* Summer 1979, 25. http://www.aka1908.com.

87. Boston and others, 9-10.

88. Ibid., 10.

89. Ibid., 10-11.

90. Ibid., 11.

91. Ibid.

92. Ibid., 12.

93. Ibid.

94. Ibid., 13.

95. Ibid., 14.

96. "Workshops Featured at Cluster VI Meeting." *Ivy Leaf,* Spring 1981, 37.

97. Boston and others, 14.

98. Ibid.

99. Ibid.

100. Ibid., 16-17.

101. Ibid., 15.

102. Ibid.

103. Ibid.

104. Ibid., 16.

105. Ibid.

106. Ibid.

107. Ibid., 17-18.

108. Ibid., 18.

109. Ibid.

110. Ibid., 18-19.

111. Ibid., 19.

112. Ibid.

113. Ibid., 21.

114. Ibid.

115. "Report of the South Atlantic Regional Director." Minutes presented at the Forty-Eight Boule of Alpha Kappa Alpha Sorority, Inc. Houston, Texas. July 16-21, 1978, 43. http://www.aka1908.com.

116. "Lambda Kappa Chartered." *Ivy Leaf*, Fall 1977, 84-85. http://www.aka1908.com.

117. Ibid.

118. Boston and others, 17.

119. Ibid,

120. Ibid., 24.

121. Ibid., 24-25.

122. Ibid., 25-26.

123. Ibid., 26.

124. Ibid., 26-27.

125. Ibid., 27.

126. Ibid.

127. Ibid., 27-28.

128. Ibid., 29.

129. Ibid., 30.

130. Ibid.

131. Ibid.

132. Ibid.

133. Ibid., 30-31.

134. Ibid., 31.

135. Ibid.

136. Ibid., 31-32.

137. Ibid, 32.
138. Ibid., 33.
139. Ibid., 34.
140. Ibid., 33-34.
141. Ibid., 34.
142. Ibid.
143. Ibid.
144. Ibid., 35.
145. Ibid.
146. Ibid.
147. Ibid., 36.
148. Ibid.
149. Ibid., 36-37.
150. Ibid., 37.
151. Ibid., 37-38.
152. Ibid., 37.
153. Ibid.
154. Ibid., 38.
155. Ibid., 38-39.
156. Ibid., 39.
157. Ibid., 40.
158. Ibid.
159. Ibid.
160. Ibid., 40-41.
161. Ibid., 43.
162. Ibid.
163. Ibid.
164. Ibid.
165. Ibid., 44.
166. Ibid.

167. Ibid.

168. Ibid.

169. Ibid.

170. Ibid.

171. Ibid., 45.

172. Ibid.

173. Ibid.

174. Ibid., 45-46.

175. Ibid., 46.

176. Ibid.

177. Ibid., 46-47.

178. "Gamma Sigma Omega Retreat a Success." *Ivy Leaf*, Winter 1992, 35. http://www.aka1908.com.

179. Boston and others, 45.

180. Ibid., 46.

181. Ibid., 48-49.

182. Ibid., 51.

183. Ibid., 49.

184. Ibid.

185. Ibid.

186. Ibid., 50.

187. Ibid.

188. Ibid.

189. Ibid.

190. Ibid.

191. "Gamma Sigma Omega Serves the Community." *Ivy Leaf*, Winter 1993, 11. http://www.aka1908.com.

192. Boston and others, 50-51.

193. Ibid., 51.

194. Ibid.

195. Ibid., 51-52.

196. Ibid., 52.

197. Ibid.

198. "Cluster VI Founders' Day Luncheon Held." *Ivy Leaf,* Fall 1994, 46. http://www.aka1908.com.

199. Boston and others, 53.

200. Ibid., 54.

201. Ibid.

202. Ibid.

203. Ibid.

204. "Gamma Sigma Omega Walks in Relay for Life." *Ivy Leaf,* Fall 1994, 23. http://www.aka1908.com.

205. Boston and others, 55.

206. "South Atlantic Regional Director is Speaker at Gamma Sigma Omega's Founders' Day." *Ivy Leaf,* Summer 1995, 53-54. http://www.aka1908.com.

207. Boston and others, 56.

208. "South Atlantic Regional Director is Speaker at Gamma Sigma Omega's Founders' Day," 53-54.

209. Boston and others, 57.

210. Ibid.

211. Ibid., 57-58.

212. Ibid., 58-59.

213. Ibid.

214. Ibid., 56-57; 59.

215. Ibid., 59.

216. Ibid.

217. Ibid., 62.

218. Ibid.

219. Ibid., 63.

220. Ibid.

221. Ibid., 62.

222. Ibid., 62-63.

223. Ibid., 64.

224. Ibid.

225. Ibid., 64-65.

226. Ibid., 65.

227. Ibid., 64.

228. Ibid., 65.

229. Ibid., 66.

230. Ibid., 67.

231. Ibid., 67-68.

232. Ibid., 68.

233. Ibid.

234. Ibid., 69.

235. Ibid., 70.

236. Ibid., 69.

237. Ibid., 70-71.

238. Ibid., 69.

239. Ibid., 70, 71

240. Ibid.

241. Ibid., 70.

242. Ibid., 68-69.

243. Ibid., 72.

244. Ibid.

245. Ibid., 74.

246. Ibid., 74-75.

247. Ibid., 75.

248. Ibid.

249. Ibid., 73-74.

250. Ibid., 82.

251. Ibid., 75-76.

252. Ibid., 76.

253. Ibid.

254. Ibid., 76-77.

255. Ibid., 77.

256. Ibid.

257. Ibid., 77-78.

258. Ibid., 82-83.

259. Ibid., 83.

260. Ibid., 80-81.

261. Ibid., 78.

262. Ibid.

263. Ibid., 78-79.

264. Ibid., 79.

265. Ibid.

266. Ibid., 81-82.

267. Ibid., 82.

268. Ibid.

269. Ibid., 81.

270. Ibid., 83.

271. Minutes. Chapter meeting. Gamma Sigma Omega Chapter. January 11, 2003.

272. Ibid., February 8, 2003.

273. Carolyn H. Bell. *The Spirit of AKA*. January 2003.

274. Ibid. June 2003.

275. Ibid.

276. Minutes. Chapter meeting. Gamma Sigma Omega Chapter. May 10, 2003.

277. Carolyn H. Bell. *The Spirit of AKA*. September 2003.

278. Minutes. Chapter meeting. Gamma Sigma Omega Chapter. September 14, 2003.

279. Carolyn H. Bell. *The Spirit of AKA*. September 2003.

280. Ibid., November 2003.

281. Ibid.

282. Ibid., March 2004.

283. Ibid., November 2003.

284. Ibid., April 2004.

285. Ibid., May 2004.

286. Minutes. Chapter meeting. Gamma Sigma Omega Chapter. February 14, 2004.

287. Carolyn H. Bell. *The Spirit of AKA*. June 2004.

288. Ibid., May 2004.

289. Minutes. Chapter meeting. Gamma Sigma Omega Chapter. January 11, 2003.

290. Ibid., April 5, 2003.

291. Carolyn H. Bell. *The Spirit of AKA*. May 2003.

292. Ibid., August 2004.

293. Ibid., September 2003.

294. Ibid., March 2003.

295. Ibid.

296. Ibid., June 2003.

297. Ibid., October 2003.

298. Ibid.

299. Ibid., November 2003.

300. Ibid., October 2004.

301. Ibid., May 2003.

302. Ibid., November 2003.

303. Ibid., May 2003.

304. Ibid., May 2004.

305. Ibid., March 2003.

306. Ibid.

307. Ibid., March 2003.

308. Ibid., May 2003.

309. Ibid. September 2003.

310. Minutes. Chapter meeting. Gamma Sigma Omega Chapter. September 14, 2003.

311. Carolyn H Bell. *The Spirit of AKA*. December 2003.

312. Ibid.

313. Minutes. Chapter meeting. Gamma Sigma Omega Chapter. December 13, 2003.

314. Gamma Sigma Omega Update. July 2003.

315. Carolyn H. Bell. *The Spirit of AKA*. October 2003.

316. Ibid., November 2003.

317. Ibid., March 2004.

318. Ibid., November 2004.

319. Ibid., May 2003.

320. Ibid., June 2003.

321. Minutes. Chapter meeting. Gamma Sigma Omega Chapter. April 2003.

322. Carolyn H. Bell. *The Spirit of AKA*. June 2003.

323. Ibid., May 2003.

324. Ibid., October 2003.

325. Minutes. Chapter meeting. Gamma Sigma Omega Chapter. June 14, 2003.

326. Ibid., May 10, 2003.

327. Ibid.

328. Carolyn H. Bell. *The Spirit of AKA*. September 2003.

329. Ibid.

330. Ibid., October 2003.

331. Minutes. Chapter meeting. Gamma Sigma Omega Chapter. September 14, 2003.

332. Ibid., May 10, 2003.

333. Ibid.

334. Minutes. Chapter meeting. Gamma Sigma Omega Chapter. October 11, 2013.

335. Carolyn H. Bell. *The Spirit of AKA*. April 2004.

336. Gamma Sigma Omega Update. July 2003.

337. Minutes. Chapter meeting. Gamma Sigma Omega Chapter. April 10, 2004.

338. History of Sigma Tau, Alpha Kappa Alpha Sorority, Inc.

339. Carolyn H. Bell. *The Spirit of AKA*. May 2003.

340. Minutes. Chapter meeting. Gamma Sigma Omega Chapter. June 14, 2003.

341. Carolyn H. Bell. *The Spirit of AKA*. August 2004.

342. Ibid, December 2004.

343. "The Heart of ESP An Extraordinary Service Program," 4.

344. Ibid., 2.

345. Patricia Clark. "Program." August 2006.

346. Minutes. Chapter meeting. Gamma Sigma Omega Chapter. September 9, 2006.

347. "The Spirit of Alpha Kappa Alpha Sorority, Inc., An Engaging Experience," *Ivy Leaf.* Spring 2007, 72, http://www.aka1908.com.

348. Ibid.

349. Ibid.

350. Emma Jean Conyers. Report. Gamma Sigma Omega Chapter. October 8, 2005.

351. Patricia Clark. "Program." *Alpha Kappa Alpha Sorority, Inc.* February 2006.

352. Ibid., October 2006.

353. Ibid.

354. Minutes. Chapter meeting. Gamma Sigma Omega Chapter. December 9, 2006.

355. Ibid.

356. Emma Jean Conyers. Report. Gamma Sigma Omega Chapter. May 5, 2005.

357. Minutes. Chapter meeting. Gamma Sigma Omega Chapter. June 11, 2005.

358. Patricia Clark. "Program." *Alpha Kappa Alpha Sorority, Inc.* December 2005.

359. Emma Jean Conyers. Report. Gamma Sigma Omega Chapter. March 2, 2006.

360. Patricia Clark. "Program." *Alpha Kappa Alpha Sorority, Inc.* June 2006.

361. Ibid., March 2006.

362. Patricia Clark. "Soror Emma Conyers-Anti-Basileus/Program Chairman." *Alpha Kappa Alpha Sorority, Inc.* Savannah, GA. September 2005.

363. Emma Jean Conyers. Report. Gamma Sigma Omega Chapter. August 31, 2006.

364. Patricia Clark. "Program." *Alpha Kappa Alpha Sorority, Inc.,* 2006.

365. Minutes. Chapter meeting. Gamma Sigma Omega Chapter. December 9, 2006.

366. Patricia Clark. "Program." *Alpha Kappa Alpha Sorority, Inc.,* November 2006.

367. Emma Jean Conyers. Report. Gamma Sigma Omega Chapter. May 14, 2005.

368. Minutes. Chapter meeting. Gamma Sigma Omega Chapter. June 11, 2005.

369. Patricia Clark. "Program." *Alpha Kappa Alpha Sorority, Inc.,* May 2006.

370. Emma Jean Conyers. Report. Gamma Sigma Omega Chapter. June 1, 2006.

371. Ibid., March 3, 2005.

372. Ibid., May 5, 2005.

373. Patricia Clark. "Program." *Alpha Kappa Alpha Sorority, Inc.,* October 2006.

374. Ibid., May 2006.

375. Patricia Clark. "Committee Information and Reports." *Alpha Kappa Alpha Sorority, Inc.* Savannah, GA. February 2005.

376. Emma Jean Conyers. Report. Gamma Sigma Omega Chapter. February 12, 2005.

377. Ibid., May 14, 2005.

378. Patricia Clark. "Program." *Alpha Kappa Alpha Sorority, Inc.,* November 2005.

379. Sharon Stallings. Report. "Black Family Committee Event." October 2005.

380. Patricia Clark. "Program." *Alpha Kappa Alpha Sorority, Inc.,* February 2006.

381. Ibid., June 2005.

382. Minutes. Chapter meeting. Gamma Sigma Omega Chapter. June 11, 2005.

383. Patricia Clark. "Program." *Alpha Kappa Alpha Sorority, Inc.,* February 2005.

384. Emma Jean Conyers. Report. Gamma Sigma Omega Chapter. May 5, 2005.

385. Patricia Clark. "Program." *Alpha Kappa Alpha Sorority, Inc.,* May 2006.

386. Ibid., October 2006.

387. Ibid., November 2005.

388. Minutes. Chapter meeting. Gamma Sigma Omega Chapter. December 10, 2005.

389. Patricia Clark. "Program." *Alpha Kappa Alpha Sorority, Inc.,* February 2006.

390. Ibid., June 2006.

391. Ibid., February 2006.

392. Emma Jean Conyers. Report. Gamma Sigma Omega Chapter. March 2, 2006.
393. Minutes. Chapter meeting. Gamma Sigma Omega Chapter. December 9, 2006.
394. Emma Jean Conyers. Report. Gamma Sigma Omega Chapter. March 2, 2006.
395. Minutes. Chapter meeting. Gamma Sigma Omega Chapter. December 9, 2006.
396. Emma Jean Conyers. Report. Gamma Sigma Omega Chapter. March 3, 2005.
397. Ibid., March 2, 2006.
398. Ibid., May 5, 2006.
399. Patricia Clark. "Program." *Alpha Kappa Alpha Sorority, Inc.,* May 2006.
400. Emma Jean Conyers. Report. Gamma Sigma Omega Chapter. May 5, 2005.
401. Ibid.
402. Patricia Clark. "Program." *Alpha Kappa Alpha Sorority, Inc.,* June 2005.
403. Ibid., June 2006.
404. Emma Jean Conyers. Report. Gamma Sigma Omega Chapter. April 2, 2005.
405. Ibid., March 2, 2006.
406. Patricia Clark. "Program." *Alpha Kappa Alpha Sorority, Inc.,* June 2005.
407. Minutes. Chapter meeting. Gamma Sigma Omega Chapter. March 11, 2006.
408. Emma Jean Conyers. Report. Gamma Sigma Omega Chapter. March 30, 2006.
409. Patricia Clark. "Program." *Alpha Kappa Alpha Sorority, Inc.,* June 2006.
410. Zena McClain. Report. Gamma Sigma Omega Chapter. June 2006.
411. Emma Jean Conyers. Report. Gamma Sigma Omega Chapter. August 31, 2006.
412. Patricia Clark. "Program." *Alpha Kappa Alpha Sorority, Inc.,* November 2006.
413. Melinda Pippen-Miller. 12th Annual AKA Day at the Capitol, February 21, 2005. Report presented at Chapter Meeting, Gamma Sigma Omega Chapter. Savannah, GA.
414. Minutes. Chapter meeting. Gamma Sigma Omega Chapter. May 14, 2005.
415. Melinda Pippen-Miller. Report. Gamma Sigma Omega Chapter. November 10, 2005.
416. Ibid., November 2, 2006.
417. Minutes. Chapter meeting. Gamma Sigma Omega Chapter. January 14, 2006.
418. Melinda Pippen-Miller. Report. Gamma Sigma Omega Chapter. November 2, 2006.

419. Minutes. Chapter meeting. Gamma Sigma Omega Chapter. February 12, 2005.

420. Chappell-Stevens, Kimberly. Report. Gamma Sigma Omega Chapter. April 2005.

421. Ibid., October 26, 2005.

422. Ibid., February 6, 2006.

423. Emma Jean Conyers. Report. Gamma Sigma Omega Chapter. April 2, 2005.

424. Patricia Clark. "Program." *Alpha Kappa Alpha Sorority, Inc.*, June 2006.

425. Patricia Clark. "Committee Information and Reports." *Alpha Kappa Alpha Sorority, Inc.* Savannah, GA. April 2005.

426. Minutes. Chapter meeting. Gamma Sigma Omega Chapter. June 11, 2005.

427. Patricia Clark. "Patricia J. Clark, 2005-2006." September 2012.

428. "Sigma Tau Chartered in South Atlantic Region." *Ivy Leaf,* Winter 2005, 69, http://www.aka1908.com.

429. Ibid.

430. Patricia Clark. "Accolades." *Alpha Kappa Alpha Sorority, Inc.* Savannah, GA. May 2005.

431. Patricia Clark. "Summer of 2005-National & Local." *Alpha Kappa Alpha Sorority, Inc.* Savannah, GA. September 2005.

432. Minutes. Chapter meeting. Gamma Sigma Omega Chapter. May 2005.

433. Patricia Clark. "Gamma Sigjma Omega Soror Registered to Attend the Regional Conference," *Alpha Kappa Alpha Sorority, Inc.* Savannah, GA. April 2006.

434. Chappell-Stevens, Kimberly. Report. Gamma Sigma Omega Chapter. May 13, 2006.

435. Patricia Clark. "Patricia J. Clark, 2005-2006." September 2012.

436. Ibid.

437. Minutes. Chapter meeting. Gamma Sigma Omega Chapter. September 9, 2006.

438. Patricia Clark. "Program." *Alpha Kappa Alpha Sorority, Inc.*, June 2006.

439. Founders' Day Committee Report. Gamma Sigma Omega Chapter. January30, 2005.

440. Minutes. Chapter meeting. Gamma Sigma Omega Chapter. January 10, 2006.

441. Patricia Clark. "Announcements." *Alpha Kappa Alpha Sorority, Inc.* Savannah, GA. March 2006.

442. Patricia Clark. "Patricia J. Clark, 2005-2006." September 2012.

443. Ibid.

444. Minutes. Chapter meeting. Gamma Sigma Omega Chapter. December 9, 2006.

445. Alpha Kappa Alpha Sorority, Inc., *Manual of Standard Procedure 2012.* Corporate Office: Chicago, Illinois.

446. Minutes. Chapter meeting. Gamma Sigma Omega Chapter. January 14, 2006.

447. Ibid., September 9, 2006.

448. Ibid., October 14, 2006.

449. Patricia Clark. "Announcements." *Alpha Kappa Alpha Sorority, Inc.* Savannah, GA. March 2005.

450. Angela Grant. Report. Gamma Sigma Omega Chapter. March 2, 2006.

451. Patricia Clark. "Announcements." *Alpha Kappa Alpha Sorority, Inc.* Savannah, GA. June 2006.

452. Glenda James. Report. Gamma Sigma Omega Chapter. November 2, 2006.

453. Patricia Clark. The Review-During the two years. 2007.

454. Patricia Clark. "Patricia J. Clark, 2005-2006." September 2012.

455. Cathy Cox. "Certificate of Incorporation." Secretary of State. September 15, 2005.

456. Minutes. Chapter meeting. Gamma Sigma Omega Chapter. December 9, 2006.

457. Ibid.

458. Ibid.

459. "Every Soror Proficient in Chapter Operations." *Centennial.* Gamma Sigma Omega Chapter. Savannah, GA. April 12, 2008, 1.

460. "Every Soror Is A Pearl." *Centennial.* Gamma Sigma Omega Chapter. Savannah, GA. November 10, 2007, 1,3.

461. "Are You Ready for Boule?." *Centennial.* Gamma Sigma Omega Chapter. Savannah, GA. March 8, 2008, 3.

462. "GSO at Centennial Boule 2008." *Centennial.* Gamma Sigma Omega Chapter. Savannah, GA. September 13, 2008, 3.

463. "Countdown to Centennial Boule." *Centennial.* Gamma Sigma Omega Chapter, Savannah, GA. September 13, 2008, 3.

464. "Get Ready for the Countdown." *Ivy Leaf,* Fall 2006, 19-20.

465. Minutes. Chapter meeting. Gamma Sigma Omega Chapter. January 4, 2007. Savannah, GA.

466. Ibid., February 10, 2007.

467. "Congratulation." *Centennial.* Gamma Sigma Omega Chapter. Savannah, GA. February 10, 2007.

468. Clemontine F. Washington. Program. Centennial. March 10, 2007, Savannah, GA.

469. *Savannah Herald.* Savannah, GA., July 2, 2008, 2.

470. "Voter Registration Drive." *Centennial.* Gamma Sigma Omega Chapter. Savannah, GA. October 14, 2008,3.

471. "Connection Committee." *Centennial.* Gamma Sigma Omega Chapter. Savannah, GA. November 10, 2007, 3.

472. "Our Children in Attendance at Elegant Sweetthang." *Centennial.* Gamma Sigma Omega Chapter. Savannah, GA. November 10, 2008, 3.

473. "Social Committee." *Centennial.* Gamma Sigma Omega Chapter. Savannah, GA. November 10, 2007, 3.

474. Ibid.

475. Clemontine F. Washington. Program. *Centennial.* January 12, 2008, 2. Savannah, GA.

476. "Alpha Kappa Alpha and the City of Savannah in Partnership The Economic Smart Fair: ESP, Earn Save Prosper." *Centennial.* Gamma Sigma Omega Chapter. Savannah, GA. October 13, 2007, 1.

477. Ibid., 3.

478. Clemontine F. Washington. Program. *Centennial.* June 9, 2007, 2. Savannah, GA.

479. Ibid., May 10, 2008.

480. Ibid., February 10, 2007.

481. Ibid., September 13, 2008.

482. Ibid., November 8, 2008.

483. "South Atlantic Region." Ivy Leaf, Summer 2008, 17-18.

484. "Congratulation." *Centennial.* Gamma Sigma Omega Chapter. Savannah, GA. April 14, 2007, 4.

485. "Alpha Kappa Alpha Sorority, Inc. 55th South Atlantic Regional Conference." *Centennial.* Gamma Sigma Omega Chapter. Savannah, GA. June 14, 2008, 1,3.

486. "Post Boule Trip South Africa Pilgrimage." *Centennial.* Gamma Sigma Omega Chapter. Savannah, GA. September 13, 2008, 3.

487. "Our Undergraduates." *Centennial.* Gamma Sigma Omega Chapter. Savannah, GA. October 13, 2007, 1,3.

488. Ibid.

489. "Sisterliness Gamma Upsilon and Sigma Tau." *Centennial.* Gamma Sigma Omega Chapter. Savannah, GA. May 10, 2008, 3.

490. "Attendance, 2008 Cluster VI Conference, December 5-6." *Centennial.* Gamma Sigma Omega Chapter. Savannah, GA. December 13, 2008, 1.

491. "Greeks Providing Service Collaborative Projects." *Centennial.* Gamma Sigma Omega Chapter. Savannah, GA. January 12, 2008, 1.

492. "The Savannah Pan-Hellenic Council Babes and Tots Contest Little Miss AKA Contestant, Nia Ayanna Brown, Wins." *Centennial.* Gamma Sigma Omega Chapter. Savannah, GA. November 8, 2008, 1.

493. "Honey Dos." *Centennial.* Gamma Sigma Omega Chapter. Savannah, GA. June 9, 2007, 4.

494. "The Basileus Report." *Centennial.* Gamma Sigma Omega Chapter. Savannah, GA. December 13, 2008, 2.

495. Clemontine F. Washington. "Clemontine F. Washington, 2009-2010." September 2012.

496. Ibid.

497. Ibid.

498. Ibid.

499. Carolyn House Stewart. "The President's Desk." *Ivy Leaf.* Alpha Kappa Alpha Sorority, Inc. Chicago, Illinois. Fall 2010.

500. Kimberly Chappell-Stevens. Report. Gamma Sigma Omega Chapter. October 1, 2009.

[501.] Clemontine F. Washington. "Clemontine F. Washington, 2009-2010." September 2012.

[502.] Ibid.

[503.] Ibid.

[504.] Ibid.

[505.] Minutes. Chapter meeting. Gamma Sigma Omega Chapter. April 11, 2009. Savannah, GA.

[506.] Ibid., October 17, 2009.

[507.] Ibid., November 14, 2009.

[508.] Ibid., April 10, 2010.

[509.] Zena McClain. Report. Gamma Sigma Omega Chapter. December 12, 2009.

[510.] Ibid., November 5, 2009.

[511.] Ibid., April 1, 2010.

[512.] Ibid., April 29, 2010.

[513.] Ibid., April 2, 2009.

[514.] Ibid., September 3, 2009.

[515.] Ibid., April 2, 2009.

[516.] Ibid.

[517.] Ibid., December 12, 2009.

[518.] Ibid.

[519.] Ibid., February 13, 2010.

[520.] Ibid., November 12, 2010.

[521.] Ibid., April 2,2009.

[522.] Minutes. Chapter meeting. Gamma Sigma Omega Chapter. June, 2010. Savannah, GA.

[523.] Ibid., May 9, 2009.

[524.] Ibid., October 17, 2009.

[525.] Zena McClain. Report. Gamma Sigma Omega Chapter. June 4, 2009.

[526.] Ibid., September 3, 2009.

[527.] Minutes. Chapter meeting. Gamma Sigma Omega Chapter. October 17, 2009. Savannah, GA.

528. Zena McClain. Report. Gamma Sigma Omega Chapter. December 12, 2009.

529. Minutes. Chapter meeting. Gamma Sigma Omega Chapter. February 14, 2009. Savannah, GA.

530. Gwendolyn Johnson. Report. Gamma Sigma Omega Chapter. May 7, 2009.

531. Clemontine F.Washington. "Clemontine F. Washington, 2009-2010." September 2012.

532. Ibid.

533. Ibid.

534. Johnye Gillans. Report. Gamma Sigma Omega Chapter. February 13, 2010.

535. Ibid., March 4, 2010.

536. Ibid., April 1, 2010.

537. Ibid., April 29, 2010.

538. Clemontine F. Washington. Report. Gamma Sigma Omega Chapter. April 2, 2009.

539. Minutes. Chapter meeting. Gamma Sigma Omega Chapter. May 9, 2009. Savannah, GA.

540. Ibid., February 13, 2010.

541. Minutes. Chapter meeting. Gamma Sigma Omega Chapter. January 8, 2009. Savannah, GA.

542. Ibid., February 14, 2009.

543. Sonia Renee Grant. Standards Report. September 3, 2009.

544. Minutes. Chapter meeting. Gamma Sigma Omega Chapter. February 14, 2009. Savannah, GA.

545. Tarangula Barnes Scott. Report. Gamma Sigma Omega Chapter. November 14, 2009.

546. Maxine Jackson and Alvernia Jackson. Report. Gamma Sigma Omega Chapter. June 4, 2009.

547. Marjorie Varnedoe and Joyce Dingle. Report. Gamma Sigma Omega Chapter.

548. Lakyah Hatcher. Report. Gamma Sigma Omega Chapter. November 5, 2009.

549. Minutes. Chapter meeting. Gamma Sigma Omega Chapter. May 8, 2010. Savannah, GA.

550. Latondia Gadson. Report. Gamma Sigma Omega Chapter. September 3, 2009.

551. Delegate Certificate Form. March 1, 2009.

552. Clemontine F. Washington. Report. "56th South Atlantic Regional Conference."

553. Ibid.

554. Minutes. Chapter meeting. Gamma Sigma Omega Chapter. April 11, 2009. Savannah, GA.

555. Ibid., May 8, 2010.

556. Ibid., April 10, 2010.

557. Clemontine F.Washington. "Clemontine F. Washington, 2009-2010." September 2012.

558. Connie Cooper and Clemontine F.Washington. Report. Gamma Sigma Omega Chapter. March 4, 2010.

559. Bernice Wall. Email, Bernice.Wall@savannah.chatham.k12.ga.us. June 5, 2009.

560. Clemontine F.Washington. "Clemontine F. Washington, 2009-2010." September 2012.

561. Ibid.

562. Ibid.

563. Zena McClain. "GSO Announcements." E-mail. January 3, 2011.

564. Zena McClain. Report. Gamma Sigma Omega Chapter. January 4. 2011.

565. Denise Weems-White. Report. Gamma Sigma Omega Chapter. January 8, 2011.

566. Minutes. Chapter meeting. Gamma Sigma Omega Chapter. September 10, 2011. Savannah, GA.

567. Taqwaa F. Saleem. Report. Gamma Sigma Omega Chapter, January 5, 2012.

568. McClain, Zena. "January's Sisterly Relations Activity." *The Vintage Pearl.* Gamma Sigma Omega Chapter. Savannah, GA. February 7, 2011.

569. Ibid., "And the Survey Says…"

570. Zena McClain. "Message from Basileus." *The Vintage Pearl.* Gamma Sigma Omega Chapter. Savannah, GA. April 8, 2011.

571. Flyer, Membership Committee, 2012.

572. Lorna Jackson. Report. Gamma Sigma Omega Chapter. February, 2011.

573. Zena McClain. Report. Gamma Sigma Omega Chapter. March 3, 2011.

574. Ibid.

575. Emma Jean Conyers. Report. Gamma Sigma Omega Chapter. February 3, 2011.

576. Ibid., March 31, 2011.

577. Ibid., August 13, 2011.

578. Minutes. Chapter meeting. Gamma Sigma Omega Chapter. November 12, 2011. Savannah, GA.

579. Emma Jean Conyers. Report. Gamma Sigma Omega Chapter. April 10, 2012.

580. Ibid., October 4, 13, 2012.

581. Connie Cooper. Report. Gamma Sigma Omega Chapter. March 3, 2011.

582. Sheila Hutcherson. Report. Gamma Sigma Omega Chapter. January 31, 2012.

583. Courtney Eaton. Report. Gamma Sigma Omega Chapter. March 31, 2011.

584. Zena McClain. "Message from Basileus." *The Vintage Pearl.* Gamma Sigma Omega Chapter. Savannah, GA. April 8, 2011.

585. Tarangula Barnes Scott. Report. Gamma Sigma Omega Chapter. February 12, 2011.

586. Ibid., May 5, 2011.

587. Ibid., June 2, 2011.

588. Ibid., September 10, 2011.

589. Tarangula Barnes Scott. Report. Email. November 21, 2012.

590. Tarangula Barnes Scott. Report. Gamma Sigma Omega Chapter. September 10, 2011.

591. Ibid.

592. Ibid., October 8, 2011.

593. Ibid., November 1, 2011.

594. Ibid., December 10, 2011.

595. Ibid., January 14, 2012.

596. Ibid., February 11, 2012.

597. Ibid., March 1, 2012.

598. Ibid., April 10, 2012.

599. Ibid,. May 3, 2012.

600. Ibid., June 9, 2012.

601. Ibid.

602. Ibid., October 13, 2012.

603. Ibid., November 1, 2012.

604. Ibid., February 12, 2011.

605. Zena McClain. "Our Chapter Edifying the Mind and Soul." *The Vintage Pearl*. Gamma Sigma Omega Chapter. Savannah, GA. April 8, 2011.

606. Tarangula Barnes Scott. Report. Gamma Sigma Omega Chapter. June 2, 2011.

607. Ibid., April 10, 2012.

608. Ibid., June 2, 2011

609. Ibid.

610. Ibid., December 1, 2011.

611. Ibid., February 11, 2012.

612. Ibid., November 1, 2012.

613. Ibid., February 12, 2011.

614. Zena McClain. "A Day of Service." *The Vintage Pearl*. Gamma Sigma Omega Chapter. Savannah, GA. February 7, 2011.

615. Zena McClain. Report. Gamma Sigma Omega Chapter. March 3, 2011.

616. Tarangula Barnes Scott. Report. Gamma Sigma Omega Chapter. March 1, 2012.

617. Ibid., May 14, 2011.

618. Ibid., March 1, 2012.

619. Ibid., April 10, 2012.

620. Ibid., June 9, 2012.

621. Ibid., December 1, 2011.

622. Ibid.

623. Ibid.

624. Ibid., March 3, 2011.

625. Ibid., May 14, 2011.

626. Ibid., February 11, 2012.

627. Ibid., April 10, 2012.

628. Ibid., February 12, 2011.

629. Zena McClain. "Message from Basileus." *The Vintage Pearl.* Gamma Sigma Omega Chapter. Savannah, GA. April 8, 2011.

630. "Facing the Rising Sun." Program. March 27, 2011.

631. Tarangula Barnes Scott. Report. Gamma Sigma Omega Chapter. October 8, 2011.

632. Ibid., December 1, 2011.

633. Ibid., November 1, 2011.

634. Minutes. Chapter meeting. Gamma Sigma Omega Chapter. June 11, 2011. Savannah, GA.

635. Tarangula Barnes Scott. Report. Gamma Sigma Omega Chapter. June 9, 2012.

636. Ibid., Januaary 14, 2012.

637. Johnye Gillans, Charlene Jones, Emma Conyers. Report. Gamma Sigma Omega Chapter. February 3, 2011.

638. Ibid., March 3, 2011.

639. Johnye Gillans. Report. Gamma Sigma Omega Chapter. May 5,14, 2011.

640. AKA's Precious Gems 16th Annual Junior Debutant Cotillion. Program. June 11, 2011.

641. Johnye Gillans, Charlene Jones, Emma Conyers. Report. Gamma Sigma Omega Chapter. September 24, 2011.

642. Minutes. Executive meeting. Gamma Sigma Omega Chapter. September 1, 2011.

643. Minutes. Chapter meeting. Gamma Sigma Omega Chapter. October 8, 2011. Savannah, GA.

644. Founders' Day Celebration. Program. March 19, 2011.

645. Alvernia Jackson. Report. Gamma Sigma Omega Chapter. March 31, 2011.

646. Joint Founders' Day Observance. Program. January 21, 2012.

647. Kimberly Chappell-Stevens. Report. Gamma Sigma Omega Chapter. February 2, 2012.

648. Minutes. Executive meeting. Gamma Sigma Omega Chapter. February 2, 2012.

649. Minutes. Chapter meeting. Gamma Sigma Omega Chapter. February 12, 2011. Savannah, GA.

650. Tarangula Barnes Scott. Report. Gamma Sigma Omega Chapter. May 14, 2011.

651. Minutes. Chapter meeting. Gamma Sigma Omega Chapter. February 11, 2012. Savannah, GA.

652. Zena McClain. Report. Gamma Sigma Omega Chapter. March 10, 2012.

653. Tarangula Barnes Scott. Report. Gamma Sigma Omega Chapter. June 9, 2012.

654. Zena McClain. Report. Gamma Sigma Omega Chapter. September 29, 2011.

655. Ibid., October 4, 2012.

656. Ibid., March 10, 2012.

657. Minutes. Executive meeting. Gamma Sigma Omega Chapter. May 31, 2012.

658. Ibid., August 30, 2012.

659. Zena McClain. Report. Gamma Sigma Omega Chapter. September 29, 2011.

660. Agenda. Chapter meeting. Gamma Sigma Omega Chapter. March 12, 2011.

661. Minutes. Chapter meeting. Gamma Sigma Omega Chapter. September 10, 2011. Savannah, GA.

662. "Mrs. Johnye W. Gillans." Program. June 10, 2012.

663. Zena McClain. Report. Gamma Sigma Omega Chapter. November 1, 2011.

664. Minutes. Chapter meeting. Gamma Sigma Omega Chapter. October 13, 2012. Savannah, GA.

665. "Soror Zena McClain." Flyer.

Bibliography

Agenda. Chapter meeting. Gamma Sigma Omega Chapter. March 12, 2011.

AKA's Precious Gems 16th Annual Junior Debutante Cotillion. Program. June 11, 2011.

"Alpha Centennial Celebration Gala." *Ivy Leaf.* Spring 2008.

"Alpha Kappa Alpha and the City of Savannah in Partnership The Economic Smart Fair: ESP, Earn Save Prosper." *Centennial.* Gamma Sigma Omega Chapter. Savannah, GA. October 13, 2007.

Alpha Kappa Alpha Sorority, Inc. *Constitution and Bylaws 2010.* Corporate Office: Chicago, Illinois.

Alpha Kappa Alpha Sorority, Inc., *Manual of Standard Procedure 2012.* Corporate Office: Chicago, Illinois.

"Alpha Kappa Alpha Sorority, Inc. Gamma Sigma Omega, an Oscar Winning Chapter." *Centennial.* Gamma Sigma Omega Chapter. Savannah, GA. April 14, 2007.

"Alpha Kappa Alpha Sorority, Inc. 55th South Atlantic Regional Conference." *Centennial.* Gamma Sigma Omega Chapter. Savannah, GA. June 14, 2008.

Archives of Greenbriar Children's Center. 3709 Hopkins Street, Savannah, GA. May 21, 2013.

Archives of Savannah State University. Asa H. Gordon Library. Savannah, GA. August 2, 2013.

"Are You Ready for Boule?" *Centennial.* Gamma Sigma Omega Chapter. Savannah, GA. March 8, 2008.

"Attendance, 2008 Cluster VI Conference, December 5-6." *Centennial.* Gamma Sigma Omega Chapter. Savannah, GA. December 13, 2008.

"The Basileus Report." *Centennial.* Gamma Sigma Omega Chapter. Savannah, GA. December 13, 2008.

Bell, Carolyn H. *The Spirit of AKA.* Gamma Sigma Omega Chapter, Savannah, GA. January 2003.

---. *The Spirit of AKA.* Gamma Sigma Omega Chapter, Savannah, GA. February, 2003.

---. *The Spirit of AKA*. Gamma Sigma Omega Chapter, Savannah, GA. March, 2003.

---. *The Spirit of AKA*. Gamma Sigma Omega Chapter, Savannah, GA. April, 2003.

---. *The Spirit of AKA*. Gamma Sigma Omega Chapter, Savannah, GA. May, 2003.

---. *The Spirit of AKA*. Gamma Sigma Omega Chapter, Savannah, GA. June, 2003.

---. *The Spirit of AKA*. Gamma Sigma Omega Chapter, Savannah, GA. September, 2003.

---. *The Spirit of AKA*. Gamma Sigma Omega Chapter, Savannah, GA. October, 2003.

---. *The Spirit of AKA*. Gamma Sigma Omega Chapter, Savannah, GA. November, 2003.

---. *The Spirit of AKA*. Gamma Sigma Omega Chapter, Savannah, GA. December, 2003.

---. *The Spirit of AKA*. Gamma Sigma Omega Chapter, Savannah, GA. January, 2004.

---. *The Spirit of AKA*. Gamma Sigma Omega Chapter, Savannah, GA. February, 2004.

---. *The Spirit of AKA*. Gamma Sigma Omega Chapter, Savannah, GA. March, 2004.

---. *The Spirit of AKA*. Gamma Sigma Omega Chapter, Savannah, GA. April, 2004.

---. *The Spirit of AKA*. Gamma Sigma Omega Chapter, Savannah, GA. May, 2004.

---. *The Spirit of AKA*. Gamma Sigma Omega Chapter, Savannah, GA. June, 2004.

---. *The Spirit of AKA*. Gamma Sigma Omega Chapter, Savannah, GA. September, 2004.

---. *The Spirit of AKA*. Gamma Sigma Omega Chapter, Savannah, GA. October, 2004.

---. *The Spirit of AKA*. Gamma Sigma Omega Chapter, Savannah, GA. November, 2004.

---. *The Spirit of AKA*. Gamma Sigma Omega Chapter, Savannah, GA. December, 2004.

Bhanoo, Sindya N. and Keith L. Alexander. "Sorority Leads March for Change." *Washington Post*. July 18, 2008.

Boston, Albertha E. Dr, Emma J. Conyers, and Virginia M. Parham. *Gamma Sigma Omega Chapter of Alpha Kappa Alpha Sorority, Inc.*. Savannah, GA: Gamma Sigma Omega Chapter, 2003.

Boyd, Norman E. "Report of National Non-Partisan Council on Public Affairs." Minutes presented at the Twenty-Fifth Annual Boule of Alpha Kappa Alpha Sorority, Inc. Chicago, Illinois. Feb. 18-20, 1944. http://www.aka1908.com.

"Chapter News Highlights." *Ivy Leaf,* Spring 1974. http://www.aka1908.com.

Clarke, Irma F. "Report of the Supreme Grammateus." Minutes presented at the Twenty-Fifth Annual Boule of Alpha Kappa Alpha Sorority. Feb. 18-20, 1944. Chicago, Illinois. http://www.aka1908.com.

Clark, Patricia. "Accolades." *Alpha Kappa Alpha Sorority, Inc.* Savannah, GA. March 2005.

---. May 2005.

---. "Announcements." *Alpha Kappa Alpha Sorority, Inc.* Savannah, GA. March 2005.

---. March 2006.

---. June 2006.

---. "Committee Information and Reports." *Alpha Kappa Alpha Sorority, Inc.* Savannah, GA. February 2005.

---. April 2005.

---. "Gamma Sigjma Omega Soror Registered to Attend the Regional Conference," *Alpha Kappa Alpha Sorority, Inc.* Savannah, GA. April 2006.

---. "Summer of 2005-National & Local." *Alpha Kappa Alpha Sorority, Inc.* Savannah, GA. September 2005.

---. "Soror Emma Conyers-Anti-Basileus/Program Chairman." *Alpha Kappa Alpha Sorority, Inc.* Savannah, GA. September 2005.

---. "Patricia J. Clark, 2005-2006." September 2012.

---. "Program." *Gamma Sigma Omega Chapter.* October 2006.

---. November 2006.

---. "Program." *Alpha Kappa Alpha Sorority, Inc.* November 2005.

---. December 2005.

---. January 2006.

---. February 2006.

---. March 2006.

---. May 2006.

---. June 2006.

---. August 2006.

---. "Program Committee Reports." *Alpha Kappa Alpha Sorority, Inc.* Savannah, GA. June 2005.

---. The Review-During the two years. 2007.

"Cluster VI Founders' Day Luncheon Held." *Ivy Leaf,* Fall 1994. http://www. aka1908.com.

"Congratulations." *Centennial.* Gamma Sigma Omega Chapter. Savannah, GA. January 13, 2007.

"Congratulations." *Centennial.* Gamma Sigma Omega Chapter. Savannah, GA. February 10, 2007.

"Congratulations." *Centennial.* Gamma Sigma Omega Chapter. Savannah, GA. April 14, 2007.

"Connection Committee." *Centennial.* Gamma Sigma Omega Chapter. Savannah, GA. November 10, 2007.

Conyers, Emma Jean. Report. Leadership Seminar. August 2007. Report presented at Chapter Meeting, Gamma Sigma Omega Chapter. Savannah, GA.

---. Report. Gamma Sigma Omega Chapter. February 12, 2005.

---. March 3, 2005.

---. April 2, 2005.

---. May 5, 2005.

---. May 14, 2005.

---. October 8, 2005.

---. March 2, 2006.

---. March 30, 2006.

---. May 4, 2006.

---. June 1, 2006.

---. August 31, 2006.

---. February 3, 2011.

---. March 31, 2011.

---. August 1, 2011.

---. August 13, 2011.

---. April 10, 2012.

---. October 4, 13, 2012.

---. *100 Years Commemorative Directory Alpha Kappa Alpha Sorority, Inc. Gamma Sigma Omega Chapter.* Savannah, GA. 2008.

Cooper, Connie. Report. Gamma Sigma Omega Chapter. March 3, 2011.

Cooper, Connie and Clemontine Washington. Report. Gamma Sigma Omega Chapter. March 4, 2010.

"Countdown to Centennial Boule." *Centennial.* Gamma Sigma Omega Chapter, Savannah, GA. September 13, 2008.

Cox, Cathy. "Certificate of Incorporation." Secretary of State. September 15, 2005.

Crank, Sujette Foutain. Report. Minutes presented at the Thirty-Eight Annual Boule of Alpha Kappa Alpha Sorority, Inc. Cincinnati, Ohio. December 26-30, 1959 http://www.aka1908.com.

Delegate Certificate Form. March 1, 2009.

Dougherty, Jill. "Sisterhood Turns 100." CNN Website. July 20, 2008.

Eaton, Courtney. Report. Gamma Sigma Omega Chapter. March 31, 2011.

"Economics, Sisterhood, Partnerships." *Ivy Leaf,* Fall 2006.

"Every Soror Is A Pearl." *Centennial.* Gamma Sigma Omega Chapter. Savannah, GA. November 10, 2007.

"Every Soror Proficient in Chapter Operations." *Centennial.* Gamma Sigma Omega Chapter. Savannah, GA. April 12, 2008.

"Facing the Rising Sun." Program. March 27, 2011.

"Fashionetta Held at Savannah, GA." *Ivy Leaf,* March 1952. http://www.aka1908.com.

Flyer. Membership Committee, 2012.

Founders' Day Celebration. Program. March 19, 2011.

Founders' Day Committee Report. Gamma Sigma Omega Chapter. January30, 2005.

Gadson, Latondia. Report. Gamma Sigma Omega Chapter. September 3, 2009.

"Gamma Sigma Omega." *Ivy Leaf,* September 1943. http://www.aka1908.com.

"Gamma Sigma Omega." *Ivy Leaf,* March 1944. http://www.aka1908.com.

"Gamma Sigma Omega." *Ivy Leaf,* February 1961. http://www.aka1908.com.

"Gamma Sigma Omega." *Ivy Leaf,* Summer 1979. http://www.aka1908.com.

"Gamma Sigma Omega and Gamma Upsilon Give Resume of Activites." *Ivy Leaf,* June 1957. http://www.aka1908.com.

"Gamma Sigma Omega and Gamma Upsilon Host Neighborhood Meeting." *Ivy Leaf,* Spring 1978. http://www.aka1908.com.

"Gamma Sigma Omega Chapter." *Ivy Leaf,* March 1946. http://www.aka1908.com.

"Gamma Sigma Omega Chapter Initiates Two." *Ivy Leaf,* March 1948. http://www.aka1908.com.

"Gamma Sigma Omega Chapter, Savannah, Georgia." *Ivy Leaf,* June 1946. http://www.aka1908.com.

"Gamma Sigma Omega Gives $500 to Charity." *Ivy Leaf*, March 1953. http://www.aka1908.com/

"Gamma Sigma Omega in Pan-Hellenic Organization." *Ivy Leaf*, June 1947. http://www.aka1908.com.

"Gamma Sigma Omega Notes." Ivy Leaf, September – December 1950. http://www.aka1908.com.

"Gamma Sigma Omega Planning to Present Fashionetta." *Ivy Leaf*, December 1951. http://www.aka1908.com.

"Gamma Sigma Omega Retreat a Success." *Ivy Leaf*, Winter 1992. http://www.aka1908.com.

"Gamma Sigma Omega Serves the Community." *Ivy Leaf*, Winter 1993. http://www.aka1908.com.

"Gamma Sigma Omega: Sisterhood at Work." *Ivy Leaf*, Spring 1977. http://www.aka1908.com

"Gamma Sigma Omega Tutorial Reading Program." *Ivy Leaf*, Fall 1977. http://www.aka1908.com.

Gamma Sigma Omega Update. Letter. July 2003.

"Gamma Sigma Omega Walks in Relay for Life." *Ivy Leaf*, Fall 1994. http://www.aka1908.com.

"Gamma Upsilon Set up at Savannah State College." *Ivy Leaf*, March 1950. http://www.aka1908.com.

"Get Ready for the Countdown." *Ivy Leaf*, Fall 2006.

"Gift Wrapping for the Children of Greenbriar." *Centennial*. Gamma Sigma Omega Chapter. Savannah, GA. December 1, 2007.

Gillans, Johnye. Report. Gamma Sigma Omega Chapter. February 13, 2010.

---. March 4, 2010.

---. April 1, 2010.

---. April 29, 2010.

---. May 5/14, 2011.

Gillans, Johnye. Charlene Jones, Emma Conyers. Report. Gamma Sigma Omega Chapter. February 3, 2011.

---. March 3, 2011.

---. September 24, 2011.

Grant, Angela. Report. Gamma Sigma Omega Chapter. March 2, 2006.

Grant, Sonia Renee. Standards Report. September 3, 2009.

---. October 1, 2009.

"Greeks Providing Service Collaborative Projects." *Centennial*. Gamma Sigma Omega Chapter. Savannah, GA. January 12, 2008.

"Greenbriar Children's Center Orphanage Built by Sorority Dedicated." Ivy Leaf, September 1949. http://www.aka1908.com.

"Greenbriar Foundation is Organized." Verticlal Files. April 3, 1961. The Live Oak Public Library. Savannah, GA.

"GSO at Centennial Boule 2008." *Centennial.* Gamma Sigma Omega Chapter. Savannah, GA. September 13, 2008.

Hatcher, Lakyah. Report. Gamma Sigma Omega Chapter. November 5, 2009.

"Health News." *Ivy Leaf,* March 1956. http://www.aka1908.com.

"The Heart of ESP An Extraordinary Service Program." *Ivy Leaf.* Fall 2006.

History of Sigma Tau Chapter, Alpha Kappa Alpha Sorority, Inc. Armstrong Atlantic State University. Savannah, GA. 2004.

"Honey Dos." *Centennial.* Gamma Sigma Omega Chapter. Savannah, GA. June 9, 2007.

Hutcherson, Sheila. Report. Gamma Sigma Omega Chapter. January 31, 2012.

Jackson, Alvernia. Report. Gamma Sigma Omega Chapter. March 31, 2011.

Jackson, Ida L. "Report of the Mississippi Health Project." Minutes presented at the Twenty-Fifth Annual Boule of Alpha Kappa Alpha Sorority, Inc. Chicago, Illinois. Feb. 18-20, 1944. http://www.aka1908.com.

Jackson, Lorna. Report. Gamma Sigma Omega Chapter. 2011.

---. February 2011.

---. March 3, 2011.

Jackson, Maxine, Alvernia Jackson. Report. Gamma Sigma Omega Chapter. May 7, 2009.

---. June 4, 2009.

James, Glenda. Report. Gamma Sigma Omega Chapter. November 2, 2006.

Johnson, A. Cathryn. "South Eastern Region." Minutes presented at the Thirty-Third Annual Boule of Alpha Kappa Alpha Sorority, Inc. Dec. 26-30, 1953. St. Louis, Missouri.

---. Thirty-fourth Boule, 1954, 12-13.

Johnson, Gwendolyn. Report. Gamma Sigma Omega Chapter. May 7, 2009.

Joint Founders' Day Observance. Program. January 21, 2012.

Jones, Charlene. Report. Gamma Sigma Omega. October 1, 2009.

Jones, Ella Springs. The South Atlantic Perspective for Chapter Histories. Alpha Kappa Alpha Sorority, Inc. Email. August 12, 2013.

"Lambda Kappa Chartered." *Ivy Leaf,* Fall 1977. http://www.aka1908.com.

McClain, Zena. "GSO Announcements." E-mail. January 3, 2011.

---. Report. Gamma Sigma Omega Chapter. June 2006.

---. April 2, 2009.

---. June 4, 2009.

---. September 3, 2009.

---. November 5, 2009.

---. December 12, 2009.

---. February 13, 2010.

---. April 1, 2010.

---. April 29, 2010.

---. November 12, 2010.

---. January 4, 2011.

---. March 3, 2011.

---. September 9, 2011.

---. September 29, 2011.

---. November 1, 2011.

---. March 10, 2012.

---. October 4, 2012.

---. "A Day of Service." *The Vintage Pearl.* Gamma Sigma Omega Chapter. Savannah, GA. February 7, 2011.

---. "And the Survey Says…"

---. "January's Sisterly Relations Activity."

---. "Message from Basileus." April 8, 2011.

---. "Our Chapter Edifying the Mind and Soul." April 8, 2011.

McNealey, Ernestine Green. AKA International Historical Perspective for Timeless Histories. Alpha Kappa Alpha Sorority, Inc. Email. August 21, 2013.

Mercer, Virginia A. "Gamma Sigma Omega." *Ivy Leaf,* March 1963. http://www.aka1908.com.

Miller, Melinda P. 12th Annual AKA Day at the Capitol, February 21, 2005. Report presented at Chapter Meeting, Gamma Sigma Omega Chapter. Savannah, GA.

---. Report. Gamma Sigma Omega Chapter. November 10, 2005.

---. November 2, 2006.

Minutes. Chapter meeting. Gamma Sigma Omega Chapter. January 11, 2003. Savannah, GA.

Minutes. Chapter meeting. Gamma Sigma Omega Chapter. February 8, 2003. Savannah, GA.

Minutes. Chapter meeting. Gamma Sigma Omega Chapter. March 8, 2003. Savannah, GA.

Minutes. Chapter meeting. Gamma Sigma Omega Chapter. April 5, 2003. Savannah, GA.

Minutes. Chapter meeting. Gamma Sigma Omega Chapter. May 10, 2003. Savannah, GA.

Minutes. Chapter meeting. Gamma Sigma Omega Chapter. June 14, 2003. Savannah, GA.

Minutes. Chapter meeting. Gamma Sigma Omega Chapter. September 14, 2003. Savannah, GA.

Minutes. Chapter meeting. Gamma Sigma Omega Chapter. October 11, 2003. Savannah, GA.

Minutes. Chapter meeting. Gamma Sigma Omega Chapter. November 1, 2003. Savannah, GA.

Minutes. Chapter meeting. Gamma Sigma Omega Chapter. December 13, 2003. Savannah, GA.

Minutes. Chapter meeting. Gamma Sigma Omega Chapter. January 10, 2004. Savannah, GA.

Minutes. Chapter meeting. Gamma Sigma Omega Chapter. February 14, 2004. Savannah, GA.

Minutes. Chapter meeting. Gamma Sigma Omega Chapter. March 13, 2004. Savannah, GA.

Minutes. Chapter meeting. Gamma Sigma Omega Chapter. April 10, 2004. Savannah, GA.

Minutes. Chapter meeting. Gamma Sigma Omega Chapter. May 8, 2004. Savannah, GA.

Minutes. Chapter meeting. Gamma Sigma Omega Chapter. June 12, 2004. Savannah, GA.

Minutes. Chapter meeting. Gamma Sigma Omega Chapter. September 11, 2004. Savannah, GA.

Minutes. Chapter meeting. Gamma Sigma Omega Chapter. October 9, 2004. Savannah, GA.

Minutes. Chapter meeting. Gamma Sigma Omega Chapter. November 13, 2004. Savannah, GA.

Minutes. Chapter meeting. Gamma Sigma Omega Chapter. December 11, 2004. Savannah, GA.

Minutes. Chapter meeting. Gamma Sigma Omega Chapter. January 8, 2005. Savannah, GA.

Minutes. Chapter meeting. Gamma Sigma Omega Chapter. February 12, 2005. Savannah, GA.

Minutes. Chapter meeting. Gamma Sigma Omega Chapter. May 14, 2005. Savannah, GA.

Minutes. Chapter meeting. Gamma Sigma Omega Chapter. June 11, 2005. Savannah, GA.

Minutes. Chapter meeting. Gamma Sigma Omega Chapter. September 10, 2005. Savannah, GA.

Minutes. Chapter meeting. Gamma Sigma Omega Chapter. December 10, 2005. Savannah, GA.

Minutes. Chapter meeting. Gamma Sigma Omega Chapter. January 14, 2006. Savannah, GA.

Minutes. Chapter meeting. Gamma Sigma Omega Chapter. March 11, 2006. Savannah, GA.

Minutes. Chapter meeting. Gamma Sigma Omega Chapter. April 8, 2006. Savannah, GA.

Minutes. Chapter meeting. Gamma Sigma Omega Chapter. September 9, 2006. Savannah, GA.

Minutes. Chapter meeting. Gamma Sigma Omega Chapter. October 14, 2006. Savannah, GA.

Minutes. Chapter meeting. Gamma Sigma Omega Chapter. December 9, 2006. Savannah, GA.

Minutes. Chapter meeting. Gamma Sigma Omega Chapter. January 4, 2007. Savannah, GA.

Minutes. Chapter meeting. Gamma Sigma Omega Chapter. February 10, 2007. Savannah, GA.

Minutes. Chapter meeting. Gamma Sigma Omega Chapter. April 14, 2007. Savannah, GA.

Minutes. Chapter meeting. Gamma Sigma Omega Chapter. January 8, 2009. Savannah, GA.

Minutes. Chapter meeting. Gamma Sigma Omega Chapter. February 14, 2009. Savannah, GA.

Minutes. Chapter meeting. Gamma Sigma Omega Chapter. April 11, 2009. Savannah, GA.

Minutes. Chapter meeting. Gamma Sigma Omega Chapter. May 9, 2009. Savannah, GA.

Minutes. Chapter meeting. Gamma Sigma Omega Chapter. October 17, 2009. Savannah, GA.

Minutes. Chapter meeting. Gamma Sigma Omega Chapter. November 14, 2009. Savannah, GA.

Minutes. Chapter meeting. Gamma Sigma Omega Chapter. April 10, 2010. Savannah, GA.

Minutes. Chapter meeting. Gamma Sigma Omega Chapter. February 12, 2011. Savannah, GA.

Minutes. Chapter meeting. Gamma Sigma Omega Chapter. April 9, 2011. Savannah, GA.

Minutes. Chapter meeting. Gamma Sigma Omega Chapter. June 11, 2011. Savannah, GA.

Minutes. Chapter meeting. Gamma Sigma Omega Chapter. September 10, 2011. Savannah, GA.

Minutes. Chapter meeting. Gamma Sigma Omega Chapter. October 8, 2011. Savannah, GA.

Minutes. Chapter meeting. Gamma Sigma Omega Chapter. November 12, 2011. Savannah, GA.

Minutes. Chapter meeting. Gamma Sigma Omega Chapter. January 14, 2012. Savannah, GA.

Minutes. Chapter meeting. Gamma Sigma Omega Chapter. February 11, 2012. Savannah, GA.

Minutes. Chapter meeting. Gamma Sigma Omega Chapter. June 9, 2012. Savannah, GA.

Minutes. Chapter meeting. Gamma Sigma Omega Chapter. October 13, 2012. Savannah, GA.

Minutes. Executive meeting. Gamma Sigma Omega Chapter. September 1, 2011.

Minutes. Executive meeting. Gamma Sigma Omega Chapter. February 2, 2012.

Minutes. Executive meeting. Gamma Sigma Omega Chapter. May 31, 2012.

Minutes. Executive meeting. Gamma Sigma Omega Chapter. August 30, 2012.

Minutes presented at the Thirty-Six Boule of Alpha Kappa Alpha Sorority, Inc. Dec. 28-31, 1956. Atlanta, GA. http://www.aka1908.com.

Minutes presented at the Thirty-Eight Boule of Alpha Kappa Alpha Sorority, Inc. Dec. 26-30 1959. Cincinnati, Ohio. http://www.aka1908.com.

Minutes presented at the Twenty-Nineth Annual Boule of Alpha Kappa Alpha Sorority, Inc. December 27-30, 1949. Houston, Texas. http://www.aka1908.com.

Minutes presented at the Twenty-Seventh Annual Boule of Alpha Kappa Alpha Sorority, Inc. August 18-23, 1947. Cleveland, Ohio. http://www.aka1908.com.

"Mrs. Johnye W. Gillans." Program. June 10, 2012.

National Pan-Hellenic Council, Incorporated. Mission. http://www.nphchq.org/mission.htm.

"Negro Children's Need is Shown." Verticlal Files. November 5, 1947. The
   Live Oak Public Library. Savannah, GA.
"New Orleans Leadership Conference Hailed as a Success." *Ivy Leaf.* Fall 2007.
"One Hundred Years of Service: The Alpha Kappa Alpha Story." *Ivy Leaf,*
   Winter 2006.
"Our Children in Attendance at Elegant Sweetthang." *Centennial.* Gamma
   Sigma Omega Chapter. Savannah, GA. November 10, 2008.
"Our Undergraduates." *Centennial.* Gamma Sigma Omega Chapter.
   Savannah, GA. October 13, 2007.
Parham, Virginia. Report. Standards Committee. Chapter Meeting, April 14,
   2007. Savannah, GA. Print.
Parker, Marjorie H. Parker. *Alpha Kappa Alpha Sorority 1908 – 1958.* Alpha
   Kappa Alpha Sorority, Inc. 1958.
Patri, Angelo. "Our Children." *Savannah Morning News.* January 1, 1943, 4.
---. May 29, 1943.
"Post Boule Trip South Africa Pilgrimage." *Centennial.* Gamma Sigma
   Omega Chapter. Savannah, GA. September 13, 2008.
"Preliminary Report of Evaluation Committee." Minutes presented at the
   Twenty-Ninth Annual Boule of Alpha Kappa Alpha Sorority. Houston,
   Texas. Dec. 27-30, 1949. http://www.aka1908.com.
Program. Committee Report. January 11, 2013.
"Report of the South Atlantic Regional Director." Minutes presented at the
   Forty-Eight Boule of Alpha Kappa Alpha Sorority, Inc. Houston, Texas.
   July 16-21, 1978. http://www.aka1908.com.
"Report of the Supreme Basileus." Minutes presented at the Thirteenth Annual
   Boule of Alpha Kappa Alpha Sorority, Inc. Dec. 28-31, 1930. Marshall,
   Texas. http://www.aka1908.com.
Riley, Collye Lee. "Report of the Southeastern Region." Minutes presented
   at the Twenty-Fifth Annual Boule of Alpha Kappa Alpha Sorority. Feb.
   18-20, 1944. Chicago, Illinois. http://www.aka1908.com.
Rossiter, Frank. "Neglected Negro Children May Get Overdue 'Break'.
   "Verticlal Files. November 27, 1947. The Live Oak Public Library.
   Savannah, GA.
Saleem, Taqwaa F. Report. Gamma Sigma Omega Chapter, January 5, 2012.
Savannah Herald. Savannah, GA. July 2, 2008, 2.
"The Savannah Pan-Hellenic Council Babes and Tots Contest Little Miss
   AKA Contestant, Nia Ayanna Brown, Wins." *Centennial.* Gamma Sigma
   Omega Chapter. Savannah, GA. November 8, 2008.

Savannah Tribune. Savannah, GA. August 20, 2008, 11.
Barnes-Scott, Tarangula. Email. November 21, 2012.
---. Report. Gamma Sigma Omega Chapter. November 14, 2009.
---. February 12, 2011.
---. March 3, 2011.
---. May 5, 2011.
---. May 14, 2011.
---. June 2, 2011.
---. September 10, 2011.
---. October 8, 2011.
---. November 1, 2011.
---. December 1, 2011.
---. December 10, 2011.
---. January 14, 2012.
---. February 11, 2012.
---. March 1, 2012.
---. April 10, 2012.
---. May 3, 2012.
---. June 9, 2012.
---. October 13, 2012.
---. November 1, 2012.
"Sigma Tau Chartered in South Atlantic Region." *Ivy Leaf,* Winter 2005. http://www.aka1908.com.
Singleton, Audrey. Report. Gamma Sigma Omega Chapter. September 10, 2011.
"Sisterliness Gamma Upsilon and Sigma Tau." *Centennial.* Gamma Sigma Omega Chapter. Savannah, GA. May 10, 2008.
"Social Committee." *Centennial.* Gamma Sigma Omega Chapter. Savannah, GA. November 10, 2007.
"Soror Margaret C. Robinson." *Ivy Leaf,* May-June 1969. http://www.aka1908.com.
"Soror Zena McClain." Flyer.
"South Atlantic Region." *Ivy Leaf,* Summer 2008.
"South Atlantic Regional Director is Speaker at Gamma Sigma Omega's Founders' Day." *Ivy Leaf,* Summer 1995. http://www.aka1908.com.
"The Spirit of Alpha Kappa Alpha Sorority, Inc., An Engaging Experience," *Ivy Leaf,* Spring 2007. http://www.aka1908.com.

Stallings, Sharon. Report. "Black Family Committee Event." October 2005.
Chappell-Stevens, Kimberly. Report. Gamma Sigma Omega Chapter.
April 2005.
---. October 26, 2005.
---. February 6, 2006.
---. October 1, 2009.
---. February 2, 2012.
Stewart, Carolyn House. "The President's Desk." *Ivy Leaf.* Alpha Kappa Alpha
Sorority, Inc. Chicago, Illinois. Fall 2010.
---. October 26, 2005.
---. February 6, 2006.
---. May 13, 2006.
Tiggett, Jimmie C. "Gamma Sigma Omega." *Ivy Leaf,* March 1960. http://
www.aka1908.com.
"[Twenty-Third] 23rd South Atlantic Regional Conference." *Ivy Leaf,* Fall
1976. http://www.aka1908.com.
"Undergraduate Round Up, 2008." *Centennial.* Gamma Sigma Omega
Chapter. Savannah, GA. October 4, 2008.
Varnedoe, Marjorie, Joyce Dingle. Report. Gamma Sigma Omega Chapter.
"Voter Registration Drive." *Centennial.* Gamma Sigma Omega Chapter.
Savannah, GA. October 14, 2008.
Wall, Bernice. Email, Bernice.Wall@savannah.chatham.k12.ga.us. June
5, 2009
Washington, Clemontine F. Program. *Centennial.* February 10, 2007.
Savannah, GA.
---. March 10, 2007.
---. May 19, 2007.
---. January 12, 2008.
---. May 10, 2008.
---. June 14, 2008.
---. November 8, 2008.
---. "Clemontine F. Washington, 2009-2010." September 2012.
---. Report. Gamma Sigma Omega Chapter. April 2, 2009.
---. Report. "56th South Atlantic Regional Conference."
Weems-White, Denise. Report. Gamma Sigma Omega Chapter. January
8, 2011.
White, Linda M. "Message from the Supreme Basileus." *Ivy Leaf,* Fall, 2002.

Wilson, Martha. Obituary. November 13, 2010. St. Matthew Episcopal Church. Savannah, GA.

"Workshops Featured at Cluster VI Meeting." *Ivy Leaf,* Spring 1981.

"WWII and Roosevelt's Last Days." Franklin D. Roosevelt. http://www.sparknotes.com/biography/fdr/section12.rhtml.

Young, Lydia. Treasurer, M.A.R.T.H.A. Inc. July 2012.

"1908 Centennial Walk Kickoff." *Centennial.* Gamma Sigma Omega Chapter. Savannah, GA. March 10, 2007.

Index

Erica Benjamin | 193, 195, 208, 209, 210, 212, 213, 218, 228, 258

Ericka Coleman Washington | 174, 179, 196, 249, 259, 281

Erline Simms | 8

Ernestine Bertrand | 6, 133

Ernestine Green McNealey | xxi

ESP | 103, 104, 107, 110, 118, 119, 147, 148, 149, 150, 152, 153, 154, 155, 157, 158, 159, 160, 161, 163, 166, 171, 172, 188, 189, 191, 192, 197, 198, 200, 312, 318, 327, 333

Esther F. Garrison Elementary School | 82, 104, 108, 224, 293

Ethel Gibbs | 17, 71, 75, 258

Ethel Hedgeman | xxi, 151, 153

Ethel Hunter | 68, 69, 70, 74, 78, 83, 86, 90, 91, 92, 93, 97, 106, 108, 110, 111, 114, 163, 168, 170, 176, 177, 192, 194, 195, 196, 199, 209, 210, 211, 213, 218, 237, 259

Eudora M. Allen | 23, 27, 77, 88, 89, 90, 93, 94, 97, 98, 99, 107, 111, 116, 119, 120, 125, 126, 128, 151, 163, 164, 167, 172, 174, 175, 176, 177, 181, 199, 208, 216, 217, 218, 221, 252, 257, 258, 279, 280, 282, 286

Eunice Washington | 27, 32, 34, 260, 261, 262

Evanel Renfrow | 9, 10

Evanel Terrell | 29, 32, 35, 37, 38, 39, 262, 264, 297

F

"Facing the Rising Sun" | 35, 41, 56, 66, 74, 90, 111, 113, 116, 142, 163, 214, 224, 324, 331

Fashionetta | 10, 11, 13, 17, 48, 51, 224, 301, 331, 332

Florence Fonielle [Fonvielle] | 7

Founders' Day | xviii, 6, 12, 23, 24, 25, 26, 28, 29, 33, 34, 37, 38, 40, 41, 42, 43, 44, 48, 53, 54, 55, 57, 62, 63, 67, 70, 74, 79, 97, 126, 133, 151, 171, 172, 189, 190, 216, 217, 255, 262, 267, 269, 274, 277, 281, 284, 286, 307, 308, 316, 325, 330, 331, 334, 340

Frances Clarke Dye | vii, viii, 5

Freddie L. Pippen | 17, 25, 29, 37, 38, 51, 82, 106, 120, 165, 166, 209, 211, 213, 218, 244, 259, 262, 267, 269, 270

G

Gamma Upsilon | xxvii, 9, 10, 11, 12, 13, 14, 16, 20, 22, 23, 27, 28, 31, 34, 35, 36, 45, 46, 49, 53, 55, 57, 61, 70, 79, 93, 95, 99, 101, 106, 112, 124, 128, 133, 148, 153, 156, 173, 178, 179, 180, 181, 182, 183, 184, 188, 190, 193, 197, 199, 200, 213, 214, 215, 217, 219, 220, 221, 225, 227, 229, 230, 231, 232, 233, 234, 235, 240, 244, 245, 246,

347

274, 276, 279, 282, 284, 285, 288, 292, 322, 331

Membership Intake | xvii, 17, 19, 26, 50, 63, 70, 79, 99, 121, 122, 124, 178, 256

Mentoring Committee | 158, 198

Merdis Lyons | 17, 26, 45, 50, 257, 265

Michelle Mincey-Gwyn | 156, 165, 166, 196, 199, 218, 242, 259

Michelle Williams | 23, 250

Minnie Smith | 5

Miss Pink and Green | 30, 67, 69, 111, 120, 132, 153, 154, 157

Monifa I. Johnson | 212, 239, 259

Mozella Gaither Collier | xviii, 25, 26, 29, 34, 37, 39, 54, 58, 190, 224, 225

Muriel King | 6

N

Nadine Lewis | 26, 27, 29, 30, 45

Natatia VanEllison | 88, 91, 92, 93, 97, 98, 106, 121, 162, 259, 278, 279

Nathaniel Little | 5

Neldra Jewel Flint | 258

Nellie Quander | xxi

Nicole A. Neal | 211, 243, 259

Nicole Fields | 68, 98, 149, 213, 258, 273

Nicole M. Williams | 98, 125, 127, 128, 159, 174, 176, 179, 199, 200, 210, 217, 218, 220, 221, 260, 279, 280, 281, 283, 285

Nominating Committee | 80, 81, 87, 282

Norman E. Boyd | 3, 300

Norma S. White | 20, 30, 31, 54, 62, 74, 77, 151, 178

O

Ogeecheeton | 18, 19, 20, 21, 224

Olga Musgrow | 26, 29

Onnye Jean Sears | 17, 24, 26, 30, 32, 50, 264

ON TRACK | xxix, 66, 71, 72, 78, 82, 83

Orphanage | xxxvi, 2, 3, 4, 5, 8, 301, 333

Ouida Frazier Thompson | xix

Ouida Thompson | 6, 13, 16, 252

P

Pan-Hellenic | 7, 8, 9, 37, 41, 47, 57, 62, 67, 73, 79, 128, 185, 186, 198, 206, 221, 224, 255, 256, 267, 269, 280, 282, 284, 286, 301, 319, 332, 338, 339

Patricia J. Clark | v, 61, 103, 124, 125, 126, 176, 181, 200, 225, 252, 258, 278, 280, 282, 285, 315, 316, 329

Patricia J. Mincey | 44, 49, 74, 75, 77, 84, 97, 99, 120, 148, 149, 157, 165, 168, 172, 174, 176, 199, 201, 257, 259, 266, 267, 268, 269, 273, 274, 275, 276, 278, 280, 281

PIMS (Partnership in Mathematics and Science) | xxxi, 59, 60, 62, 64

P.I.N. | 18

U

Undergraduates | xxv, xxvi, xxviii, xxxii, 16, 34, 35, 52, 57, 61, 76, 99, 118, 127, 178, 179, 180, 183, 184, 199, 200, 219, 227, 228, 229, 230, 231, 232, 233, 234, 235, 236, 237, 238, 239, 240, 241, 242, 243, 244, 245, 246, 247, 248, 249, 250, 251, 260, 261, 294, 297, 340

United Negro College Fund | xxiii, 17, 30, 38, 55, 59, 66, 73, 79, 100, 101, 170, 185, 220, 224, 242, 288

V

Valencia R. Thomas Austin | 227, 258

Vanessa Miller Kaigler | 68, 69, 70, 71, 75, 76, 79, 98, 99, 148, 149, 162, 168, 170, 174, 175, 176, 177, 191, 193, 197, 199, 211, 259, 276, 282

Vernice Whitfield | 49, 53, 54, 55, 58, 60, 268, 269, 270

Violet Singleton | 6, 8, 11, 16, 17, 23, 27, 29, 30, 33, 132, 253

Virginia Annette Mercer Parham | v, 244

Virginia Mercer Parham | 17, 66, 275, 289, 290

Virginia M. Parham | viii, xiii, xiv, xv, 16, 35, 68, 69, 84, 94, 96, 175, 187, 201, 213, 252, 259, 265, 267, 275, 279, 280, 283, 299, 329

W

Wanda Williams | 67, 68, 72, 78, 97, 106, 126, 160, 162, 169, 203, 211, 259, 279

Wesley Community Center | 41, 211, 212

William Kenneth Payne | 9

Willie Mae Patterson | 17, 22, 29

Y

Young Authors | 85, 86, 111

Z

Zena E. McClain | v, 89, 106, 115, 117, 120, 124, 125, 126, 128, 130, 148, 149, 151, 156, 162, 174, 175, 176, 179, 180, 181, 185, 187, 189, 191, 197, 198, 199, 200, 202, 218, 221, 241, 252, 259, 281, 282, 283, 284, 285, 314, 319, 320, 321, 322, 323, 324, 325, 339